THE
REIKI
SOURCEBOOK

Reviews

What an incredible work. A must for all Reiki people.
Mari Hall, founder and director of the
International Association of Reiki

A gift to humanity. It de-clutters and demystifies so many misconceptions about Reiki. A "must" for fellow healthcare practitioners.
Neil Anthony, UK Reiki Federation Chair and co-founder

You will find EVERYTHING you would like to know about Reiki in this book, for this is the most updated and extensive work. This book will be highly appreciated and treasured.
Hyakuten Inamoto, Japanese Reiki Master
and founder of Komyo Reiki

Very impressed.
Patrick Zeigler, founder of SKHM/Sekhem/Seichem/Seichim

An asset to the Reiki community worldwide.
Maureen Kelly, author of Reiki and the Healing Buddha

One of the few Reiki books I can recommend. Excellent.
Reiki Evolution eZine

It is time that such a book be written.
Australian Yoga Life Magazine

The definitive manual for teacher, student and general reader alike.
Adyar Book News

I love your book, The Reiki Sourcebook. *You have done an excellent job of research and writing for this sensitive but important material. Thank you for your meticulous effort to provide unbiased information on Reiki, which will help to keep Reiki alive.*
Nina Paul, author of Reiki for Dummies

*Heralded around the world as **the** Reiki book.*
WellBeing Magazine

The most comprehensive book on the system of Reiki ever produced.
Nature and Health Magazine

THE
REIKI
SOURCEBOOK

Revised Edition 2008

BRONWEN and FRANS STIENE

**Founders of the International House of Reiki
Sydney, Australia**

info@reiki.net.au
www.reiki.net.au

BOOKS

Winchester, U.K.
New York, U.S.A

First published by O Books, 2003
Reprinted 2004 (twice), 2005 (twice), 2006,
2007
Revised edition published 2008
O Books is an imprint of John Hunt Publishing
Ltd., The Bothy, Deershot Lodge, Park Lane,
Ropley, Hants, SO24 0BE, UK
office1@o-books.net
www.o-books.net

Distribution in:

UK and Europe
Orca Book Services
orders@orcabookservices.co.uk
Tel: 01202 665432 Fax: 01202 666219 Int.
code (44)

USA and Canada
NBN
custserv@nbnbooks.com
Tel: 1 800 462 6420 Fax: 1 800 338 4550

Australia and New Zealand
Brumby Books
sales@brumbybooks.com.au
Tel: 61 3 9761 5535 Fax: 61 3 9761 7095

Far East (offices in Singapore, Thailand, Hong
Kong, Taiwan)
Pansing Distribution Pte Ltd
kemal@pansing.com
Tel: 65 6319 9939 Fax: 65 6462 5761

South Africa
Alternative Books
altbook@peterhyde.co.za
Tel: 021 555 4027 Fax: 021 447 1430
Text copyright Bronwen and Frans Stiene,
2003 and 2008

Design: Jim Weaver
Illustrations: Lolly Ellena Rados

ISBN: 978 1 84694 181 8

A CIP catalogue record for this book is
available from the British Library.

Printed in the US by Maple Vail

O Books operates a distinctive and ethical publishing philosophy in

all areas of its business, from its global network of authors to

production and worldwide distribution.

No trees were cut down to print this particular book. The paper is

100% recycled, with 50% of that being post-consumer. It's processed

chlorine-free, and has no fibre from ancient or endangered forests.

This production method on this print run saved approx. 13 trees,

4,000 gallons of water, 600 pounds of solid waste, 990 pounds of

greenhouse gases and 8 million Btu of energy. On its publication a

tree was planted in a new forest that O Books is sponsoring at The

Village www.thefourgates.com

Table of Contents

Preface

To collate all of the information that you are about to read has not been an easy task. We experienced a multitude of setbacks. On top of the list was our lack of understanding of the Japanese culture (you can stop that knowing laughter now). It is true, the culture is renowned as being notoriously difficult for foreigners to comprehend and, well – we can vouch for that. In times of need, determination and faith were our only assets.

We were determined that this book would be written. The confusion that we experienced as fledgling Reiki teachers in 1998 encouraged us to seek out the truths and fictions that surrounded Mikao Usui's early teachings and the modern system of Reiki. This was for our own benefit and for those who are interested in or involved in the system of Reiki as it stands today. We tackled Japanese customs, learning that information is only given when the right question is asked. We fell down when we didn't understand that a Japanese lack of enthusiasm actually meant 'NO!' We never wish to hear the words, 'think laterally' again and are glad that we continued asking and shaking the tree till some information fell from its branches. This is an ongoing task and we hope to zealously continue researching in the future.

There was also our faith that this book would be fleshed out from a Japanese perspective. Thankfully along came some very patient colleagues and teachers some of whom we studied with or interviewed and others who have made invaluable resources available such as informative books and websites. Our thanks go to H.E. Davey, Hiroshi Doi, Andrew Gordon, Hyakuten Inamoto, Daniel Lee, Chris Marsh, Patrick McCarthy, Stanley Pranin, Reverend Jion Prosser, Professor Judith Rabinovitch, Miek Skoss, John Stevens, Seiji Tabatake, Seikou Terashima, Tokushin, Stephen Turnbull, Vikki Quill and anyone else we may have forgotten to mention.

Other aspects of the Japanese language left us dumbfounded until we came across our translator, Anne Radovic, whose love of the intricacies of the Japanese culture and language was a blessing. Extra translations from Japanese books were also supplied by the lovely Tokiko Minamida.

Some aspects of this book were easy. The perfect illustrations were designed and drawn up by a wonderful Australian artist and Reiki practitioner, Lolly Ellena Rados. Thanks to Michiko Honda for her calligraphy work too.

The writing in itself was a clarification and joy for us as eternally self-learning human beings.

Our teachers, students and friends who provided us with a great deal of information and support – we sincerely thank.

There are also major contributions in this sourcebook from many Reiki practitioners the world over. To them we are extremely thankful for providing to the Reiki community material which, in our case, has allowed us to attempt to create a book that is the ultimate in Reiki knowledge.

Thanks to Nevill Drury, our agent, for his simple faith in us, and *The Reiki Sourcebook*. Thanks too, to John Hunt and his team for making the publishing of this book a pleasure.

Editing of the first edition was supported by Maurizio Floris. This second edition has undergone a committed and careful editing process by New York Reiki teacher and The Reiki Digest editor, Janet Dagley Dagley; thank you Janet for bringing the readability of *The Reiki Sourcebook* to the fore.

We would never have begun this journey without the support of our friends and families, especially our mothers – Elaine Voll and

Henny Stiene. Thank you. Our fathers who are no longer with us, especially Jan Stiene who we know would have loved to be researching alongside us. The most special thanks of all goes to our precious daughter, Bella – for simply bringing us joy.

And thank you to those, too, who wished not to have their names mentioned.

There is one more important thank you – to Mikao Usui and those who practice his teachings, in whatever form, everywhere.

There is a common saying in Japanese that we think is highly appropriate at this point in the book. We hope it expresses our desire to achieve great things for Mikao Usui's teachings by bringing information together in one easily accessible tome. We do not wish to harm anyone or anything and would like to apologize in advance for any inconsistencies, or mistakes that may be found within the text. To the best of our knowledge, we have accurately portrayed the information that we have read or received.

Let us begin the book by writing:

mangaichi ayamariga arimashitara goyousha kudasai

Please forgive us if we have made a mistake

Do not believe in anything (simply) because you have heard it.
Do not believe in traditions because they have been handed
down for many generations.
Do not believe in anything because it is spoken and rumored
by many.
Do not believe in anything (simply) because it is found written
in your religious books.
Do not believe in anything merely on the authority of your
teachers and elders.
But after observation and analysis, when you find that
anything agrees with reason and is conducive to the good and
benefit of one and all then accept it and live up to it.

Gautama Buddha
Anguttara Nikaya Vol. I, pp. 188–193, R.T.S. Ed.

Introduction

The system of Reiki is changing.

Why, you may wonder. Why should the teachings that were started in the early 1900s by a Japanese man called Mikao Usui need to change? Perhaps because they have already been changed – many, many times. Mikao Usui's teachings have constantly been altered and adapted to suit the people who have practiced them and the worlds they live in.

The real change that is taking place with these teachings today is that practitioners are returning to its origins. In this cyclical return to the roots of the system of Reiki, we encounter the many diversions that have taken place over the last 100 years. In this edition we take this further by moving our focus from the past into the future to see where the many diversions will lead us.

This is the second edition of *The Reiki Sourcebook* and, as you will see, both the content and setup are quite different from that of the original, which we began writing back in 2002. This 2008 edition takes on the challenge to move with the changes in the Reiki community. We believe that the popularity of the 2002 edition was due to the timeliness of its content; this edition continues in this tradition by addressing the timely issues of now.

The Reiki Sourcebook has been written to guide you on your journey. It aims to be a complete resource for all aspiring Reiki practitioners throughout the world, including Japan.

To begin the book we look at what is understood by the word Reiki. Translated it means 'spiritual energy', yet at the same time it also represents the system of Mikao Usui's teachings in their modern form. Following this brief explanation is detailed information about the teachings today in the guise of Reiki treatments and Reiki courses, for the benefit of those who are interested in or are currently practicing the system of Reiki.

The next section of *The Reiki Sourcebook* is broken up into three sections; Reiki Past, Reiki Present, and Reiki Future. It begins by taking a deeper look into Mikao Usui's teachings with a concise history of Reiki as seen through the eyes of its numerous practitioners. To create a clear understanding for the reader of what is to come, there is a Reiki Timeline and Lineage Chart. Many of the historical notes included are the results of our own research, which took us, naturally, to Japan. There we met with a variety of traditional and non-traditional Japanese Reiki practitioners and viewed some of the sites that are relevant to Reiki's history, such as Mikao Usui's gravesite and memorial stone, *kurama yama* (Mt. Kurama) and *hiei zan* (Mt. Hiei). Research into Japanese books and the Japanese culture and philosophy supported the process of delving into the life of Mikao Usui and following his students and the influence of Japanese traditions on the system.

Reiki Present addresses current happenings in the Reiki world, where the different branches are at and what global Reiki movements are at play.

Moving into our Reiki Future, discussion is encouraged through topical subjects such as the evolving structure of the Reiki community, climate change and how personal practice can make a difference to the world we live in.

Major Reiki techniques, both traditional and non-traditional, are explained. Reiki terminology is available in an extensive glossary and there is much more. In the last couple of years the Internet has become an undeniable monster of information. This edition of *The Reiki Sourcebook* holds more Internet references than ever before due to this fact.

The system of Reiki continues to change.

There will always be more information to add to this journey and new questions to ask. Mikao Usui's teachings are a practice in motion, which means that in each moment we capture a picture perfect shot of its truth. But there are many of these moments and therefore many truths. It all depends on what sort of camera you use, when you use it, and from which angle it is photographed. We have tried to capture as many sides as possible of this wonderful technique for you in this practical, comprehensive, and intriguing book.

There is a truth to these teachings that cannot be negated no matter which branch you may associate yourself with. This truth can be described as belonging to the energy of the universe, or that of Earth and Heaven, the yin and the yang, the soul connection, or simply the spiritual or healing energy. No matter which language you choose to describe these teachings, there will always be the sense of what that truth is: Reiki is far greater than us as individuals. Our desires and needs are impotent when faced with Reiki – it renders them powerless. Our intent opens us up to accept Reiki through us. It washes us, and others, clear. No life force is unaffected by Reiki.

We practice these teachings so that we may heal inside and out, let go and be One with the universe, reconnect with the path of our inevitable enlightenment and help others. To experience this we need to know that it is also our personal awareness of Reiki that creates an even more effective technique.

Controversy abounds concerning individual teaching methods and yet we all take this energy into our lives with the intent to evolve and heal. Reiki is far greater than our concerns of time, money and power. As humans, we are challenged by ourselves every step of the way. Reiki is our magical tool, proffering us strength, calm and light. We must take what we can with gratitude and work on ourselves, knowing that we can do this. We are empowered and the world can only become a more beautiful place through this knowing and the practice of Mikao Usui's teachings.

This versatile, free-flowing method is perfect for our times in that it is ultimately simple. Children can learn about Reiki, it is switched on with a thought, and the practice of it can take place in bed or on the bus. This simplicity makes it accessible to our 'busy, busy' lifestyles that 'don't have time for spirituality'. Conversely, the complexity of understanding Reiki is beyond the ability of our technical 21st century mind. The challenge for us, then, is to just let go and to see what we will discover. Letting go is not as easy as it sounds. If we can learn to let go and resist controlling ourselves, our situations, and others, we might find a peaceful beauty of contentment in our lives; one that, in turn, might result in world peace.

The intent of *The Reiki Sourcebook* is to link together information that has been spread far and wide by time and circumstances. By capturing the results of this systematic global research, it aims to share the information and to promote and stimulate discussion in the global Reiki community. It is not necessarily about 'new' information but the bringing together of histories and anecdotes to create a cohesive understanding of what has happened to and been said about the teachings during the past 100 years.

It is hoped that this will be a valuable resource for anyone interested in the history of Mikao Usui, his teachings, Reiki and related practices. It is also for beginners or those who feel lost and confused by the myriad of choices that are presented to them as Reiki in today's society.

This is an attempt to create unity rather than dissension – unity for all who work with this wondrous energy. Do not be distracted by the human frailties you will encounter within these pages; just remember that it is human strength that initially formed the teaching's solid base. If we can see where we came from, we can see clearer where we are heading.

Respect is a word that must be remembered and practiced by all when dealing with such a pure and beautiful energy. Correspondingly, we have attempted to retain this respect for the sacredness of the teachings by not baring the traditional mantras and symbols or attunement processes to the general public. The research information in this book is not just about what is taught but, most importantly, where these teachings originated. We respect that methods often involve the student completing certain energetic levels before being handed specific information.

The scientist and author of *The God Delusion*, Richard Dawkins, claims his issue with religion comes down to rationalism versus superstition. This is also an issue within many contemporary beliefs regarding the system of Reiki. Although Reiki practitioners are often at pains to clarify that the system of Reiki is not a religion, it is still often treated as a pseudo-religion by some practitioners. Instead of working with facts, truths are plucked from the air and expected to be treated as fact by all who come in contact with them. Our aim has always been to bring a sense of rationalism back into the system of Reiki, to afford it the respect that such a wonderful healing system deserves.

Verification of historical material about Mikao Usui and his teachings is a continuing struggle. Hawayo Takata taught her history of the system of Reiki. Her historical anecdotes, though entertaining, have unfortunately appeared to be unreliable. In the aftermath of her death in 1980, modern eyes turned to Japan for answers and discovered a country quietly practicing Mikao Usui's teachings. This was a great surprise, as it had been understood that the system of Reiki was 'dead' in Japan.

Information is gradually seeping through to the rest of the world although cultural and linguistic differences have made this far more difficult than it might sound. The result is that the information coming out of Japan is only doing so through limited channels – those who have the contacts and the language. Japan has also readily adopted many of the modern forms of the system of Reiki and it is now difficult for foreigners to know what the differences are between Japanese and non-Japanese practices. This is aggravated by a few instances where apparently 'old' teachings from Japan turned out to be hoaxes. Verification is required when dealing with the history of Mikao Usui's life and teachings, although you must never discount following your heart and placing trust in its inner sense.

To present objective viewpoints, information from many sources has been used and footnoted (where possible) in *The Reiki Sourcebook*. Information that is knowingly incorrect or untruthful has not deliberately been included as fact.

It is good to remember that Mikao Usui's teachings cannot be learnt from a book. The information that has been gathered here is not an alternative to seeking out a teacher.

How to read this book:
• An asterix (*) before the name of a technique indicates that it can be found in Part V – Reiki Techniques.

- Japanese words are italicized. The *kanji* plus the translation or description of the word can be found in the Reiki Glossary in the Appendix.
- The Reiki Glossary in the Appendix includes descriptions of people, places, techniques, branches and associated material concerned with Mikao Usui's early teachings and the system of Reiki. This is a useful tool for understanding any unfamiliar terminology in *The Reiki Sourcebook*.
- The use of upper case is a non-Japanese notion. When printing Japanese words the authors have taken the liberty of using capitals for people's names and places for added clarity.
- This book may be used solely as a reference material for Reiki practitioners or as a comprehensive manual for beginners that can be read from cover to cover.
- We would advise all Reiki practitioners to take note of Part II – Reiki Past, as this information continues to change due to ongoing research.

The contents of this book are for general information only. The authors do not endorse the methodology, techniques or philosophy of individual modalities detailed herein, and accept no liability for the use or misuse of any practice or exercise in this book.

We invite those who possess credible information about Mikao Usui's teachings or other relevant research knowledge to share it via *The Reiki Sourcebook* so that this awareness can flow back into the Reiki community.

Japanese Pronunciation:

> a is similar to the *a* in father
> i is similar to the *ea* in eat
> u is similar to the *oo* in look
> e is similar to the *e* in egg
> o is similar to the *o* in go

> (From *An Introduction to Modern Japanese* by Osamu and Nobuko Mizutani)

Part I

Approaching Reiki

Many people have heard the word Reiki but have no idea of what it actually is. Is it a religion, a massage procedure or could it even be dangerous? 'No', is the answer to all three questions. It is neither a belief system nor a physically manipulative technique and it is completely safe. The system of Reiki is a method of working with energy that allows the body to clear itself, leaving one feeling lighter, healthier and happier.

The origins of the word Reiki are discussed in Part 1. Reiki represents both the name of the system that is practiced today and the concept of spiritual energy. The system of Reiki is best known for its delicious treatments and eye-opening courses and it is through these avenues that the system is explored. Sound information about the workings of this system from a modern perspective are looked at in depth from both the practitioner/client and teacher/student viewpoints. There are many beliefs about Reiki and this section is intended to clarify what is, and what is not, a part of the modern practice of Reiki.

1   Reiki, the Word

Reiki Translated

Reiki, the word, is Japanese. It is written with two Japanese *kanji*, 霊気, meaning 'spiritual energy'. Below are some literal translations from Japanese dictionaries.

霊 is *rei*
- A spiritual entity believed to exist within or without our physical body. The Soul.
- Spiritual.
- Sacred, divine and miraculous.
- Departed spirit.
- That which possesses an infinite power. An invisible and wondrous power or the source of it.
- Reverence. Sacredness. Blessing.

気 is *ki*
- Something unseen.
- Atmosphere.
- Vital energy.
- Vapor.
- Breath.
- The energy of the universe.

In more recent times, these 2 *kanji* have also been described as meaning 'Universal Energy' (or 'Universal Life Force Energy'). This appears to be a translation of the second *kanji*, *ki*, only. *Ki* is the energy of everything including Heaven and Earth; the entire universe.

The first *kanji, rei,* may have been left out of earlier English translations due to the fact that the term 'spiritual' was not the focus of the modern practice in the 20th century. At the time the system was more prominently promoted as a hands-on healing, rather than spiritual, practice.

One will find more detailed explanations relating to the origins of *kanji,* how to draw *kanji* (especially helpful for working with Reiki symbols) and the etymological origins of the word Reiki in chapter 7.

There are only a smattering of works translated into English on the subject of Japanese arts and ways. Yet there is an abundance of translated material from Chinese resources that relate specifically to traditional energetic practices. Using Chinese resources to research some aspects of the system of Reiki can be helpful in piecing together a more complete understanding of what Reiki is through an Asian historical perspective. For example, the two *kanji* that represent the word Reiki originated in China. Their Chinese counterparts are called *Ling Chi* (*Chi* may also be written as *Qi*).

> The *Ancient Book of Lu* states that "even a blade of grass or clump of dirt contains *Ling Qi.*" *Ling Qi* is the spiritual energy that envelops and forms all things. In order to connect with and perceive the *Ling Qi* contained within the environment, an individual must first cultivate his or her own personal *Ling Qi.*
>
> (Excerpt from *Chinese Medical Qigong Therapy*
> *Volume 1* by Professor Jerry Alan Johnson)

This Chinese understanding of *Ling Chi* relates directly to the Japanese use of the word Reiki as spiritual energy. Reiki is the energy (or spirit or essence) of everything. There are not different flavors of Reiki—rather different flavors of thought, practice and intention. It is the 'energy that envelops and forms all things' including humankind. The system of Reiki, too, teaches that when humans work consciously with Reiki they begin to evolve and strengthen their connection with the universe.

Pronouncing Reiki

To pronounce the word Reiki in Japanese it is necessary to forego any preconceptions about language. The first sound in *rei* is neither an 'R' nor an 'L' as some believe. In Japanese the sound is, in fact, somewhere in between the two letters. The Japanese language has no correlation with English or its pronunciations.

The first time that the government initiated a standardized system and *romanji*[1] were introduced was in 1885. The *kanji* for *rei* is officially spelled with an 'R' when translating into English and is therefore pronounced with an 'R' by English speakers.

The word Reiki is commonly pronounced as *Ray Kee.*

A System and an Energy

Although the word Reiki has its own unique meaning in the Japanese language, the same word has been adopted throughout the rest of the world to represent a healing system; the system of Reiki.

Mikao Usui, the founder of this system, did not call his teachings by this name. Reiki appeared written in conjunction with his teachings but this was merely to point out that the teachings worked with spiritual energy. This was common practice at that time.

Japanese Reiki teacher Hiroshi Doi[2] stated that from the beginning of the Meiji era in 1868 through to the modern day, Japanese spiritual therapists commonly used the term *Reiki Ryôhô* to refer to their therapies. An example of this can be seen in the title of the work *Reiki Ryôhô To Sono Koka* (*Reiki Ryôhô and its Effects*) which was published in 1919 and written by a therapist called Mataji Kawakami who was unrelated to Mikao Usui and his teachings.[3]

Other spiritual healing groups of the early 1900s took on titles such as *Reiki Kangen Ryôin* and *Dainihon Reigaku Kenkyû Kai* (Japanese Institute of Studies of the Spirit).

An appropriate name for Mikao Usui's teachings would have been *Usui dô* meaning 'the Way of Usui'. According to H.E. Davey, author of *The Japanese Way of the Artist*, the word *dô* originates from the Chinese word *Dao.*

---

[1] *Romaji* are the English letters used to translate *kanji.*
[2] Hiroshi Doi is a modern day Reiki teacher in Japan who has studied both more traditional and modern forms of the system of Reiki.
[3] *Usui Reiki Ryôhô* International (URRI) Conference 2003 in Denmark.

The ancient meaning conveyed by this ideograph [*dao*] can be translated as "the way that one comes to see and understand oneself in relationship with the universe or cosmos (Heaven), environment (Earth) and the Divine".

(Excerpt from *Chinese Medical Qigong Therapy Vol. 1* by Professor Jerry Alan Johnson)

It would also have been appropriate to call his healings *Usui teate* which translates as 'Usui hands-on healing'.

The title on the Mikao Usui Memorial Stone, which was erected in 1927, one year after the death of Mikao Usui by his students, is inscribed *Reiho Choso Usui Sensei Kudoko No Hi*. Hyakuten Inamoto has translated this as 'Memorial of the Merits of Usui *Sensei*, the founder of *Reiho*'. The direct translation of *Reiho* is 'spiritual method' and Hyakuten Inamoto clarifies that in Japan today it would represent the more commonly used term of *Reiki Ryôhô*, 'spiritual energy healing method'.

Reiki, the word, is found in the names of the branches that developed from Mikao Usui's teachings. Both the *Usui Reiki Ryôhô Gakkai*[4] (Society of the Usui Spiritual Energy Healing Method) and, one of its offshoots, the *Hayashi Reiki Kenkyû Kai* (Hayashi's Spiritual Energy Research Society) used the word Reiki to signify that they worked with 'spiritual energy'.

Hawayo Takata was the first student of these teachings outside of Japan. Chûjirô Hayashi, a teacher student of Mikao Usui was her teacher. He, along with his daughter, travelled with her to Hawaii to help her set up her practice. At his farewell dinner in 1938, he presented her with a Western-style certificate. This official gesture ensured that she was viewed as a legal teacher and practitioner in these teachings under American law. The certificate states in English that Hawayo Takata 'has passed all the tests and proved worthy and capable of administering the treatment and of conferring the power of Reiki on others'. This appears to refer to the word Reiki as meaning 'spiritual energy' rather than the name of a system. The certificate also states in English that she was a 'Master of the Usui

---

[4] The *Usui Reiki Ryôhô Gakkai* is registered in Japan as *Shinshin Kaizen Usui Reiki Ryôhô Gakkai*.

Reiki system of drugless healing'. Here the word 'system' appears to have been translated from the Japanese word *Ryôhô* while the word Reiki has been left as is. In neither instance does the certificate convey that the system was called Reiki by Chûjirô Hayashi.

Throughout the next 40 years the system, under Hawayo Takata, formally became known as *Usui Shiki Ryôhô*[5] which does not mention Reiki at all. This was the official title which Hawayo Takata printed on her students' certificates. She was also known to refer to it as *Usui Reiki Ryôhô*[6] and as the Reiki method of natural healing.

Eventually the word Reiki jointly came to represent the system based on Mikao Usui's teachings as well as the energy that 'envelops and forms all things'.

The disadvantage of using the word Reiki to indicate both 'spiritual energy' and a system is that no one is certain as to what the name refers to. Is it referring to the energy (which belongs to no culture, belief or place) or the system (which has a founder and a specific structure)? Lack of clarity on this subject has meant that in recent times people have become unsure as to what particular practices fall within the system of Reiki. Varied systems calling themselves Reiki may claim to utilize spiritual energy yet the system itself may not stem from the teachings of Mikao Usui. Without a strong definition of the system, the door is left wide open for individual interpretations.

Traditional and Non-Traditional Systems

The system of Reiki as it is taught today is often roughly broken up into Japanese or Western methods. It is the Western or modern method that has swept across the planet over the last couple of decades. This method originated with Chûjirô Hayashi and his student Hawayo Takata and, on returning to Japan from the West in the 1980s, has highly influenced most modern Japanese systems of Reiki. Therefore to call a system, merely because it is taught by Japanese, 'traditional' would be incorrect.

True Japanese practices are almost impossible to find anywhere

---

[5] *Usui Shiki Ryôhô* translates as 'Usui Way Healing Method'.
[6] From a transcript of Hawayo Takata talking about the system of Reiki in 1979.

today, yet researched courses are available that have been developed to offer students a greater sense of connectedness to the teachings of Mikao Usui. The authors of this book, Bronwen and Frans Stiene, teach well-researched Reiki courses from a Japanese perspective without New Age add-ons.

2 Treatments

The Reiki Treatment Experience

Ki is the basic unit of the universe.
It is the infinite gathering of infinitely small particles.
Everything is ultimately composed of *Ki*.

If you pursue this concept to the depth of human consciousness, you will understand the universal mind which governs all creation, loving and protecting all life ...

Everything originates from the *Ki* of the universe.

(Excerpt from the *Book of Ki* by Koichi Tohei)

Ki is at the base of all energy work including the popular aspect of the system of Reiki – Reiki treatments. They can be found advertised in magazines, health food stores, libraries or just discussed between friends.

Reiki treatments should probably be regarded as a by-product of the system of Reiki. Prior to a treatment, a student has studied the system of Reiki with a teacher and worked through various practices to develop skill, knowledge and experience. The practitioner then becomes available to fulfill the role of practitioner for friends and family and eventually as a professional for clients if so desired.

A Reiki treatment may be experienced in numerous ways. Some treatments are provided in a professional setting while others embody a gentle connection between acquaintances.

Perhaps at work a colleague, who has studied the system of Reiki, extends a hand to an aching shoulder muscle. Before long the pain has miraculously melted away.

Even better is the luxury of a one-hour Reiki treatment. The client lies on a professional practitioner's Reiki table with relaxing music and soft lighting as the mind and body float off.

Then there is self-treatment where a practitioner treats him or herself using various elements of the system of Reiki.

Reiki treatments come in all shapes and sizes.

Practitioners

A professional practitioner is generally someone who has completed at least the second level of a Reiki course. Ideally, a professional Reiki practitioner should have basic counseling, first-aid and business skills with a sound knowledge of physiology and anatomy. Information should be on hand to be able to refer the client on to a professional healthcare worker where appropriate. Professional practitioners should have a developed personal self-healing regime that enables them to work effectively as knowledgeable, experienced and energetically clear practitioners.

There is more to a professional practice than just placing hands on the body. Most countries have Reiki associations for practitioners to register with. Ideally these associations promote a high standard of Reiki training along with a set Code of Ethics and Practice that practitioners are required to abide by.

A practitioner who does not work professionally can also perform Reiki treatments for the self, friends and family. These treatments can be just as effective and enjoyable as professional treatments. Clinical professionalism does not necessarily denote a specific quality of energetic expertise.

Clients

Anyone can receive a Reiki treatment, from a child in the womb through to someone in the precious last moments of life. There are no requirements except an open mind and the intent to heal.

A practitioner will adjust a client's treatment depending upon the environment and the individual. For example, a child may not sit still for long and therefore a treatment would need to be quick and to the point. Someone in a wheelchair might be unable to lie down and then a treatment would be delivered with the client seated. Most any situation can be catered for.

Everyone knows of someone who would benefit from a Reiki treatment. This person, though, may not be a willing participant in a Reiki treatment. It is important that the client (or friend or family member) is not pushed into receiving the treatment. A practitioner cannot heal – that is the client's responsibility. Practitioners must always respect the wishes of those around them.

Remember that life is continually changing. So, a client may refuse a treatment one day and yet happily accept one another day.

The Procedure

To experience a Reiki treatment the client lies or sits and the practitioner's hands are placed on, or just above, the body. It is unnecessary for the client to remove any clothing and no private parts of the body need ever be touched. *There is no place for sexual contact or inference within the system of Reiki.*

Quiet and comfort during a Reiki treatment are an asset for both the practitioner and the client. The practitioner reaches a meditative state quite quickly and the client eventually lets go of the busy mind and tense physicality.

This sense of utter relaxation is, in fact, a healing state. It is often likened to being in the womb. There is consciousness, yet the client feels enclosed and safe from outside influences. It is also in this state that the client may glean spiritual guidance.

The system of Reiki is not a manipulative one. Energy knows its true path. Reiki is not different from one's energy; there is no cut-off point or disconnection. Existence is a continuous flow of energy without beginning or end. A client simply draws on more of the same energy, building personal resources and clearing energy – balancing the body at all levels.

The practitioner offers energy to the client which moves through the hands and into the client's body supporting the client's healing process. The hands do not manipulate the Reiki, they are merely a vessel for the Reiki to flow through. Hand positions can be held roughly from one minute to half an hour or longer – depending upon what the practitioner can sense in the body.

A general rule of thumb is that as long as the practitioner can sense something like a cool breeze, vibrating, moving, heating up, tingling (or whatever the energetic sensation is) then the practitioner remains in that position. Clients, too, may sense the movement of energy in their bodies.

These sensations are the side effects of energy clearing in the body. Descriptions of the effects of sensing energy might be twitching or involuntary movement; the 'seeing' of colors or a visual journey while the eyes are closed; the gaining of an intuitive knowledge or understanding. As these sensations are but side effects and not the healing itself, the practitioner and client learn that no matter whether something is sensed or not, the treatment is still effective.

A clear understanding of what a Reiki treatment is results from undergoing the holistic experience of a treatment rather than responding to select sensations only.

Reiki's Path

A Reiki treatment realigns one with one's true path, source and spirit.

It must be conceived that everything has energy or *ki* in it—even a piece of paper or a plant, the items in the room, the building itself, the city, the country, the world, the universe and on and on. Gradually, comprehension dawns that there exists an unlimited amount of energy. This energy may seem invisible or elusive, but it is, instead, all-encompassing. It is this energy that makes not just humans, but worlds, function. It is the fuel that drives humans and gives ultimate structure and purpose in life. This is Reiki.

Occasionally, humans get a bit of dirt in the fuel line. A better way to explain it is perhaps by envisaging a free-flowing river. This beautiful river is like energy flowing easily down through the body. Occasionally a pebble, or even a rock, will fall into that river making the flow of the water a little more difficult. These pebbles are human worries, fear and anger. Each pebble builds on top of the other. Soon there is only a trickle of water running in that once beautiful free-flowing river. And so it is with energy in the human body.

During a Reiki treatment the pure flow of energy is realigned within the body. It washes down, clearing obstructions and strengthening the flow of energy. This kindles a connection to the understanding of one's purpose on Earth and the easiest, most successful way of achieving it.

Working with Intent

At the base of all Reiki treatments is intent. Both practitioners and clients can support their treatments by working consciously with intent.

Intent is the initial, directed thought that flickers across the mind – often before there is a conscious awareness that the thinking process has begun.

This directed thought sets a process in motion. It stimulates energy to trigger an action. The action might be picking up a tea cup, talking to someone or allowing a healing process to initiate.

As an often unconscious act, intent can be vague and unclear or misdirected due to pre-set judgments and understandings that have accumulated during one's lifetime. This can weaken one's intent and the resulting process.

When working with energy, the base of this energy needs to be clear. And at the very base of this energy is intent. Once intent is crystal clear, energy can move freely through the body.

But what intent should practitioners and clients consciously hold throughout a Reiki treatment?

Healing intentions are most effective when there are no limitations and one gives over to the flow of the universe. In this state the unlimited power of the universe can truly enter one's world and affect change.

During a treatment, practitioners and clients need to let go of judging sensations and focusing on outcomes. Attachment to any outcome leads practitioners to desire specific results in a treatment. Perhaps the practitioners are attempting to prove to both themselves and others that they have an intellectual and technical control of Reiki. Such an attitude aims at boosting the ego with a sense of personal validation rather than supporting the practitioners' practice or clients' healing journey.

To support their practice, practitioners may consciously hold this intent: 'May my client receive whatever it is that he/she may need at this exact moment in his/her life.'

Practitioners hold a responsibility to effectively connect with this pure intent. They must delve deep inside themselves using the five elements of the system of Reiki; the meditations, symbols and mantras, precepts, hands-on healing for the self and the attunement. From this space of Oneness where intent is pure and clear, there are no practitioners, no clients and no universal energy – just Oneness. It is in this Oneness that deep healing can occur.

Clients, on the other hand, can support the healing process by consciously setting their intent to be open and without attachment. It is the clients' self-responsibility to be as open as possible to healing. Clients, however, may desire a repeat of a similar treatment experience due to the pleasure or relief that they had felt in past treatments and this will only obstruct the free flow of energy.

To support their Reiki treatment, clients may consciously hold this intent: 'I am open to receive whatever it is that I may need at this exact moment in my life.'

Clients will only draw the amount of energy that is needed. Therefore, if the client consciously or unconsciously does not want to draw on the energy there will be little or no effect. In this way the client is in control of what is happening with the Reiki, albeit at an often unconscious level. This allows one's own nature to do the healing and one's own nature does no harm. It is only when humanity tries to control nature and develop rules and regulations that work against its natural flow that harm can occur. Any fear that is introduced into the system of Reiki is therefore a human concoction.

By letting go of making conscious decisions the pressure to perform is taken off, the ego is sent on vacation and the practitioner and client can get to work on what is integral to one's well being.

Once this is accepted by both the practitioner and client, the energy is allowed to support the natural healing process and the benefits will become apparent.

Benefits of Treatments

The purpose of a Reiki treatment is to support healing. To heal means 'to make whole'. This understanding lies at the foundation of the system of Reiki. Becoming whole entails drawing varied aspects of the self together; allowing them to collaborate with one another, helping 'the whole' function to its best ability. That is THE benefit of receiving a Reiki treatment.

Specific results from working with the system of Reiki cannot be guaranteed. Any outcome depends upon each individual's current situation and life experience. Individuals draw on the energy that they require at that moment in time. It is therefore not helpful to create an inflexible treatment plan. A practitioner must work intuitively, sensing where and when to move the hands during the treatment. The hands are listening to the client's body as it determines what it requires to become whole. By body, this includes every aspect of the self; the physical and non-physical. For this reason no two Reiki experiences are alike.

All illnesses can be treated with Reiki, even though it is impossible to predict an outcome. The Reiki itself will work away on wherever the body draws it at the time. This might be a physical problem, an emotional imbalance, a busy mind or the sense of a lack of connection to life.

Basically, a Reiki treatment supports each person in healing themselves.

> Each of us has his or her own natural pharmacopoeia – the very finest drugstore available at the cheapest cost – to produce all the drugs we ever need to run our bodymind in precisely the way it was designed to run over centuries of evolution. Research needs to focus on understanding the workings of these natural resources – our own endogenous drugs – so that we can create the conditions that will enable them to do what they do best.
>
> (Excerpt from *Molecules of Emotion: The Science Behind Mind-Body Medicine* by Candace B. Pert)

Benefits may include experiencing mental clarity and pain relief, or feeling relaxed and more deeply connected to one's spiritual nature. It may also help deal with acute or chronic illnesses.

A good example is of a client who has experienced a chronic illness over many years and is near death. A practitioner cannot predict or calculate whether there will be recovery, how long recovery might take or if death is imminent. Instead, the practitioner lets the Reiki do what is needed; it may be to emotionally settle the person, to relieve pain or to offer spiritual insight. The client and doctors may not expect recovery but a Reiki practitioner is always open to the possibility of a miracle. Depression, insomnia and fear-based illnesses and other non-physical illnesses can also benefit from Reiki.

Reiki works with acute problems too. As a first-aid tool, it offers pain relief while attempting to return the body to its most natural state. Stress is a word that is familiar in all sectors of the community today. When stressed the immune system weakens leaving humans prone to ill health. Reiki brings about calm and thus deals effectively with stress. Reiki assists clarity of thought and ease of decision-making.

Not only does Reiki support self-healing, it also enhances whatever it is used on – attempting to bring everything back to a natural, balanced state.

Experiencing Clearing

Reiki clears and enhances energy according to the needs of the body. It is a non-manipulative, non-invasive and non-diagnostic practice. To begin to bring the body back into balance the journey toward becoming whole is all that can occur and, as stated earlier, this cannot be harmful. Listening to the body is, in fact, the most sensible thing anyone can do for premium health and the system of Reiki is founded on this principle.

After a Reiki treatment, it is advisable to drink lots of water to continue the clearing that was initiated by the Reiki.

Although not a contraindication, clients should be aware that, due to a natural clearing process, there may be temporary discomfort. Some symptoms may be slightly exaggerated. This is, in fact, a very positive sign indicating that the Reiki is moving things in the body.

If this is the case, it is beneficial to receive more Reiki to follow up on the work already done.

Clients may also feel the need to review their medication, in conjunction with their healthcare worker, to assist the natural rebalancing of the body that has been initiated by the Reiki.

Number of Treatments

Practitioners often suggest three initial Reiki treatments if the client wishes to work on a specific issue. This issue may be of an emotional, physical, mental or spiritual nature. If, after three treatments, the symptoms are still apparent, treatments may be continued.

Practitioners should work within timeframes as it gives clients the chance to work toward recovery by a particular date. Unlimited Reiki treatments may mean unlimited ill health for some.

Reiki treatments are also an excellent tool for relaxation and can be experienced in the same manner as, for example, a one-off Swedish massage – for pure enjoyment. Don't forget that Reiki will always be working on re-balancing even if the client is not consciously aware of it.

Animals, Plants and More

Animals, plants and other 'things' can also draw on Reiki. Science tells us that everything has energy in it, whether it is a human, a cat, a coffee mug or a thought form. When Reiki is drawn upon, it clears and enhances the existing energy, bringing it back into balance. This is beneficial to all things.

For animals, a treatment is practiced in much the same way as on humans. Reiki practitioners physically approach animals and offer their energetic services. Hands should be placed on or near the animal depending on the animal's response.

Be assured that an animal will signal if it does or does not want the Reiki. Generally, animals are attracted to energy and will attempt to get into whatever position is best to draw maximum benefit from the treatment. If the animal just walks (or runs) away, a later attempt might be more successful. The animal may then feel less nervous about this new experience.

Plant life flourishes with Reiki. Treating the seeds is just the first step. As the plant grows, the hands are placed above the leaves or wrapped around the pot. A trick to using Reiki in a house filled with potted plants is to first use Reiki on the bucket of water. This can then be used for watering the plants.

Food and drink can be enhanced energetically with Reiki too. Imagine eating food that is energetically heightened! Many people find that such food immediately tastes better. The food is coming into a heightened vibration through the energetic balancing that Reiki supports and therefore any elements that may be less than fresh or have stayed too long on the shelf or in the freezer may improve. Each day that a piece of fruit or vegetable is away from its plant it is fast losing nutrients and goodness.

The same can be said for allopathic[1] medicines or herbal remedies. By lifting the vibration level of allopathic medicines into a more balanced state, clients claim the side effects have less impact. Herbal remedies draw on Reiki to become more effective.

Stones, crystals and other natural elements are felt to draw great amounts of energy. Reiki does not take away from their own natural abilities—it just enhances them.

People have also been known to use Reiki on computers, batteries, wallets and the list goes on.

The only limit is imagination.

---

[1] Allopathy: That system of medical practice that aims to combat disease by the use of remedies which produce effects different from those produced by the special disease treated. Webster Dictionary.

3   Courses

Choosing Self-Healing

> The process of healing a personal illness is, in fact, a rite of
> passage, designed by yourself as one of the greatest learning
> tools you will ever encounter.
>
> (Excerpt from *Light Emerging* by Barbara Ann Brennan)

Treating the self is the most important aspect of Mikao Usui's
teachings.

Learning to treat the self is actively taking one's health into one's
own hands. This fearless act of self-responsibility changes how a
life situation is experienced. Reiki practitioners no longer need be
victims of their circumstances but can choose to live optimally at
every level. Life becomes easier as stress dissolves and perceptions
alter. The immune system strengthens and illness takes a back seat
in life. Most importantly, the connection to one's true spiritual
nature is re-established.

Feeling strong in the self also gives one the ability to help others.
Reiki courses teach not only how to heal the self, but how to support
the healing process of others too.

Before embarking on this journey, the student will need to find
an appropriate teacher.

Teachers

To find a Reiki teacher, the potential Reiki student needs to research
the choice and availability of teachers in the area.

Within the system of Reiki there are different styles of teaching, different attitudes and different methods. According to the level of dedication to personal practice undertaken by the teacher there are even different energetic abilities. As with anything in this life, the more one practices, the more one improves. Reiki itself, however, never changes what it is: the energy of everything. One teacher explains this by writing that people are 'higher vibrations' while systems are not. Meaning that no system is better than another – only individual practitioners can be 'better' by improving through their practice of the system.

There are different titles adopted by Reiki teachers. These include Reiki Master, Reiki Master/Teacher, *Shihan* or Reiki Teacher. The levels they are said to have completed might be called either Level 3 or *shinpiden*. These are names used by different branches to indicate that the individual has the ability to 'pass on' the system of Reiki which in some cases may only indicate that the person knows how to perform an attunement, the teacher's method of connecting to students. Due to a general lack of regulation, the title given to a Reiki teacher might not necessarily mean that this individual can guide students on their spiritual path or even understand the concept of Reiki. A few sub-branches may only teach the attunement to their teacher students while others may offer extensive training that includes thorough training in all five elements of the system of Reiki. Some have added more levels to a Reiki course, but this in itself does not indicate that the more levels one takes the more advantageous it is. Added levels may not teach the essence of becoming a professional Reiki teacher, but simply focus on add-ons to the system. It is the quality, rather than the quantity, of training that is important.

Reiki associations are available to support teachers and students. There may, however, be a great disparity in the standards offered by associations. Ideally, an association should be a place where Reiki practitioners and teachers are open to scrutiny by their peers in an effort to continue to raise standards. The Code of Ethics and Practice proposed by associations should also support high standards for practitioners and teachers.

Students

The system of Reiki has been developed in such a way that it is accessible to people of most any age. There are courses created specifically for children and, as long as one has the ability to comprehend the teachings, there are no age limitations. Physical handicaps need not be an issue as a course can be developed around individual needs where required. As a non-religious practice, it is open to men and women from every country the world over.

Selecting a Beneficial Course

Students must find out what qualifications in, and outside of, the system of Reiki the prospective teacher has and if the branch of Reiki feels right for them. It is recommended to personally meet teachers and, if possible, their students prior to studying with them.

Students should be aware (or beware) that some systems of Reiki have been known to make outrageous claims along the lines of 'we are the only ones who can use Reiki', 'our Reiki is the only real Reiki' or more simply that 'our Reiki is better than yours'. These attitudes are the result of active egos and display a lack of connection to the system of Reiki and its practices. Such claims are generally employed as tactics to promote insecurities in the minds of students to manipulate them to sign up to a course or to ensure that they remain exclusively with the one teacher.

Most importantly, don't be fooled by teachers who say they no longer need to work on themselves. Enlightenment is not so easily come by!

Steer clear of those who promote secrecy as a part of their training. This is generally a method to keep the sheep in the flock. If a branch is using the concept of secrecy as a technique to keep knowledge intact, as is often claimed, it must be realized that such a method is only as trustworthy as the trustworthiness of its students. Humans are fallible and such an excuse for creating secrets is a weak one. Secrecy and the forbidding of discussion with outsiders or the gaining of knowledge of other's ways and methods tend toward sect-like activities and misuse of power. Neither of these have any place in the system of Reiki.

This is not to say that there is not an appropriate time for students to learn different skills according to their abilities. Humans learn step by step and knowledge is best received in sequential steps; it is useless to learn step 3 before completing steps 1 and 2.

Many roads can be taken. Students need to be discerning and to choose the road that is appropriate for them.

Reiki Levels

Due to individual teachers' interests, motivations, or beliefs, there are infinite varieties of Reiki courses available today. Therefore, the number of levels and what is taught within them can vary extensively.

The structure of the system of Reiki includes three levels. Research shows that the levels Mikao Usui taught were spaced out over time, with students being required to work hard at each level before moving on to receive more teachings. This can be seen by the number of students who began each of his three levels. Only 1 percent or less went on to study Level 3. If the practices had been simple, the flow-through rate would have been much higher.

If these levels are taught close together, there is a limit to the amount of energy that a student can adjust to within a short period. Each student adjusts and builds on energy in his or her own time and forcing this process works for no one. Completing Levels 1 and 2 together in a weekend (a few modern courses may even include Level 3 in this 'package') is pointless and leaves students feeling powerful (temporarily) without actually becoming empowered.

The system of Reiki is not about paperwork or a timetable or any other man-made schedule. It is an energetic practice and therefore can only be experienced energetically. Some branches of Reiki may provide time limits for when it is appropriate to move on to a new level but for each individual this will be different. It is only through energetic practice that a student can come to the decision to move on to a new level of training.

Working with Reiki may appear extremely simple to a beginner and this in itself can create problems for students. By studying the system of Reiki in too short a course it is difficult to grasp its uniqueness and profundity. It is tempting to think that Reiki is too simple to have an impact and consequently disregard it. This is part of the true nature of Reiki. Scratch its surface and it takes one deeper and deeper spiritually, emotionally and intellectually.

Level 1

Shoden in Japanese. It is the beginning of a student's journey in self-healing using Reiki practices. It should teach a foundation of the system and how to work with Reiki on the self; how to strengthen one's inner energy and begin a personal healing process. It should also give one the confidence to work with friends and family using Reiki techniques. Students should also receive four attunements at this level.

Level 2

Okuden in Japanese. This is where students learn three mantras and symbols that aid the students in focusing and developing a strength and connection to energy. A student may continue developing a personal practice to develop skills as a professional practitioner. Students receive three attunements at this level.

Level 3

Shinpiden in Japanese. Traditionally this would be an ongoing level where the student continues building a strong connection with the teacher. This focuses on personal development and teaches one mantra and one symbol plus how to perform the attunement on others. At this level a student receives one attunement.

In modern courses, an approximate length of time for Level 1 is a minimum of 14 hours and for Level 2 is a minimum of seven hours. Level 3 is commonly taught from the perspective of providing ongoing support to the teacher student. Ongoing practice at all levels, either alone or with a group, is imperative.

> After practicing for a while, if we feel discouraged or tired because of how far we are from the goal of our spiritual journey, we should look back at our life in the days before we started training and celebrate any progress we have made.
>
> (Excerpt from *The Healing Power of The Mind* by Tulku Thondup)

At each level of the system of Reiki the student is brought into a fuller understanding of the workings and meaning of the five elements of the system of Reiki. These elements are the system's building blocks and they continue to be refined throughout each of the teachings and the ensuing personal practice that these teachings promote.

Course Costs

Costs will vary for Reiki courses. Some courses are plain cheap and others exclusively expensive. Human nature may tell us that expensive means better but that is not always true. Hawayo Takata introduced a system where it is claimed she asked her students to charge set prices, including a US$10,000 fee to complete a Level 3 course. Very few teachers charge these prices today and there is also no guarantee that what is taught for that price is any better than some other courses that are offered.

Students need to find out what they are paying for. Is there a manual? Are there experienced (technically and energetically) teachers, a suitable venue, post-course support and practice groups for students?

The Five Elements of the System of Reiki

Within the system of Reiki there are five major elements that a Reiki practitioner will learn, practice and experience. They are:

- The spiritual and mental connection using the five precepts.
- Hands-on healing for the self and others.
- Techniques.
- Four mantras and symbols.
- Attunements.

Each of these elements works together with the others to create a whole system for spiritual development and healing that is unique.

There are many other variables to the system of Reiki depending upon who the teacher and what the branch is, but these five elements are consistent throughout all Reiki courses – whether they developed in Japan or further evolved elsewhere in the world. The historical origins of the five elements of the system of Reiki are researched in detail later in *The Reiki Sourcebook*.

The Five Precepts

> For today only:
> Do not anger
> Do not worry
> Be humble
> Be honest in your work
> Be compassionate to yourself and others

This is a simple translation of the five precepts that are associated with the teachings of Reiki. They were introduced by Mikao Usui and are universal teachings.

These precepts should be kept in mind throughout each day. This is the beginning of the student's spiritual journey.

Hand Positions

> Everyone needs to be touched, stroked, cuddled, fondled, and held. Without this tactile stimulation, children and adults do not grow in a healthy way. Their emotional selves grow gnarled, crooked, bent, and deformed. They can be smoothed, straightened, and supported by touch.
>
> (Excerpt from *Time In: A Handbook for Child and Youth Care Professionals* by Michael Burns)

Hand positions are specific places on the body where students are taught to place their hands. This is for the purpose of assisting the energy to move through the body, clearing and strengthening one's spiritual and energetic connection.

In modern courses, students practice this on themselves and on others. A one-hour Reiki treatment is made up of a practitioner placing hands on (or off) the body of the client. The energy moves through the practitioner and is drawn by the client into the body. This is the same concept when practiced on oneself.

Some teachers' instructions about hand positions are very strict while others work from a solely intuitive perspective. There is no right or wrong, though it is useful to have some guidelines to follow as a beginner. Guidelines initially build confidence to a point where students can eventually break away from them.

A seminar is very pleasant to sit and listen to, but it is personal experience gained during a course that is truly enriching. For this reason it is integral that a Reiki course allows time for experiential work. Within the course it is most beneficial if the student is given the opportunity to work with Reiki on different people – this immediately broadens the experience and helps build confidence.

Techniques

> Techniques employ four qualities that reflect the nature of our world. Depending on the circumstance, you should be: hard as a diamond, flexible as a willow, smooth-flowing like water, or as empty as space.
>
> (From *The Art of Peace* by Morihei Ueshiba)

A number of techniques were used in Mikao Usui's early teachings. Only a very few of these made it across the ocean to America in the late 1930s with Hawayo Takata.

Since that time a great variety of techniques have been added to the system of Reiki. Many of these techniques have no foundation in the Japanese culture and the majority have been introduced through the New Age movement. A good example of this is the chakra system that is taught almost across the board in the system of Reiki, as it is known today. Traditionally, the Japanese used the *hara* center as a method to stimulate and balance energy in the body, not the chakra system[1].

Techniques are included in the system of Reiki for a number of reasons. They strengthen the connection to the energy, to build one's own energy, to create focus, and to support a spiritual journey.

---

[1] Research indicates that Hawayo Takata did not use the chakra system. In a 1935 diary entry she writes of the 'meaning of Reiki' being the Reiki meditation that lets the true 'energy' come out from within. 'It lies in the bottom of the stomach about 2 inches below the naval.' This correlates to the *hara* center.

Some 'new' techniques support these aims while others seem to complicate the system of Reiki needlessly – giving the teacher more 'power'.

One key reason why 'new' techniques have been added to the system of Reiki is that there has been limited understanding as to what Mikao Usui's original teachings entailed. This lack of understanding has been exacerbated by insufficient historical documentation. This does not mean that many of these techniques are not of value, although it does mean that they do not belong to the early teachings of Mikao Usui or the system of Reiki.

Mantras and Symbols

> ... Since the stars have fallen from heaven and our highest symbols have paled, a secret life holds sway in the unconscious. That is why we have a psychology today, and why we speak of the unconscious. All this would be quite superfluous in an age or culture that possessed symbols ...
>
> (Excerpt from C. G. Jung – *Psychological Reflections, an Anthology of his Writings 1905—1961*, edited by Jolande Jacobi)

There are only four mantras and symbols in traditional forms of the system of Reiki. Here again, there has been great change in the use of mantras and symbols since Mikao Usui began his teachings. Their meanings have changed and many new symbols have either been created or taken from other cultures and systems and added to the system of Reiki.

Mantras and symbols have also had a certain mysticism attributed to them. This has even led to the meanings behind the four traditional symbols gaining in significance over the years. At first, they were provided, like training wheels, for students to discard once they had become the appropriate energy. Today, they are credited with ideals such as protection, bringing in power, enhancing, manifesting and healing karma. These were never the major focus of the mantras and symbols and yet it is true some of these ideals are by-products of their practice. There is a misunderstanding here about the basic reason for the introduction of mantras and symbols into the teachings. Initially, Mikao Usui introduced symbols for those who had difficulty invoking the energy – that was all.

Attunements

> 'Initiation' is, first and foremost, a means calculated to induce the novice to discover for himself certain facts that are not directly revealed to him but which, by the aid of symbolical rites, he will eventually perceive himself... It is not intended to enlighten the novice but rather to lead him to become conscious of what has hitherto been hidden from him because his mental eye has not been capable of perceiving it.
>
> (Excerpt from *Initiations and Initiates* in Tibet by Alexandra David-Neel)

Attunements are integral to Mikao Usui's teachings. To practice the system of Reiki, students must first receive attunements. Methods differ, but the purpose is the same: to strengthen the students' connection with spiritual energy and to raise their personal energy levels.

An attunement is where a teacher completes a physical ritual around a seated student. The student generally has his/her eyes closed, concentrating on breathing or another form of meditation. There have been many variations on this. Some teachers touch the body and others do not, some move around the front and back of the body and some claim to even 'attune' the feet. An attunement is relatively short – a couple of minutes in length – but it is a pleasant experience for the student to sit and enjoy the sensation of energy in the body.

Attunements were initially called *reiju* in Japan and when the system moved out of the country they became known as initiations, empowerments or attunements.

There have been many claims made about the effects of an attunement. The hunt for the perfect explanation of what an attunement 'does' is ongoing. Some traditional teachings explain the attunement with the words 'more practice'. In other words 'if you keep practicing, then you will discover the answer for yourself'. Something as profound as an attunement is difficult to analyze at a human level. In essence the purpose of an attunement is:

- A sense of reconnection to one's true self.
- A clearing of the meridians allowing the student to conduct more energy through the body.
- A method a teacher uses in order to communicate with individual students on an energetic level.

Though attunements may vary from branch to branch they all seem to work to some degree – provided there is a perceptible basic core of the ritual coupled with clarity of intent. This occurs due to the fact that everything is made of energy and everyone has an innate ability to heal both themselves and others.

There are different set-ups that teachers will use when performing attunements on students. Most teachers perform the complete attunement on one student at a time. Some may even go so far as to take each student into a separate room, performing a complete attunement on the back and front in one go.[2]

When working with a large group of students some teachers have been known to walk down the front row of students completing only the front section of the ritual and then walk down the back of the row, completing only the back section. The attunement ends with the person they began with. It has been suggested that this method creates an incomplete energetic connection between the teacher and student.

Students may also receive as many attunements as they wish – in fact, the more the better. In Japan, these are repeated on a weekly or monthly basis and are not aligned to receiving new levels of certification, which is often believed to be the case in modern teachings. They do not appear to change the ritual for separate levels either, as is also often done today. The differences in understanding relate back to the traditional belief that a student will only ever take in the amount of energy from an attunement that is required by the student at that particular time. This is often disregarded today with the teacher being given more 'power'.

At no point should an attunement rely on the 'power' of the teacher. Modern teachers have been known to announce that the

---

[2] There are NO sexual connotations or suggestions in the system of Reiki whatsoever. If a teacher acts suggestively or inappropriately it is imperative that the student notify the appropriate authorities immediately.

Level 1 attunement works on the physical level, while the Level 2 attunement works on the emotional level and so on. These are examples of New Age mystification where teachers pretend to control the attunement process with their 'power'. In reality, an individual will draw the energy to wherever the body decides – this is not for the teacher to decide.

As an attunement is a powerful clearing of the body's energy, it is impossible to undo this or 'wipe it out'. Each attunement received takes the student a step further to re-aligning oneself with the natural functioning of the body.

For this reason it is also impossible to 'make' an attunement last for a limited period of time. Some crafty individuals have been known to say that a free 'sample' attunement will only last for four (or five or six or seven…) days. Students believe they are given something wonderful and then it is taken away again. If students did not know any better and wanted to continue receiving the benefits of Reiki they would then need to pay (maybe again) to do a course with the teacher. Apart from the fact that an attunement cannot 'wear out' within a pre-arranged time – energy doesn't wear a watch! – there is also a major misconception about Reiki here.

Attunements are beneficial and integral to the system of Reiki but it is the personal practice that rains blessings down upon the student.

> Attunement is just a beginning and the real ability is to develop on your own [with personal practice].

> (Excerpt from *Modern Reiki Method for Healing* by Hiroshi Doi)

Post-Course Experiences

As with a Reiki treatment, there is also a clearing experienced by students after completing a Reiki course. Life itself, is in fact one great cleansing process. Humans are continually working through things, whether it is a tiny revelation about an issue or a massive change that throws life into disarray. These are clearings where the old moves out and the new takes over. Reiki definitely aids this process, but the concept of clearing is certainly not unique to this system. This is a natural way for the body to heal and become whole.

Today, some teach that there is a three-week cleansing process after completing a Reiki course. Though this time allotment is a recent addition to the system of Reiki, it certainly has had its share of esoteric interpretations. There is no direct correlation between the three-week cleansing process and the 21-day meditation undertaken by Mikao Usui. This meditation would have been one of many meditations undertaken by Mikao Usui and was a part of a *shûgyô* or austerity practice. One does not undertake a 21-day practice without prior meditation training. Basically the popularity of the three-week cleansing process concept can be put down to the fact that it is successful: it achieves its aim. That aim is to get people practicing. Some smart individual knew that human nature takes 21 days to break a habit and therefore also takes 21 days to *make* a habit. After practicing the system of Reiki for three weeks students do not want to stop practicing – it feels too good!

Working with the system of Reiki does increase the effect of the cleansing process and often students will have quite immediate results (life turned into disarray!) a day or two after beginning their practice. The key is to keep practicing, allowing the energy to keep moving.

Becoming One with Reiki

During a student's practice of the system of Reiki, different personal stages are discovered. A path is unearthed and those who conscientiously practice the five elements of the system of Reiki gradually see where it is heading.

To tap into this spiritual energy, in its completeness, is to have arrived at the advanced stages of one's personal spiritual practice. To paraphrase, the experience of receiving the full effect of the system of Reiki actually means to achieve *satori*[3].

At this stage all ordinary perceptions are transformed and there is a realization of one's true potential as a human being.

Attaining this enlightened state of mind and becoming pure light is the ultimate goal of a Reiki practice. This is reflected by the mantra and symbol that are practiced at the third and final level of

---

[3] *Satori* means Enlightenment

the system. The mantra literally translated from the Japanese means 'great bright light'. So the goal is to become this great bright light by achieving a state of nonduality or *satori*.

Although students work with Reiki, in effect they only tap into a small amount of this spiritual energy until their energy is strong enough to allow pure spiritual energy through. As long as a student's true realization of this state is limited, then so too is the ability.

To achieve *satori* may take years and years of practice and there is no shortcut by means of using secret symbols or mantras. What is required, though, is perseverance and the right understanding of how to work with the five elements in order to reach, or become One with, the Great Bright Light of the system of Reiki.

Part II
Reiki Past

The history of the system of Reiki in general is sketchy. Much of the early Japanese information has been hard to come by and much of the factual history taught since the system's arrival in Hawaii in the late 1930s can be relegated to myth or unverifiable facts. Reasons for this are varied:

- Each individual will retell history according to his or her own experience, situation and agenda.
- There has been a lack of solid factual information for Reiki teachers to pass on to students.
- The introduction of historical material to the system of Reiki that is unverified.
- The difficulty in researching information in Japan. This is due to issues inherent in translating Japanese (especially pre-1940s Japanese) into English, and the unique Japanese culture.
- Many old Chinese, Tibetan and Indian books and manuscripts have been translated into English and other languages. Translated Japanese historical materials are not so readily available.
- The restrictions placed on the Japanese themselves (based on cultural mores and Eastern religious mystery teachings). Japanese do not conduct research as a non-Japanese would. There are many cultural limitations to contacting previously unknown individuals and to requesting relevant information, hence poor research results.
- At the turn of the century no photocopying machines existed to pass on course notes. Early methods required that students copied what notes there were by hand. Symbols were also copied from the teacher in this manner.

Fortunately there have recently been some redeeming factors to the system's history. These include the revelation of the existence of Mikao Usui's memorial stone in 1994; Japanese teaching manuals; early students who are still alive and the *Usui Reiki Ryôhô Gakkai*[4].

---

[4] The *Usui Reiki Ryôhô Gakkai* (Society of the Usui Spiritual Energy Healing Method) claims to have been created by Mikao Usui in 1922. The society still exists today, and has its seventh president. Its membership to date has not included any foreigners. Members are asked not to discuss the details of the society with non-members.

Part II begins with a timeline and a lineage chart to aid reader orientation on the history and development of Mikao Usui's teachings. These pages can be utilized as reference points. For more detailed reference information about people, places, events, techniques and branches readers should refer to the extensive Reiki Glossary in the Appendices.

Following on from this reference material the reader can trace the life of Mikao Usui through the numerous facts and fictions that have been told, and written, about him.

Mikao Usui (1865–1926), the founder of the system of Reiki, was born into a world of radical change. The Meiji Emperor (1852–1912) introduced Japan to modernization and industrialization after more than two centuries of national isolation or *sakoku* from the rest of the human race. Even Christianity, which had been banned during this time of isolation with punishment by death, was legalized in 1877. This environment explains certain developments in Mikao Usui's teachings, as does the impact of World War II on the evolution of the system of Reiki.

The actual practice of the teachings is dissected here and then restored in a logical order, which allows the reader to follow its many digressions. Further explored are the origins of the five precepts which aid students' spiritual development; the use of *gyosei*[5] as practiced at traditional gatherings; the hand positions, as taught by various Japanese teachers; the practice (and non-practice) of meditations, mantras and symbols; to the practice and variations of *reiju* or attunements in Japan.

The lives and practices of the students that followed in Mikao Usui's footsteps including the *Usui Reiki Ryôhô Gakkai* and Chûjirô Hayashi are also discussed.

The Reiki system that has evolved outside of Japan has its own history which began in the late 1930s. In Hawaii the system thrived under the care of Hawayo Takata[6] for many years until her death in 1980. The system she developed has had an enormous impact on what is taught in the present day in both Japan and the rest of the world as the system of Reiki.

---

[5] *Gyosei* means *waka* (poetry) written by an Emperor.

[6] Hawayo Takata was born in Hawaii to Japanese parents. She brought the system of Reiki to Hawaii from Japan in 1938 and was a major influence on the system's modern form.

4   Historical Facts

Lineage Chart

Mikao Usui created the origins of the system that is called Reiki today. There are a great many offshoots from these initial teachings. To give a quick and clear overview of the branches and their influences, we have drawn up a Reiki lineage chart. This chart incorporates two methods to simplify the reading of it.

To begin with, Mikao Usui and his teacher students have been named in person (where known). The naming of teachers continues on through the lineages until the teachings leave Japan. At that point, instead of following the path of individuals, the major branches are followed and their influence on one another. It is impossible to include the names of all of the students of each lineage leading up to a new branch.

[Authors' note: Hiroshi Doi, *Usui Reiki Ryôhô Gakkai* member, states that Kaiji Tomita and Toshihiro Eguchi did not study to the teacher level with Mikao Usui. Mariko Obaasan, Yuri in and Suzuki san have yet to be verified as teacher students of Mikao Usui.]

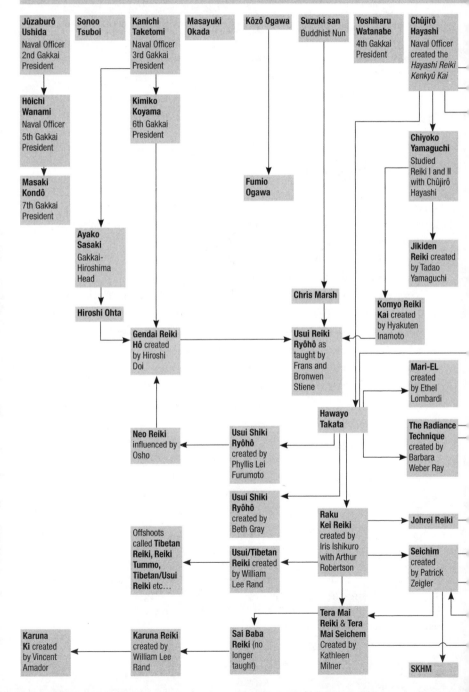

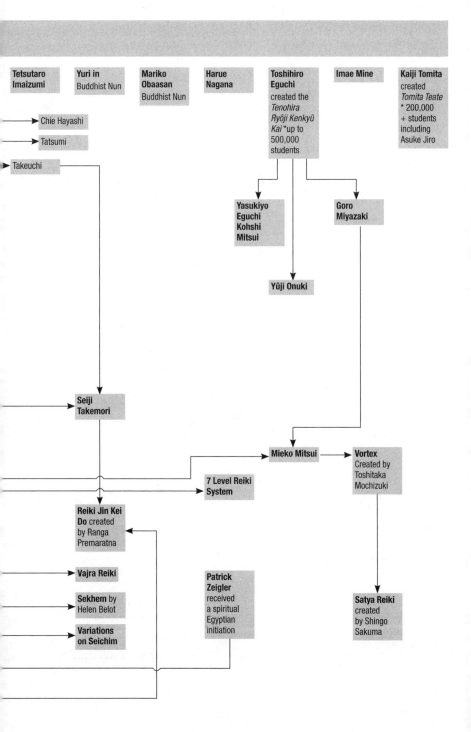

Timeline

Reiki Events		**Japanese Events**
	550	**550 ca:** Buddhism enters Japan via Korea
800: Japanese Buddhist precepts are written that are the base for Mikao Usui's precepts (SS)	800	**800:** Buddhism becomes the state religion of Japan
1865: 15 August, Mikao Usui is born in *Taniai mura, Yamagata gun, Gifu ken* (MUMS)	1865	**1865:** Japan opens its ports, etc. after a self-imposed isolation of over 200 years
		1868: Meiji Emperor moves the capital from *Kyôto* to *Edo*, now named *Tôkyô*
		1870: Commoners are permitted to take surnames
		1871: *Samurai* are ordered to cut off their topknots
		1871: First Japanese-language daily newspaper, *Yokohama Mainichi Shimbun*, begins publication
		1871: An 18-month tour to study the social systems of the United States and European nations is sponsored by the Japanese government
		1872: Compulsory elementary education is established
1873: 11 April, Toshihiro Eguchi is born (JR)	1873	**1872:** Army and Navy ministries are established
		1874-1877: *Samurai* protest movements
		1877: Christianity is legalized
1880: 15 September, Chûjirô Hayashi is born (CY)		
1883: Kôshi Mitsui is born (JR)		
1889: Mikao Usui receives *menkyo kaiden* in martial arts (SS)		
1887: Chie Hayashi is born (CY)		
		1890: Imperial Rescript on Education is written
1895: Suzuki san is born, cousin of Mikao Usui's wife (SS)	1895	**1894-1895:** Sino-Japanese War
1896: Yuri in, *Tendai* nun and student of Mikao Usui is born (unverified)		**1907:** U.S. President Theodore Roosevelt bans Japanese from immigrating to the United States

Reiki Events		Japanese Events
1897: Mariko Obaasan (Buddhist name is Tenon in) *Tendai* nun and student of Mikao Usui is born (unverified)	**1897**	
1900: 24 December, Hawayo Takata is born in Hawaii (HT)		
1906: Kimiko Koyama is born (HD)		
1908: Fuji, Mikao Usui's son is born (MUMS and gravesite)		**1909:** Jigorô Kanô, founder of *jûdô*, becomes the first Japanese member of the International Olympic committee
		1910: Korea is made a colony of Japan
1913: Toshiko, Mikao Usui's daughter is born (MUMS and gravesite)	**1913**	**1912:** 6 July, Japans first entry in the Olympic games held in Stockholm, Sweden
1914: 28 December, *Kenzen no Genri* (*The Principles of Health*), written by Bizan Suzuki, includes precepts that are similar to those of Mikao Usui (JR)		**1914–1918:** WWI. Japan sides with the 'Allies', seizing German island colonies in the Pacific and German concessions in the Shandong Peninsula
1915: Suzuki san starts her training with Mikao Usui (SS)		
1915: Mikao Usui begins teaching the five precepts (SS)		
1917: Mikao Usui becomes well known as a healer (SS)		
1917: Hawayo Takata marries Saichi (HT)		
		1918: High rice prices incite riots throughout Japan
1920: Chiyoko Yamaguchi is born (CY)		**1920:** Shinpei Goto becomes Mayor of *Tôkyô*
1920: Mariko Obaasan and Yuri in begin their study with Mikao Usui		
1922: March, Mikao Usui completes his *shûgyô* training, the 21-day meditation on *kurama yama* (MUMS)	**1922**	**1922:** First national athletic exhibition in *Tôkyô* where many martial artists are asked to perform
1922: April, Mikao Usui opens his seat of learning in Harajuku, *Aoyama, Tôkyô* (MUMS)		

Reiki Events		Japanese Events
1922: April, *Usui Reiki Ryôhô Gakkai* is created by Mikao Usui (HD)	**1922**	
1923: Symbols are introduced in Mikao Usui's teachings (SS)		**1923:** 1 September, the great *Kanto* earth quake in *Tôkyô* and surrounds
1923: *Torii* gate erected by Mikao Usui and his family in *Taniai mura* (HD)		
1925: February, Mikao Usui moves his *dôjô* to a suburban house at Nakano (MUMS)		
1925: Kaiji Tomita studies with Mikao Usui (HD)		
1925: May, Chûjirô Hayashi studies with Mikao Usui		
1925: November, Jûzaburô Ushida and Kanichi Taketomi study with Mikao Usui		
1926: 16 February, Photo of Mikao Usui and his students and family is taken (Toshitaka Mochizuki's book, *Chô Kantan Iyashi No Te*)		
1926: 9 March, Mikao Usui dies of a stroke in *Fukuyama* in *Hiroshima* (MUMS)		
1927: February, the *Usui Reiki Ryôhô Gakkai* erects the memorial stone of Mikao Usui (MUMS)	**1927**	**1927:** Severe depression (which has been in place since the 1920s) causes many commercial banks to collapse
1927: Tatsumi receives the teacher level from Chûjirô Hayashi		
1927–1928: Toshihiro Eguchi establishes his own center, *Tenohira Ryoji Kenkyû Kai* (Hand Healing Research Center) (HD)		
1928: Wasaburo Sugano (Chiyoko Yamaguchi's uncle) studied Level 1 with Chûjirô Hayashi (CY)		
1928: Shûô Matsui writes an article about Chûjirô Hayashi, his teacher and the system of Reiki (article www.reiki.net.au)		

Reiki Events	1930	Japanese Events

Reiki Events

1930: Toshihiro Eguchi and Kôshi Mitsui write a book together called *Te No Hira Ryôji Nyûmon (Introduction to Healing with the Palms)*

1931: Chûjirô Hayashi names his own clinic *Hayashi Reiki Kenkyû Kai* (Hayashi Spiritual Energy Society) (HD)

1933: Kaiji Tomita, a student of Mikao Usui, writes a book called *Reiki To Jinjutsu: Tomita Ryû Teate Ryôhô (Reiki and Humanitarian Work: Tomita Ryû Hands Healing)*

1935: Hawayo Takata becomes a client of Chûjirô Hayashi (HT)

1935: 23 September, Mikao Usui's daughter Toshiko dies (MUMS and gravesite)

1937: Hawayo Takata returns to the USA to begin teaching the system of Reiki. Chûjirô Hayashi and his daughter accompany her and help her to begin her practice (HT)

1938: 21 February, Chûjirô Hayashi awards Hawayo Takata a Master certificate before returning to Japan (HT)

1938: Chiyoko Yamaguchi studies *shoden* and *okuden* with Chûjirô Hayashi (CY)

1940: 10 May, Chûjirô Hayashi commits suicide (CY and HT)

1940: Chie Hayashi, Chûjirô Hayashi's wife becomes the president of his organisation (HD and CY)

1942: Fumio Ogawa joins the *Usui Reiki Ryôhô Gakkai* (FAP)

1946: 10 July, Mikao Usui's son Fuji dies (MUMS and gravesite)

1946: 17 October, Mikao Usui's wife, Sadako Suzuki, dies (MUMS and gravesite)

Japanese Events

1931: Manchurian Incident: Japan sends troops into southern Manchuria 1932: Shanghai Incident: Japan sent troops into Shanghai China

1937–1945: Second Sino-Japanese War

1939–1945: WWII

1941: Pearl Harbor is attacked. Many Japanese and Japanese-Americans living in the USA are placed in internment camps as a result

1945: Atomic bombs dropped on *Hiroshima* and *Nagasaki*

Reiki Events

1975: Advertising Poster for a workshop by Hawayo Takata states; The Only Teacher of the Usui System of Reiki in the World Today

1976: Hawayo Takata teaches her first official Reiki teacher student, Virginia Samdahl, for US$10,000

1980: 11 December, Hawayo Takata dies of a heart attack

1982: Hawayo Takata's teacher students meet to compare mantras, symbols and attunements

1983: The Reiki Alliance standardizes mantras, symbols and attunements at their official inaugural meeting at Barbara Brown's house in British Columbia (Carel Anne Farmer, student of Phyllis Lei Furumoto and John Harvey Gray)

1983: The Reiki Alliance chooses Phyllis Lei Furumoto to become the lineage bearer of their system of Reiki. She receives the 'title of holder' of the 'Office of the Grandmaster' (The Reiki Alliance)

1985: Mieko Mitsui begins teaching Levels 1 and 2 in Japan

1991: Frank Arjava Petter and his then-wife, Chetna Kobayashi, begin teaching all three levels in Japan (FAP)

1993: 22 October, Hiroshi Doi received *shoden* from the *Usui Reiki Ryôhô Gakkai* (HD)

1995: Toshitaka Mochizuki's book is published, *Iyashi No Te* (*Healing Hands*)

1997: Yuri in, *Tendai* nun and student of Mikao Usui, dies

1952

1975

Japanese Events

1952: End of Allied Occupation of Japan

1964: Olympics held in *Tôkyô*

Reiki Events		Japanese Events
1997: Historic meeting between Phyllis Lei Furumoto and Kimiko Koyama cancelled (HD)	**1997**	
1997: Rejection of Phyllis Lei Furumoto's application to trademark the words *Usui Shiki Ryôhô* and Usui System in the USA and internationally		
1997: Frank Arjava Petter's first book, *Reiki Fire*, is published		
1998: January, Masaki Kondô becomes the seventh president of the *Usui Reiki Ryôhô Gakkai*		**1998:** Olympic games held in *Nagano* prefecture
1999: September, Kimiko Koyama, the sixth president of the *Usui Reiki Ryôhô Gakkai*, dies		
1999: Hiroshi Doi teaches a *reiju* at the URRI (*Usui Reiki Ryôhô International*) in Vancouver		
2000: Hiroshi Doi's book is translated into English and called *Modern Reiki Method for Healing*		
2000: Chris Marsh meets with Suzuki san, a cousin of Mikao Usui		
2001: Chris Marsh meets another 11 students of Mikao Usui		
2000: The URRI takes place in *Kyôto*		
2001: The URRI takes place in Madrid		
2002: The URRI takes place in Toronto		
2003: The URRI takes place in Denmark		
2003: Bronwen and Frans Stiene's first edition of *The Reiki Sourcebook* is published by O Books		
2003: 19 August, Chiyoko Yamaguchi dies		
2005: *The Japanese Art of Reiki* by Bronwen and Frans Stiene is published by O Books		

Reiki Events	Japanese Events
2006: *A-Z of Reiki Pocketbook* by Bronwen and Frans Stiene is published by O Books	**2006**
2006: *Reiki Techniques Card Deck* by Bronwen and Frans Stiene is published by O Books	
2007: *Your Reiki Treatment* by Bronwen and Frans Stiene is published by O Books	
2008: *Reiki Meditations for Self Healing* CD by Bronwen Stiene is published by Sounds True	▼

Key to Sources of Information for Timeline

MUMS – Mikao Usui Memorial Stone in *Tôkyô*.

SS – Suzuki san, a *Tendai* nun and a cousin of Mikao Usui's wife. She was born in 1895 and is said to be still alive today. Information about Suzuki San is supplied by Chris Marsh. He states that in 2001 there were also 11 other students of Mikao Usui alive. They are said to have possessed some of Mikao Usui's notes and teachings. A number of these have since passed on. Chris Marsh's information is currently uncollaborated.

HD – Hiroshi Doi, member of the *Usui Reiki Ryôhô Gakkai*.

FAP – Frank Arjava Petter.

CY – Chiyoko Yamaguchi was a student of Chûjirô Hayashi.

HT – Hawayo Takata, an American citizen of Japanese descent who brought the system of Reiki to the USA in 1938.

5   Mikao Usui's Teachings

Mikao Usui, his Life and Times (1865–1926)

Like stars, mists and candle flames
Mirages, dewdrops and water bubbles
Like dreams, lightning and clouds.
In that way I will view all existence.

(Taken from the notebook of Mikao Usui,
dated 1923)[1]

The main source of factual history about Mikao Usui, at present, is written in stone – literally. This is the carved memorial stone of Mikao Usui's life at his gravesite at the Pure Land[2] Buddhist *Saihôji* Temple in *Tôkyô*.[3] It was placed there by a number of his students just one year after his death in 1927. The memorial stone is one aspect of Mikao Usui's life as seen through the eyes of his students from the *Usui Reiki Ryôhô Gakkai*.

Apart from this information there are very few historical facts about Mikao Usui's teachings that can claim authenticity through verification. That is not to say that there are not a great many stories told about Mikao Usui and his teachings – there are.

[1] The quote is an extract from an eighth-century Buddhist prayer /contemplation on the nature of impermanence. Chris Marsh states that it was written in Mikao Usui's notes and may have been translated by him into Japanese. Chris Marsh provided the English translation.

[2] Information supplied by Hyakuten Inamoto, Pure Land monk and Reiki Teacher.

[3] There is a full translation of the Mikao Usui Memorial Stone, translated by Hyakuten Inamoto on page 391.

When the teachings were brought across to Hawaii by Hawayo Takata they were adapted to suit the political situation of World War II through her fascinating anecdotes and 'parables'. For 40 years she employed the method of storytelling to teach people about the system she called *Usui Shiki Ryôhô* and its history. It is difficult today to verify much of this information; however, it is certain that some of it is incorrect. Hawayo Takata's anecdotes were perhaps appropriate for her at that particular period in her life and for the world in which she lived. It would be mistaken to downplay the fact that through her strength as a Reiki teacher, her system of Reiki is now practiced in every country of the world.

Since the rekindled interest in the teachings of Mikao Usui there have been many theories and histories coming out of the woodwork. Some have been proven false, causing havoc, while others have yet to be verified. It is wiser to believe that which can be verified and at some level is open to perusal by others.

Frank Arjava Petter, a Reiki teacher and researcher, said that he and his then-wife, Chetna Kobayashi, contacted a relative of Mikao Usui who explained that a female relative had left a clause about Mikao Usui in her will. The clause mysteriously stated that his name should never be spoken again in her house. This may have also added to the lack of information available about Mikao Usui's personal life.

The most straightforward information to be found, as mentioned earlier, is that from Mikao Usui's memorial stone. This was written just one year after his death and therefore leaves little leeway for the historical information to have changed drastically. Unfortunately, the students who wrote this information up are said to not have consulted Mikao Usui's family and therefore may have left out information that would be relevant in a truly comprehensive memorial to Mikao Usui.[4]

Hiroshi Doi is yet another source of historical information. His status as a *Usui Reiki Ryôhô Gakkai*[5] member means that he has access to historical information that is not available to non-members. Hiroshi Doi has studied many styles of Reiki, New Age and more

[4] Information supplied to the authors by Chris Marsh.
[5] The *Usui Reiki Ryôhô Gakkai* claims to have been created by Mikao Usui in April 1922.

traditional, as well as numerous energetic and spiritual techniques and does not speak English. The *Usui Reiki Ryôhô Gakkai* is believed to restrict what he does pass on. This has caused confusion in the past with some information not being as 'original' as initially believed.

Frank Arjava Petter and Hyakuten Inamoto have also researched aspects of Mikao Usui's teachings in Japan through their own contacts.

A nun called Suzuki san, the cousin of Mikao Usui's wife and one of his students, is said to still be alive today. She was born in 1895 and is in contact with Chris Marsh[6]. Suzuki san's information has not been taught widely in the greater Reiki community in Japan or any other country. There is also said to be another nun called Mariko Obaasan[7] who studied with Mikao Usui. This, too, is unverified information at present.

To show an objective view, information from most sources has been utilized with appropriate footnotes where possible.

It is good to remember that it is impossible to know the full story behind Mikao Usui, his life and teachings. The remnants that still exist of both can be somewhat pieced together but they will never create a whole. One must be satisfied with the little available knowledge and take advantage of the practices that have been left for one's spiritual development.

To clearly illustrate the history of Mikao Usui direct quotes from his memorial stone have been used. Any historical background has been italicized.

> …the *samurai*, (who) commonly wanted to be known both
> as swordsmen and poets … The greatest warriors of feudal
> Japan were therefore also men of the mind, the spirit and the
> cultivated senses.
>
> (Excerpt from *A History of Warfare* by John Keegan)

Born into a Samurai Family

Mikao Usui was born on 15 August 1865 in the village of *Taniai* (now called *Miyama cho*) in the *Yamagata* county of the *Gifu* Prefecture in Japan.

---

[6] Chris Marsh claims to be a student of Suzuki san, an early student of Mikao Usui.

[7] Obaasan is a term used in Japan for Grandmother or old woman.

Japan was just opening up in 1865 after a self-imposed isolation that had left it culturally prosperous though far behind most of the world technologically and militarily. Kyôto was the capital of Japan and remained so until 1868 when the advent of the Meiji Restoration moved it to Tôkyô.

Today in *Miyamo cho*, Mikao Usui's name can be found carved on a large *torii*[8] at the *Amataka* shrine close to where his home once stood. The three Usui brothers donated the stone *torii* in April 1923. Mikao Usui's brothers, Sanya and Kuniji, grew up to become a physician and a policeman respectively. There was also an older sister called Tsuru.[9] Mikao Usui's father's name was Uzaemon[10] and his mother was from the Kawai family.

Mikao Usui was born into a society based on a class system. There was the privileged class to which he belonged and then there were the common people. Common people were not even permitted the luxury of surnames until 1870. Mikao Usui's family was *hatamoto samurai* – a high level within the ranks of *samurai*.[11]

The hatamoto were the shôgun's personal guard. During the Tokugawa shôgunate (1600–1867), the hatamoto were direct vassals of the shôgun, and their annual revenue was less than 10,000 bushels of rice.

Due to the major changes that were happening in Japan from the 1860s onwards, the samurai class were no longer required. In 1871, samurai were ordered to cut off their topknots and cast aside their swords. Topknots were considered a symbol of maturity, virility and manhood. These clans were offered positions as public servants instead. This certainly did not satisfy the majority of the samurai clans and for many years there remained struggles between the privileged class and the law.

The memorial stone states that the famous *samurai* Tsunetane Chiba (1118 to 1201), was Mikao Usui's ancestor. Hiroshi Doi noted

[8] *Torii* is a shrine gate.

[9] Hiroshi Doi, member of the *Usui Reiki Ryôhô Gakkai*, received this information from a relative of Mikao Usui.

[10] Information supplied to the authors by Chris Marsh states that his father's name was Uzaemon Tsunetane. Hiroshi Doi and Hyakuten Inamoto have both translated the memorial stone to read that his father's name was Taneuji. Chris Marsh explains that this is a diminutive of a name with the -tane suffix. Research shows that it may in fact mean Mr. Tane. It has also been suggested that Mikao Usui used a different name for a portion of his lifetime. If this is so, then it is likely to have hampered many research efforts in the past.

[11] Information supplied by Chris Marsh.

that this was incorrect and that it was in fact Toshitane Chiba, a famous *samurai* warlord from the 1500s. In 1551 he conquered the city *Usui* and thereafter all family members acquired that name. Whether the ancestor was Tsunetane or Toshitane or both is inconsequential: both were from the *Chiba* clan, as was Mikao Usui.[12]

The Chiba clan was once an influential samurai family in Japan according to Chiba family records. The Usui family crest, otherwise known as the Chiba crest, is designed using a circle with a dot at the top. The circle represents the universe, and the dot (a Japanese representation for a star) represents the North Star. The North Star never moves while the universe must move around it.

Mikao Usui was born a *Tendai* Buddhist and as a young child studied in a *Tendai* monastery.[13] Hawayo Takata, however, invented the tale that he was born a Christian. This is thought to have been created as a self-preservation response to the anti-Japanese sentiment in the USA during and after World War II. Christianity was actually outlawed in Japan at the time Mikao Usui was born.

From 1639 to 1854, Japan was shut under a policy called sakoku or 'national isolation'. Foreigners were forbidden to enter Japan and trade. Only the Dutch and Chinese were excluded from this ban. Through the small port of Dejima in Nagasaki, the traders became Japan's single link to anything foreign for more than two centuries. This privilege was only extended to contact with Japanese merchants and prostitutes. Any Japanese who dared to venture abroad during this period were executed on their return to prevent any form of 'contamination'.

At present there is little known about Mikao Usui's personal life. What can be told, though, are experiences from other Japanese who were of a comparable age and born under similar conditions.

Three well-known Japanese *budô* masters[14] lived in the same era

---

[12] Even if this is a technical fault it does not automatically negate other facts inscribed on the memorial stone.

[13] Information supplied by Chris Marsh.

[14] In Toshitaka Mochizuki's book, *Iyashi No Te*, there is a group photo in which Mikao Usui, friends, family and students are gathered together on 16 January 1926. It has been suggested that Jigorô Kanô was standing at the furthest right hand side of the photo. Although there is a slight resemblance, this has been denied by every martial arts source contacted by the authors. This includes respected authorities such as the *Kodokan Jûdô* Institute in Japan, Stanley Pranin of the *Aikidô* Journal and Miek Skoss of Koryu Books. Morihei Ueshiba and Gichin Funakoshi are also not in the photo.

as Mikao Usui and are even said to have known of him.[15] Gichin Funakoshi, the founder of modern *karate*, was born into a *samurai* family in 1868 (three years after Mikao Usui). Jigorô Kanô[16], born in 1860, was the son of a wealthy family. Morihei Ueshiba was slightly younger, born in 1883, and belonged, too, to a wealthy and prominent *samurai* family.

During this period, young children from the privileged class all began their studies with the Chinese classics. The classical elements of Japanese culture were still retained in their early training. Traditional Japanese flute playing and the recitation and writing of poetry were just a few hobbies of the well-to-do youth of that time.

Gichin Funakoshi passed his test to enter medical school but due to the fact that he still had his samurai topknot was not accepted as a student of the school. Many gentrified families were unhappy with the changes that were taking place in Japan. They refused to accept the changes around them and consequently joined what was known as The Obstinate Party.

Martial Arts Training

At the age of 12 Mikao Usui began with the practice of a martial art called *aiki jutsu*. He also studied a form of *yagyu ryû* and gained *menkyo kaiden* (the highest license of proficiency) in weaponry and grappling.[17] There are a great many forms of *yagyu ryû* practiced today. The *yagyu ryû* tradition entails both life-giving and life-taking (*kappo* and *sappo*)[18] and includes exercises such as grappling, *taijutsu* and *katsu*. *Katsu* is a method of infusing life into a person and is mentioned on page 35 of the Chûjirô Hayashi *Ryôhô Shishin*[19] as a method to aid resuscitation.

It is certain that a lifetime practice such as this would have influenced and informed the spiritual practice of Mikao Usui and the system that has come to be known as Reiki today.

---

[15] Information supplied by Chris Marsh.
[16] Jigorô Kanô was the founder of *jûdô*.
[17] Information supplied by Chris Marsh.
[18] Life-giving means utilizing healing practices while life-taking means the art of killing.
[19] This is the *Healing Method's Guideline* created by Chûjirô Hayashi.

Family Life[20]

Mikao Usui married Sadako Suzuki and they had two children, a boy, Fuji, and a girl, Toshiko. Fuji (1908–46) went on to teach at *Tôkyô* University and Toshiko lived a short life, dying at the age of 22 in 1935. The entire family's ashes are buried at the gravesite at the *Saihôji* Temple in *Tôkyô*.

Mikao Usui had children late in life according to the times he lived in. He was 43 when his first child, Fuji, was born and it was another six years before Toshiko was born.

Gichin Funakoshi wrote in his autobiography, Karate dô – My Way of Life, that he did not marry and have children until he was over 20 'quite an advanced age for marriage' in those days in his area.

Career

> From his youth he surpassed his fellows in hard work and endeavor. When he grew up he visited Europe and USA, and studied in China. He was by nature versatile and loved to read books. He engaged himself in history books, medical books, Buddhist scriptures, Christian scriptures and was well versed in psychology, Taoism, even in the art of divination, incantation, and physiognomy.
>
> (Excerpt from the Mikao Usui Memorial Stone, 1927)

Due to the fact that he traveled greatly through Japan and overseas his career was also varied. At one point he was a private secretary to a politician called Shinpei Goto, who, among other positions, was Governor of the Standard of Railways and became the Mayor of *Tôkyô* in 1920.

Men of Mikao Usui's class were trained well in the arts.

Gichin Funakoshi wrote that he went to a 'moon viewing party' when he was a young karateka.[21] This consisted of martial artists sitting around chatting about karate and reciting poetry under a full moon.

---

[20] There is little information on the memorial stone about Mikao Usui's family as his students, not family members, wrote it.

[21] *Karateka* is a *karate* student.

Mikao Usui has shown his leaning toward poetry by his inclusion of 125 *waka*, or poems, into his teachings. In his notes it is claimed that he wrote his own form of *waka* and jotted down poetry written by others that he had enjoyed.[22] Toshitaka Mochizuki wrote in his book, *Iyashi No Te* (*Healing Hands*), in 1995 that it was quite a common and natural thing to read and recite poetry at that period in time. During Japan's 'national isolation' there had been a great focus on the arts. In a book from 1933[23], a student of Mikao Usui's describes a technique called **hatsurei hô*. Here *waka* is recited silently to oneself in an attempt to become One with the essence, or perhaps the energy, of the poem.

Religion

Mikao Usui was never a doctor[24] as Hawayo Takata was known to call him but he is said to have been a *zaike*, a lay *Tendai* priest[25]. A *zaike* could remain in his own home with his family without having to reside in a temple as is commonly expected of priests. Although there is currently no verification of this, it has also been said that at the time he became a *zaike* he took the Buddhist name, or extra name, of Gyoho, Gyohan or Gyotse.

Tendai Buddhism was brought to Japan by Saichô in the early 9th century and names Nagarjuna as its patriarch. Apart from the belief that the Lotus Sutra is Buddha's complete and perfect teaching it also teaches meditation based on esoteric elements like mudras and mandalas.

In the time of Mikao Usui a practice called *Shugendô* was also taught within *Tendai* Buddhism. Many spiritual communities that were established in the late 1800s/early 1900s utilized *Shugendô* as a platform for their teachings. It is believed that Mikao Usui also studied *Shugendô*. His oft discussed practice on *kurama yama*, mentioned on the memorial stone as *shûgyô* or severe discipline, is likely

---

[22] See poem at the beginning of this chapter.

[23] This book was written by Kaiji Tomita and is called *Reiki To Jinjutsu–Tomita Ryû Teate Ryôhô*.

[24] Mikao Usui never studied to become a doctor and there is no documentation of him ever being called by this title in Japan. It is thought to be an inaccurate translation by Hawayo Takata of the respectful term of *sensei* into English. Mikao Usui's brother was a physician.

[25] Information supplied to by Chris Marsh.

to have been one of the set 21-day *Shugendô* practices.

Shugendô is a mix of Buddhism, Shintôism, Taoism and shamanic practices. Its practitioners were known as shugenja and yamabushi (mountain warriors).

The influence of *Tendai* Buddhism and *Shugendô* can be clearly seen in the depths of the teachings of Mikao Usui. For example the *reiju* and mantras and symbols have direct links to these Japanese traditions. The teachings of Mikao Usui were also influenced by *Shintô* practices – many of which were also elements of *Shugendô*.[26] This can be seen in some of the traditional techniques and mantras taught within the system of Reiki.

Shintô (the way of the gods) is the indigenous faith of the Japanese people, and it is as old as the culture itself. The kami, or gods, are the objects of worship in Shintô. It has no founder and no sacred scriptures like the sutra or the Bible. Initially, it was so unselfconscious that it also had no name. The term Shintô came into use after the sixth century when it was necessary to distinguish it from the recently imported Buddhism.

Its origins are of a people who were sensitive to nature's spiritual forces and believed that every rock and pebble could speak. The kami are sacred spirits and can take the form of natural elements like the sun, mountains, trees, rocks, and the wind. They can also be abstract things like fertility, ancestors or protectors of family clans.

It is not unusual for Japanese people to be followers of both Buddhism and Shintôism as the two have come to co-exist and complement each other throughout the years. Shintôism uses its festivals and shrines to celebrate its kami while Buddhism works from within a wealth of religious literature and an elaborate body of doctrine. Buddhism in Japan has actually integrated the Shintô kami by naming them as manifestations of various Buddhas and bodhisattvas.

A Healing Path to Enlightenment

It is impossible to offer a commencement date for Mikao Usui's teachings. He was 35 years old at the turn of the century and was

---

[26] *Shintô* priests practice **kenyoku hô* or the dry bath method, a purifying technique according to some *Usui Reiki Ryôhô* teachers. One *Shintô* practitioner said that he performed a similar ritual with a group of men from his village where they wore only a red loincloth at the *hekogaki* festival (putting on the loincloth festival).

apparently proficient in martial arts from his mid-20s. Suzuki san is said to have been aware of Mikao Usui her whole life as she was his wife's cousin. Her formal training with him began in 1915 when she was 20 years old and her relationship with him continued on a less formal basis until his death in 1926.[27] It is understood that Suzuki san and her fellow students preserved a collection of papers including the precepts, *waka,* meditations, and teachings.[28]

In a 1928 Japanese article[29] a student of Chûjirô Hayashi states that the system was founded decades ago.

For these reasons it is believed the teachings of Mikao Usui existed prior to 1922 when he opened his official seat of learning and the *Usui Reiki Ryôhô Gakkai* claims to have been created.

Early students did not relate the word Reiki to the entirety of Mikao Usui's teachings. The two *kanji* for Reiki are extremely common in Japan and can be found in a variety of situations unrelated to the word, Reiki, as it is understood today. It was also often used in conjunction with Mikao Usui's teachings but not as the name of them; merely in its literal form meaning 'spiritual energy'.

> Eguchi[30] did not practice 'reiki' per se and did not use the term, any more than Usui did. The term *rei/reiki* was of course widely known and had many meanings in the healing world, connoting spiritual matters/spiritual forces of various sorts.
>
> (Quote from Professor Judith Rabinovitch. Ph.D., Harvard University; Currently Karashima Professor of Japanese Language and Culture Department of Foreign Languages and Literatures, University of Montana, USA)

Only once the teachings left Japan was the word 'Reiki' turned into the name for a system.

The aim of these teachings was to provide a method for students

---

[27] Information supplied to the authors by Chris Marsh.

[28] Information supplied to the authors by Chris Marsh.

[29] 'A Treatment to Heal Diseases, Hand Healing' by Shûo Matsui in the magazine *Sunday Mainichi,* 4 March, 1928, translated by Amy to be viewed at www.reiki.net.au.

[30] Toshihiro Eguchi was a friend and student of Mikao Usui and a famous Japanese healer.

to achieve enlightenment. Unlike religion, however, there was no belief system attached.

Though enlightenment was the aim, the healing that was taking place for students was a wonderful 'side effect'. What sets Mikao Usui's teachings apart from other hands-on healing methods is his use of *reiju* or attunement to remind students of their spiritual connection.[31] It seems that all students of Mikao Usui received *reiju* and the five precepts and those with a further interest in the teachings became dedicated students. There does not appear to have been a distinction between clients and students in the beginning though this changed in 1917.[32] People began coming to Mikao Usui for different purposes – some for healing and others for the spiritual teachings.

The *reiju* appears to have links to practices from within the more esoteric elements of *Tendai* called *Mikkyô*.[33]

Early on in the history of Tendai, a close relationship developed between the Tendai monastery complex, hiei zan (Mt. Hiei), and the imperial court in Kyôto. As a result, Tendai emphasized great reverence for the Emperor and the nation. There are five general areas taught in Tendai. They are the teachings of the Lotus Sutra; esoteric Mikkyô practices; meditation practices; Buddhist precepts; and Pure Land teachings.

Mikao Usui initially gave mantras to students as a device for tapping into specific elements of energy. As each individual learns in his or her own unique manner just one device was impractical to serve the whole of mankind. Meditations too, became integrated into the teachings.[34]

Once the *Usui Reiki Ryôhô Gakkai* was formed the teachings became more formalized. A manual including a healing guide, *Ryôhô Shishin*, plus interesting information about the system in its early days was created at the 50 year anniversary of the *Usui Reiki Ryôhô Gakkai*. This manual is called the *Reiki Ryôhô Hikkei*. Hand positions were taught

---

[31] The use of *reiju* though was not totally unheard of at that time – the Japanese spiritual practice Johrei also uses a *reiju* of some kind. Toshihiro Eguchi performed a form of *reiju* on a group which was called *kosho michibiki* (Illuminating Guidance).

[32] Information supplied to the authors by Chris Marsh.

[33] *Mikkyô* is an esoteric form of Buddhism and can be translated as 'the secret teaching'. The *reiju* has similarities to the *Mikkyô* practice called *Go Shimbô* (Dharma for Protecting the Body).

[34] Information supplied to the authors by Chris Marsh.

to those who found working intuitively difficult. Symbols were also added to the mantra recitations as a helpful tool to evoke specific energy. The introduction of symbols was useful for those whose experiences with spiritual work had previously been limited or those who had difficulty sensing the energy.

Whether mantras, meditations, or mantras and symbols together were practiced it did not matter as all were focused on working with the same energy.

Chûjirô Hayashi, who broke away from the *Usui Reiki Ryôhô Gakkai*, naturally emerges as the individual who created a structured system of healing that did not principally focus on spiritual development. His teachings are the forerunner to what is known as the system of Reiki today. Chûjirô Hayashi created his own manual which he passed on to his students. This manual is similar to the healing guide section of the manual that the *Usui Reiki Ryôhô Gakkai* uses. As an original member of that society and a doctor it is thought Chujiru Hayashi was probably the author of both healing guides. This healing guide may well have been created after Mikao Usui's death. Mikao Usui's interest appeared to lay in spiritual growth rather than teaching people to treat others.

Mountains and Divine Inspiration

> Now and again, it is necessary to seclude yourself among
> deep mountains and hidden valleys to restore your link to the
> source of life. Breathe in and let yourself soar to the ends of
> the universe; breathe out and bring the cosmos back inside.
> Next, breathe up all the fecundity and vibrancy of the earth.
> Finally, blend the breath of heaven and the breath of earth
> with that of your own, becoming the Breath of Life itself.
>
> (Quote by Morihei Ueshiba from *The Art of Peace*
> by John Stevens)

As *hiei zan* is the main *Tendai* complex in Japan, and is very close to *Kyôto*, it has been surmised that Mikao Usui practiced there as a lay priest. A *Tendai* meditation practice called *zazen shikan taza*[35] may well have inspired him and his teachings either on *hiei zan* or *kurama*

---

[35] For the complete *zazen shikan taza* meditation see Appendix C.

yama.[36] It has been suggested that old *sutra* copies on *hiei zan* have Mikao Usui's Buddhist name on them of Gyoho or Gyotse.[37]

According to the memorial stone Mikao Usui's teachings were developed, almost miraculously, during a meditation in 1922. The concept of Divine Inspiration is a must for the founder of any Japanese art.

> One day, he climbed *kurama yama* and after 21 days of a severe discipline without eating, he suddenly felt One Great Reiki over his head and attained enlightenment and he obtained *Reiki Ryôhô*. Then, he tried it on himself and experimented on his family members. The efficacy was immediate.
>
> (Excerpt from the Mikao Usui Memorial Stone, 1927)

Mount Kurama, or kurama yama as it is called in Japan, is 570 meters above sea level and is 12 kilometers due north of the Kyôto Imperial Palace. It can be reached in 30 minutes from Kyôto by car or train. The main Kurama Temple was founded in 770 as the guardian of the northern quarter of the capital city (Heiankyo) and is located halfway up the mountain. The temple formerly belonged to the Tendai sect of Buddhism, but since 1949, it has been included in the newly founded kurama kokyo sect as its headquarters.

The legend behind kurama yama is that more than six million years ago Maô son (the great king of the conquerors of evil and the spirit of the Earth) descended upon kurama yama from Venus with a great mission – the salvation of mankind.

Since then, Maô son's powerful spirit emanates from kurama yama and governs the development and evolution, not only of mankind but, also, of all living things on Earth.

Maô Son, Bishamon Ten, and Senju Kannon are the symbols of the universal soul, forming a Trinity known as Sonten or the Supreme Deity. These three are the symbols of power, light, and love.[38] Sonten is the creator of the universe, and cultivates the development of everything all over the Earth.[39]

---

[36] Information supplied to the authors by Chris Marsh.

[37] Information supplied to the authors by Chris Marsh.

[38] Interestingly, some modern Reiki practitioners have used 'love and light' as a salutation for a number of years. How this came about is unknown and it does not seem to have been a salutation used by Hawayo Takata.

[39] Information supplied by *kurama yama* tourist information pamphlet.

Mikao Usui's 21-day practice on *kurama yama* was called *kushu shinren*,[40] (which is a form of *shûgyô*[41], or severe discipline or training) according to the memorial stone. *Kurama yama* was also well known for its *yamabushi* or mountain ascetics. These were men who practiced martial arts and also spent time in the mountains for solitude and personal practice. It was a sort of quest where they pitted themselves against the elements in order to seek some sort of revelation or to test their mettle. This practice would not have been a one-off training but a part of a system of meditations and training enabling the practitioner to be able to survive 21 days of meditation in the mountains.

Both Hawayo Takata and the memorial stone have stated that Mikao Usui had a strong connection with *kurama yama* and its temple. According to the Kurama Temple, there are no records of his having undertaken any form of ascetic training at the temple itself. The temple goes on to say that Mikao Usui has 'no special connection to Kurama Temple whatsoever'.[42]

The memorial stone was written and erected by students of the *Usui Reiki Ryôhô Gakkai*. This society was set up one month after Mikao Usui's experience on *kurama yama*. For the *Usui Reiki Ryôhô Gakkai*, the experience on *kurama yama* defines the society's creation and purpose. Therefore it has been acknowledged in detail on the memorial stone.

The memorial stone's text grants that Mikao Usui was an avaricious learner of anything spiritual from all cultures throughout his whole life. Even from the society's stance he may well have taught before his experience at *kurama yama*. It certainly does not discount earlier anecdotes about Mikao Usui's teachings. His experience at *kurama yama* may have brought him a new understanding of energy and his methods of teaching.

Whether Mikao Usui practiced on *hiei zan* or *kurama yama* is relatively unimportant. His teachings are the focus of modern research. It is true that if he practiced on *hiei zan* or *kurama yama* it is likely that *Tendai* Buddhism would have heavily influenced his developing teachings.

---

[40] On the memorial stone the term *kushu shinren* is used. Hyakuten Inamoto states that *kushu* literally means painful discipline and *shinren* means difficult training.

[41] *Shûgyô* is also written as *shyu gyo* as seen in some memorial stone translations.

[42] Letter from Kurama Temple to the authors, 2002.

Reiki Ryôhô

Sensei thought that it would be far better to offer it widely to the general public and share its benefits than just to improve the well-being of his own family members. In April of the eleventh year of *Taisho* (1922 A.D.) he settled in *Harajuku, Aoyama, Tôkyô* and set up the Gakkai to teach *Reiki Ryôhô* and give treatments. Even outside of the building it was full of pairs of shoes of the visitors who had come from far and near.

(Excerpt from the Mikao Usui Memorial Stone, 1927)

Mikao Usui's move to *Tôkyô* is guessed to have come through his connection with Shinpei Goto who was Mayor of the city. *Harajuku* became Mikao Usui's first official seat of learning.

This *Reiki Ryôhô* or 'spiritual energy healing method' that people lined up for was most likely the *reiju*[43] and the spiritual teachings of Mikao Usui. It is believed that Mikao Usui did not need to perform a long ritual when performing *reiju* himself but could just become One with a student by standing near them or touching them. This would be enough for them to strengthen their energy.[44] This way of working with the *reiju* corresponds with the third symbol and mantra utilized at Level 3 which means non-duality, void and emptiness. When one is truly in this space of interconnectedness, energy becomes more direct making ritual almost unnecessary.

In September of the 12th year (1923 A.D.) there was a great earthquake and a conflagration broke out. Everywhere there were groans of pains from the wounded. *Sensei*, feeling pity for them, went out every morning to go around the town, and he cured and saved an innumerable number of people. This is just a broad outline of his relief activities during such an emergency.

(Excerpt from the Mikao Usui Memorial Stone, 1927)

[43] The Japanese word *reiju* is known as an attunement today.
[44] Hiroshi Doi stated that Mikao Usui would sit opposite his students without any ritual to perform *reiju*. This is also stated by Chris Marsh.

On 1 September 1923, just before noon, an earthquake measuring 8.3 on the Richter scale occurred near the modern industrial cities of Tôkyô and Yokohama, Japan. This was not the largest earthquake to ever hit Japan, but its proximity to Tôkyô and Yokohama and the surrounding areas, with combined populations numbering 2 million, made it one of Japan's most devastating earthquakes. Tôkyô's principle business and industrial districts lay in ruins. There was an estimation of nearly 100,000 deaths with an additional 40,000 missing. Hundreds of thousands were left homeless in the resulting fires.

Gichin Funakoshi was also living in Tôkyô at that time. He wrote in his autobiography, 'We who survived did all we could to succor the injured and the homeless in the days immediately following the terrible disaster... I joined other volunteers to help provide food for the refugees, to clear the rubble and to assist in the task of disposing of the dead bodies.'

This earthquake may well have been the background inspiration for Hawayo Takata's well-known 'beggar story'.[45] There was a great deal of poverty in Japan at that time due to the depression. After the earthquake in 1925, Mikao Usui moved his home and *dôjô* to *Nakano ku*, outside of *Tôkyô*. Selection of this particular house was decided through the art of divination.[46] He was often invited to travel throughout Japan treating people and teaching students. Mikao Usui had over 2000 students in total[47], about 60 to 70 *okuden* students and 21 teacher students who reached *shinpiden*.[48]

> *Sensei's* personality was gentle and modest and he never behaved ostentatiously. His physique was large and sturdy. He always wore a contented smile.
>
> (Excerpt from the Mikao Usui Memorial Stone, 1927)

---

[45] Most modern practitioners know this beggar story as a parable. It teaches practitioners that Reiki must be paid for or it will not be respected. Many teachers dispute this concept today and there exist groups of teachers and practitioners who offer Reiki for free. There is an account of the 'beggar story' in *Living Reiki, Takata's Teachings* by Fran Brown.

[46] Information taken from the Mikao Usui Memorial Stone.

[47] Information taken from the Mikao Usui Memorial Stone.

[48] Information supplied to the authors by Hyakuten Inamoto. The *Usui Reiki Ryôhô Gakkai* has 11 of these listed by name in their booklet called *shiori*.

Spiritual Healers

At the turn of the century hands-on-healing or *teate* was very popular in Japan. Toshihiro Eguchi was a friend of Mikao Usui and studied with him in the 1920s.[49] He created the *Tenohira Ryôji Kenkyû Kai* (Hand Healing Research Center), wrote a number of books and ran a healing community for a number of years.

Law and order had largely broken down in the late 1800s and ronin[50] roamed the streets. Martial arts practices from all over the country joined together in the cities, where respectable schools developed such as Kodokan Jûdô. There was a definite code of ethics and honor attached to early martial arts practices that often verged on the spiritual. Morihei Ueshiba taught a spiritual martial arts called aikidô, the Art of Peace. This may largely have been due to his involvement with a religion called the Oomoto sect.

This link between martial arts and spirituality had always been a quest for the samurai. It was also a reflection of the cultural period itself, which held the antithesis of military action and spiritual healing together in one hand. Of the many naval personnel in Japan, a number were interested in martial arts and intrigued by spiritual healing. This interest was to form a further historical element to the journey of Mikao Usui's teachings.

Shinpei Goto, Mikao Usui's boss, wrote a calligraphic work in the foreword to Gichin Funakoshi's first book in 1922. Gichin Funakoshi also taught Jigorô Kanô for a number of months. Jigorô Kanô would send his students to either Morihei Ueshiba or Gichin Funakoshi for further study.[51] There are numerous connections between these figures during Mikao Usui's lifetime.

> Due to his respected and far-reaching reputation many people from local districts wished to invite him. *Sensei*, accepting the invitations, went to *Kure* and then to *Hiroshima* and *Saga*, and reached *Fukuyama*. Unexpectedly he became ill and passed away there. It was 9 March of the 15th year of Taisho (1926 A.D.), aged 62.[52]

> (Excerpt from the Mikao Usui Memorial Stone, 1927)

---

[49] Hiroshi Doi states that Toshihiro Eguchi was involved with the teachings from 1925 to 1927.

[50] A *ronin* is a masterless *samurai*.

[51] *Three Budô Masters*, John Stevens, Kodansha International, 1995.

[52] During Mikao Usui's lifetime the age of a Japanese person was counted not on the birthday, but on a New Year's Day without regard to one's actual birthday. Today he is considered to have died at the age of 61.

Mikao Usui died of a stroke.

> These are truly great teachings for cultivation and discipline
> that agree with those great teachings of the ancient sages and
> the wise. *Sensei* named these teachings Secret Method to Invite
> Happiness and miraculous Medicine to Cure All Diseases;
> notice the outstanding features of the teachings. Furthermore,
> when it comes to teaching, it should be as easy and common
> as possible, nothing lofty. Another noted feature is that during
> sitting in silent meditation with *Gasshô* and reciting the Five
> Precepts mornings and evenings, the pure and healthy minds
> can be cultivated and put into practice in one's daily routine.
> This is the reason why *Reiho* is easily obtained by anyone.
>
> (Excerpt from the Mikao Usui Memorial Stone,
> 1927)

Gichin Funakoshi wrote that, 'Times change, the world changes,
and obviously the martial arts must change.' Mikao Usui's own
teachings appeared to have gone through many changes during his
lifetime and were set to continue to change.

Reiki Precepts

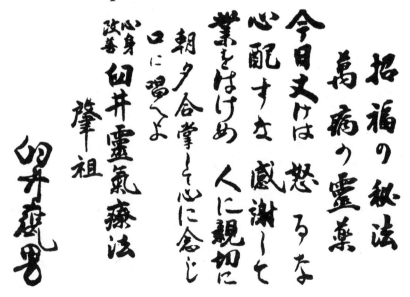

The secret of inviting happiness through many blessings
The spiritual medicine for all illness

For today only:
Do not anger
Do not worry
Be humble
Be honest in your work
Be compassionate to yourself and others

Do *gasshô* every morning and evening
Keep in your mind and recite[53]

Improve your mind and body

Usui Reiki Ryôhô Founder Mikao Usui

What are the Five Precepts?

The five precepts[54], or *gokai* as they are called in Japan, are a foundation to aid students in their journey toward spiritual development. They are one of the five basic elements of the system of Reiki today.

Mikao Usui taught them from as early as 1915.[55] The *Usui Reiki Ryôhô Gakkai* perform *gokai sansho*, or the chanting of the five precepts three times, at the end of their regular group meetings. They are also printed in the *Reiki Ryôhô Hikkei*.[56]

The five precepts are the six sentences in the center of the entire teaching found at the beginning of this chapter. The teaching consists of an introduction, the five precepts themselves, directions on how and when to use them and what the result of this practice will be. An old Japanese version of the five precepts was in the top left-hand corner of a photo of Mikao Usui that was provided to Frank Arjava Petter by Tsutomu Oishi.[57]

[53] This translation was supplied to the authors by Chris Marsh.

[54] A precept is a general rule that helps you decide how you should behave in particular circumstances. (Collins Essential English Dictionary, 1989.)

[55] Information supplied to the authors by Chris Marsh.

[56] Information taken from the *Reiki Ryôhô Hikkei* (*Spiritual Energy Healing Method Manual*), a manual that is given to *Usui Reiki Ryôhô Gakkai* members in Japan.

[57] There is uncertainty whether these precepts are written in Mikao Usui's handwriting. It was initially believed that this was so by non-Japanese. Though that was probably due to Mikao Usui's name written in the last sentence, not unlike how signatures are written outside of Japan.

Origins of the Five Precepts

The origins of the precepts are uncertain. The memorial stone states that Mikao Usui requested that his students' practice two things:

> Thus, before the teachings, the '*ikun*' (admonition) of the
> Meiji Emperor should reverently be told and Five Precepts be
> chanted and kept in mind mornings and evenings.

Here it is likely that there are two different teachings being described – the '*ikun*' and the precepts.

According to the translator of this copy of the memorial stone, Hyakuten Inamoto, '*ikun*' is, in fact, referring to the Meiji Emperor's *waka* (poetry). This would indicate that the precepts are a separate teaching.

Frank Arjava Petter states in his books, *Reiki Fire* and *Reiki – The Legacy of Dr. Usui* that the precepts originated from the Meiji Emperor's *Imperial Rescript on Education*.[58] It seems that he has linked the two teachings that were written about on the memorial stone together.

The Imperial Rescript was written by the Meiji Emperor in 1890 and is an edict that became a fundamental Japanese moral code until the end of World War II. The rescript was treated with quasi-religious reverence and in schools was kept, together with the picture of the Emperor and Empress, in a special safe.[59] There are elements of the five precepts taught by Mikao Usui in this edict but it is certainly not a direct translation. It is only natural that there is some connection as all moral and civic instruction after 1890 was based on the rescript's principles.

Jigorô Kanô, who is believed to have known Mikao Usui, introduced a very similar system of cultural and moral codes to *jûdô*.[60] Traditional *jûdô* teachings claim that the purpose of training is the

---

[58] A rescript is an edict or decree. For two English translations of the rescript (one formal and one less formal) see Appendix D.

[59] It was taken so seriously the story goes that School Principals were known to have committed suicide if they mispronounced a word in reciting the rescript or if it perished in a fire.

[60] Jigorô Kanô, the founder of *jûdô*, was also a great sportsman, teacher and philosopher – he was a member of the International Olympic Committee for 23 years.

cultivation of the perfection of character. Therefore, in order to perfect the personality students must first learn and understand the *Imperial Rescript on Education* by the Meiji Emperor. These codes, he taught, included filial piety to parents, friendship to the siblings, harmony between husband and wife and trust between friends. It was also necessary to be modest and respectful to others, and to love mankind.

Due to the rescript's nationalistic focus it may have been obligatory for all official schools to teach at that particular stage in history.

Jigorô Kanô's precepts resemble those of Mikao Usui in a broad sense only and appear to be excerpts from the rescript. Mikao Usui's precept of 'do not worry' and the unique concept of 'just for today' are not mentioned.

Suzuki san has said that the precepts were taught from as early as 1915 to students. Hiroshi Doi, however, writes that they were officially introduced in April 1922 when Mikao Usui created the *Usui Reiki Ryôhô Gakkai*.[61] Hiroshi Doi also claims that the book, *Kenzen no Genri*, written by Bizan Suzuki[62] in 1914 may have inspired the writing of them.

A translation of the piece in Bizan Suzuki's book is:

> Today do not be angry,
> do not worry and be honest,
> work hard and be kind to people

Though the exact same *kanji* are not used, this reflects the same five precepts as taught by Mikao Usui. The vital element, today, has interestingly taken the same placement in the poem. Professor Judith Rabinovitch states: The language is extremely close and it was common in those times to pick up such language 'as one liked' and revise it for one's own purposes. Western notions of 'plagiarism' simply never prevailed. This is not a traditional *waka* (or *tanka* poem) but is modern style free verse.

---

[61] *Modern Reiki Method for Healing*, Hiroshi Doi, Fraser Journal Publishing, 2000.
[62] Published by Teikoku Kenzen Tetsugakkan (The Imperial Philosophy of Health Institute).

It has also been asserted that the origins of the five precepts actually date back to 9th century Japanese Buddhist precepts.[63]

Perhaps Bisan Suzuki influenced Mikao Usui (or was it the other way around?) who, in turn, was originally influenced by these early Buddhist teachings.

The five precepts as taught by Mikao Usui, no matter what their history, are universal and valuable to all regardless of religion or creed. They are spiritual teachings rather than religious teachings and all students were asked to practice them in their daily lives.

The precepts have the syllabic regularity of 6-4-6-6-7-8 denoting that they fall into the category of a Japanese poem (this is not *waka*). The word for 'poem' in Japanese is also the word for 'song' and this lack of distinction may verify that the precepts were always sung or chanted.

The Five Precepts in Detail

Here is a look at some meanings that may lay behind the five precepts:

> The secret of inviting happiness through many blessings
> The spiritual medicine for all illness

This first paragraph introduces the 'secret'. It alludes to spirituality being an instrument to good health. The 'many blessings' may be the benefits of the repeated receiving of the *reiju*. Mikao Usui and the *Usui Reiki Ryôhô Gakkai* performed *reiju* on a regular basis, believing that many *reiju* lead to enlightenment. After many years of personal practice and the receiving of *reiju* it is understood that the practitioner becomes One with the universe. A more appropriate viewpoint may see the practitioner being showered with the blessings that the universe has to offer when practicing the teachings.

> For today only:
> Do not anger
> Do not worry

---

[63] Information supplied to the authors by Chris Marsh.

Be humble
Be honest in your work
Be compassionate to yourself and others

For today only is a practical sentence to keep the practitioner's minds focused on the NOW. It is a typical Buddhist stance. By focusing on tomorrow – well, tomorrow never comes. Each moment of life is NOW. If these precepts are practiced NOW then they are being practiced in each and every moment of the practitioner's life.

> If you no longer want to create pain for yourself and others, if you no longer want to add to the residue of past pain that still lives on in you, then don't create any more time, or at least no more than is necessary to deal with the practical aspects of your life. How to stop creating time? Realize deeply that the present moment is all you ever have. Make the NOW the primary focus of your life.
>
> (Excerpt from *The Power of NOW* by Eckhart Tolle)

Do not anger is a basic Buddhist principle. Anger not only hurts those in the practitioner's vicinity but the practitioner him or herself. It is the antithesis of balance. Once the practitioner is no longer a victim to the senses then focus can energetically be placed on the spiritual path.

> Sometimes people feel that anger is useful because it brings extra energy and boldness. When we encounter difficulties, we may see anger as a protector. But though anger brings us more energy, that energy is essentially a blind one. There is no guarantee that that energy will not become destructive to our own interests. Therefore, hatred and anger are not at all useful.
>
> (Excerpt from the *Power of Compassion* by His Holiness the Dalai Lama)

Do not worry as this causes stress at all levels. Stress lowers the immune system opening the practitioner up to the possibility of disease. To worry is a lack of faith. Fearfulness is a reaction that does not trust the universe to provide what is best for the practitioner.

... Shantideva says:
If you can solve your problem,
Then what is the need of worrying?
If you cannot solve it,
Then what is the use of worrying? ...

(Excerpt from *The Healing Power of Mind* by Tulku Thondup)

Be humble and the practitioner will find this humbleness and thankfulness permeating each and every aspect of his or her life. Thoughts will be of a life of abundance rather than want. The importance of material circumstances will no longer be the gauge that existence is based on.

... True happiness relates more to the mind and heart.
Happiness that depends mainly on physical pleasure is
unstable; one day it's there, the next day it may not be ...

(Excerpt from *The Art of Happiness* by His Holiness the Dalai Lama and Howard C. Cutler)

Be honest in your work is asking for the practitioner to be truthfully dedicated to spiritual progress by not becoming a 'spiritual materialist'.[64]

... Understanding the energy consequences of our thoughts
and beliefs, as well as our actions, may force us to become
honest to a new degree. Lying, either to others or to ourselves,
should be out of the question. Genuine, complete healing
requires honesty with oneself. An inability to be honest
obstructs healing as seriously as the inability to forgive.
Honesty and forgiveness retrieve our energy – our spirits –
from the energy dimension of 'the past.'

(Excerpt from *Anatomy of the Spirit* by Carolyn Myss, Ph.D.)

---

[64] A term coined by Chogyam Trungpa that relates to one who gathers spiritual knowledge in the same manner as one who constantly buys the latest shopping trend. It is the gathering of spiritual knowledge to prove how 'spiritual' one really is.

Be compassionate to yourself and others and the practitioner will remember the connection of all things under the universe.

> … numberless times in previous lives we have each fulfilled the role of a mother. The feeling of a mother for a child is a classic example of love. For the safety, protection and welfare of her children, a mother is ready to sacrifice her very life.
>
> (Quote by His Holiness the Dalai Lama)

Mindfulness brings peace to life. This thought reminds human nature that it is compassionate and to understand and experience connectedness. Oneness can be experienced through working with the precepts that lie at the base of all the teachings. These precepts form the foundation for a successful working relationship with each of the other four elements of the system of Reiki. If the practitioner can live these precepts, the system of Reiki becomes complete.

> Do *gasshô* every morning and evening
> Keep in your mind and recite

Gasshô is the placing of both palms together in front of the chest. It is a sign of respect for oneself, the action and the energy. This simple act balances both the mind and body.

Keep these precepts in the mind throughout the day. They are not just for reading but also for living.

> Improve your mind and body
>
> *Usui Reiki Ryôhô* Founder Mikao Usui

The last three sentences name the motto, the system and its founder.

Precepts in one's Daily Life

It is almost impossible to keep focused on these five precepts 100 percent of the time. Therefore it must not be considered a 'sin' when the practitioner is unsuccessful in following each one. Buddhist thought offers the idea that when a precept is 'broken', focus can be placed on forgiveness and kindness towards oneself. This contemplation brings the practitioner full circle back to focus on compassion; one of the five precepts.

> It is like the precepts. Even though it is almost impossible to observe them, we must have them. Without an aim or the precepts ... we cannot actualize our way.
>
> (Excerpt from *Crooked Cucumber* by David Chadwick)

Waka

> Poetry has its seed in the human heart and blossoms forth in innumerable leaves of words ... it is poetry which, with only a part of its power, moves heaven and earth, pacifies unseen gods and demons, reconciles men and women and calms the hearts of savage warriors.
>
> (Excerpt from the preface of *Kokinshû* [*Collection of Waka of Ancient and Modern Times*] by *Ki* no Tsurayuki (884–946))

What is Waka?

A component of Mikao Usui's teachings was the recitation of *waka* as written by the Meiji Emperor. Once again, there is this natural link between the Japanese culture and Mikao Usui's teachings.

Waka is a purely Japanese phenomenon and like the *Shintô kami* it, too, is without Chinese precedents.[65] This cultural poetic purity meant that it was considered to be the equivalent to the Indian *dharani* spells.

> *Waka* came to be seen as Japanese-language spells infused with the same magical powers that characterised the *dharani* and mantra of esoteric Buddhism – and, indeed, *waka* served as such spells in medieval *Shintô* and *Shugendô* traditions.
>
> (Excerpt from *Shintô* by Mark Teeuwen, John Breen, Nobutaka Inoue, Satoshi Itō)

---

[65] *Shintô* by Mark Teeuwen, John Breen, Nobutaka Inoue, Satoshi Itō.

The word *waka* is made up of two parts: *wa* meaning 'Japanese' and *ka* meaning 'poem' or 'song'. The word may have been written to distinguish between the poetry written by the Japanese in their own language to differentiate from that which they read and wrote in Chinese.

A certain portion of the Japanese community commonly recited *waka* at the turn of the 20th century. It was a remnant of the strong cultural base that Japan had built up throughout its 250 years of national isolation.

A contemporary of Mikao Usui, the modern founder of *karate*, Gichin Funakoshi, advised in his book *Tapenshu* that students ponder the words of a classical poem used by a fierce swordsman, Jigenryu:

> Spring blossoms.
> Autumn moon.
> Conditions.
> Confrontation.
> Swordsmanship.
> No conditions.

Mikao Usui, having lived under the reign of the Meiji Emperor, must have been highly influenced by the Emperor's spiritual insight. He asked his students to realize the Emperor's teachings and to chant or sing his poetry. The Japanese believed that the monarchy was in fact godly and in that context it is easy to see how the Emperor could exert such great power over the people.

Mikao Usui placed over 125 *gyosei* from the Meiji Emperor in the *Reiki Ryôhô Hikkei*.[66] His recommendation was that all students recite these *gyosei* as a form of self-development. In this way students would not only be practicing energy enhancement with his meditations and techniques but also mind expansion.

The power of *waka* was evident to Mikao Usui and it is taught today that he even wrote his own *waka*.

A student of Mikao Usui's called Kaiji Tomita wrote a book in 1933

---

[66] Information taken from the *Reiki Ryôhô Hikkei* (*Spiritual Energy Healing Method Manual*), a manual that is given to *Usui Reiki Ryôhô Gakkai* members in Japan.

called, *Reiki To Jinjutsu – Tomita Ryû Teate Ryôhô* (*Reiki and Humanitarian Work-Tomita Ryû Hands Healing*). In a technique called **hatsurei hô*, he asks the students to become One with the Meiji Emperor's *waka*.

Today, *waka* is not commonly taught within the system of Reiki, although some teachers do acknowledge *waka* as a founding practice. The reason for this is likely that coming from such a specific cultural background it may not be well understood by the modern student (or teacher for that matter). To work directly with the *waka* that Mikao Usui recommended, one must also be able to read pre-1940s Japanese. Prior to World War II there were about 50,000 *kanji* in use. After the war the Japanese went from having to know about 4,000 *kanji* to read a newspaper to 1,850. A Japanese person of average education today would be familiar with about 3,000 *kanji* rather than the previous number of 50,000.

Origins of Waka

In the historical Japanese *Hotsuma Tsutae*, or *The Hotsuma Legends*[67], there is a legend about the origins of *waka* poetry. Princess *Waka*, or *Wakahime*, was very skilled in writing a particular style of song. She inscribed these songs onto wooden tablets, sending them to her lovers. One of her lovers was supposedly moved to distraction by her written love songs. On the strength of her skill and ability this style of song or poetry eventually became recognized as *waka*.

Waka is a short form of poetry that contains 31 syllables. In English it is typically divided into five lines of 5,7,5,7 and 7 syllables.

Apart from the esoteric use of *waka* as a type of magically infused language linked to *kami* and the power of nature, it was often performed on public occasions at the Imperial court. In fact, many Emperors were renowned for their *waka*. It also became an essential skill for noblemen, women and *samurai*. *Waka* were often composed as a kind of finale to every sort of occasion – no experience was

---

[67] Its first parts, 'Book of Heaven' and 'Book of Earth', were recorded and edited around 660 B.C. (according to the *Nihonshoki* calendar) by Kushimikatama-Wanihiko. His descendant, Ootataneko, recorded the third part, 'Book of Man', which contains the stories after Emperor Jinmu (660 B.C.), and offered the complete *Hotsuma Tsutae* to Emperor Keiko (the 12th Emperor) in 126 A.D.. The origin of the *Hotsuma Tsutae* is controversial. It is guessed to be very old while some researchers challenge the dates written above.

complete until one had been written about it. In the fourteenth century, a competition developed where one person would write the first half of a *waka* and another would complete it with the last two 7-syllable stanzas. Up to four people took part in these games with the rules becoming extremely complex ensuring that a courtly standard was preserved.

Meiji Emperor and Waka

The Meiji Emperor ruled Japan from 1867 to 1912 and is said to have written over 100,000 *waka* and his Empress Shôken over 30,000. These *waka* are not only excellent as literary works but also constitute significant teachings to enhance national moral character'.[68] *Waka* written by Emperors are called *gyosei,* meaning 'created by the Emperor'.

The Meiji Emperor was the first Emperor ever to be seen by foreigners. Hiroshi Doi stated at a URRI[69] workshop that when politicians visited the Meiji Emperor they would begin to sweat – not just because they were nervous but because of the great amount of energy he exuded.

Waka Today

Today, *waka* has become outdated and such poetry is more commonly expressed in its modern form as *tanka.* The best-known poetry outside of Japan is neither the *waka* nor *tanka* but the *haiku. Haiku* is said to have also originated from *waka.* It is shorter still and consists of three lines of 5, 7 and 5 syllables and traditionally focuses on nature using descriptive seasonal terms. *Haiku* are popular throughout the world and are written in numerous languages.

Although this may be the case, there are a few rare Reiki practitioners whose interest in the traditional aspects of the teachings has encouraged them to write *waka* as a practice to support their spiritual connection to the teachings. Below is an example of *waka* written by writer and Reiki practitioner Michael Dagley:

---

[68] Information supplied by website: www.meijijingu.or.jp/english.
[69] *Usui Reiki Ryôhô* International.

Diamond
A diamond's hard face
Can by mere dust be obscured,
Its true reflections
Dimmed, as a heart burdened
By powdery motes of doubt.

Hand Positions

> *Reiho* puts special emphasis not just on curing diseases but
> also on enjoying well-being in life with correcting the mind
> and making the body healthy with the use of an innate
> healing ability.
>
> (Excerpt from the Mikao Usui Memorial Stone)

What is a Hand Position?

Since the beginning of time humans and animals have instinctively used touch – to comfort, support, connect, rejuvenate and heal. It is not 100 years old or even 5,000 years old – it is as old as our living planet.

From the beginning, as a baby, humans have drawn on the energy of those around them while being held, cuddled and fed. Premature babies are known to gain weight faster when touched and held.[70] As humans grow older the power of touch remains integral to their wellbeing. In everyday life it continues to express intention in an energetic manner. By reaching out humans transfer energy from one person to another; the comforting pat on the shoulder; the compassionate look; welcoming, open arms or the healing kiss on a child's sore finger. Natural, intuitive actions that are used to connect on an energetic level – this is the concept behind hand positions.

Hand positions are one of the five foundation elements of the system of Reiki. Mikao Usui is believed to have taught students to place their hands on or near the body, to pat, stroke, gaze at and blow on

---

[70] Field, T.M., S.M. Schanberg, et al. 1986. Tactile/kinesthetic stimulation effects on preterm neonates. *Pediatrics* 77: pp. 654-58.

the body[71] – all with the intention that the body would restore its balance. This physical action brings awareness to a natural skill and with practice, a stronger connection to this innate healing ability.

It is probable that Mikao Usui never used set hand positions himself. More likely he would have simply performed *reiju*. He would do this by being either near, or touching, the recipient. For him the ability to become One with the energy of others was his form of healing.

Hand positions were created later in his life, in the same manner as the mantras and symbols, to be training wheels for those who could not yet accomplish Mikao Usui's energetic prowess. When experiencing difficulty in intuiting where the hands should be placed on the body hand positions were taught as a useful tool.

The Origins of Treating Others

Zentô bu – Forehead
Sokutô bu – Both temples
Kôtô bu – Back of your head
Enzui bu – Either side of neck and forehead
Tôchô bu – Crown on top of head

There are a number of versions of set hand positions for treating others that have been used in Mikao Usui's teachings at one time or another. Mikao Usui apparently taught five hand positions around the 1920s. These were centered solely on the head. The rest of the treatment for the body was intuited, if treated at all.[72] These hand positions may have been the positions used for the physical *reiju* which have since that time been interpreted as mere hand-positions.

Similar head positions were also written up in the healing guide of the *Reiki Ryôhô Hikkei* used by the *Usui Reiki Ryôhô Gakkai* and Chûjirô Hayashi's own healing guide *Ryôhô Shishin*. Toshihiro Eguchi, a well-known healer around the time of Mikao Usui, used a

---

[71] Information taken from the *Reiki Ryôhô Hikkei* (*Spiritual Energy Healing Method Manual*), a manual that is given to *Usui Reiki Ryôhô Gakkai* members in Japan.
[72] Information supplied to the authors by Chris Marsh.

Zentô bu – Forehead

Sokutô bu – Both temples

Kôtô bu – Back of your head and forehead

Enzui bu – Either side of neck

Tôchô bu – Crown on top of head

similar set of hand positions in his manuals. He studied with Mikao Usui and was a good friend of his.[73]

Frank Arjava Petter in his book, *The Original Reiki Handbook of Dr. Mikao Usui*, states that Mikao Usui mainly used his left hand when treating people.[74] This book relates to a manual used in the *Usui Reiki Ryôhô Gakkai* called the *Reiki Ryôhô Hikkei*.

Head positions focus on the mind because once it is calm and balanced the rest of the body naturally returns to its original state. Humanity today spends a great deal of its time working with the head using computers and ipods and basically being largely intellectually based rather than working with the natural connection to the Earth. The first four positions appear to balance the energy. By the time the fifth and last position is reached, on top of the crown, the mind is relaxed and the energy is easily drawn down and into the whole body. The crown is also our connecting point to spirit. Working on the crown strengthens this spiritual connection. In the *Reiki Ryôhô Hikkei* it states that if the spirit is healthy and connected to the truth, the body will naturally become healthy.

These positions can be performed while the recipient is seated. The hands are held in place for as long as the energy is felt to flow – this could take a couple of minutes or up to half an hour. Some versions of this method rest the hands physically on the person while others hold them 2 to 3 inches (5 to 8 cm) off the body.

When the practitioner has finished the five positions the hands are moved to the part of the body where an imbalance is sensed.

Apart from these head positions the *Reiki Ryôhô Hikkei* also contains over 20 pages of specific hand positions for certain illnesses. It is believed that Chûjirô Hayashi compiled this guide as it matched his own healing guide, the *Ryôhô Shishin*, which he provided students with just a few years later. His medical background would explain the technical, less intuitive, qualities of these manuals.Whether the original healing guide was created during or after Mikao Usui's life-

[73] Information supplied to the authors by Chris Marsh and Judith Rabinovitch.

[74] The title of this book is misleading as it is named after the manual which the *Usui Reiki Ryôhô Gakkai* uses. This manual, the *Reiki Ryôhô Hikkei*, was actually put together for the society's 50th anniversary. There is no authentication that it was written by Mikao Usui. In fact, the section of the manual that is a healing guide was likely put together by Chûjirô Hayashi and this may have occurred after Mikao Usui's death while Chûjirô Hayashi was a member of the *Usui Reiki Ryôhô Gakkai*.

time is unknown. Alongside the creation of Chûjirô Hayashi's hand position method was the development of his official clinic called the *Hayashi Reiki Kenkyû Kai* or Hayashi Spiritual Energy Research Society. Clients paid money for treatments and there existed a system where students would complete an internship that included working as volunteers at the clinic. Fran Brown states that Chûjirô Hayashi never changed the system but simply brought it inside the clinic.[75]

When Hawayo Takata first came to him as a patient he had a clinic that had eight beds with two practitioners working at each bed. One practitioner would begin at the abdomen or *hara* and the other would begin at the head. Neither of the healing guides mentioned this particular method of treating people with two practitioners. Most probably elements of the healing guides were practiced during treatments.

Hawayo Takata was taught where and how to place her hands on the body during her training with Chûjirô Hayashi in Japan. After a one-year internship she returned to the USA where she worked intuitively with clients from the late 1930s into the 1970s. She did not appear to use one particular hand position method. After her death, a number of her students came together to create an organization that taught a strict set of 12 hand positions which began at the head. Other students of Hawayo Takata argued that she had taught them to start at the abdomen. Both of these systems, plus totally intuitive systems, are taught today.

Researchers place the beginning of the importance of hand positions with Chûjirô Hayashi. This could mean that what is practiced as Reiki today has its origins in Chûjirô Hayashi's system rather than that of Mikao Usui.

The Origins of Self-Treatment

Parallel to the development of hand positions as a means to heal others, the concept of self-treatment naturally developed. This is where students place their hands on their own bodies in a systemized fashion.

---

[75] *Living Reiki – Takata's Teachings*, Fran Brown, Life Rhythm, 1992.

Self-treatment by placing hands on one's own body was not taught directly by Mikao Usui. The recitation of *waka* and the five precepts along with mantras and meditation techniques were the earliest forms of self-development taught to students.

Self-treatment with hand positions is not mentioned in any original texts, such as the two healing guides referred to previously. It is natural though to place the hands on an area of the body where there is a corresponding problem. There does not appear to have been any formalized teaching of this practice until the system of Reiki left Japan. The memorial stone from 1927 describes self-practice as 'sitting in silent meditation with *gasshô* and reciting the five precepts mornings and evenings'.

Going deeper into one's inner self using the practices suggested on the memorial stone triggers energy to flow more freely through the body. This in turn leads to a state that does not need hand positions to support the movement of energy in the body. The physicality of working with the hands triggers the mind to sense that place which then allows the energy to also flow to that area. Once a practitioner is experienced such a support may no longer be required. From this it can be seen that hand positions are merely a tool and a training aid.

Hawayo Takata emphasized that first one must become whole by practicing on oneself and then one can move on and help others.

Healing Touch in Japan

Using hands to heal is not considered extraordinary in Japan. It was a very popular technique in Japan at the beginning of the 20th century and it has always been popular through the Japanese deity *Binzuru*. *Binzuru* is known as the 'master of remedies' and is the Buddha of healing. It is believed that he promised to find remedies for human kind for all disease. His abilities are recognized in Japan and many festivals are held yearly in his honor.

In his hands he holds a medicine jar made of precious stone emerald. By being bathed in this Emerald Radiance all illness can be cured. But it is his touch that offers benefits to all who come to him.

From a culture that is grounded in such a strong connection with touch and healing it is easy to imagine the ease with which a healing system using hand positions has evolved.

In *Nara*, an unusual statue stands just outside the great doors of one of the world's largest wooden structures. This is the *Todai ji* Temple and it is *Binzuru*, made of wood that has split with age, who is seated there. He wears a cotton cloth cap and shawl with one palm facing towards his followers and the other holding his wooden bowl. Visitors to the temple rub the region of *Binzuru*'s body that corresponds to their own illness or pain. *Binzuru* consequently relieves them of their problem whether it is physical, mental, emotional or spiritual.

Meditations, Mantras and Symbols

> It [mantra] is a source of spiritual energy, and sometimes even the inspiration that unleashes the power of spiritual healing.
>
> (Excerpt from *The Essence of Shintô* by Motohisa Yamakage)

What are Meditations, Mantras and Symbols?

Meditations, mantras and symbols all work on the same principle. Each method is a different approach yet the end result is the same – eventual enlightenment.

The meditations (and other techniques listed in the Techniques section) plus the mantras and symbols are two of the foundation practices of the five elements of the system of Reiki.

The Origins of Meditations, Mantras and Symbols

Meditations, mantras and symbols appear to have been gradually introduced into Mikao Usui's initial teachings. Much of the information provided in this chapter is sourced from research into the Japanese culture and philosophy and the influences on Mikao

Usui's life. These facts are then cross-checked against information provided by those claiming to be students of Mikao Usui.

The earliest history begins around 1915 where the mantras and meditations were the first of these three practices to be taught. The purpose of the teachings was solely to develop spiritual growth. Only later in Mikao Usui's life, around 1922 (once he began working with lay people who were not involved in spiritual practices), were symbols introduced.

The symbols were extra tools that made it easier for students to practice Mikao Usui's spiritual teachings.

The *Usui Reiki Ryôhô Gakkai* and Chûjirô Hayashi did not seem aware of these early teachings. They were known to have worked with the mantras and the symbols as taught by Mikao Usui from 1922 onwards. The mantras and symbols were not included in the *Reiki Ryôhô Hikkei* but were copied by students from their teachers.

According to the student's ability either a meditation, a mantra, or a symbol and mantra would be given. These are all different paths leading toward the same destination. The paths are chosen according to the student's abilities.

Another link between these devices is that the energy evoked by some meditations, mantras, and mantras and symbols is of the same quality. The system offers diverse approaches for different people.

The Use of Meditations

Students received a meditation for their own personal practice. On a regular basis the teacher, Mikao Usui, would discuss their progress and eventually teach them a new follow-up meditation. This device is not unlike teaching Zen through the use of koans. Here the answer is not reached by logic but rather through an experience, a realization. Depending on the student's ability it may take from a couple of months to a number of years before receiving the new meditation. These meditations are not the same as the known techniques practiced by the *Usui Reiki Ryôhô Gakkai*. There is a small group of teachers who teach these meditations. The meditations are required to be taught one-on-one.

Many traditional and non-traditional techniques are listed in the techniques section.

The Use of Mantras

In Japan the word for mantra is either *kotodama*[76] or *jumon*[77]. The terms *kotodama* and *jumon* accentuate a slightly different aspect of working with sound. For ease of understanding the word mantra is used to cover all aspects of *kotodama* and *jumon*.

According to Suzuki san's teachings, the mantras (rather than symbols) were the first to be introduced to Mikao Usui's teachings. The mantras taught at this time were pronounced differently to how they are pronounced today, often focusing more on vowel sounds than on the consonants. She also said it was Mikao Usui's friend Toshihiro Eguchi who was responsible for adding the three mantras from Shintôism into Level 2 of the system of Reiki.

Eventually symbols in conjunction with mantras were added for those students who were not sensitive enough to the energy (generally non-Buddhist and non-martial arts practitioners).

Morihei Ueshiba, founder of *aikidô* and said to be an acquaintance of Mikao Usui, was another martial arts practitioner who worked from a spiritual viewpoint. He, too, used the chanting of vowel sounds in his spiritual teachings. He was involved with the *Oomoto* sect who had formulated a number of effective meditation techniques and powerful chants based on *kotodama* theory.[78]

Mantras invoke a specific vibration through sound. Therefore it is most effective when spoken out loud. Mantras must be uttered correctly as a slight alteration creates a different vibration thus producing a different manifestation.[79]

> Since we chant these words with energy from the abdomen, it naturally creates repetition of deep breathing from the belly: this way of breathing is called the 'the long breathing method' (*okinagaho*) in *Shintô*. Through this breathing the power in the physical body is increased.
>
> (Excerpt from *The Essence of Shintô* by Motohisa Yamakage)

[76] *Kotodama* means words carrying spirit. Hiroshi Doi, teacher of *Gendai Reiki Hô* and member of the *Usui Reiki Ryôhô Gakkai*, uses the word *kotodama* in place of the word mantra.

[77] *Jumon* is a sound that invokes a specific energetic vibration.

[78] *Three Budô Masters*, John Stevens, Kodansha International, 1995.

[79] Authors' discussion with Hyakuten Inamoto about mantras.

Kotodama and *jumon* were ancient *Shintô* practices that used vibrations to interact with the natural environment. To understand sound's importance it is necessary to experience and learn about vibration. Imagine that you are interested in studying a tree. You could approach it in a number of ways. First you could read a book about it written by someone else (most probably a non-tree), then you could cut a tree down and study it yourself, or lastly you could ask the tree – commune with the tree – go to its vibration and listen.

> Primordial sounds are the vibrations of nature that structure the universe. They are the root sounds of every language. We can hear these sounds in the songs of birds, the rushing of streams, the crashing of waves and in the whispering breezes in the leaves of a tree … listening to primordial sounds restores our sense of connection to the whole and enlivens our inner healing energy.
>
> (Excerpt from *The Wisdom of Healing* by David Simon)

The Use of Symbols

In Japan each symbol is known as a number. For example: Symbol 1, Symbol 2, Symbol 3 and Symbol 4. In the modern world they are generally called by the name of the mantra, which is incorrect as the mantra is a separate device.

The focus today is also mainly on the symbols rather than the mantras. The 'power' of the symbols has gained in importance over the years. This emphasis has meant that throughout the last 20 years as more and more people have created new Reiki systems, many new symbols have also been invented.

Hiroshi Doi writes that, 'Searching for more additional symbols or regarding symbols as a holy thing is meaningless.'[80]

The symbols have no power of their own – they act merely as a focus for one's intent. Until recently, however, the mantras and symbols were not taught, outside Japan, as tools to help one focus. The misguided motivation behind creating more mantras and sym-

---

[80] *Modern Reiki Method for Healing*, Hiroshi Doi, Fraser Journal.

bols was that it was thought that mantras and symbols would make one's Reiki 'more powerful'. This thought process existed because the original understandings behind these devices had not yet been explored or understood.

According to Hiroshi Doi, the symbols are the training wheels of a bicycle – and once the bike can be ridden the training wheels are taken away. This is the same with the mantras and symbols, but it is necessary to be very careful and not to throw them away too soon. The vibrations must be fully understood before moving on – this may take years and years of practice.

When drawing symbols a few aspects need to be kept in mind by the practitioner. Knowledge of what the action is affects the quality of the outcome. The strength of this outcome is determined by the student's inner connection to the symbol. Ignorance allows for mistakes and a poor bonding with the symbol.

The Use of Mantras and Symbols

There are no traditional Reiki mantras written in *The Reiki Sourcebook* – pseudonyms are used in their place. These are CKR, SHK, HSZSN and DKM.

Symbols have also not been printed on the pages of this book. The rationale behind this is one of respect for Mikao Usui's teachings and for the beliefs of some Reiki branches. Some maintain that the mantras and symbols are secret. Yet, as can be seen in this book's research these mantras and symbols are widely and openly available in Japan in non-Reiki contexts.

As far as the symbols and Mikao Usui's teachings are concerned – the more they are practiced, the easier it becomes to sense the energy and the sooner the student will find that symbols are irrelevant.

> Progress comes
> To those who
> Train and train;
> Reliance on secret techniques
> Will get you nowhere

> (Quote by Morihei Ueshiba from *The Art of Peace* by John Stevens)

Four traditional mantras and symbols taken from Tatsumi's hand-drawn copies of Chûjirô Hayashi's symbols have recently become globally adopted. Those taught by Hawayo Takata were modified by some of her students and therefore these are the closest to the original symbols that the modern day Reiki community has to work with. In Japan it is said that the *Usui Reiki Ryôhô Gakkai* uses slightly different symbols, as does Chûjirô Hayashi's student Chiyoko Yamaguchi[81] and her students.

The mantra and the symbol are written independently of one another. In traditional Japanese branches the symbol is not called by the mantra's name as has been commonly practiced outside of Japan.

Each mantra and symbol can be practiced independently of the other mantras and symbols. For example CKR and Symbol 1 are not required to activate the other mantras and symbols as has been recently taught by some.

The Mantras and Symbols in Detail

In the following section all four traditional mantras and symbols are dissected in detail. This is a brief explanation of what to expect under each of the four groupings which include the one mantra and the one symbol. The mantra and the symbol, though different devices, work toward the same goals.

The characteristics of the mantras and symbols are the energetic vibrations that these devices evoke.

When using mantras in conjunction with symbols they must be chanted three times. Many have wondered if 'repeat three times' is a modern addition to the practice of mantras. This does not seem to be the case. In the *Usui Reiki Ryôhô Gakkai* the five precepts are also chanted three times. They use the Japanese name *gokai sansho* for this practice, which is a Buddhist term meaning to chant the precepts three times. Three is considered to be a divine number.

To draw a symbol there are various approaches that can be taken. Visualize drawing the symbol in the mind's eye, physically with the palm of the hand or with your fingers.

---

[81] Information supplied to the authors by Hyakuten Inamoto.

Many myths have been created around the mantras and symbols, perhaps because the knowledge behind their origins was unknown. It is unsubstantiated and, as can be seen, impossible that these traditional Japanese symbols and *kanji* could possibly have originated from Tibet, Atlantis, Egypt or any other country or specific culture.

All of the four symbols are recognizable in Japan. Symbol 1 (or part thereof) is often found inscribed on temple walls. Symbol 2 is related to a seed syllable[82] and can be seen in temples across Japan. Symbols 3 and 4 are Japanese *kanji* and when read are the actual names of the mantras used in modern Reiki branches. Though all four mantras are translatable, their technical meanings are less relevant than the vibrations that are invoked with their use. Mantras are simply mental vibrations and they should not carry meaning. Meaning ties us down to everyday associations. By following the vibration of the sound it is possible to cut through these mundane thoughts and reach a space of silence.

> But if we recite in a rote way, as if we are singing a popular song, we are not able to receive anything. We just drift up and down on the waves of sound without ever becoming immersed.
>
> (Excerpt from *Opening the Heart of the Cosmos
> —Insights on the Lotus Sutra* by Thich Nhat Hanh)

Symbols 1 and 2 are clearly 'real' symbols while symbols 3 and 4 are merely Japanese *kanji* that have inaccurately been termed 'symbols'. Plainly these two sets (symbols and *kanji*) have separate intentions. The first two symbols invoke an energy (Earth and Heaven or yin and yang) while the last two 'symbols' create a specific state of mind.

Only after becoming Earth energy and Heavenly energy can we experience Oneness.

---

[82] Seed symbols are letterforms drawn in a stylized manner of calligraphy to be used for meditation purposes.

The *Usui Reiki Ryôhô Gakkai* shows the mantras and symbols to members but does not actively practice them.[83] The mantra DKM is a Japanese phrase that is a goal for the members to aim toward (and the symbol is simply the *kanji* of the phrase). Chiyoko Yamaguchi also did not use this mantra or symbol.[84]

These mantras and symbols are slightly different to what has been taught in the recent past. This is not surprising, as it is known that The Reiki Alliance standardized all mantras and symbols in 1983. There have also been many variations on these 'standardized' mantras and symbols since then. Chûjirô Hayashi is also known to have used slightly different mantras and symbols to that used by the *Usui Reiki Ryôhô Gakkai*.[85]

It is essentially not necessary to know the literal translation of a mantra. Chanting is about the practice and the vibration it evokes, not the meaning behind the word itself. For interest's sake, however, *The Reiki Sourcebook* has included the literal translations for each of the mantras.

Some Japanese branches of Reiki today teach that the mantras and symbols are connected to Japanese deities.[86] These connections may differ depending on the branch of Reiki using them.

The mantras and symbols within the system of Reiki are also not unique to Mikao Usui's teachings. They were utilized in Japan long before Mikao Usui's time and have also been employed since his death by many different teachings which were never influenced by, or in contact with, the system of Reiki.

The uniqueness of the system of Reiki is thus not in the mantras and symbols but in the way Mikao Usui formulated his system.

---

[83] Stated by Hiroshi Doi, URRI, 1999.

[84] Chiyoko Yamaguchi did not complete *shinpiden* (Teacher level) fully or formally. She was taught the attunement to help a family member who was hosting a course run by Chûjirô Hayashi.

[85] Authors' discussion with Hyakuten Inamoto about mantras and symbols.   .

[86] Deities are gods (in this context – Japanese deities) and connections to them are used in *Gendai Reiki Hô, Usui Reiki Ryôhô Gakkai* and other branches.

CKR and Symbol 1

a represents Heaven *u* represents Beginning
wa represents Earth

The *Futomani* Divination Chart stems from the *Hotsuma Tsutae*[87] – it holds the ancient letters of the traditional Japanese

[87] Its first parts, 'Book of Heaven' and 'Book of Earth', were recorded and edited around 660 B.C. (according to the *Nihonshoki* calendar) by Kushimikatama-Wanihiko. His descendant, Ootataneko, recorded the third part, 'Book of Man', which contains the stories after Emperor Jinmu (660 B.C.), and offered the complete *Hotsuma Tsutae* to Emperor Keiko (the 12th Emperor) in 126 A.D.. The origin of the *Hotsuma Tsutae* is controversial. It is guessed to be very old while some researchers challenge the dates written above. Seiji Takabatake provided the *Futomani* Divination Chart from the Japan Translation Center Ltd, *Tôkyô*

god, Amemioya. The god, Amemioya, created Heaven and the Earth by blowing into the chaos of the universe. *In* and *yo* (*yin* and *yang*) were formed and light and clear substances became Heaven 'a', and heavy, turbid substances became Earth 'wa'.

Modern characteristic: Power
Traditional characteristic: Focus

The energy invoked with this mantra and symbol:
Earth energy – which is heavy, powerful and grounding. The first two mantras and symbols represent Earth and Heaven. This is a *Shintô* concept. Humanity is said to be the connection between these two energies. Working with Earth energy stimulates the *hara* enabling the student to strengthen the connection to original energy.[88]

Using the mantra in conjunction with the symbol:
Chant the mantra three times while the symbol is being drawn. It is not necessary to use this mantra and symbol to activate the other mantras and symbols.

Origin of the mantra and symbol:
CKR originates in Shintôism. The *kanji* for *choku* is used in *Shintô* purification (*misogi*). There are 4 types of purification in Shintôism and these are called *seimei seichoku*. In this context *choku* means 'straight' which conveys the idea of 'honest'.[89] This reflects upon the Reiki precepts where the practitioner is requested to be *honest in your work*.

> *Seichoku* means right action or behavior as well as the social aspect of being right, (that is, not committing any sin, crime, or offense) and behaving with honesty, openness, and frankness towards others.
>
> (Excerpt from *The Essence of Shintô* by Motohisa Yamakage)

[88] Original energy is the energy that you receive from your parents when you are conceived and most importantly it is the energetic connection between you and the universal life force.

[89] *The Essence of Shintô* by Motohisha Yamakage.

An element of Symbol 1 has similarities to symbols used in many cultures. This element is commonly utilized as an expression for movement of energy. The first symbol is usually written as a symbol of the Earth element in *Tendai* cosmology with its origins probably in *Hotsuma* symbology.

The *Hotsuma Tsutae*, a controversial historical text, is not alone in using a derivation of Symbol 1. Here the letter *wa* is translated as an early Japanese letter for 'Earth' and has a physical similarity to an element of Symbol 1.

Included in the *Hotsuma Tsutae* is *futomani* practice, which involves a divining system where the oracle uses deer bones. This practice contains some very dramatic and interesting artistic ritual.[90]

Copies of *Hotsuma Tsutae* have been stored in *iwamuro* (cave storage) in a *Tendai* temple at *enryaku ji*[91] (*hiei zan, Kyôto*). These copies were given to *Saichô* (767–822), the founding priest of *enryaku ji*. *Tendai* priests were also known to give lectures on the *Hotsuma Tsutae*. If there were any link here it would be that Mikao Usui was a practicing *Tendai* Buddhist said to have trained on *enryaku ji*. It is interesting to note that the memorial stone records that Mikao Usui practiced divination.

Other organizations/religions in Japan using this mantra/symbol:
Apart from its origins in Shintôism as mentioned above, the word CKR is practiced within other organisations in Japan such as the religion *Oomoto*. A spokesperson for *Oomoto*, Maamichi Tanaka, wrote that the CKR means literally 'Direct Spirit. It is a part (or a portion) of the Divine Spirit which all of us are bestowed from God, the Creator of the universe. This is a word (or term) we use at *Oomoto* and *Shintô*.'

Also Goi Masahisa (1916-1980), founder of the Japanese new religion *Byakkô Shinkôkai*, wrote that the meaning of CKR in his religion was 'direct spirit'.

Both these groups seem to have no concern with writing or discussing this mantra outside their own organisations unlike some Reiki branches.

---

[90] Information supplied to the authors by Jion Prosser, *Tendai* priest.
[91] Main Japanese *Tendai* Complex.

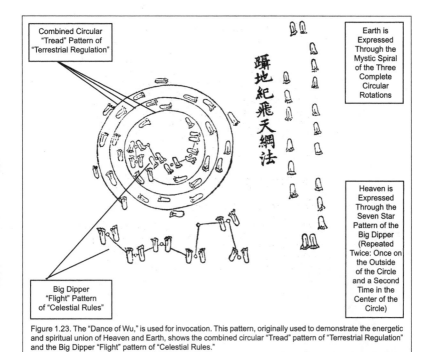

Figure 1.23. The "Dance of Wu," is used for invocation. This pattern, originally used to demonstrate the energetic and spiritual union of Heaven and Earth, shows the combined circular "Tread" pattern of "Terrestrial Regulation" and the Big Dipper "Flight" pattern of "Celestial Rules."

From *Chinese Medical Qigong Therapy – Volume 1* by Dr. Jerry Alan Johnson.

In ancient China the Daoist Rite of the Great Bear Polar circle expresses Earth energy through three anti-clockwise circular rotations. This ritual is from the Sung Dynasty (1400 A.D.) and is utilized in the Daoist Complete Reality School of Dragon Gate sect.[92]

In the Chinese *Yi-Jing* structure of the Eight Trigrams and the Sixty Four Hexagrams the energy of the Earth is also stated to flow anti-clockwise. This correlates with the *Futomani* Divination Chart.

Translation of the mantra:
There are different alternatives when translating the mantra CKR depending on the *kanji* used. Some translations of the mantra CKR are:

---

[92] *Chinese Medical QiGong Therapy – Volume 1* by Dr. Jerry Alan Johnson and *Qi Gong Master* Sat Chuen Hon.

- Direct or Straight Spirit (Spirit that directly comes from the supreme existence)
- Imperial order or command
- Supreme spiritual emptiness (void)

Deity connection:
The deity most often linked to CKR and Symbol 1 is Daiseishi Bosatsu. The name means 'He who Proceeds with Great Vigor'. This is the Buddha who, with great vigor, offers wisdom to awaken the Buddha nature and Buddha wisdom that are in everyone helping them proceed to enlightenment.

SHK and Symbol 2

The *kiriku* symbol drawn by a monk at *hiei zan*, Japan

Modern characteristic: Mental/Emotional
Traditional characteristic: Harmony

The energy invoked with this mantra and symbol:
Heavenly energy – which is light. The first two mantras and symbols represent Earth and Heaven. This is a *Shintô* concept. Humanity is said to be the connection between these two energies. The second mantra and symbol helps to increase one's intuition and stimulate the energetic center at the head, in turn creating more psychic ability and a stronger connection to spirit.

Traditionally, the characteristic is harmony because when one first becomes Earth energy and then Heavenly energy one starts to slowly move into harmony with these opposite forces. This in turn helps release bad habits. By the term bad habits, habitual practices such as smoking, drinking, etc., are not being referred to. Instead it is the bad habit of how one may see reality. After harmonizing Earth and Heavenly energy, one begins to move into the space of the third mantra and symbol, HSZSN.

Using the mantra in conjunction with the symbol:
Chant the mantra three times while the symbol is drawn.

Origin of the mantra and symbol:
Symbol 2 originated from a seed syllable from the sacred *siddham* script. The seed syllable is called *hrih* in Sanskrit and is known as *kiriku* in Japan. Seed syllables in Japanese are called *shuji*.

A seed syllable is a letterform used solely for meditation and is a part of esoteric Buddhism practiced in China and Japan. To use for the purpose of meditation, the character is drawn large in either formal or cursive style on a scroll and hung on a wall.

Siddham characters do not normally represent ideas or concepts but were originally used as signs (or expressions) of their respective linguistic sounds.[93] This means that first came the sound and this was then followed by a physical representation – the seed syllable.

Kiriku calls upon the energy of Amida Nyorai. Amida Nyorai is the main deity in Pure Land Buddhism. *Tendai* utilizes Pure Land Buddhist principles and Mikao Usui was a *Tendai* lay priest[94] therefore it would be within reason to see a connection between the two.

Other organizations/religions in Japan using this mantra/symbol:
Kiriku, the seed syllable, is utilized in Pure Land and *Tendai* Buddhism and can be found at many grave sites and in people's homes to bring good luck.

Translation of mantra:
Translations of the mantra SHK are:

- One's disposition
- Natural tendency
- Mental habit (bad habit)

[93] *Mantric Linguistics and Shittan Grammatology*, lecture by Fabio Rambelli.
[94] Information supplied to the authors by Chris Marsh. Mikao Usui was also buried in a Pure Land Buddhist graveyard and Pure Land originated from *Tendai* Buddhism.

Deity connection:
The deity most often linked to SHK and symbol 2 is Amida Nyorai.
The Sanskrit for Amida is 'Infinite Light'. Amida's compassion is
therefore also infinite. In Pure Land schools of Buddhism Amida
Nyorai is the main deity.[95] Spiritual peace of mind lies in being able
to attain salvation by relying on his powers.

HSZSN and Symbol 3

> A monk asked Ummon, What is the teaching of the Buddha's
> lifetime?
> Ummon said, 'Preaching facing Oneness.'
>
> Oneness is absolute truth.
> To face Oneness means to face everything –
> yourself, the world, every being, and everything –
> in its absolute truth.

(Koans – The Lessons of Zen)

Modern characteristic: Sending energy across a distance
Traditional characteristic: Connection

The energy invoked with this mantra and 'symbol':
A state of mind is created with this mantra and *kanji*; it is a state of
Oneness with all things. Therefore it is not about sending distance
healing but about becoming One with the recipient to allow healing
to take place. It is not possible to 'send' anything when one already
is the energy and that energy is universal. Quantum physicist David
Bohm, in his book *Wholeness and the Implicate Order*, describes how
all the fragments of our world are derived from an implicate order
of unbroken wholeness. He uses the analogy of a stream to show
how everything in the universe is a part of one flowing movement.

> On this stream, one may see an ever-changing pattern of
> vortices, ripples, waves, splashes, etc., which evidently have

---

[95] Mikao Usui's Memorial Stone is in a Pure Land Buddhist temple. Pure Land
Buddhism was propagated in Japan by the *Tendai* monk Honen in the year 1175.

no independent existence as such. Rather, they are abstracted from the flowing movement, arising and vanishing in the total process of the flow. Such transitory subsistence as may be possessed by these abstracted forms implies only a relative independence or autonomy of behaviour, rather than absolutely independent existence as ultimate substances.

(Excerpt from *Wholeness and the Implicate Order* by David Bohm)

In the modern world there is often a sense of fragmentation and disconnection with the natural elements. This tool helps the practitioner remember that connection. In fact, through the practice of this mantra and symbol the practitioner is reminded that this connection already exists.

Before being able to fully move into this space of Oneness, one must first be in harmony with Earth and Heaven and this is accomplished through the self-practice of their accompanying mantras and symbols.

Oneness comes repeatedly to the fore with any research into Mikao Usui's teachings. It is an undeniably Japanese perspective that has strong roots in Buddhism, *Shugendô*, Shintôism, and martial arts – all major influences of Mikao Usui's life.

As the two opposing forces of Earth and Heaven – one from the *hara* and one from the head – join together, it is in the Heart center that unification and balance is achieved. As HSZSN is symbolic of Oneness, within Japanese cosmology it would also be representative of Heart energy. This in turn represents the center of humanity.

Working from this Heart energy reflects the precept taught in the system of Reiki where one is requested to be *compassionate to yourself and others*.

How then, should we connect with one another? When opening a door, you have to use a key that fits. To mutually understand each other's intentions well, you need a key. The key to grasp is the heart (*kokoro*).

(Quote from Ikeguchi Ekan, the highest ranking priest in *Shingon* Buddhism 1996)

Using the mantra in conjunction with the symbol:
Chant the mantra three times while the *kanji* is drawn.

Origin of the mantra and symbol:
This 'symbol' is made up of five separate *kanji*, permitting it to be read as a sentence in either Japanese or Chinese. Clearly this could not be an Atlantean, Tibetan or Egyptian symbol as *kanji* is not at the foundation of these languages (where these languages are known). The *kanji* of Symbol 3 is the written compressed form of the mantra HSZSN – compressing *kanji* is a common practice in Japanese esoteric traditions.

Other organizations/religions in Japan using this mantra/symbol:

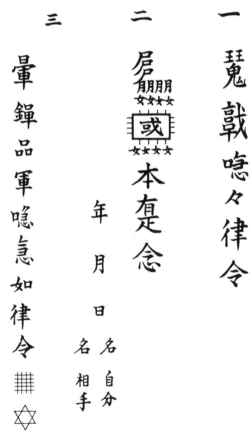

This image is an excerpt from *Ninja: The True Story of Japan's Secret Warrior Cult*, by Stephen Turnbull. The original image can be found in Maysayuki Yamaguchi's *Ninja No Seikatsu*, pp.169–170.

The *kanji* of HSZSN is written into this old Japanese charm (in its compressed form as utilized by the system of Reiki). According to the *Tendai* priest Jion Prosser, this charm has its background in *Onmyo-do* divination. *Onmyo-do* is a form of divination using both celestial clues and natural occurrences to foretell possible outcomes. The memorial stone of Mikao Usui states that he was well versed in 'the art of divination'. In the world of the esoteric *Tendai* practice called *Mikkyô*, [96] *Onmyo-do* is the only channel through which to study spirit control and spans a hefty chasm between this world and the next. Apparently, in Japan today, it is not a commonly known practice.

Translation of the mantra:
Translating *kanji* is unique. Each singular *kanji* can be translated to have many varied meanings. Depending on the translator there will be different versions of HSZSN. Here are some examples:

- My original nature is a correct thought
- I am correct consciousness
- Right consciousness is the origin of everything
- Properly thinking/cognizing/meditating, ones comes to know the True Self

By returning to one's original nature a state of correct consciousness is achieved and it is in this state that Oneness is attained. From this point, one naturally moves into a state of readiness for the fourth mantra and symbol, DKM.

Deity connection:
The deity most often linked to the HSZSN and Symbol 3 is Kannon. No other Buddha is worshipped by as many people as Kannon. This

---

[96] *Mikkyô* is an esoteric form of Buddhism used in *Tendai* that is passed on, not only through teachings, but through active ritual.

is the 'Bodhisattva who Perceives the Sounds of the World'. Kannon made a vow to hear the voice of the people and the sounds of the conditions of the world. Salvation was immediately granted to the suffering and the afflicted as well as dispelling the evil and calamities that surround them.

DKM and Symbol 4

> To unify mind and body and become One with the universe is the ultimate purpose of my study.
>
> (Motto of Koichi Tohei)

Modern characteristic: Embodiment of Mastership
Traditional characteristic: Empowerment

The energy invoked with this mantra and symbol:
A state of mind is created with this mantra and *kanji*. The state of mind is one of enlightenment; becoming One with the void, realizing our full potential as human beings. And it is in this state that the practitioner empowers him or herself.

It is important to note that on the Mikao Usui Memorial Stone it states: One day, he climbed *kurama yama* and after 21 days of a severe discipline without eating, he suddenly felt One Great Reiki over his head and attained enlightenment and he obtained *Reiki Ryôhô*.

This means that for Reiki practitioners to be able to fully integrate the system of Reiki (*Reiki Ryôhô*), one must first attain enlightenment through the elements that the system teaches. This has generally been overlooked in modern forms of the teachings with some people teaching that this level of consciousness and commitment within the system is unnecessary, unrealistically likening the system to a magical pill. Such an attitude has enjoyed a faddish popularity as it temporarily satisfies a modern need for instant gratification. Though thankfully, in more recent times, this shallow approach has stimulated an opposing need for serious practice within the system of Reiki bringing about a new respectability and understanding of the system's true roots and purpose.

Using the mantra in conjunction with the symbol:
Chant the mantra three times while the *kanji* is drawn.

Origin of the mantra and symbol:
This 'symbol' is made up of three separate *kanji* permitting it to be read as a sentence in either Japanese or Chinese. The *kanji* of symbol 4 is the written form of the mantra DKM. If students wish to know if they have the correct 'symbol' simply have DKM (the complete mantra – not this pseudonym) written into Japanese *kanji*.

Other organizations/religions in Japan using this mantra/symbol:
This *kanji* is found across Japan in temple complexes and even on *kurama yama*. It symbolizes the concept of enlightenment.

DKM can be found in a text of the *Mikkyô* tradition of *Tendai* called *ko myo ku*. This text is practiced in *ju hachi dô*, a traditional *Mikkyô* style that is common to all esoteric ritual patterns in Japan. In the *ko myo ku* one merges with the 'Light Wisdom' of the original Buddha nature (Dainichi Nyorai). This manifests as the pure light of one's radiant self; a natural energetic force. Reaching this purity in one's life ties in with using light as a healing force and one's work toward enlightenment.

Many different Japanese traditions practice DKM; from martial arts to *Shugendô* to Buddhism.

In some Japanese martial arts schools, DKM can be found written on a scroll hanging on the *dôjô* wall. It is written within this Japanese sentence: *shikin haramitsu daikomyo*. Masaaki Hatsumi Soke[97] explained this to mean 'Let the training be safe and enjoyable'. Another meaning comes from martial arts teacher Richard Ray, who states that *shinkin* means Heart and *haramitsu* is the Japanese phonetic rendering of the Sanskrit word *paramita*[98]. *Daikomyo*, he says, is a great, large radiating light. Therefore once one's Heart develops the *paramita*, one radiates light; this is merely another way to express one's evolution into enlightenment.

---

[97] Masaaki Hatsumi Soke is the current head of the *Bujinkan Dôjô* martial arts organization. He is also a practitioner of mending bones and his predecessor, Toshitsugu Takamatsu, was the last known active *ninja* before and during World War II,.

[98] The *paramita* are Buddhist virtues.

Translation of the mantra:
Translating *kanji* is unique. Each singular *kanji* can be translated to
have many varied meanings.

The *kanji* for *myo* for example has a number of meanings. It can be
seen as an abbreviation of *myoshu* meaning a spell. It also holds the
meaning of brightness which is a translation of the Sanskrit *vidya*.
This indicates that the mantric formulae represents (and reproduces)
the wisdom of a Buddha or a Bodhisattva. *Myo* can therefore elimi-
nate all obstacles on the path.[99]

The last two *kanji* in DKM are symbolic of the sun and moon
in Buddhism. This represents, once again, the coming together of
opposite forces such as Earth and Heaven.

Here are some translations of DKM:

- Great enlightenment
- Zen expression for one's own true nature or Buddha nature
  of which one becomes cognizant in the experience of
  enlightenment
- Great Bright Light (void)

Deity connection:
The deity most often linked to the DKM and Symbol 4 is Dainichi
Nyorai. This is the Great Shining Buddha because this Buddha is the
life force of the Buddhas that illuminates everything. Dainichi Nyorai dispels the darkness of the world by casting light everywhere,
giving life to and nurturing all living things.

> What is a Buddha? A Buddha is nothing other than the light of
> mindfulness, and that light, wherever it shines, is able to show
> us the wonderful truth, the ultimate dimension of whatever it
> illuminates.
>
> (An excerpt from *Opening the Heart of the Cosmos –
> Insights on the Lotus Sutra* by Thich Nhat Hanh)

The wrathful face of the Buddha Dainichi Nyorai is Fudô Myôô.

---

[99] *Mantric Linguistics and Shittan Grammatology* by Fabio Rambelli.

Fudô Myôô is often depicted with flames (to consume passions), a sword in his right hand (to conquer and cut through ignorance, greed, anger and injustice), and a rope in his left hand (to bind demons). According to Karen Mack, a translator for the *Jôdo Shû* Research Institute in Tokyo, Fudo Myôô is also invoked in Pure Land Buddhism for rebirth.

Reiju and Attunements

reiju – (lit. Japanese) spiritual offering/blessing
attunement – an initiation ritual for students of the system of Reiki

What is a Reiju or an Attunement?

Reiju is a ritual initially used and taught by Mikao Usui. It is one of the five foundation elements of the system of Reiki. The Japanese term *reiju* was first known as an initiation in English and is often called an attunement today. There are differences in the actual rituals behind these practices depending upon who performs them and at what point they are performed within the system's teachings.

Ritual

Ritual is in use by every living being throughout our planet. Often there is no awareness of this or the effect it creates. By working consciously with ritual an even stronger effect can be achieved.

The purpose of ritual can be seen from a number of different levels:

- The mind's fundamental method of learning is through symbolism. Ritual uses symbolism. The mind responds quickly to this as communication is taking place in its own language. An example is where the baby falls asleep quickly when rocked. In fact the baby will fall asleep with or without the rocking but it is the ritual that brings about the state of mind faster.
- When ritual is based on movement then that movement

is used as a focusing point. Eventually the movement may be left out when the intent becomes clear enough to focus on its own. Learning the movement of ritual without the intent is ineffective. Intent needs to be focused and clear and this grows with the repetition of ritual.

- Ritual provides a structured approach to experiential learning. This can be seen as a form of protection against drifting off into a fantasy world. It keeps practitioners on track so that the learning that others may have begun (perhaps centuries earlier) is continued.
- Gaining an understanding of the meaning behind the physical movement or ritual can expand knowledge of the method as a whole. It is not often that a challenge to complete something so structured and rigid is taken on. On true understanding of this structural conformity the exact nature can be hit upon.

It is easy to fall in love with a ritual or the idea of ritual and to let it rule the entire process. Inability to work without ritual is pure attachment and attachment distracts one from inner work. It is wrong to invest *reiju* with more 'power' than it actually contains. By holding onto the physicality of *reiju*, complete Oneness may never occur as the ritual may eventually come to stand between the practitioner and this attainment.

When one begins to consciously remove ritual from one's life, this action resonates through all aspects of existence; opening doors unseen and previously unheard of. But to do so prematurely is to jump off the train before arriving at the station; leaving one feeling confused, unsure and with nowhere to go.

Origins of the Reiju

The non-physical *reiju*
It is believed that Mikao Usui would sit opposite a student, create an energetic space and *reiju* would transpire. There was no physical ritual and no symbols and mantras were involved. Usui was likely able to perform this non-physical *reiju* due to a life that had centered intently on continual spiritual development.

The realm of the highest vehicle of empowerment is called "Mind taking in spiritual understanding." Speech and action are both unnecessary; the subtlety of the operation lies in mind alone. At this juncture there is a transition from external movement to internal movement, from internal movement to movement of the spirit; both sides communicate mentally by means of spirit, combining in unspoken communion.

(Excerpt from Opening the Dragon Gate by
Chen Kaiguo and Zheng Shunchao)

During *reiju*, Mikao Usui became a vehicle for Dainichi Nyorai, or, in other words they became One. This was a result of Mikao Usui's personal practice where he merged with Dainichi Nyorai and DKM, the 4th mantra and symbol in the system of Reiki. In this space there are unlimited possibilities.

Toshihiro Eguchi, a friend and student of Mikao Usui, was also known to work with a relatively non-physical energetic practice. Professor Judith Rabinovitch writes of her teacher: Miss Endo [a student of Toshihiro Eguchi] (then aged around 97 in 1994) ... initiated me without my knowing it, just by putting my hands under hers (I had no idea what for at the time) for a longish period of time and then telling me just to 'keep practicing', saying my hands were very good.

The physical *reiju*

A *reiju* with physical movement was used by some of Usui's teacher students. This method is a precursor to the *reiju* that is taught today. It is unsure whether Usui actually taught the physical ritual for *reiju* or if the students themselves introduced it in an effort to replicate their energetic experience with Usui.

The physical *reiju* appears to originate from *Tendai* Buddhism. This is not surprising as Mikao Usui is believed to have been a *Tendai* practitioner as would some of his early students have been. Two separate respected *Tendai* teachers have related that the *reiju* mirrors a *Tendai* ritual called *Go Shimbô*, Dharma for Protecting the Body. *Go Shimbô* is a purification process and is one of the first *Mikkyô* rituals that one completes. These esoteric teachings are passed from teacher to student and are not available for the general public.

Another Japanese *Tendai* teacher explained that over the years there have been many small healing practices that in some way are offshoots of the *Mikkyô* tradition, and that they all claim connection to *Tendai* for their orthodoxy.

Hiroshi Doi writes, 'As a result of extensive study and experiments, he [Mikao Usui] successfully developed techniques for passing on *Reiki hô* (*reiju*) and for heightening spirituality (*hatsurei hô*). In these techniques, some of the techniques in ... *Mikkyô* are incorporated.'[100]

Within *Go Shimbô* there are certain concentration points. These are – depending on the lineage and teacher – the heart, forehead, throat, and crown of the head. According to ritual manuals these points represent Dainichi Nyorai, the deity of the corresponding 4th mantra and symbol within the system of Reiki. These gestures are said to cause the body to emit an unbearable light which blinds demons and causes pain to dissipate. These concentration points are similar to the hand positions used with the physical *reiju*. Could this physical *reiju* be the forerunner to the five hand positions that were performed around the head and thought to be a Reiki treatment?

Some modern Reiki researchers claim that the *reiju* has similarities to the Japanese practice of *kaji*.

> *Kaji's* power lies in the enlightened and enlightening transference of power from Dainichi to the individual and vice versa.
>
> (*Curing with Kaji Healing and Esoteric Empowerment in Japan* by Pamela D. Winfield)

There is the possibility that this relationship exists, yet, at this moment in history, it is unlikely that any Reiki teacher is in such a space as to be able to perform *kaji*. Oda Ryûkô, former head priest of the *Shingon* sect, had this to say about *kaji*: In order to effectively administer *kaji* one has to be an enlightened Buddhist practitioner.

Using a physical ritual helped Usui's teacher students to be able to recreate the energetic space that Usui managed to accomplish. Often a physical link can help to find one's way and enable one to focus intent clearly. It does not take away the requirement that one work on oneself – in fact it is an encouragement toward that

---

[100] *Modern Reiki Method for Healing*, Hiroshi Doi, Fraser Journal Publishing, 2000.

constant goal. Ritual is structure, and structure gives something to hold on to when one feels unable to perform the task alone. After many years of solid personal work, when confidence has grown and the ritual and its energetic practice become second nature there is another step one must take – removal of the ritual.

Purpose of Reiju

Reiju appears to have a number of purposes

- A sense of reconnection to one's true self.
- A clearing of the meridians allowing the student to conduct more energy through the body.
- A method a teacher uses in order to communicate with individual students on an energetic level.

Reconnection
Mikao Usui used the *reiju* to help students (and perhaps clients) remember their inner connection; a connection to their true selves. *Reiju* was, however, just the first step. The recipients were also asked to practice with the mind and the body using the five precepts and *waka*, and the physical techniques respectively. Those that repeatedly practiced these elements and received ongoing *reiju* naturally became students of Mikao Usui.

Clearing
During the physical *reiju*, the student sits in meditation while the teacher performs a specific pattern of movement around him or her. As with the non-physical *reiju* no mantras and symbols are used and the *reiju* does not 'attune' the student to the symbols as is sometimes believed with attunements today. There are also no differences in *reiju* for various levels as has developed with attunements. This is because each *reiju* supports the student in clearing stagnant energy and deepening the understanding of energetic work. Therefore, the more often one receives *reiju*, the deeper one can go into the system of Reiki. It is the student's ability to experience more energy that creates perceived differences, not the *reiju* itself.

The same *reiju* is repeated at each meeting of the student and teacher. This confirms the understanding that students take in as much energy as they can at each *reiju*. By receiving repeated *reiju* the students enhance their own energy levels. This also supports the notion that the teacher does not have any special 'power' over the students – personal development is solely up to the student and the amount of work that the student completes.

Communication
Reiju is a concentrated energetic communication between teacher and student. The teacher and student reach out to each other and in moments of true connection, with the support of *reiju*, they and the universe become One energetically.

It is a potent tool for Reiki teachers to support students in developing their skills and working toward replicating the expertise of energetic practitioners such as Morihei Ueshiba (*aikidô's* founder) or Mikao Usui.

For *reiju* to be truly effective there needs to be active participation in the ritual from both the teacher and student.

The student may think, 'I just have to be here and the teacher will make it all happen.'

The teacher may think, 'I just have to do the ritual and something will happen.'

Such thoughts by the teacher and student do not lead to optimal energetic communication.

The Experience of Reiju

During *reiju* students may experience themselves as being One with the universe; that the universe is them and they are the universe. Or perhaps there is a complete sense of profound inner peace. This type of experience is not unusual during *reiju* and is usually temporary rather than permanent. It can be labeled as an initial experience. This initial experience is a reference point for students' inner Reiki work. It offers students insight into where solid practice with the elements of Reiki can lead them. It is the metaphysical carrot dangling in front of the human donkey.

Initial Experience
The words 'initial' and 'initiation' both come from the same Latin

word meaning 'beginning'. For this reason it is possible to see how the word *reiju* may be translated into English as initiation. With the student being able to recall the fleeting experience from *reiju* at any time, there is produced an initial place to begin; a place where students can formulate their current understandings and discover a path to follow.

The Blessing

A Japanese book on Toshihiro Eguchi's life called *Tenohira-ga Byoki-o Naosu* (*Cure Your Illness with Your Palms*) relates that he performed a type of *reiju* called *kosho michibiki*. It quotes Toshihiro Eguchi as saying that everyone can do hands-on healing once it is opened up. The way to open it is to do *gasshô* and meditate and then someone with a stronger power connects with you. This is a good description of *reiju*. That 'stronger power' is the teacher who has practiced the techniques and meditations and *reiju* for an extended period, knowing how to connect strongly with the energy and others. When this teacher steps into the energy field of a student with the intent to become One with that student, then the opportunity for a spiritual blessing occurs.

Student's Responsibility

The student's responsibility is to him or herself: to be as open as possible in order to access the healing and deeper understandings that energetic practice can provide. There needs to be a willingness and openness to self-heal rather than a waiting for others to do the healing. This motivated approach opens students to the possibility of complete communication with the teacher. It is where two consciousnesses share the same experience. The more energetically developed that students are, the more aware and conscious they will become. Receiving *reiju* regularly is an ingenious method to continue this development.

Teacher's Responsibility

The teacher's responsibility is to perform the *reiju* effectively. This requires self-responsibility. Teachers need to develop their skills and strengthen Reiki (spiritual energy) within their own lives before they can support others in the process. This is achieved by gradually moving through the levels of the system of Reiki and fully integrating the teachings with ongoing personal practice at each step. Otherwise the performance of *reiju* is perfunctory; an outer shell without any center. An 'empty' *reiju* may trigger a student's awareness that energy 'exists' but it cannot facilitate a student to a heightened level of knowledge and awareness. A teacher must not be tricked into thinking that because the student felt something that a physical ritual without soul is 'working'. Fluffing up a student's energy field may mislead both the teacher and student into believing that something happened – but this sensation is in fact simply an awareness that energy has been stirred.

Types of Reiju and Attunements

Below are three major directions that have evolved from the teachings within Japan.

Mikao Usui and Early students
Mikao Usui would sit opposite students and performed *reiju* without a physical ritual. Suzuki san taught the physical *reiju* as a tool to familiarize students with the energetic process until they could reach a point in their experience where they could summon the correct intent. The early students of Mikao Usui did not use a physical *reiju*.

Usui Reiki Ryôhô Gakkai
The *Usui Reiki Ryôhô Gakkai* performs a physical *reiju* at each gathering of their members. This is not to say that this society uses the exact *reiju* that Mikao Usui developed. Within the society it is also likely that changes have been made throughout the last century.

Hiroshi Doi claims that the *reiju* is the same for each level – there are no differences as it is the student's ability to draw on more energy that creates the differences, not the *reiju* itself. No symbols or mantras are used in the *reiju* and it is definitely not based on the Indian chakra system.

At the URRI[101] workshop in 1999, Hiroshi Doi taught a *reiju* that he said was re-created from that used by Kimiko Koyama, sixth

---

[101] *Usui Reiki Ryôhô* International.

president of the *Usui Reiki Ryôhô Gakkai*. There are also similarities between this 'created' *reiju* and the *reiju* used by Suzuki san. Hiroshi Doi has also stated that the *reiju* he taught in 1999 had been taught to him by a son of an *Usui Reiki Ryôhô Gakkai* teacher.

At the URRI workshop in 2002, Hiroshi Doi taught what he called the 'Original Usui *Reiju* Used in Gakkai'. It is a different *reiju* from his earlier presentation in 1999.

Whichever *reiju* the *Usui Reiki Ryôhô Gakkai* practice, it is likely to be closer to the original than that taught in most modern Reiki branches as it has been kept within the one community.

Chûjirô Hayashi
Chûjirô Hayashi performed a physical *reiju* with symbols and mantras which, today is called an attunement. He was a student of Mikao Usui and was also a member of the *Usui Reiki Ryôhô Gakkai*. He broke away from it in 1931 to create his own clinic.

Hawayo Takata studied with Chûjirô Hayashi from 1936 to 1938 and thereafter took the teachings to Hawaii.

Today, what is called an attunement might be one of a multitude of different attunement versions. There are in fact so many that are being taught that no one is really sure what the 'original' is. Most are re-creations of re-creations of re-creations. Some practitioners have added more symbols to the attunements, others extend the process to include extra movements and unending repetition, link individual attunements to chakras or include the playing of singing bowls, etc.

This uncertainty promotes a disregard for this mystical process leaving it open for more distortions.

Albeit that there are so many versions of attunements, there are also some similarities:

• The use of mantras and symbols
• Each level has a slightly altered attunement

These similarities suggest a distinctly different ritual to the *reiju* taught by Mikao Usui, which indicates one thing: the practice called an attunement (and all its variations) has come from one source – Chûjirô Hayashi via his student Hawayo Takata.

To further back this up there are the similarities of attunements from two more students of Chûjirô Hayashi. One is Tatsumi who taught a simpler, non-elaborate attunement. The other is Chiyoko Yamaguchi who, although she had learnt Reiki in her late teens, didn't start teaching until she was in her late 70s. She also taught a simple attunement with just two hand positions. Both Tatsumi and Chiyoko Yamaguchi used mantras and symbols and altered the attunement for each level. Therefore, the attunement process can be traced back to Chûjirô Hayashi. Though it is interesting to note that Chiyoko Yamaguchi did not use Symbol 4 in her attunement.[102]

It is unknown whether Mikao Usui taught Chûjirô Hayashi this ritual or if he created it himself. It is known that Japanese practitioners today say that the modern teachings are Hayashi's Reiki not Usui's teachings. It may be the case that Chûjirô Hayashi took the *reiju* and adapted it to fit in with his idea of teaching over a short period of time. This is unlike the *Usui Reiki Ryôhô Gakkai* who repeat *reiju* at each meeting.

Chûjirô Hayashi may have believed that he made the *reiju* more 'powerful' by including the symbols and mantras into the process. This, therefore, allowed students to receive their certificates at the end of the 5-day training without the obligation of any ongoing meetings, tutoring or repeated performing of *reiju*.

This particular arrangement is very much a forerunner to the modern style of teaching where there is no continuity of study with the teacher. It is also representative of the concept that symbols add more 'power' to one's Reiki practice. Traditionally, mantras and symbols are not considered to be 'powerful' but simply to aid in the understanding of energy. This modern misconception may very well have begun in the practice of Chûjirô Hayashi.

There have been suggestions that Chûjirô Hayashi was actually unaware of the exact workings of the *reiju* and therefore created his own ritual and that is what is called an attunement today. The basis for this statement is that he only studied with Mikao Usui for the limited period of 10 months. According to Chris Marsh, there is a record stating that Chûjirô Hayashi started *shinpiden* in 1925. As

---

[102] Chiyoko Yamaguchi did not teach DKM and Symbol 4 or use them in the attunement – this might be because she was taught by a relative and never formally learnt *Shinpiden*.

Mikao Usui died not long after this there is the suggestion that he may not have finished this training and therefore may not have learnt the *reiju*. Toshitaka Mochizuki states in his 1995 book, *Iyashi No Te* (*Healing Hands*), that Chûjirô Hayashi was one of 19 teachers appointed by Mikao Usui before he died.

The name of Chûjirô Hayashi's organization, *Hayashi Reiki Kenkyû Kai*, indicates that he adapted Mikao Usui's teachings. In Japan, it is customary to keep the teachings' title intact. This would only change if the teachings were altered. From this early title change it is possible to see that Chûjirô Hayashi had created his own teachings and system.

Saihôji Temple

> Of late the fellow disciples consulted with each other about building the stone memorial in a graveyard at *Saihôji* Temple in *Toyotama gun* so as to honor his merits and to make them immortalized.
>
> (Excerpt from Mikao Usui's Memorial Stone)

Mikao Usui's memorial is at the Pure Land Buddhist *Saihôji* Temple in *Tôkyô*. The exact address is *Toyotama* district, 1-4-56 *Umesato, Suginami Ku, Tôkyô*.

Here stands the memorial stone that was engraved and erected by Mikao Usui's students in February 1927, one year after his death. The ashes for the Usui family are also placed here.

All students of Mikao Usui's teachings would do well to visit this site. The peace and serenity of the *Saihôji* Temple is a wonderful reminder of the origins of these teachings. The connection to their past is here to be experienced, steeped in Japanese culture.

Most funeral ceremonies held in Japan are Buddhist. The body is first cremated with the relatives picking the bones out of the ashes with chopsticks and passing them from person to person.

A meal may be offered to the guests at the crematorium. The actual funeral then takes place. Guests offer money to the relatives and receive a small gift in return. A final meal is taken.

The urn, filled with ashes, is placed upon an altar at the family's house for 35 days. Incense sticks are burned around the clock and, during this period, visitors drop by to burn a stick of incense and extend their sympathy to the family.

Finally, after the 35 days, the urn is buried at a Buddhist gravesite. There are many occasions throughout the year when family members visit their ancestors' gravesites.

Directions to the Gravesite

To find Mikao Usui's gravesite take the metro to the *shin koenji* station. Leave the station through the south exit. If you are arriving from the *Tôkyô* central direction then exit from the left side of the train.

At the south exit turn to the right and follow the sidewalk.

At the first main road, cross the street to your right. Here there is a small side street with the numbers 1-4-56 written on the signpost.

Walk down this street until you arrive at its end. To your right is the shingled roof of the entrance gate to the *Saihôji* Temple.

Walk under the gate and straight ahead of you is the main temple. To your right is the central path of the memorial grounds. Begin to walk along this central path and immediately to your right you will find an alcove where you can purify yourself with the aid of a wooden ladle and water from the temple well.

This method of purification is offered to all who visit the *Saihôji* Temple (and is a general rule of etiquette in temples throughout Japan). The ladle is provided to scoop up the water to wash the visitors' hands and mouth. Do remember that it is impolite to drink this water. The correct custom is to scoop water holding the ladle in your right hand and wash your left hand. Take the ladle in your left hand and now wash the right hand. Return the ladle to your right hand and place some water in your left hand using it to rinse your mouth out. Shake the ladle sideways. The little remaining water will remove any dirt that may have become attached to your hands from the handle.

Wooden pails line the walls of the alcove and visitors pump them full of water from the temple well.

Carry the pail of water and ladle with you as you return to walking down the central path. This graveyard is cool and green, being dotted with large trees. People wander along its cobbled pathways visiting those who are no longer with them in their daily lives. When you pass a red wall, turn to the left. Follow this path and then take the second path to the left. You are almost there. Look up and you will see the large memorial stone dedicated to the life and works of Mikao Usui peering through the pine trees. It is the second site on your right.

Follow the short path into the gravesite. It is about 10 x 10 feet (3½ × 3½ meters) in size. To your right a red berry tree stands next to a stone lantern or *tôrô*.

Tôrô were first brought to Japan from China in the sixth century along with the introduction of Buddhism. Though they come in all shapes and sizes their one common factor is the hollow upper tier that is used for illumination purposes where a candle or oil lamp can be placed.

There is also a great granite-like stone on the ground with a fist sized indentation in its center that gathers the daily dew dripped from overhanging pine trees.

In front of you is the altar and gravesite marker. Students come here to demonstrate their respect to the man who has reminded them of their connection to the source.

Purify the altar with the water ladled from your pail. Light your incense and place flowers in both of the vases.

Below, and in front of, this altar, the Usui family *Chiba* crest or *mon* can be seen elegantly carved out of stone. The *Chiba* crest is a circle with a dot at the top. The circle represents the universe, and the dot or Japanese star represents the North Star. The North Star never moves while the universe circumambulates it. These crests are handed down from generation to generation and originated in the eleventh century. Soldiers would affix them to the banners that they carried into battle. There are around 200 basic crests in Japan today with about 4000 individual variations. The most famous crest is the 16-petalled chrysanthemum inherited by the Imperial family.

At the back of Mikao Usui's altar is a rectangular pole about 6 feet high. On the front side it states that this marker is the gravestone for the entire Usui family. This marker was erected one month after the memorial stone had been placed at the site by students from the *Usui Reiki Ryôhô Gakkai*.

On the left side of the marker are the posthumous names of both Mikao Usui and his wife, Sadako. Mikao Usui's name, given after his death, is *Reizan-in shuyo tenshin koji* and his wife's name was *Teshin ing on ho jo ning dai shi.*

The back of the marker explains when the marker was erected and by whom. Fuji Usui, Mikao Usui's son, erected the marker on 9 March 1927, exactly one year after Mikao Usui's death. On the left side of the marker is the inscription recording the date of the death of their daughter, Toshiko Usui.

Between the *tôrô* and the gravesite marker is a small square tablet raised off the ground. This is Fuji Usui's own gravesite marker.

Turn to your left and there facing you is the great monolithic memorial stone. The text was composed by Masayuki Okada with brush strokes written by Jûzaburô Ushida[103] in 1927.

This memorial relates the story of Mikao Usui's life – his trials and accomplishments. It also recounts his basic teachings of the five precepts, and reminds all that the purpose of his teachings was not just to heal illnesses but also to combine a right mind and a healthy body. This in turn creates enjoyment and happiness in life.[104]

Mikao Usui
9 March 1926

Toshiko Usui
23 September 1935 (22 years old)

Sadako Usui
17 October 1946

Fuji Usui
10 July 1946 (39 years old)

Healing Manuals

Reiki Ryôhô is something absolutely original and cannot be compared with any other (spiritual) path in the world.

(Excerpt from the *Reiki Ryôhô Hikkei* as translated in
Frank Arjava Petter's book, *Reiki – The Legacy of Dr. Usu.*)

---

[103] Jûzaburô Ushida was the second president of the *Usui Reiki Ryôhô Gakkai.*
[104] There is a full translation of the Mikao Usui Memorial Stone in the Appendix.

Traditional Healing Manuals and Books

There are a number of traditional healing manuals and books that can be accessed today by Reiki practitioners.

- The most well known is the *Reiki Ryôhô Hikkei* which is now available to Reiki practitioners around the world. It was put together by members of the *Usui Reiki Ryôhô Gakkai*.
- The *shiori* is a manual that *Usui Reiki Ryôhô Gakkai* members only may access.
- *Tenohira-ga Byoki-o Naosu* (*Cure Your Illness with Your Palms*) written by Mihashi Kazuo sheds some light on what was taught and practiced by a student and friend of Mikao Usui called Toshihiro Eguchi.
- Kaiji Tomita's book *Reiki To Jinjutsu–Tomita Ryû Teate Ryôhô* (*Reiki and Humanitarian Work-Tomita Ryu Hands Healing*) from 1933 was re-published in 1999 with the help of Toshitaka Mochizuki, and includes practices taught and practiced by him.

Reiki Ryôhô Hikkei

Frank Arjava Petter first wrote about the manual he came across in Japan in his book *Reiki, The Legacy of Dr. Usui* in 1998. This was yet another eye-opener for modern Reiki practitioners. First there had been the discovery of the wonderfully informative memorial stone and now there were actual written notes from the Japanese society, *Usui Reiki Ryôhô Gakkai*. The surprise was great, namely, because Hawayo Takata had said that the system of Reiki was an oral tradition and allowed no note-taking in her classes.[105]

The *Reiki Ryôhô Hikkei* (*Spiritual Energy Healing Method Manual*) is a 68-page document divided up into four sections that is handed out to *shoden* (Level 1) members.[106] It is comprised of an introduc-

[105] Though this is said to be the case, a number of her students did receive a manual called the *Ryôhô Shishin* written by Chûjirô Hayashi. It appears to be almost identical to the healing guide in the *Reiki Ryôhô Hikkei*.

[106] Frank Arjava Petter included only three sections in the book *Reiki – the Legacy of Dr. Usui* and placed the fourth section, the *Ryôhô Shishin*, in a later book called *The Original Reiki Handbook of Dr. Mikao Usui*.

tion or explanation by Mikao Usui with the five precepts; a question and answer section with Mikao Usui; the *Ryôhô Shishin*, or *Healing Method's Guideline*, with specific hand positions; and the *gyosei* (*waka* written by the Meiji Emperor).

Kimiko Koyama[107] published this teaching manual for the 50th anniversary of the *Usui Reiki Ryôhô Gakkai*. It is still handed out to members today. As this is a collection of materials it is unclear if all of the material originates from the time of Mikao Usui or not. Both Part I and Part II of the manual appear to be written in the time of Mikao Usui. Part III, the healing guide, may well have been written after the death of Mikao Usui by an early member of the *Usui Reiki Ryôhô Gakkai*, Chûjirô Hayashi especially as Part II states that in 1922 the Japanese Government's position, as far as Reiki was concerned, was that this method had nothing to do with the medical faculty. This makes it appear unlikely that a 'medicalized' healing guide such as is included in Part III would have been acceptable within the system. Part IV includes poetry from the early 1900s which was definitely used by students of Mikao Usui as can be seen in the book by Kaiji Tomita.

Below is a brief summary of what is included in the *Usui Reiki Ryôhô Gakkai* manual called the *Reiki Ryôhô Hikkei*.

Part I – *Usui Reiki Ryôhô Kyôgi* or *Usui Spiritual Energy Healing Method Doctrine*
This is an explanation by Mikao Usui as to why he taught publicly.

He maintains that the happiness of humanity is based on two elements: working together and the desire for social progress. This cannot happen if any one individual attempts to possess Reiki.

This method is original and cannot be compared with any other spiritual path and therefore it should be available for all.

Through this spiritual method people will become happy and healthy and that is something that is clearly needed today (there was a great deal of military action at the turn of the 20th century in Japan).

Part II – Explanation of Instruction for the Public
The origins of this section may lie in the system where students

---

[107] Kimiko Koyama was the sixth president of the *Usui Reiki Ryôhô Gakkai*.

wrote their questions for Mikao Usui in their 'manuals' and consequently also wrote the answers once they were provided. In those
days there were no photocopiers to quickly print off information
for students and everything was hand written. Below is a condensed
version of Mikao Usui's responses:

- Mind and body are one. Once the spirit is healed, humanity
  will find its true path resulting in a healthy body.
- The method is a spiritual secret of freeing the body and
  mind.
- It is a spiritual and a physical method. Physical in that
  energy and light radiate from the mouth, the eyes and the
  hands of the practitioner. This can heal chronic and acute
  illnesses.
- It is unnecessary to believe in it. Though, even after the first
  treatment the benefits are noticed and therefore it is only
  natural to come to believe in it.
- It not only works on physical illness but also bad habits and
  psychological imbalances. By practicing, students become
  aligned with God energy, which in turn gives a desire to
  help fellow human beings.
- Mikao Usui was not initiated into the method by anyone.
  During fasting he sensed an intense energy and thereafter
  realized he had been given the spiritual art of healing. He
  cannot explain how it works scientifically.
- The method does not use medication.
- It is a spiritual method not a scientific one. The part of the
  body that has the problem just needs to be touched, that's
  all.
- Allopathic medicine does not treat the spiritual aspect of
  human beings.
- In 1922, the Japanese Government's position as far as Reiki
  was concerned was that this method had nothing to do with
  the medical faculty as it then stood.
- Anyone can learn it; men, women, old and young. Mikao
  Usui had at the time of writing taught over one thousand
  students and not one had been unable to practice it. It is
  simple to learn yet effective to perform.

- First, healing one's self must take place before healing others.
- *Okuden*, the second level, consists of techniques such as tapping, stroking, pressing and distant healing. First enthusiasm for the method must be learnt with much personal practice.

Part III – *Ryôhô Shishin* or Healing Method's Guideline
This guide is split into 11 chapters as listed below:

1. Basic Treatment of Specific Body Parts
2. Nerve Disorders
3. Respiratory Disorders
4. Digestive Disorders
5. Circulatory and Cardiovascular Disorders
6. Metabolic Imbalances and Blood Disorders
7. Urogenital Disorders
8. Surgical and Dermatological Disorders
9. Pediatric Disorders
10. Gynecological Disorders
11. Contagious Diseases

Part IV – 125 *Gyosei* (*waka*, poetry written by the Meiji Emperor)

Akino yono tuskiwa mukashini kawaranedo yoni nakihito no ooku narinuru (*Tsuki*)
　　While a moon on an autumnal night remains just
　　the same as ever,
　　in this world the number of the deceased
　　has become larger. (Moon)

Asamidori sumiwataritaru ohzorano hiroki onoga kokoro to mogana (*Ten*)
　　As a great sky in clear light green
　　I wish my heart would be as vast. (Sky)

Atsushitomo iware zarikeri niekaeru
mizutani tateru shizu wo omoheba (*Orinifurete*)
　　Thinking of lowly people standing in a boiling hot

paddy field
I hesitate to utter "it's hot". (Upon occasion)

Amata tabi shigurete someshi momijiba wo tada hitokaze no chirashi keru-kana (Rakuyou-fu)
Maple leaves tinted by frequent showers
in late autumn
just a whiff of wind scattered. (Fallen Leaves-Wind)

Shiori

Along with this manual, *Usui Reiki Ryôhô Gakkai* members also receive the *shiori*. This is a booklet exclusively for members and was written by Hôichi Wanami[108] and Kimiko Koyama. It contains:[109]

- The purpose, history and administrative system of the *Usui Reiki Ryôhô Gakkai* and includes the names of 11 of the 21 *shinpiden* students taught by Mikao Usui.
- How to strengthen Reiki and includes techniques such as *byôsen reikan hô*, *gedoku hô*, *kôketsu hô*, and *nentatsu hô*.
- A teaching from Mikao Usui.
- A guide to treatment.
- Characteristics of *Reiki Ryôhô* (Spiritual Energy Healing Method).
- Remarks by medical doctors.
- Explanation of the *Ryôhô Shishin* (*Healing Method's Guideline*).

Tenohira-ga Byoki-o Naosu

In 2000 a book by Mihashi Kazuo called *Tenohira-ga Byoki-o Naosu* (*Cure Your Illness with Your Palms*) shed some light on what was taught and practiced by a student and friend of Mikao Usui called Toshihiro Eguchi.

Toshihiro Eguchi believed that everyone could do hands-on heal-

---

[108] Hôichi Wanami was the fifth president of the *Usui Reiki Ryôhô Gakkai*.
[109] Information supplied to the authors by Hyakuten Inamoto.

ing once their energetic path was open. The way to open or fully clear this path was very easy: practitioners must *gasshô* and meditate with someone who was more energetically experienced for 30 to 40 minutes over three consecutive days. This helped strengthen the practitioner's own energetic connection and build the confidence to carry out hands-on healing.

Professor Judith Rabinovitch states that he writes of going into people's home, showing them 'how,' and bidding them to practice faithfully. Spiritual and meditative practices were used, however, to advance those who came to take his course.

Much of Toshihiro Eguchi's practice was based on self-development and he advised his students to follow these seven Principles to encourage an ascetic lifestyle:

1. Deep compassion needs to be felt for clients.
2. Keep the body clean, be honest, be kind and don't get angry.
3. When training: eat *shojin ryori* (type of Buddhist meal without meat) and eat lightly.
4. To remain healthy: take light from the sun, fresh air, good water and good food.
5. By only focusing on the body it is impossible to get healthy. Students must also think and act well.
6. Read *waka* from the Meiji Emperor every day.
7. If we become sick we must first say to ourselves from the bottom of our heart, 'I sincerely apologise if I have done something wrong'.

A specific aspect of Toshihiro Eguchi's hands-on healing technique was the use of the right hand only – as this was for giving while the left hand was for receiving (though in some cases he did advise practitioners to use the left hand). Practitioners must make sure that the client feels balanced during the treatment, e.g., if you treat the left arm, the right must also be treated. Talking must be kept to a minimum during the treatment and a prayer is said at its commencement. An example of a prayer might be: may my hands help this person that he/she may become well. Toshihiro Eguchi also believed that the illness itself should not be mentioned in the prayer.

When treating people, Toshihiro Eguchi taught to begin with the head using five head positions with one last position on the stomach. The first five head positions correlate with the five head positions as taught by Mikao Usui. The treatment would generally take about 30 to 40 minutes.

Below in italics is a verbatim translation by Professor Judith Rabinovitch of Toshihiro Eguchi's head 'method' taken from the 1930 book co-written with Kôshi Mitsui called *Tenohira Ryôji Nyûmon*. After the head (including the stomach position) the Professor states that specific parts of the body would be touched focusing on the organs. Hand placement directions for organs are given as well as placements for specific illnesses that are diverse as asthma, cerebral hemorrhage, female hysteria, and hiccups. At the same time it should be noted that Toshihiro Eguchi did not believe that the 'method' was as important as the practitioner's spiritual connection in bringing about healing.

Hand Positions for the Head

1. Hairline (*haegiwa*)
2. Temples (*komekami*) 'you can do both sides with both hands at once'
3. Rear of head, high up (*kôtôbu no takai tokoro*)
4. Nape of neck (*kubisuji*)
5. Top of head (crown) (*atama no chôjô*)
6. Stomach, intestines (*ichô*)

Perform practices 1–6 for approximately 30 or 40 minutes for healing to take place. This treatment is also effective in reducing fever. Before starting treatment, take the body temperature of the patient, and you will be able to measure the drop in fever.

Reiki To Jinjutsu – Tomita Ryû Teate Ryôhô

Kaiji Tomita was a student of Mikao Usui. He wrote a book called, *Reiki To Jinjutsu – Tomita Ryû Teate Ryôhô* (*Reiki and Humanitarian Work-Tomita Ryu Hands Healing*) in 1933. The book was re-published in 1999 with the help of Toshitaka Mochizuki.

Included in his book are case studies, the technique *hatsurei hô* (which includes the use of *waka*) and hand positions for specific illnesses.

Techniques of one kind or another have always been used in conjunction with the system of Reiki. *Hatsurei hô* is one of the early techniques. Below is a translation of this technique from Kaiji Tomita's book which is much simpler than what is practiced. The chanting of *gyosei*, poetry written by the Meiji Emperor, is not practiced in the modern form of *hatsurei hô*.

To begin this practice one is required to sit and concentrate (unify) the mind and body. To do this, choose a quiet place or somewhere comfortable where you can relax. Included in the text are 2 different readings of the word *seiza*. One means to sit still and is the first part of the technique, the other relates to the physical action of sitting in *seiza*.

Seiza (lit. Japanese to sit still)

Sit in the *seiza* position and *gasshô* with the objective to gather/concentrate the energy from the heart into the palms of the hands. Hold the hands together without using force from the arms or the shoulders. Drop the shoulders and clasp the hands, joining the fingers lightly and feel the alignment of the posture. Close your eyes.

Jôshin hô (Mind purification method)

The aim of *jôshin hô* is to unify and purify the mind. Once the sitting upright is achieved, recite (in your head) some *waka* poetry and feel at One with its meaning. The poetry in Part IV of the *Reiki Ryôhô Hikkei* can be utilized for this practice.

Hatsurei hô

If you have followed the previous steps and stayed focused on the palms of your hands they start to become warm. This is what (*Tomita ryû*) calls *reiha* (wave of *rei*). It describes the tingling sensation as comparable to an electrical current. The heat created and the wave of rei are what constitute spiritual energy. Even if the sensations are weak at first, they should become stronger as you keep concentrating.

5-Day plan

Repeat the above steps for 5 consecutive days, and concentrate for at least 30 minutes (progressively increasing, eventually reaching an hour).

6 Reiki in Japan

Post-Mikao Usui

The Private Teachings

Mikao Usui died in 1926, leaving his legacy, his teachings, to the world. He once said that he wished to 'release this method to the public for everyone's benefit'.[1] His intention has been realized with practitioners in every country of the world today. Yet, in Japan itself, there has been a reticence to bring his teachings into the public eye by many traditional Japanese practitioners.

There were only a handful of books written by Mikao Usui's students in the first half of the last century. Some of these were:

- *Te No Hira Ryôji Nyûmon* (*Introduction to Healing with the Palms*), Toshihiro Eguchi and Kôshi Mitsui, 1930
- *Reiki To Jinjutsu – Tomita Ryû Teate Ryôhô* (*Reiki and Humanitarian Work – Tomita Ryû Hands Healing*), Kaiji Tomita, 1933
- *Te No Hira Ryôji Wo Kataru* (*A Story of Healing with the Palms*), Toshihiro Eguchi, 1954

Looking at what is called the system of Reiki today, it can be difficult to see where it connects to what was once practiced in Japan in the early 1900s. So many alterations and additions by so many individuals have created a method that Mikao Usui would not

---

[1] Information supplied by the *Reiki Ryôhô Hikkei*.

recognize as his teachings. Aura cleansings, dragon breaths and the chakra system were not a part of his vocabulary.

These changes may also not have been welcomed by traditional Japanese practitioners. Fundamental Japanese culture is based on respect. Within that there is a deep respect for the *kokoro* or the true nature of Mikao Usui's teachings. Traditional Japanese practitioners are respectful and protective of them. For this reason it has been difficult to trace the teachings in Japan. Once they moved outside the country they spread like a wildfire that could not be contained (especially after Hawayo Takata's death in 1980). The system of Reiki as it is practiced today is perceived to have lost touch with its *kokoro*. For example, in the USA one teacher has 'Reiki Master' on the number plates of his car. This type of foreign approach has validated and strengthened many traditional Japanese practitioners' beliefs that Mikao Usui's teachings should be practiced quietly, without advertising and within the parameters of the culture.

> Focus on your feet rather than getting on a horse
> Focus on your *ki* rather than your feet
> Focus on kokoro rather than your *ki*
>
> (Excerpt from Funakoshi Gichin in *Tanpenshu* by
> Patrick and Yuriko McCarthy)

When the American born Hawayo Takata wanted to learn Chûjirô Hayashi's teachings in Japan in 1935–1936, she was told that she could not become a practitioner because she was a foreigner. After proving her sincerity and commitment to his teachings, she was made an exception to the rule. An article written by a student of Chûjirô Hayashi in Japan in 1928[2] (just two years after Mikao Usui's death) said that *Usui Reiki Ryôhô Gakkai* members did not like to advertise or to make their teachings public. It seems their attitude has changed little.

Traditional Teachers

Exactly who these traditional Japanese practitioners are today is somewhat unclear because of their lack of interest in standing in

[2] 'A Treatment to Heal Diseases, Hand Healing', Shûô Matsui in the magazine *Sunday Mainichi*, 4 March 1928, translated by Amy, to be viewed at www.reiki.net.au.

the public arena. Interest in traditional Japanese practitioners has been steadily growing since the mid 1990s. Prior to this there was little curiosity due to a claim in the USA that Hawayo Takata was the only Reiki Master in the world.[3]

The names of 11 of approximately 21[4] teacher students of Mikao Usui have been recorded in a booklet used by the *Usui Reiki Ryôhô Gakkai* called the *shiori*. From those 21 stem a small number of traditional Japanese practitioners claiming to teach what he taught without outside influences. There have been many other Japanese offshoots of Mikao Usui's teachings but they are no longer directly linked to him.

The most well known group, though reclusive, stemming directly from Mikao Usui is the *Usui Reiki Ryôhô Gakkai*. The *Usui Reiki Ryôhô Gakkai* was comprised of naval officers as its senior members plus Mikao Usui himself (according to the *Usui Reiki Ryôhô Gakkai*). Thanks to Hiroshi Doi there has been a better understanding globally of how that society practices and what this might mean for the system of Reiki in general. Interestingly, in the 1930s it was one of the *Usui Reiki Ryôhô Gakkai*, Chûjirô Hayashi, who traveled to Hawaii with his American student, Hawayo Takata. This was the first step out of Japan for these teachings.

Another student of Chûjirô Hayashi was Chiyoko Yamaguchi[5] who passed away in her 80s in 2003. She had been taught Levels 1 and 2 by Chûjirô Hayashi. Many of her family members were practitioners and from one of them she had been taught to perform the attunement.

Over the last decade there has been research into living students of Mikao Usui. No solid proof has come to light in regards to these claims. Some of these students are:

- Suzuki san, born in 1895 said to be still alive (2008).
- Mariko Obaasan, also known as Tenon in, born in late 1897 and is claimed to have died in 2005.

---

[3] Advertising Poster for a workshop by Hawayo Takata states: The Only Teacher of the Usui System of Reiki in the World Today, 27-31 July 1975.

[4] Hiroshi Doi states that there were 21 teacher students of Mikao Usui while Toshitaka Mochizuki suggests 19 in his book, *Iyashi No Te*.

[5] Chiyoko Yamaguchi died at the age of 82 in August, 2003.

- Yuri in, who was born in 1896 and is said to have died in 1997.

There are also other claims to the existence of more traditional teachers in Japan. Masaharu Ueno (a president of Cosmo Bright) and Mr. Okajima (manager of Modern Reiki Healing Center in Osaka) both claim to have received *reiju* early on in their lives.[6]

Popularity of Hands-on Healing

According to Toshitaka Mochizuki's book, *Iyashi No Te* (*Healing Hands*), tens of millions of people have been affected by Mikao Usui's teachings over the past 100 years.

Some of the better-known hands- on healers who trained with Mikao Usui in Japan were Toshihiro Eguchi, Kaiji Tomita, and their students.

Toshihiro Eguchi
Toshihiro Eguchi is believed to have been a friend of Mikao Usui. He studied from 1925 to 1927, first with Mikao Usui and then, after his death, with the *Usui Reiki Ryôhô Gakkai*.[7] In 2000, a book was published in Japan about Toshihiro Eguchi and his healing techniques called *Tenohira-ga Byoki-o Naosu* (*Cure Your Illness with Your Palms*) written by Mihashi Kazuo. This book sheds some light on what was taught and practiced by him. It also briefly discusses Toshihiro Eguchi's dealings with a group called *Usui Reiki Ryôhô* from 1926 onwards. This name refers to the *Usui Reiki Ryôhô Gakkai* (Usui Spiritual Energy Healing Method Society) that still exists in Japan today. The author's knowledge of Toshihiro Eguchi was drawn from a number of out-of-print books, written by Toshihiro Eguchi and others.

Toshihiro Eguchi was born on 11 April 1873 in Kumamoto, Japan and died on 10 June 1946. Around 8 years Mikao Usui's junior, his health had never been very good and he often fainted and had chest problems. At one point in his youth he was not accepted into the Army Cadet School due to problems encountered in the physical

---

[6] *Modern Reiki Method for Healing*, Hiroshi Doi, Fraser Journal Publishing, 2000.
[7] *Modern Reiki Method for Healing*, Hiroshi Doi, Fraser Journal Publishing, 2000.

entry test. Later when he was admitted to the University of *Tôkyô* he fainted during the University examination. Toshihiro Eguchi was known to have dropped some subjects due to his weak health yet he still managed to graduate eventually becoming a principal of a school in *Nagano*.

According to *Tenohira-ga Byoki-o Naosu*, a lady called Tamura introduced Toshihiro Eguchi to *Usui Reiki Ryôhô* in 1926; he was 53 years old at the time. Toshihiro Eguchi was living in *Shibuya, Tôkyô*, and wrote of this society that '50 yen was/is a high price to pay for admission to the group [*nyûkai* is the term], and moreover, at each meeting, one has to pay 1 yen further. So, while I thought that this [my training] was very important, having to pay 50 yen for this kind of thing just didn't make sense to me.' Toshihiro Eguchi believed that people practicing hands-on healing should never ask large fees for the service as it is a natural gift that everyone is born with and he also believed it may have been possible to collect a person's karma. He also noted that the current teacher of the *Usui Reiki Ryôhô Gakkai* was Taketomi Kanichi (1878-1960) who, as a Rear Admiral in the Japanese Navy, was well off financially. After two years Toshihiro Eguchi took action saying he had 'seen through to the unjustness [*iwarenaki wo*] of the high fees', writing a formal letter of resignation [*taikai-todoke*] from the group and submitting it to Naval Officer (Rear Admiral) Ushida Jûzaburô (1865-1935), 'head of the *Usui-Kai*'.

Moving on to begin his own teachings, with his own ideas and his 'declared independence', Toshihiro Eguchi created the *Tenohira Ryôji Kenkyû kai* (Hand Healing Research Centre). He moved to the city of *Kôfu* where, to house the hundreds who came for his public service, he took a meeting room near the *Kôfu* station. 'This,' Professor Judith Rabinovitch states, 'was the beginnings of Toshihiro Eguchi's flourishing practice, which attracted thousands of people from all across the land for decades.' She also said of his nature that 'he is said to have been a deeply religious man who practiced a meditative healing grounded in prayer without symbols or attunements'.

As far as fees were concerned Toshihiro Eguchi and his brother Shunpaku apparently did not take fixed fees for training others, but Professor Judith Rabinovitch believed that they did receive small contributions.

Mikao Usui, personally, is not mentioned in *Tenohira-ga Byoki-o*

Naosu but according to Professor Judith Rabinovitch, 'Eguchi was a student of Usui *sensei's* for about two years and a close personal friend for much longer'. It is unknown whether he actually studied through to the teacher level with Mikao Usui. Hiroshi Doi has stated that he did not study to this level. Perhaps official teacher levels were only introduced with the establishment of the *Usui Reiki Ryôhô Gakkai* and, as he himself states, he did not finish his training with this society.

Professor Judith Rabinovitch goes on to say that 'since Eguchi in particular studied under Usui with such seriousness, his writings are especially valuable in tracing early proto-Reiki and better understanding the Buddhist and spiritual underpinnings of hand healing.' There are also said to be records and a journal of Toshihiro Eguchi's that have survived the decades detailing information about his relationship with Usui.

Tenohira-ga Byoki-o Naosu states that Eguchi's center became very popular by 1929 with about 150 new people joining each month to learn his techniques. Eguchi and some of his students developed 3-day seminars that they took to *Tôkyô* and *Osaka* with around 300 people attending each seminar. Toshihiro Eguchi introduced hundreds of thousands of students to his style of hands-on healing. Toshihiro Eguchi also ran a healing community called *Ittôen* for a number of years.

Of his students the most well known were Kôshi Mitsui and Gorô Miyazaki.

In Japan today, Mihashi states that there are still people teaching Eguchi's method with one of them being Kijima Yasu.

Kôshi Mitsui
Kôshi Mitsui, a poet and one-time village Mayor, helped Toshihiro Eguchi with his lectures and meetings and was well respected for his writing of *waka* poetry; classical Japanese poetry that Mikao Usui and some of his contemporaries combined with their spiritual teachings. The *Usui Reiki Ryôhô Gakkai* have a list of 125 *waka* poems written by the Meiji Emperor (1852-1912) that were used by Usui in his teachings. 'The important thing during training,' Mitsui wrote, 'is to reach unity and to reach this you must practice *gasshô*, or during your normal daily life – *waka*'. Mitsui published quite a few

books discussing the Meiji Emperor's *waka*. In 1930 he co-wrote a book about *tenohira ryôji* with Eguchi called *Tenohira Ryôji Nyûmon* (*Introduction to Healing with the Palms*).

Kaiji Tomita

Kaiji Tomita studied Mikao Usui's teachings around 1925 and founded *Tomita Teate Ryôhô* (Tomita Hands-on Healing Method). Kaiji Tomita taught Reiki in four levels: *shoden, chuden, okuden* and *kaiden*. Each level required five days (two hours each day) to be completed. The last level, *kaiden*, required 15 days. Kaiji Tomita wrote a book in 1933 called *Reiki To Jinjutsu – Tomita Ryû Teate Ryôhô* (*Reiki and Humanitarian Work – Tomita Ryû Hands Healing*). It describes around 20 case histories, a major technique that he used to generate energy called *hatsurei hô*, and a five-day plan to work on oneself. It is a technical book with many hand positions for specific illnesses listed. Kaiji Tomita is believed to have had more than 200,000 students and his most famous student was Asuke Jiro, who wrote *Therapy with Hands*.[8]

Usui, the Nucleus

Toshitaka Mochizuki actually claims that Mikao Usui was the nucleus from which many other forms of spiritual healing took place in the early 1900s in Japan. Some other spiritual healing groups working at the time were:[9]

Tairedô by Morihei Tanaka
Jintai Rajiumu Gakkai (Human Radium Society) by Dobetsu Matsumoto
Shinnôkyô Honin by Taiman Nishimura
Toyo Jindo Kyokai by Shunnichi Ema
Teikoku Shinrei Kenkyû Kai (Imperial Society of the Spirit) by Kinji Kuwata
Dainihon Tenmei Gakuin (Japanese Tenmei Institute) by Kumagoku Hamaguchi
Shurei Tanshinkai by Saiko Fujita
Seido Gakkai by Reizen Ôyama

[8] *Modern Reiki Method for Healing*, Hiroshi Doi, Fraser Journal Publishing, 2000.
[9] *Iyashi No Te*, Toshitaka Mochizuki, Tama Shuppan, 1995.

Reiki Kangen Ryôin by Koyo Watanabe
Nipon Shinrei Gakkai (Japanese Society of the Spirit) by Tôko
   Watanabe *Shinshin Kaizen Kôshû Kai* (Psychophysical
   Improvement Academy) by Reizen Yoshiwaza
Reidô Shûyô Kai by Shûsen Oguri
Shizen Reinô Kenkyû Kai (Institute of Investigation of the
   Natural Mystical Capacity) by Reikô Takeda
Shizenryô Nôryokuhô Denshû Kai (Institute of the Capacity of
   Natural Therapies) by Reijin Oze
Seiki Ryôhô Kenkyû Jo (Institute of Treatment of Spirit) by Jôzô
   Ishi
Katsurei Kai by Yoshikatsu Matsuda
Dainihon Reigaku Kenkyû Kai (Japanese Institute of Studies of
   the Spirit) by Reikô Saito
Yôki Jutsuryôin by Yoshitaro Ueda
Reinôin by Reisei Katayama

Many of the founders of these hands-on healing organizations
changed their first names to indicate the field that they worked in.
For example the names Reizen, Reikô, Reijin and Reisei all allude to
working with spirit.

At the turn of the 20th century in Japan spiritual movements
were influencing one another, such as *Seiki* therapy, *Fuji System*, *Ishii*
system and the Master Masaharu Taniguchi's *Seicho No Ie* (The Home
of Infinite Life, Wisdom, and Abundance).[10]

Usui Reiki Ryôhô Gakkai[11]

> … the Society's goal was 'keeping good health and
> enhancement of body and spirit. Peace prosperity and
> happiness in family, society, country and world'.
>
> > (Excerpt from *Modern Reiki Method for Healing* by
> > Hiroshi Doi)

---

[10] *Iyashi No Te*, Toshitaka Mochizuki, Tama Shuppan, 1995.
[11] Much of the information gathered in this chapter about the *Usui Reiki Ryôhô Gakkai* has been passed down from Hiroshi Doi.

Usui Reiki Ryôhô Gakkai Members

The memorial to Mikao Usui, which was erected in 1927, writes that Mikao Usui's students remained in *Tôkyô* and carried on practicing and teaching after his death. Their group was called the *Usui Reiki Ryôhô Gakkai* or Society of the Usui Spiritual Energy Healing Method. This society, they claim, began with Mikao Usui as president in April 1922[12] followed, after his death, by Jûzaburô Ushida.[13] Today this society has its seventh president.

Some researchers believe that Mikao Usui was not the first president of the *Usui Reiki Ryôhô Gakkai* and that it was in fact founded after his death. It is understood that Mikao Usui formalized his teachings after his meditation on *kurama yama* in March 1922 but whether this was the inauguration of the *Usui Reiki Ryôhô Gakkai* or simply the creation of his official seat of learning is as yet unknown. If the *Usui Reiki Ryôhô Gakkai* was created by Mikao Usui then the following president, Jûzaburô Ushida, would have been his successor – not another member, Chûjirô Hayashi, as some modern teachers would like to believe.

The early members of the *Usui Reiki Ryôhô Gakkai* appear to mainly be naval officers. The military was quite powerful at this period in Japanese history. First there was World War I and then there was a build-up toward the military conflict with China in Manchuria. Japan was expanding its borders and a large sum of the male Japanese population was involved. The military held influential positions in the society. It has been suggested that Mikao Usui was pressured into teaching many of the naval men. This may be a reason for the more practical and basic elements of his teachings that evolved, such as the hand positions.

Here is a list of presidents and their details from Mikao Usui to modern day:[14]

1. Mikao Usui (1865–1926)
2. Jûzaburô Ushida (Rear Admiral 1865–1935)

---

[12] *Modern Reiki Method for Healing*, Hiroshi Doi, Fraser Journal Publishing, 2000.
[13] Jûzaburô Ushida wrote the brushstrokes for the text for Mikao Usui's Memorial Stone.
[14] *Iyashi No Te*, Toshitaka Mochizuki, Tama Shuppan, 1995.

3. Kanichi Taketomi (Rear Admiral 1878–1960)
4. Yoshiharu Watanabe (Schoolteacher ? –1960)
5. Hôichi Wanami (Vice Admiral 1883–1975)
6. Kimiko Koyama (1906–99)
7. Masaki Kondô (University Professor)

There is little historical information regarding membership of this society. An ex-naval surgeon called Chûjirô Hayashi joined the *Usui Reiki Ryôhô Gakkai* in May 1925. He broke away in 1931 further developing his own branch called the *Hayashi Reiki Kenkyû Kai*.

In November 1925 Jûzaburô Ushida and Kanichi Taketomi, both naval men, became members of Mikao Usui's seat of learning.

Fumio Ogawa joined the *Usui Reiki Ryôhô Gakkai* in 1942 and completed six levels in 14 months. His certificates were published in a Japanese magazine called *Twilight Zone* in 1986.

Hiroshi Doi said that during World War II the *Usui Reiki Ryôhô Gakkai* moved quite often because of aerial bombing. It has also been suggested that the *Usui Reiki Ryôhô Gakkai* needed to be careful in case it became associated with the underground peace movement. During World War II, naval members could no longer participate in meetings but the *Usui Reiki Ryôhô Gakkai* did have members who were not naval men and has continued through to modern times.

Usui Reiki Ryôhô Gakkai Teachings

There are three major levels in the *Usui Reiki Ryôhô Gakkai*. These are *shoden, okuden,* and *shinpiden,* the teacher level. Within these levels there are six levels of proficiency; with the lowest being six and the highest one. Mikao Usui rated himself as a two with the acknowledgement that one should always leave the possibility to continue to develop oneself. *Shoden* includes the first four levels of proficiency. At each stage new techniques are learnt, with the member progressing to the next level of proficiency on satisfactorily accomplishing the technique.

The society's meetings, or *kenkyû kai*, are held three times a month in *Tôkyô*. Once new members receive the regular *reiju* they begin at the sixth level of proficiency.

The *reiju* does not change with each level – it remains the same.

No mantras or symbols are used in the *Usui Reiki Ryôhô Gakkai's reiju* either. In fact the society does not use mantras and symbols but members are made aware of them.[15] The mantras and symbols are different from those taught in the system of Reiki today.

At each meeting, *gyosei* (*waka*, poetry, written by the Meiji Emperor) is read aloud by all members and **hatsurei hô* is practiced. Members receive *reiju* from the *shihan* or senior teacher. At the end, the *gokai* (five precepts) are repeated three times by all present.[16] After the *shûyô kai*[17] there is the *jisshû kai*, the practical gathering, where some techniques are practiced.

Each member is supplied with the *Reiki Ryôhô Hikkei*, which contains the five Reiki precepts, an interview with Mikao Usui, a guide to healing using specific hand positions and *gyosei*. Booklets, called *shiori*, are also provided exclusively for *Usui Reiki Ryôhô Gakkai* members. They were written by Hôichi Wanami and Kimiko Koyama and contain information including original teachings and techniques such as **byôsen reikan hô*, **gedoku hô*, **kôketsu hô*, and **nentatsu hô*.[18]

Usui Reiki Ryôhô Gakkai Protocol

The *Usui Reiki Ryôhô Gakkai* has no foreigners as members and is a very private society. Members are not meant to discuss the society with non-members.[19] Many requests have been made to the society from foreigners intrigued to understand it better but few have met with its members.

A Reiki teacher contacted Hiroshi Doi on 14 December 1996 on behalf of Hawayo Takata's granddaughter, Phyllis Lei Furumoto. She requested a meeting in Japan with then-president Kimiko Koyama, who was 91 at the time. This would have been an historic visit of West meets East, but one of Phyllis Lei Furumoto's teacher students apparently made claims that insulted Kimiko Koyama and the meeting was cancelled.[20]

[15] Information supplied to the authors by Hyakuten Inamoto.
[16] *Modern Reiki Method for Healing*, Hiroshi Doi, Fraser Journal Publishing, 2000.
[17] *Shûyô* means to cultivate one's mind or improve oneself.
[18] Information supplied to the authors by Hyakuten Inamoto.
[19] Information supplied to the authors by Hyakuten Inamoto.
[20] *Modern Reiki Method for Healing*, Hiroshi Doi, Fraser Journal Publishing, 2000.

The *Usui Reiki Ryôhô Gakkai* may be joined by invitation only. At this point the person becomes an honorary member until full membership is offered. At the turn of the 21st century, the society was charging members US$90 to register with the society and just US$15 for each meeting.[21] There were once 80 divisions of the *Usui Reiki Ryôhô Gakkai* throughout Japan but today there are but a few. All the teaching takes place in *Tôkyô* itself. As of 2002 there were 11 *shinpiden* in the *Usui Reiki Ryôhô Gakkai* and that included the five *shihan* or teachers. The majority of members are longstanding and there are only about 500 throughout the whole of Japan.

The society's function today is generally described as a support group for its members. Hiroshi Doi's first impression on joining the society was his amazement at how different it was from the system of Reiki he had been taught (he has also studied a number of modern Reiki teachings) and yet they all came from the same roots.

Chûjirô Hayashi (1880–1940)

Family and Career

Chûjirô Hayashi was born on 15 September, 1880 in *Tôkyô*. He was a *Sôtô Zen* practitioner who naturally included *Shintô* practices, as is common in Japan, into his religious routine.[22] He was not a Christian. He was also married with two children. His son, Tadayoshi, was born in 1903 and his daughter, Kiyoe, was born in 1910. In 1902, Chûjirô Hayashi was on harbour patrol during the Russo-Japanese War. In 1918 he became commander of the defence station of Port Owinato.[23]

A student of Chûjirô Hayashi described him as 'a serious, warmhearted person as if he was destined from birth for the Reiki work'.[24]

---

[21] Information supplied by website: www.threshold.ca/reiki.

[22] Information supplied to the authors by Hyakuten Inamoto.

[23] *Hayashi Reiki Manual: Traditional Japanese Healing Techniques*, Frank Arjava Petter & Tadao Yamaguchi, Lotus Press, 2003.

[24] 'A Treatment to Heal Diseases, Hand Healing' by Shûô Matsui in the magazine *Sunday Mainichi*, 4 March 1928, translated by Amy to be viewed at www.reiki.net.au.

Meeting Mikao Usui

In May 1925, he became a student of Mikao Usui's seat of learning in *Tôkyô*.[25] He was a retired naval officer (still in the reserves) and surgeon and was about 45 years old when he met Mikao Usui.[26] He had but 10 months to learn the complete teachings before Mikao Usui died of a stroke.

A number of other naval officers joined the same society not long after Chûjirô Hayashi. Once Mikao Usui died they continued on with his work using the title *Usui Reiki Ryôhô Gakkai*. Chûjirô Hayashi was not Mikao Usui's successor, as is sometimes believed today, but remained a regular member of the society until 1931 when he began developing his own clinic and branch called the *Hayashi Reiki Kenkyû kai* or Hayashi Spiritual Energy Research Society. He is said to have left the *Usui Reiki Ryôhô Gakkai* due to differences with then-president Jûzaburô Ushida.

Chûjirô Hayashi's Clinic

Unique to the system at this time, his clinic was known to have a treatment room where eight clients could be treated. These clients would lie down on futons or low tables and have two practitioners working on them. According to Hawayo Takata one would begin at the abdomen and the other at the head. Chûjirô Hayashi's wife, Chie, was the receptionist and hostess. She continued on with his work after he died.[27]

Chûjirô Hayashi's Teachings

Chûjirô Hayashi was known to have a healing guide called the *Ryôhô Shishin*. It appears to be an almost exact copy of the *Reiki Ryôhô Hikkei's* own healing guide. Today researchers believe that Chûjirô Hayashi wrote the *Reiki Ryôhô Hikkei's Ryôhô Shishin* as well as his own healing guide. As he was a doctor and both healing guides are

[25] This seat of learning may well have been called the *Usui Reiki Ryôhô Gakkai* at this stage.

[26] Transcript of tape of Hawayo Takata telling the story of Dr. Hayashi, 1977.

[27] Information supplied to the authors by Chiyoko Yamaguchi.

similar and written with knowledge of anatomy and human disease, this is not an illogical assumption. The timing of the writing of the manuals would have been different. One for the *Usui Reiki Ryôhô Gakkai* (created during Chûjirô Hayashi's membership up until 1931) and one for his own branch.

Another student of Chûjirô Hayashi, Tatsumi, trained in 1927 to become a teacher. Tatsumi did not appreciate the changes that Chûjirô Hayashi had made and finally left in 1931. Tatsumi said he was initially taught in a class with five other students and he often saw Jûzaburô Ushida and Kanichi Taketomi (*Usui Reiki Ryôhô Gakkai* presidents) there. Kanichi Taketomi was also an officer in 1918 at Port Owinato with Chûjirô Hayashi. Students volunteered in Chûjirô Hayashi's clinic practicing for eight hours a week on clients. After three months it was possible for them to move to the second level. Nine months later they might progress to the third level and aid in the running of the clinic. After two years students would achieve *shinpiden* with the knowledge of how to teach and perform attunements. Students received *reiju* in a dark room while sitting in *seiza*. *Waka* poetry, was then recited before *reiju* was performed. The 5 precepts were then chanted and *reiki mawashi* would be practiced.[28]

Shûô Matsui became a student of Chûjirô Hayashi in 1928. The first level was completed in five lots of 90-minute sessions. He wrote that it was very expensive and was surprised that the modest people who ran the clinic would charge money and have a grading system. He said he did not intend to begin the second level but shared many stories of people he had helped, over 100 to be exact. Shûô Matsui also mentions that there are more grades but claims that he was unaware of exactly how many there were.[29]

Hawayo Takata's experience with Chûjirô Hayashi was a little more difficult, apparently because she was considered to be a foreigner. First, she received treatments for ill health for six months in 1935. In 1936 she volunteered at the clinic over the period of a year while staying at the Hayashis' home. On 21 February 1938, as Chûjirô Hayashi was leaving Hawaii after having helped her to set up a

---

[28] *Hayashi Reiki Manual: Traditional Japanese Healing Techniques*, Frank Arjava Petter & Tadao Yamaguchi, Lotus Press, 2003.

[29] 'A Treatment to Heal Diseases, Hand Healing' by Shûô Matsui in the magazine *Sunday Mainichi*, 4 March 1928, translated by Amy to be viewed at www.reiki.net.au.

clinic, he awarded her a Master certificate.

Chiyoko Yamaguchi studied with Chûjirô Hayashi in 1938.[30] Many of her family members were already practitioners by that time. She said that she learnt both *shoden* and *okuden* together over five consecutive days when she was in her late teens.[31] The cost at that time was 50 yen, which was extremely expensive for that period (the equivalent of thousands of US dollars today).[32]

This leads to the conclusion that Chûjirô Hayashi taught *shoden* independently from *okuden* in 1927 with Tatsumi, 1928 with Shûô Matsui and between 1936 and 1938 with Hawayo Takata. In 1938, Chiyoko Yamaguchi was taught *shoden* and *okuden* together over a five-day period.

Unfortunately, Chiyoko Yamaguchi no longer had her certificates and other notes, as they were lost when she and her late husband fled Manchuria at the end of World War II.[33] She only began teaching students in her late 70s with her son, Tadao, in a branch they have called *Jikiden Reiki*. It appears she never learnt to become an official teacher but was taught the attunement from a relative who was hosting a course for Chûjirô Hayashi. The mantras and symbols Chiyoko Yamaguchi used were slightly different to those taught by Tatsumi as well as to those taught by the *Usui Reiki Ryôhô Gakkai*. Interestingly, she was also not taught Symbol 4. This may be because she did not officially study to become a teacher.[34] It may also indicate that there was no Symbol 4 used in the attunement process at that time by Chûjirô Hayashi, however it was roughly the time that Hawayo Takata studied with Chûjirô Hayashi and yet she *was* taught Symbol 4.

What is considered to be the modern system of Reiki is proposed by traditional Japanese practitioners to be Chûjirô Hayashi's teachings rather than Mikao Usui's.

The attunement process that is performed today, in all its variations, utilizes mantras and symbols. This is not the case in the *Usui Reiki Ryôhô Gakkai* or other traditional Japanese teachings where

---

[30] Chiyoko Yamaguchi died at the age of 82 in August, 2003.
[31] Information supplied to the authors by Chiyoko Yamaguchi.
[32] Information supplied to the authors by Hyakuten Inamoto.
[33] Information supplied to the authors by Chiyoko Yamaguchi.
[34] Information supplied to the authors by Hyakuten Inamoto.

these methods of attunement are called *reiju* and are practiced without mantras and symbols. This is a major difference between what Chûjirô Hayashi taught and Mikao Usui's teachings.

Mantras and symbols were only taught to those who had difficulty with sensing the energy. Chûjirô Hayashi may have believed that his students who did not have enough experience with energy work were aided by the inclusion of symbols into the ritual. Though Chûjirô Hayashi changed the teachings, his respect for Mikao Usui remained. Even after leaving the *Usui Reiki Ryôhô Gakkai*, a scroll of the *gokai* was hung in his clinic.

Chûjirô Hayashi's Legacy

Chûjirô Hayashi wrote in 1938 that he had trained 13 Reiki Masters.[35]

On 10 May 1940 Hawayo Takata reported that he died ceremoniously of a self-induced stroke in his country house in Atami with his family, colleagues and friends around him. Hayashi's student Chiyoko Yamaguchi emphatically recounts that Chie Hayashi had personally told her that he had killed himself by 'breaking an artery'.[36] Others say that as he was a military man, the honourable method of death would certainly have been *seppuku* (the cutting of the *hara* or abdomen). Chûjirô Hayashi informed his wife and Hawayo Takata that his reason for suicide was that he did not wish to be called upon to enter World War II.

Chie Hayashi stayed on at her husband's clinic, becoming the second president of the *Hayashi Reiki Kenkyû Kai*.[37] Hawayo Takata told a story that she was, in fact, the successor but felt that she could not remain in Japan and asked Chie Hayashi to manage it for her. After World War II, Hawayo Takata stated that she returned it to Chie Hayashi, as she had no desire to live in Japan. There was also no indication on the certificate she received from Chûjirô Hayashi that she was his successor, but rather that she was one of a number of Reiki Masters to be trained by him.

---

[35] Hawayo Takata's Master certificate.
[36] Information supplied to the authors by Chiyoko Yamaguchi.
[37] Information supplied to the authors by Chiyoko Yamaguchi.

Japanese Reiki Levels

Japanese words are increasingly being incorporated into the modern-day system of Reiki. This can create confusion especially when one is trying to work out which level is being referred to within the teachings. Here is some insight into the names of various Japanese levels attributed to the teachings of Mikao Usui.

At the turn of the 20th century when Mikao Usui first started teaching he had no need for recognized levels – it was just the teachings and students would be given further teachings after they had progressed on their spiritual path.

Mikao Usui's close association with members of the martial arts world and his own experience within it may have led him to create levels once the teachings became more formalized.[38]

In 1928, Shûô Matsui, a student of Chûjirô Hayashi, writes about the levels *shoden* and *okuden* and mentions that there were further unknown levels.[39]

Kaiji Tomita, founder of *Tomita Teate Ryôhô*, studied with Mikao Usui around 1925 and created his own *Teate Ryôhô Kai* after Mikao Usui's death. The levels he taught were *shoden, chuden, okuden* and *kaiden*.[40]

The levels on Fumio Ogawa's certificates read *rokkyû, gokyû, yonkyû, sankyû, okuden zenki* and *okuden kôki*. These dated from 1942 to 1943.[41] Here the first four certificates may well account for *shoden*. His stepfather, Kôzô Ogawa – a senior member of the *Usui Reiki Ryôhô Gakkai*, was his teacher.

The terms *shodan, okudan* and *shinpeten* were written in Hawayo Takata's diary notes and were most likely spelling mistakes that should have been noted as *shoden, okuden* and *shinpiden*.[42] These

---

[38] Information from Chris Marsh states that Mikao Usui received *menkyo kaidan* in martial arts. Some of the martial arts people he apparently knew were Morihei Ueshiba (founder of *aikidô*), Jigorô Kanô (founder of *jûdô*) and Gichin Funokoshi (the father of modern *karate*).

[39] 'A Treatment to Heal Diseases, Hand Healing', Shûô Matsui in the magazine Sunday Mainichi, 4 March 1928, translated by Amy, to be viewed at www.reiki.net. au.

[40] *Modern Reiki Method for Healing*, Hiroshi Doi, Fraser Journal Publishing, 2000.

[41] Information from www.threshold.ca/ reiki.

[42] *The Gray Book – Reiki*, Alice Takata Furumoto, 1982.

slight spelling changes represent different understandings of the terms in the first two cases. Hawayo Takata did spell some Japanese terms incorrectly in her diary notes (the incorrect spelling of *shinpe-ten* was crossed out and replaced with the almost correct *shinpeden*) and therefore it might simply have been a spelling error. *Dan* (rather than *den*) is for levels that are used in Japanese martial arts such as *karate, aikidô* and *jûdô*. *Dan*, therefore, means level while *den* means teachings.

Each of the levels used in Mikao Usui's teachings represent that the student is beginning that level rather than having already achieved it.

The levels taught in the *Usui Reiki Ryôhô Gakkai* today are:

- *Shoden* – (lit. Japanese) first teachings. It can also mean the receiving of the first full transmission.
- *Okuden zenki* – (lit. Japanese) first stage of hidden teachings.
- *Okuden kôki* – (lit. Japanese) second stage of hidden teachings.
- *Shinpiden* – (lit. Japanese) mystery teachings.

These levels have within them different levels of proficiency that need to be accomplished. In total, it is understood that there are six levels of proficiency in the *Usui Reiki Ryôhô Gakkai* teachings. The teacher measures the progress of the student/member allowing them to move on to the next level when ready.

Certification in *Usui Reiki Ryôhô*, taught globally today, generally uses the three levels *shoden, okuden* (incorporating both *zenki* and *kôki*) and *shinpiden*.

7   Japan and Traditions

The Three Diamonds

Those who work with the Japanese practice of the system of Reiki will find that they are always being directed back to a place of energy in the body called the *hara*. The *hara* is often translated as belly and sometimes center.

Yet, the *hara* is just one aspect of the Japanese energetic system. There are in fact three energetic centers and in this book these are called The Three Diamonds.

These Three Diamonds correspond to the energy of Earth, Heaven and Oneness or Heart.

The Earth center is located just below the navel at the *hara*, the Heavenly center is located in the head and the Oneness center is located in the Heart (middle of the chest).

The word *hara* is the most commonly known of these energy centers and the most important. Energy is stored in this point of the body from where it expands throughout the whole body. By linking all three diamonds the practitioner creates unity and balance. It is essential that one first develop the Earth center or *hara*, as this is the body's central axis point.

A strong *hara* in a practitioner is indicated by a firm and collected stance. The shoulders are low and hanging loose. The legs are slightly apart with the body weight evenly distributed. The *sumô* wrestler is a good example as the body is large and heavy yet somehow quick and nimble. It is not one's physical strength that wins one's fights. The *hara* is like a building block. It is from this point that strength is developed. It is the base of the pyramid and it needs to be strong and stable.

Outside of Japan people are often afraid of being large and of carrying a protruding belly. The belly is culturally rejected and therefore the natural instinct for gravity within the body is lost. Instead the shoulders are built up at the gym creating a broad top of the body and a small abdomen. This is the shape of an upside down pyramid – one that is unstable and ready to topple at any time. Sticking out the chest strengthens the connection to the ego. This expresses a disconnection between mind and body with the axis of gravity in an unbalanced point of the body.

Many New Age practitioners focus on energetically building the energy in the head, the purpose being to develop the intuitive and psychic abilities. By working solely on this area of the body it is easy for the practitioner to become, once again, top-heavy and unbalanced. Though there are a great many psychics practicing today who are genuinely helping others heal and grow, it is often interesting to see that their own lives might be confused and unbalanced. This is an excellent example of the instability created by not first building the *hara*.

Re-establishing this connection with the original energy through the *hara* will ensure good health and recovery from illness. There is always access to a reliable source of strength whenever needed.

An inner attitude results from focusing on the *hara*. From this central point there is an ability to cope with everyday tasks and sudden emergencies with an ease of understanding. This allows appropriate action to be taken in a balanced and unprejudiced manner.

By understanding Mikao Usui's background in *Tendai* Buddhism, martial arts, and *Shugendô*, it is interesting to see how the energetic focal points of The Three Diamonds relate to these practices and are an integral aspect of Japanese life.

One of the *sutra* utilized in Japanese Buddhism, including *Tendai* Buddhism, states: This production of the *dharmadhâtu* [Buddhahood] flowed out of the three places (the upper, middle and lower part of the body of the Buddha). [1]

In the Japanese martial art of *aikidô*, which developed during Mikao Usui's lifetime, there is the primary concept of *tenchi*: standing firmly between Heaven and Earth.

---

[1] Mahâvairocana *sutra*.

Aikidô practitioners believe that the universe is composed of Heaven (emptiness), Earth (form) and human beings which are a combination of both elements. Human beings learn to live in harmony between these dual elements.

> Always try to remain in communion with Heaven and Earth; then the universe will appear in its true light. If you perceive the true form of Heaven and Earth, you will be enlightened to your own true self.
>
> (Quote from Morihei Ueshiba, founder of *aikidô*)

One that practices *Shugendô* is called a *yamabushi*. The first *kanji* for *yamabushi* (meaning mountain) has three vertical lines united by a horizontal line. This symbolizes that the trinity of the three learnings – morality, meditation and wisdom – are One; that Body, Speech, and Mind are One.

The Three Diamonds of Earth, Heaven, and Heart have evolved out of a distinct Japanese culture as they relate back to the foundation of Japanese cosmology and the creation of the universe. Yet, conceptually, The Three Diamonds exist in the form of other universal trinities as well, such as:

Birth, life, death
Past, present, future
Man, woman, child
Father, Son, Holy Spirit

As a universal truth, Earth and Heaven can be found in the dualism of many natural elements such as fire and water or sun and moon. The result of their integration is always unity, harmony, and enlightenment. This is also reflected in the character of the fourth Reiki symbol whose characteristic is enlightenment and nonduality. In this symbol the bottom *kanji* are symbolic of the sun and moon while the top *kanji* symbolize humanity. The *kanjis'* tale tells the practitioner that to be able to become completely human, harmony must exist between the sun and moon; the human in this *kanji* is on a journey toward realizing nonduality.

Esoteric Buddhist practices include similar concepts of a trinity that can bring about nonduality through three types of drops. There is the white drop located in the head and the red drop located 4 finger widths below the navel and the indestructible drop at the heart center. To gain a direct experience of emptiness the white drop has to first make a connection with the indestructible drop and, equally, the red drop has to make a connection with the indestructible drop. These 3 drops then melt together, resulting in emptiness.

Within yogic traditions, B.K.S. Iyengar states that yoga is derived from the Sanskrit root *yuj* meaning to bind, join, attach and yoke. What is being joined through yoga? It is the dual elements that are brought together through the practice, creating a nondual experience; thus the practitioner becomes a yogi. In hatha yoga, *ha* means sun and *tha* means moon, so Hatha Yoga is a system that links sun (fire) and moon (water), or in other words, hatha yoga brings together the union of opposites.

Also within yogic traditions there are the 3 granthi, or knots. The Rudra granthi is situated in the head area, the Vishnu granthi is in the heart area, and the Brahma granthi is located in the lower abdomen. Brahma, Vishnu and Shiva are the presiding deities of these knots and are reflections of creation, preservation and destruction. Together these three knots express the intricacy of interconnectedness and one cannot exist without the other.

Religions, too, work directly with the trinity and nonduality. These universal laws are written into their holy books and oral traditions.

In the Christian Bible, John states: 'I baptize you with water, but one is coming who will baptize you with the fire of the Holy Spirit.' (Luke 3:16)

In the Kabbala's 'Science of Prophets', Solomon's seal is used. Solomon possessed a seal ring that kept demons at bay. The seal is a pentagram and represents the combination of the dual forces of fire and water (up and down triangles) and the transformation that these bring. It is also the sign of resurrection and completeness.

The *shatkona,* in Hinduism, is a hexagram or six-pointed star which is a combination of two interlocking triangles. The upper triangle stands for Shiva and fire and the lower triangle stands for *shakti* and water. When these two opposite forces unite, they give birth to Sanatkumara, who is one of the sons of Brahma, the creator. Sanatkumara said that true knowledge is not achieved through words or reading but is accessed from within and this alone can be done through meditation. The *shatkona* is often depicted in old drawings at the heart area of human beings.

Native Incan practices include a ceremony where the Apus, sacred mountain deities, and the three levels of life are invoked. These are the world above or future, the middle or present world and the underworld or past. Once these three aspects come together human beings can access the three dimensions.

Alchemists believe in the ability to transmute or change matter. One of the most important principles that alchemists work with is the basic duality of the universe. A human who can balance the dual forces of the universe becomes the carrier of the Philosopher's Stone or Lapidis Philosophorum.

Traditional Chinese *Qi Gong* practices utilize three main energy centers called *dantian*. The lower *dantian* (*xia dantian*) lies just below the navel, the middle *dantian* (*zhong dantian*) in the middle of chest and the upper *dantain* (*shang dantian*) is at the head area.

These three centers represent Earth, humankind, and Heaven. By balancing and refining energy within these centers a practitioner becomes One with the *Dao* (divine energy).

> Only through the understanding of the natural powers of the heavens and the earth can man (humanity) exist in harmony with the *Dao*.
>
> (Excerpt from *Chinese Medical Qigong Therapy* – Volume 2 by Professor Jerry Alan Johnson)

Searchers from every tradition, not just the Japanese, look to the combining of dualistic elements to create a trinity that allows one to enter a world of enlightenment. The Japanese have merely developed their own understandings and practices based on these energetic foundations. To gain an understanding of their unique methods is to move along a path of spiritual development where a glimpse of something special awaits to take one further.

Ki

To work with The Three Diamonds an understanding of the Japanese word *ki* is invaluable. Within Japan, the concept of *ki* is an integral tradition that many modern cultures find difficult to comprehend. A deeper understanding of *ki* will support all Reiki practitioners in their practice.

Ki or Energy was first written about in a Chinese document, *Huang Ti Nei Ching Su Wen*, or The Yellow Emperor's Classic of Internal Medicine (also commonly known as the *Nei Ching*).

The *Nei Ching* was written on the subject of healing. Chinese folklore claims the *Nei Ching* was written during the mythological life of Emperor Huang Ti (2697–2599 B.C.), but the text is historically dated at approximately 300 B.C..

In the *Nei Ching*, *ki* is described as the universal energy that nourishes and sustains all life forms. It flows through the universe and each individual. An unrestricted flow of *ki* in the body allows one to remain healthy, while a diminished flow of *ki* in the body leads one to illness.

The *Nei Ching* describes how *ki* circulates through the body and is directed by invisible channels known as meridians.

Ki is considered an integral element to everyday Japanese life. Many Japanese traditions are based on a strong connection to *ki* apart from the martial arts and religious training. The success of the world-renowned tea ceremony called *sadô*, the ancient game of *go* and the art of calligraphy or *shodô* are all based on the practitioners' ability to channel free-flowing *ki*.

Teachings from the *Nei Ching* traveled from China to Korea and eventually across to Japan in the 7th century along with Buddhist *sutra*, historical books, medical books, works on astronomy, geography and the occult arts.

Ki was practiced solely for medical purposes until the 12th century when the *samurai* introduced it into their art.

Gasshô

Literally *gasshô* means 'to place the two palms together'. It actually has several interpretations at different levels.

Initially it is a sign of reverence. It also says, 'I revere the Buddha nature in you' – a non-judgmental manner of showing respect for all beings.

> This Bodhisattva constantly bowed with palms together in the act known as *gasshô* before anyone he encountered, for he recognized the potential for enlightenment in all beings.
>
> (Excerpt from *River of Fire – River of Water* by Taitetsu Unno)

The *gasshô* brings all opposites together. It creates unity within the body by bringing the left-and right-hand side together. All opposites become one.

It is possible to see how focused an individual is by their *gasshô*. If their concentration is poor, their *gasshô* will be loose and sloppy. A firm *gasshô* indicates a quiet and focused mind. This action creates the integration of mind and body as one.

There are many varieties of *gasshô*. When performing *gasshô*, the eyes must be kept on the tips of the middle fingers. One style has been included to direct practitioners in a correct application of the *gasshô*.

Formal Gasshô

The formal *gasshô* is commonly used on a daily basis in Japan and is used when entering a temple and before eating. It aids in retaining an alert mind.

Place the hands together, palm-to-palm in front of the face. The fingers are straight and palms are slightly pressed together. The elbows are not touching the body and the forearms not quite parallel to the ground. There is one fist's distance from the fingers to the tip of the nose.

Seiza

Seiza, or correct sitting, is a traditional Japanese style of sitting on top of the ankles, with the legs folded underneath and the back erect.

When sitting in *seiza* correctly, it is comfortable and easy to maintain.

To sit in *seiza* the legs bend at the knees and the left knee is placed on the floor. The right knee is placed about 8 inches (20 cms) from the left. Now the feet are positioned onto the floor so that the big toes just touch each other. The buttocks are lowered until they rest on or between the heels. If the legs tire or fall asleep then the practitioner must slightly rise up off the knees to allow better circulation. A pillow can also be placed behind the knees to help lift the pressure off the heels. The more it is practiced the easier it becomes and the longer the *seiza* position can be sustained.

The motivation behind sitting in *seiza* is that the leg that has contact with the floor along to the toes is representative of a large foot. When standing, the body's weight is on the balls of the feet rather than the soles. This is the perfect posture of balance. So the same can be said for sitting on the ground as the weight is forward rather than on the ankles.

From this position the body must feel relaxed. Relaxation should be refreshing. Relaxation is when the body is supported permitting the circulation of blood, oxygen and energy to flow with ease. The ancient Chinese believed that energy entered the body with the breath and moved through the body in the blood. When all three are free to move with ease – breath, energy, and blood – the practitioner becomes relaxed, strong, and healthy.

The spine is slightly S-shaped in a natural position. To support the head it must be balanced on top of the spine. The chin is pulled in slightly and the back of the neck stretched. It should feel as if someone has taken a strand of hair from the crown and is pulling it up, stretching the spine. Sitting supported releases stress from the body keeping it light and buoyant.

To check that the posture is relaxed, the practitioner can imagine a string attached to the crown on the inside of the head. This string drops down through the neck and torso and is attached to a weight approximately 3 inches (8cm) below the navel inside the body, the hara. By sitting too far forward or backward this string will touch the insides of the body.

The practitioner relaxes the body. Shoulders and arms are relaxed with the palms of the hands facing downward onto the knees. The eyes are either closed or gazing gently at the floor 3 feet (1 meter) in front of the body.

Quiet sitting is something that is practiced when in *seiza*. A different reading of the word *seiza* actually means 'to sit still'. This particular *kanji* is used by a student of Mikao Usui in a 1933 book describing the technique *hatsurei hô. What follows is a simple introduction to this practice.

The practitioner breathes slowly, naturally, not forcing the breath, breathing in through the nose. The lungs fill naturally in relaxation and the *hara* also responds, releasing the breath, breathing out until the need to breathe in takes over once again. The chest and shoulders are relaxed throughout. The body is imagined as a glass and a carafe of water is being poured down into it. The body begins to fill from the lower torso with life-giving air and energy. Taoist belief has it that each person has a limited number of breaths in this lifetime. By breathing slowly and calmly it was believed the length of a lifetime could be extended.

While following the breath, the practitioner counts both inhalations and exhalations. Later the exhalations only are counted and finally the practitioner just sits, without counting at all. The practitioner then counts from one to ten repeatedly. If the count is lost the practitioner begins again at one. It is not required that the practitioner remember the last number; that is not what is important; just the counting.

The practitioner relaxes the mind. All thoughts that enter float past as clouds in the sky. There is no resistance or energy put into following the thought's journey – the practitioner remains focused solely on the action of the breath. If the mind follows these thoughts, the practitioner must not berate oneself. Instead, the practitioner simply brings the attention back and focuses on breathing in and out. The practitioner is aware of the movement of energy in and around the body, keeping the memory of the sense of wholeness and light that is felt. It is there to be taken and drawn on each moment of the day. It will always be there. To help bring the practitioner back into the body, the hands are shaken a couple of times.

Etiquette in Japan

As with all things Japanese, certain traditional elements exist within the teachings of Mikao Usui. There is an uncertainty as to how these Japanese elements should be applied or dealt with. Often they are introduced into a modern Reiki course as a fad rather than something beneficial.

The Japanese are shrouded in a certain mystique as far as most non-Japanese are concerned. Their rituals are inextricably linked with so much historical and religious tradition that they may seem unfathomable to a foreigner. *Gaikokujin*, non-Japanese, can sense the beauty of these traditions and often desire to imitate them. This is the point where possible disconnection from the source may allow the original beauty of a tradition to begin to fade. Another way of looking at it is that the *ki* is being weakened.

Understanding the roots of a Japanese custom will strengthen practitioners' certainty in their practice, promising a stronger sense of connection to the source. It does not mean they must pretend to be Japanese, but a grounding in the culture will support their interaction with the teachings at many levels.

The first thing a Reiki practitioner who visits Japan, or merely communicates with someone from Japan, should understand is basic etiquette.

Name Order

In Japan the first name follows the family name. For example 'Mikao' is a first name and 'Usui' is a surname, therefore he would traditionally be called 'Usui Mikao'.[2]

Family Names

Most Japanese family names consist of two *kanji*. The meanings of many of the *kanji* used in family names are related to nature, geographical features or locations.

---

[2] *The Reiki Sourcebook* has taken the non-Japanese method of writing the surname last and the first name first throughout the book, e.g., Mikao Usui.

First Names

Japanese first names commonly consist of two *kanji*. The meanings of these *kanji* are generally positive characteristics such as intelligence, beauty, love or light, names for flowers, the four seasons, and other natural phenomena. They may also name the order of birth like first son, second son, etc. They are chosen not only for their meaning, but also for their sound.

Often, the gender of a person can be guessed by the ending of the first name. First names ending with *-ro, -shi, -ya,* or *-o* are typically male first names, while names ending in *-ko, -mi, -e* and *-yo* are typically female first names.

Titles

The Japanese commonly address each other by their surname. Only very close friends and children are usually addressed by their first name. An appropriate title is also attached to a name. These titles depend upon the gender and social position of the person being addressed. They are added to the end of the surname. Some of the most frequently used titles are:

> *san*: This is a neutral title, and can be used in most situations. In formal situations it may not be polite enough.
> *sama*: This is a more polite version of san and is commonly used in formal situations or when writing letters. It may be too polite in a casual context.
> *kun*: This title is informal and is used for boys and men that are younger than the speaker.
> *chan*: This title is informal and used for young children and very close friends or family members.
> *sensei*: This title is used for teachers, doctors and other people with a higher education and from whom the speaker receives a service or instructions. It may also be used on its own.

Sensei

A number of Reiki teachers outside of Japan have begun to call themselves *sensei*. This is an incorrect use of the word. They may have picked it up from hearing practitioners say the words 'Usui *Sensei*' when talking about Mikao Usui.

Sensei is, in fact, an honorific title given to a teacher by students out of respect. That is why students will say Usui *Sensei* but Mikao Usui would never have called himself that.

In the Japanese language ways of referring to one another depend on the context, i.e., the position of someone in comparison to the person they're talking to. So a student will call their teacher *sensei* but that same teacher might be called by their surname by a colleague.

It is always about how much respect the person talking owes to the recipient, never the other way around. *Sensei* is often used outside of Japan to propound the mystical qualities of the teacher. In reality, there are many people besides teachers whose position calls for the use of *sensei* as a form of address. Doctors are always addressed as *sensei* as are lawyers and politicians. There is no mystical element in the use of the term *sensei*.

If a teacher in the system of Reiki wished to appoint a Japanese name to reflect one's title, *kyoshi* would be appropriate. This translates as 'one who teaches' and refers to the function of teaching without any honorific aspect.

No one can claim a sign of respect; it is given to those who deserve it.

Japanese Customs

If it is a practitioner's fortune to visit Japan to see sites or to make acquaintance with Japanese practitioners, it is advisable to have a basic understanding of what will be expected of them. Fortunately for foreigners it is anticipated that they will not be able to follow all of these customs but it is respectful to at least attempt to do so.

- Stand outside the entrance to a house and call a formal greeting to announce yourself. Then slide the door open and wait inside the door. If invited into the house, take off the shoes and enter. Use the indoor slippers where provided.

- When walking on tatami mats, remove the indoor slippers (remaining barefoot or in socks).
- Bathrooms will generally also have special slippers to be worn.
- *Arigatô gozaimasu* is thank you.
- A bow instead of a handshake indicates hello and goodbye.
- People of a lower status must bow lower.
- Instead of directly saying 'no', the Japanese may sound indecisive or unassertive. This must be accepted as a 'no'.
- It is polite to present a business card in a formal situation otherwise the other person does not understand one's status. This card is offered with both hands, bowing slightly.
- A small gift or souvenir should be offered from one's country when visiting with Japanese people. Gifts are given and received with both hands.
- When dining out the bill is usually split. If change is offered it must not be counted in front of the other diners.
- Sit in *seiza* when on the ground. If this becomes uncomfortable a man may sit cross-legged and a woman may sit on the ground with her calves out to the side.
- Turn chopsticks upside down when eating from a communal bowl.
- Do not stick chopsticks into food so that they are standing up – this indicates someone has died.
- Do not pass food from chopstick to chopstick (this is traditionally done at cremations with charred bones only).
- Slurping is normal in Japan.
- Do not pour soy sauce over white rice.
- Always wash with soap and rinse the body off before entering a Japanese bath.
- Never blow your nose in public.

Good Luck!

Japanese Kanji

Kanji are made up of both pictographs[3] and ideographs[4]. In China, *kanji* originated in the Yellow River area about 2000 B.C.. During the 3rd and 4th century A.D., they were brought across from China and Korea to Japan. Until this time Japan had only ever used the spoken language. The Chinese characters were used phonetically to represent similar sounding Japanese syllables; the actual meaning of the characters was ignored.

Chinese characters are one of the earliest forms of written language in the world. The first known Chinese scripts are called Oracle Bone Inscriptions as they were often inscripted upon a shell, such as that of a tortoise. The script became more abstract over the centuries, leaving Japan with a quite different script today.

16th–11th Century B.C.: Oracle Bone Inscriptions (*Kokotsubun*)

Oracle Bone Inscriptions were inscriptions on tortoise shell and bone. They were used for divination.

Only approximately a thousand of the more than 4,000 characters inscribed on the oracle bones can be deciphered and understood today.

1122–256 B.C.: Bronze Inscriptions (*Kimbun*)

During this period Bronze inscriptions were also found on Chinese bronzes such as zhong (bells).

221–207 B.C.: Small Seal Characters (*Tensho*)

Seal script lies at the origins of the standardized, formal script used throughout China.

400 A.D.: Chinese Characters in Japan

Chinese small seal characters were known to have come to Japan as

---

[3] Pictographs are pictures that represent ideas.
[4] Ideographs are symbols (*kanji*) that represent the sounds that form their names.

early as 57 A.D. but it was from the 4th century A.D. that the Chinese written language was used in Japan. From the 6th century onwards, Chinese documents written in Japan were altered to make them more Japanese.

710 A.D. – 1185 A.D.: Hiragana and Katakana

During this period the symbols underwent a further simplification. This is what is called *hiragana* today. *Hiragana* is used to write the inflectional endings of the conceptual words that are written in *kanji*. It also is used for all types of native words not written in *kanji*. This was an attempt to cut down on the amount of *kanji* needed to express a multi-syllabic Japanese word.

Katakana was developed a little later and became phonetic short-hand based on Chinese characters. It was used by students who, while listening to classic Buddhist lectures, would make notations on the pronunciations or meanings of unfamiliar characters, and sometimes wrote commentaries between the lines of certain passages. *Katakana* is used chiefly for words of foreign origin. This style made reading and writing much less complicated, creating a higher literacy rate amongst the Japanese people.

Ling Chi

In Chinese the same two *kanji* used to represent Reiki are pronounced differently but have a similar meaning. In Chinese the Reiki *kanji* are called *ling chi*. Although each language has evolved in its own direction the root meanings is traceable.

> *Ling Chi* is the subtlest and most highly refined of all the energies in the human system and the product of the most advanced stages of practice, whereby the ordinary energies of the body are transformed into pure spiritual vitality. This type of highly refined energy enhances spiritual awareness, improves all cerebral functions, and constitutes the basic fuel for the highest level of spiritual work.
>
> (Excerpt from *Chi-gung: Harnessing the Power of the Universe*, by Daniel Reid)

Reading Kanji

There are two methods of pronouncing Japanese *kanji*. The first is *kun yomi*. This is where Chinese *kanji* are used to express Japanese words that have a similar meaning to the original Chinese word. When a Japanese word's sound uses *kanji* this is then called a *kun yomi* reading. The second is *on yomi*. Here the Chinese reading and meaning are attached to the *kanji*.

Kanji on its own generally uses *kun yomi* readings and *kanji* in compounds (more than one *kanji*) often uses *on yomi* readings. There has been such a great deal of change in the Japanese language that most modern *kanji* have two or three *kun yomi* and *on yomi* readings. This allows the language to express many varied concepts and expressions in contrast to Chinese where each character has only one reading.

By the 20th century there were around 50,000 *kanji* in use in Japan but after World War II the Japanese Ministry of Education began simplifying the language and developed the 'Tōyō Kanji Character Form List'. To be able to read a newspaper at that time the reader would have needed to know about 4,000 *kanji*. In 1946 the number of *kanji* used in official publications was limited to 1850. A Japanese person of average education would be familiar with about 3,000 *kanji*.

The *kanji* that are drawn for the word Reiki can be quite spooky for the Japanese as the *kanji rei* may also be read as the spirit of dead people. For this reason, in modern Japan today, where the modern system of Reiki has flourished, the *kanji* for Reiki is not used. Instead, the word Reiki is written in *katakana*; a phonetic writing system that holds no meaning.

Calligraphic Styles of Kanji

There are also different styles of calligraphy. Here are three modern styles and one older style. The older style would have been in use at the time Mikao Usui developed his teachings.

1) *Kaisho* modern, standard style. This style is similar to the printed style of *kanji*, and is taught in schools.

2) *Gyôsho* modern, semi cursive style. A simplification of the standard style, allowing it to be written in a more flowing and faster manner.

3) *Sôsho* modern, cursive style. This is a kind of simplified shorthand that is drawn according to aesthetic standards.

4) *Kaisho* old, standard style. This is the standard style written before World War II and was how Reiki was drawn during Mikao Usui's lifetime.

How to Draw *Kanji*

In the system of Reiki, two of the four symbols that are practiced are in fact *kanji*. These are Symbol 3 and Symbol 4. To draw these symbols correctly it is valuable to understand the basic brushstroke technique for calligraphy. *Kanji* have an exact order in which the strokes must be drawn.

Intent is clearer and stronger when there is the assurance that one is working in a correct and certain manner. There is also an added beauty to something that is drawn with accuracy and care.

The guidelines, as set out by the Japanese Ministry of Education in 1958, are summarized below. Some modern branches of Reiki have created their own *kanji*-like symbols or altered existing ones. It is possible to verify the symbols by comparing the order and directions of the brushstrokes with the official Japanese calligraphic guidelines.

Stroke direction

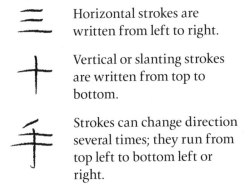

Horizontal strokes are written from left to right.

Vertical or slanting strokes are written from top to bottom.

Strokes can change direction several times; they run from top left to bottom left or right.

Stroke order (the rules are given in order of importance)

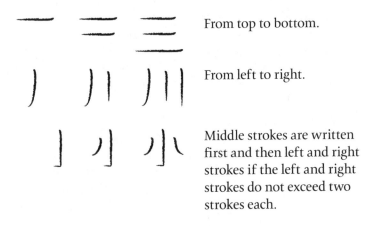

From top to bottom.

From left to right.

Middle strokes are written first and then left and right strokes if the left and right strokes do not exceed two strokes each.

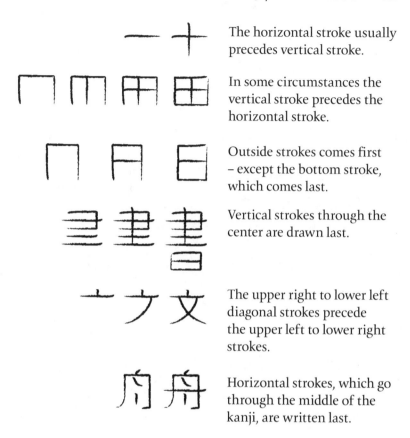

The horizontal stroke usually precedes vertical stroke.

In some circumstances the vertical stroke precedes the horizontal stroke.

Outside strokes comes first – except the bottom stroke, which comes last.

Vertical strokes through the center are drawn last.

The upper right to lower left diagonal strokes precede the upper left to lower right strokes.

Horizontal strokes, which go through the middle of the kanji, are written last.

8   Reiki leaves Japan

Hawayo Takata (1900–1980)[1]

Just do it! Do Reiki, Reiki, Reiki and then you shall know!

(Quote by Hawayo Takata from Hawayo Takata's Story, by Helen Haberly)

Her Early Life

Hawayo Takata came into this world early in the morning on Christmas Eve in 1900 at Hanamaulu on the island of Kauai, Hawaii. A midwife patted her on the head three times proclaiming that this first-generation American would be a success.[2] Hawayo Takata honored that prophecy by introducing the system of Reiki to the rest of the world and practicing it until the day she died in 1980. Hundreds of thousands of practitioners exist today thanks to the persistence and strong character of Hawayo Takata.

Mr. and Mrs. Otogoro Kawamura, Hawayo Takata's parents, had emigrated from Japan to Hawaii. This, their second daughter, was to be named after their new homeland. On the morning of her birth she was held up to the rising sun and christened Hawayo.

Hawayo Takata grew up in a simple Hawaiian village where her

---

[1] Information about Hawayo Takata is abundant. For this chapter, autobiographies, personal interviews and tape recordings have been drawn from to recreate her life and teachings. Unfortunately history has an inherent contradictory nature and therefore there are inconsistencies in some of this material. These irregularities might also be due to the fact that Hawayo Takata was an excellent storyteller.

[2] 'Mrs. Takata and Reiki Power', interview with Mrs Takata, *Honolulu Advertiser*, 25 February 1974.

father worked as a cane cutter. From the age of 12 she became an assistant teacher with the first grade as well as a shop assistant. Though working, she continued her studies at the Japanese school. An invitation from a wealthy woman to work in her household took her to a local sugar cane plantation. Hawayo Takata left school and remained with the family for 24 years. She was eventually promoted to head housekeeper, with the responsibility of supervising the 21 staff members. Here she met her husband, Saichi Takata, who worked as the plantation's bookkeeper. They were blessed with two daughters before he died at the young age of 34.[3]

By 1935, five years after her husband's death, Hawayo Takata's health was at a low point. She was suffering from asthma and abdominal problems and even found it difficult to walk. For a number of reasons she decided to return to *Tôkyô* and it was there that she went to undergo surgery for a tumor, gallstones and other physical problems.[4]

Discovering her Life's Purpose

Lying on the operating table in Japan, Hawayo Takata heard a voice telling her that the operation was unnecessary. She was instructed to ask the surgeon, Dr. Maeda, if there was an alternative to surgery. Dr. Maeda thought about her unusual request then called for his sister, Mrs. Shimura, the hospital dietician.[5] Mrs. Shimura guided Hawayo Takata to Chûjirô Hayashi's drugless treatment clinic.

The clinic's receptionist was Chûjirô Hayashi's wife, Chie Hayashi. She welcomed Hawayo Takata and led her into the clinic. Here eight clients were lying with two practitioners per person. One practitioner began at Hawayo Takata's head while the other placed his hands on her abdomen.[6] She sensed the heat and vibrations from their hands throughout the treatment.

Returning for treatment the following day Hawayo Takata checked to see if any electrical machinery was being operated to

[3] *Hawayo Takata's Story*, Helen Haberly, Archedigm Publications, 1990.
[4] *The Blue Book – Reiki*, Paul Mitchell and Phyllis Furumoto, 1985.
[5] 'Mrs. Takata opens minds to Reiki', interview with Hawayo Takata by Vera Graham, *The Times*, San Mateo, California, 17 May 1975.
[6] *Hawayo Takata's Story*, Helen Haberly, Archedigm Publications, 1990.

create the heat that she had felt. Nothing. To quieten her curiosity, Chûjirô Hayashi explained the basic concepts of his system to her. After three weeks of daily treatments Hawayo Takata felt much better and enquired about becoming a student. This technique was not taught to foreigners, she was told. Though she looked Japanese, she had been born and educated in the USA. Fortunately, Chûjirô Hayashi eventually relented and allowed her to study his teachings as an honorary member.

For six months Hawayo Takata received treatments. At the end of that period she moved in with the Hayashi family and spent another year studying and practicing. In the mornings she was a practitioner at Chûjirô Hayashi's clinic and in the afternoons she set out on house calls. At the end of this period she progressed to what she called the *okudan* level.[7] The terms *shodan* and *okudan* were written in Hawayo Takata's diary notes.

Hawayo Takata claimed that Chûjirô Hayashi had been Mikao Usui's number one disciple before his death in 1926.[8]

Today the society called the *Usui Reiki Ryôhô Gakkai* states that Mikao Usui was their first president. The second president wrote the brushstrokes for the memorial stone that stands at the *Saihôji* Temple in *Tôkyô*. If Chûjirô Hayashi were the 'number one' student, then it would be logical that he would have been the president as successor to Mikao Usui and would probably have been, in part, responsible for the text on the memorial stone. Chûjirô Hayashi was merely a regular member of the society who eventually started his own branch in 1931, which he called the *Hayashi Reiki Kenkyû kai* or Hayashi Spiritual Energy Research Center.

Introducing the System of Reiki to the USA

Once Hawayo Takata finished her practitioner training in 1937, she returned to Hawaii. Chûjirô Hayashi and his daughter followed a few weeks later and stayed for six months helping her to build her practice in Honolulu. On his departure, Chûjirô Hayashi announced publicly that Hawayo Takata had become a Master of the Usui Sys-

[7] *The Gray Book–Reiki*, Alice Takata Furumoto, 1982.
[8] Transcript of a tape of Hawayo Takata talking about Mikao Usui, 1979.

tem of Natural healing.[9] She was his thirteenth, and last, teacher student.

It is interesting to note that Chûjirô Hayashi did not use the name of his organization but that of Mikao Usui, on her certificate. Hiroshi Doi explained that in this way honor was given to Mikao Usui by crediting his original system. At the same time it was also appropriate for Chûjirô Hayashi to have his own name for his organization as he had changed its teachings to some extent.[10]

For Hawayo Takata to receive this appointment, a student of hers claimed she had had to sell her house.

At no point did Hawayo Takata ever call herself, her teacher or Mikao Usui a grandmaster. This statement can be made after listening to recordings, and reading her students' class notes, early books written by her students and article interviews where she often retold vivid and detailed histories of the system's beginnings. It was not until after she passed away that terms such as this came into use in some branches of the system of Reiki.

In Chicago, 1938, Hawayo Takata took classes in anatomy and various other therapies before continuing with her practice in Honolulu.

Hilo, on the big island of Hawaii, became her new home and practice in 1939. Here she built treatment rooms, a waiting room and private apartments for her family. Her practice was almost an instantaneous success and she soon became renowned as Mrs. Takata, Madame Takaka or just Takata.[11]

Hawayo Takata's treatments were performed for as long as a couple of hours and continued from one or two days up to as long as a year. She would give treatments sitting cross-legged on the floor.[12] In Helen Haberly's book, *Hawayo Takata's Story*, many individual cases treated by Hawayo Takata are recorded, including facts about the illnesses and length of treatments. This includes the story of a woman who had died. Hawayo Takata placed her hands on the woman's solar plexus and she came back to life after 5½ hours treatment. She was a great practitioner with extensive experience. As far as pay-

9 *The Blue Book–Reiki*, Paul Mitchell and Phyllis Furumoto, 1985.
10 Information supplied by Robert Fueston from URRI, 2002.
11 *Hand to Hand*, John Harvey Gray, Xlibris Corporation, 2002.
12 *Hand to Hand*, John Harvey Gray, Xlibris Corporation, 2002.

ment went, she appears to have been very flexible, charging those who could afford it and simply helping those who couldn't.

Her practical approach meant that she often had suggestions for her clients as to how they could improve their health apart from having treatments or learning the system of Reiki. She was always very interested in diet, though little of this has been passed down in modern branches of the system. She had begun working with nutrition at Chûjirô Hayashi's clinic in Japan (perhaps influenced by the dietitian Mrs. Shimura). There is no mention of diet in either Chûjirô Hayashi's teachings or in those taught by the *Usui Reiki Ryôhô Gakkai*. One Level 1 student of hers in California remembers her turning up to a class with what she called a 'Reiki salad'.[13] Some of her recommended recipes for better health included sunflower seeds, red beets, grape juice, and almonds.[14] Two students of Takata's master student Virginia Samdahl's wrote a book in 1984 called *The Reiki Handbook*, which includes Reiki recipes. Hawayo Takata called herself a vegetarian and yet occasionally enjoyed lamb kidneys sautéed in gin.[15]

Her Teacher's Passing

On 1 January 1940 Hawayo Takata had a premonitory dream about Chûjirô Hayashi, her teacher in Japan. It puzzled her and though the Hayashi family assured her that all was well she decided to travel to Japan in April of that year. Once there, she found out that Chûjirô Hayashi had decided to end his time in this world. He was concerned that when Japan went to war against the USA, as he was sure it would, he would be forced to fight as an officer in the Japanese Navy, killing many people. On 10 May 1940, Chûjirô Hayashi passed away from a self-induced stroke with his friends and family around him.[16]

There are a number of different accounts about Chûjirô Hayashi's death. His student, Chiyoko Yamaguchi, said that he killed himself by breaking an artery. Others say that as he was a military man the

[13] Author's interview with Exie Lockett, student of Hawayo Takata.
[14] 'Mrs. Takata opens minds to Reiki', interview with Hawayo Takata by Vera Graham, *The Times*, San Mateo, California, 17 May 1975.
[15] *Hand to Hand*, John Harvey Gray, Xlibris Corporation, 2002.
[16] Transcript of a tape of Hawayo Takata talking about Dr. Hayashi, 1977.

honorable method of death would certainly have been *seppuku* (the cutting of the *hara* or abdomen).

One of the World's Reiki Masters

Before he passed on, Hayashi said, 'My wife and five other people in Japan and yourself, that makes us seven ... will be the teachers that we will have in all Japan, including my wife.'[17]

Some of Hawayo Takata's advertising and interviews in the USA claimed that she was the only living Reiki Master in the world.[18] This has been proven incorrect by the existence of the *Usui Reiki Ryôhô Gakkai* and the possibility of other living students of Mikao Usui. Even Hawayo Takata herself mentioned the other teacher students of Chûjirô Hayashi in interviews. This may merely have been her students' desire to set her on a pedestal.

On one of about 20 audiotapes that John Harvey Gray had made during her classes, Hawayo Takata discusses meeting practitioners of Mikao Usui's teachings in Japan. She said that she actually went to Japan to teach her system of Reiki and while there spoke to these practitioners. What they taught, she explained, was highly complex and required years of training and was closely intertwined with religious practices. She felt that their approach was inappropriate for non-Japanese.[19]

Chiyoko Yamaguchi, a student of Chûjirô Hayashi, said that Chie Hayashi continued to teach after Chûjirô Hayashi's death.[20] Some of Hawayo Takata's advertising asserted, more reasonably, that she was the only Reiki Master in the USA, though this too may have been untrue. Tatseyi Nagao completed Levels 1 and 2 with Hawayo Takata in Hawaii and while in Japan in 1950 received *shinpiden* (Level 3) from Chie Hayashi. He returned to Hawaii to teach the system of Reiki to students and died in 1980, the same year as Hawayo Takata.[21] Hawayo Takata knew both Chie Hayashi and Tatseyi Nagao.

[17] Transcript of a tape of Hawayo Takata talking about Dr. Hayashi, 1977.

[18] 'Mrs. Takata opens minds to Reiki', interview with Hawayo Takata by Vera Graham, *The Times*, San Mateo, California, 17 May 1975.

[19] *Hand to Hand*, John Harvey Gray, Xlibris Corporation, 2002.

[20] Information supplied to the authors by Chiyoko Yamaguchi.

[21] *The Spirit of Reiki*, by Walter Lubeck, Frank Arjava Petter, William Lee Rand, Lotus Press, 2001.

Hawayo Takata claims to have been left the Hayashi practice and home in *Tôkyô*. She accepted it but returned to the USA leaving it in the hands of the widow, Chie Hayashi's.

Around this particular period of world history it was not a favorable time to be of Japanese origin in the USA, especially after December 1941 when Japan bombed Pearl Harbor. Americans of Japanese descent were even being placed in internment camps. Chûjirô Hayashi had told Hawayo Takata before he died that she would need to keep her 'mouth shut' or she, too, might end up in a concentration camp.[22] It is not believed that Hawayo Takata was ever placed in an internment camp.

Returning to Japan 14 years later, Hawayo Takata found the house and practice she had been left by Chûjirô Hayashi to be full of refugees. Chie Hayashi had apartmentalized the buildings to help those without any shelter in the aftermath of World War II. At this point Hawayo Takata officially handed the house and clinic back to Chie Hayashi, knowing that her own true place was in the USA.

The Growth of the System of Reiki in the USA

For the next 30 years Hawayo Takata worked from a base in Honolulu in Hawaii. She traveled regularly around the islands teaching. There are few accounts by others of Hawayo Takata in the USA leading up to the 1970s. Initially she worked with Japanese-Americans in Hawaii and appears to have been known as a Reiki practitioner, not specifically as a teacher. As she was an unconventional individual, it is likely she may have informally taught those she treated. Gradually her popularity increased and she claimed to travel with Barbara Hutton[23] and Doris Duke (the richest woman in the world at that time) around the globe as a private healer.[24] She said that she was even set up in a private spa in Palm Springs working with Hollywood celebrities such as Danny Kaye.[25]

Through her hard work and a successful practice, Hawayo Takata became wealthy. As she grew older she lived well and included a

---

[22] Transcript of a tape of Hawayo Takata talking about Dr. Hayashi, 1977.

[23] Information supplied by a student of Hawayo Takata.

[24] *Hand to Hand*, John Harvey Gray, Xlibris Corporation, 2002.

[25] Information supplied by a student of Hawayo Takata.

daily nine holes of golf in her morning routine.[26] In 1973 she also began teaching on the mainland of the USA and Canada. Now that she was in her seventies, she decided it was time to begin training her successor/s.

In 1974 Hawayo Takata told a reporter that she planned to teach until 24 December (her birthday) 1977 and that she wished to build a Reiki center on three acres of land in Olaa, Hawaii. If she could not find a replacement for herself, then the property would be turned over to the county of Honolulu.[27]

Hawayo Takata taught only the first two of the three levels of the system of Reiki until she officially taught her first Master (Level 3) student at the age of 76. By this time her sister, Kay Yamashita, had already been taught unofficially how to teach the system of Reiki according to Robert Fueston. The term Master was used by her and by her teacher on her own certificate in 1938, the first certificate written for a teacher of the system of Reiki in English. Due to the connotations that the term Master encourages, many today prefer to use the term teacher or Master/Teacher for the Level 3 teachings. *this book* uses the term teacher where appropriate.

Hawayo Takata charged US$10,000 for teacher training from 1976 until 1980. Her Level 1 was US$100 in 1975 and increased to US$125 in 1976. The second level was US$400.[28] Hawayo Takata used two moving anecdotes (one about her own family and the other known as the 'beggar story') to explain why it was necessary to pay large amounts of money to become a Reiki practitioner and eventual teacher. Both anecdotes were based on the principle of respect. Students would feel more responsible and have more respect for the system once they had paid their hard-earned money to receive it.

Wanja Twan wrote in her book, *In the Light of a Distant Star: A Spiritual Journey Bringing the Unseen into the Seen,* that she was allowed to deduct the amount she raised from bringing Hawayo Takata new students from her teacher's fee. Unfortunately, she didn't raise enough and ended up using the money she'd saved to feed her fam-

---

[26] 'Mrs. Takata and Reiki Power', interview with Hawayo Takata, *Honolulu Advertiser,* 25 February, 1974.

[27] 'Mrs. Takata and Reiki Power', interview with Hawayo Takata, *Honolulu Advertiser,* 25 February, 1974.

[28] Information supplied by a student of Hawayo Takata.

ily for the coming winter. This, she believed, was an example of trusting the universe to provide for her.

In 1976, Hawayo Takata (though born a Buddhist) became an honorary Minister for the Universal Church of the Master, a metaphysical church founded in 1908. One of her students, Reverend Beth Gray, ordained her on the basis of the spiritual nature of her teachings. After this, she began to sign her notes and certificates as Reverend Hawayo Takata.[29]

In 1975 Hawayo Takata suffered a heart attack in Honolulu and began preparations for her retirement. Rather than tell John Harvey Gray that she had a heart attack, she told him she had fallen off a ladder.[30]

According to Gretchen Munsey, she also had a mild heart attack in 1977.[31]

In a letter to a student wishing a 'Happy Prosperous 1977' she wrote that she had 'created' three Reiki Masters to carry on her 'noble work'. They were John Harvey Gray, Virginia Samdahl, and Ethel Lombardi. In fact, on the transcript of the tape of Hawayo Takata telling the life history of Chûjirô Hayashi, she appears to say goodbye to all of her students. That was her 77th year and she was planning to retire at the end of it on her birthday. None of those three students became her successor, and in 2008, John Harvey Gray is the only student of those three still alive.

After Hawayo Takata's death in 1980, two students of Hawayo Takata claimed to be her successor. One was Barbara Weber (teacher in 1979) and the other was Phyllis Lei Furumoto (teacher in 1979). Neither of them originated from these initial three and had only received their teacher certificates the year before. It is said she tried to set up her granddaughter, Phyllis Lei Furumoto, with classes on the mainland before she died.[32] Other students may have felt that they should have been the successor but nothing ever came of this, with some students going in their own directions.

Retirement was obviously not on the agenda as Hawayo Takata

[29] Information supplied to the authors by Fran Brown, a teacher student of Hawayo Takata. Fran Brown also became a Minister in Beth Gray's church in 1977.
[30] *Hand to Hand*, John Harvey Gray, Xlibris Corporation, 2002.
[31] *Reiki Magazine International*, February/March 2006.
[32] Information supplied by a student of Hawayo Takata.

taught the majority of her 22 Reiki teachers (14 of them) after 1977. In 1978, even though she was failing in health, she participated in Virginia Samdahl's class and was still teaching all levels.[33]

Hawayo Takata's Teacher Students

Below are listed the 22 teacher students of Hawayo Takata in order of their year of teacher training according to Robert Fueston[34]. Robert Fueston has the most complete research into Reiki facts regarding these 22 practitioners. The only change to the order set by him is in relation to Beth Gray. Students in Beth Gray's lineage claim that she was trained as a teacher student at the same time as her husband in 1976 but did not receive an official certificate until 1979.

According to Phyllis Lei Furumoto, Hawayo Takata did not provide an official list of the 22 teacher students to her sister Kay Yamashita before she died as was thought by some. Instead, an unofficial list of 22 teacher students is recognized by her students. There has been little, if no, conflict over this number. Hawayo Takata did not appear to consider her sister, Kay Yamashita, as an official teacher. Hawayo Takata's comments provided to John Harvey Gray prior to his Level 3 training did, however, state that her sister was able to replace Hawayo Takata as a teacher if necessary.[35] For this reason Robert Fueston has listed Kay Yamashita as '0' in the student listing of 22 as is also done here.

0. Kay Yamashita prior to 1976
1. Virginia Samdahl 1976
2. Ethel Lombardi 1976
3. John Harvey Gray October 1976
4. Beth Gray 1976 (Official certificate states 1979)
5. Dorothy Baba 1976
6. Barbara Lincoln McCullough 1977
7. Harry M. Kuboi April 1977
8. Fran Brown January 1979

---

[33] Information supplied by a student of Hawayo Takata.

[34] Consult Robert Fueston's website for more details: http://www.robertfueston. com/reiki/articles/article_on_takatas_22.html.

[35] Information supplied by Robert Fueston.

9. Iris Ishikuro 1979
10. Phyllis Lei Furumoto April 1979
11. Barbara Weber September 1979
12. Bethel Phaigh October 1979
13. Barbara Brown October 1979
14. Wanja Twan October 1979
15. Ursula Baylow October 1979
16. Paul Mitchell November 1979
17. George Araki 1979
18. Shinobu Saito May 1980
19. Patricia Bowling September 1980
20. Mary McFadyen September 1980
21. Rick Bockner October 1980

Though it took almost three years for Hawayo Takata to become a Reiki teacher, she did not have a required waiting period between levels for her own teacher students.

Rick Bockner completed Level 1 on 10 October 1979, Level 2 on 20 October 1979 and Level 3 on 12 October 1980. Bethel Phaigh wrote in her unpublished book *Journey into Consciousness*: 'The lessons (in life that I needed to learn) may have been particularly painful because my initiations had been timed so closely together. I had left Hawaii that spring not knowing of Reiki. I return this winter as a Reiki Master, a very green one.'[36]

Hawayo Takata was known to have limited the number of teachers that one Reiki teacher could teach in their lifetime. Iris Ishikuro stated that she was asked to teach just three Reiki teachers and no more in her lifetime.[37] Hawayo Takata generally taught the Level 3 students of all of her teacher students.

Hawayo Takata's Teachings

Oral Tradition
Exactly what Hawayo Takata taught her Level 1, 2 and 3 students has always been contentious. The system of Reiki, she professed, was an

---

[36] Information supplied by Robert Fueston.
[37] Information supplied by Robert Fueston.

oral tradition. As such, she could teach what she wished. Fortunately some students did take notes after her classes and these verify that her teachings were often at variance with one another. This may well have been because there was a large lapse of time, perhaps 20 or more years, between her learning the system and her teaching it.

The *Usui Reiki Ryôhô Gakkai* uses a manual called the *Reiki Ryôhô Hikkei*. It has a section where Mikao Usui answers questions about Reiki. It contains *waka* (poems) by the Meiji Emperor, the five Reiki precepts and hand positions to be used for specific illnesses.

Hawayo Takata possessed a copy of Chûjirô Hayashi's *Ryôhô Shishin* for use in the USA. Its front cover read *Healing Method's Guidelines*, explaining that it had been set up for American distribution. The branch name on the cover was the *Hayashi Reiki Kenkyû Kai* or Hayashi Spiritual Energy Research Society. It also stated that it was not for sale and was a printed copy of the original. Written in Japanese, Hawayo Takata is known to have handed it to a number of her students including Harue Kanemitsu. John Harvey Gray also received a copy from Alice Takata Furumoto, Hawayo Takata's daughter.[38]

Hawayo Takata did teach what she felt was appropriate at the time. This means that no two teachings were identical.

The Five Precepts
Hawayo Takata taught a simple version of the five precepts to all of her students. This is one aspect of the system of Reiki that has been passed from teacher to student with regularity.

Hand Positions
There has been controversy in the system of Reiki since Hawayo Takata's death regarding the hand positions that she taught. Some students say she started at the abdomen and others say the head. Perhaps her own experience taught her that both methods were valid. Her teachings about the abdomen or *hara* were, 'Spend half your treatment time here because this is the main factory. It processes the fuel taken in and delivers it to the places it is needed.'[39]

---

[38] *Hand to Hand*, John Harvey Gray, Xlibris Corporation, 2002.
[39] *Living Reiki–Takata's Teachings*, Fran Brown, Life Rhythm, 1992.

Hawayo Takata is often credited with teaching 12 hand positions, which she called the Foundation Treatment. This was made up of four positions on the head, front and back of the torso. At the end of the treatment she would often perform the *finishing treatment or *nerve stroke.

It is believed that Mikao Usui did not use hand positions when he first began teaching. The teachings developed into five hand positions for the head.[40] Chûjirô Hayashi's center used five head positions or seven positions including the head.[41]

Hawayo Takata stressed that students should treat themselves first and then their family and friends. This way, the student becomes whole and is also surrounded by harmony.[42]

Mantras and Symbols

The symbols taught by Hawayo Takata were once again not completely regimented. Yes, there were three mantras and symbols used for Level 2 and one for Level 3 but they did vary slightly (or at least the versions that her teacher students used were varied). Students were not allowed to keep copies of these mantras and symbols.

The first meeting of the teacher students was in 1982 – just over a year after Hawayo Takata's death. They compared the teachings and symbols that Hawayo Takata had given them. Each drew their symbols and were shocked to find that they were different 'similar in some respects and different in others'.[43]

There are a number of possible reasons for this: Hawayo Takata taught that Reiki was an oral tradition therefore no one had original copies of the symbols. It is easy to unintentionally change something that may not have been memorized completely or perhaps correctly. Two of the four symbols are in fact Japanese *kanji*. If a non-Japanese student is not aware that the symbol is *kanji* it may be drawn in an incorrect manner.

This particular group of teachers, not all of whom were present

---

[40] Information from the *Reiki Ryôhô Hikkei*.

[41] Information from Chûjirô Hayashi's *Ryôhô Shishin*.

[42] Information from the tapes of Hawayo Takata's teachings, compiled by John Harvey Gray.

[43] Letter written by Carrel Ann Farmer on 31 December 1997 (she was the fourth teacher initiated by Phyllis Lei Furumoto and was present at the first Reiki teacher meeting in 1982).

(though all were invited), decided to standardize the symbols. As a result none of them was ever really sure if they were using the correct symbols or not.

Attunements

Hawayo Takata practiced four attunements for Level 1, one for Level 2 and one for Level 3.[44] She taught the first level over four evenings and students received one attunement on each of these evenings.

It has been suggested that the four are representative of the four levels of proficiency of *shoden* practiced by the *Usui Reiki Ryôhô Gakkai.*[45]

The actual attunement process is so varied today that it is almost impossible to even track back to what Hawayo Takata taught. It is feasible though to pinpoint where components were added (chakras, repetition of movement, etc.) by either Hawayo Takata or her students (or their students and so on). There is also the chance that she may have varied processes according to students' abilities.

Student accounts relate that there were sometimes up to 40 or more students in a Level 1 course. For the attunement, four students would be taken into a separate room where they would sit in a row. One student said that she was asked to remove her watch as the 'teacher's power' (Hawayo Takata's) would damage the watch.[46]

She is also known to have taught the second Level in just two hours to a group of 10 students. The reason for the short length of the course, she told the group, was because they were exceptionally gifted.[47]

Techniques

In the traditional teachings of Mikao Usui there are a number of techniques practiced. These consisted of practice on others as well as meditative methods to build the practitioner's energy.

Hawayo Takata used some traditional techniques or at least versions of some of them: *ketsueki kôkan hô (she called it the *finishing treatment or *nerve stroke), *nentatsu hô (*deprogramming tech-

---

[44] Information supplied by Robert Fueston.
[45] *The Spirit of Reiki* by Walter Lubeck, Frank Arjava Petter, William Lee Rand, Lotus Press, 2001.
[46] Student notes from a Level 1 class with Hawayo Takata.
[47] Information supplied by a student of Hawayo Takata.

nique), *byôsen reikan hô* (*scanning) and *shûchû Reiki* (*group Reiki).
In her diary she wrote that Chûjirô Hayashi had bestowed upon her
the secret of *shinpiden, Kokiyu hô* (either *koki hô* or *kokyû hô*) and the
Leiji hô (*reiji hô*).[48] She also wrote that before beginning a treatment a
student should 'close your hand together'.[49] This is a traditional way
to begin all treatments using *gasshô*. When she wrote about the *hara*,
she said that to work with it would help one to concentrate, to purify
one's thoughts and to meditate letting the true energy from within
come out.[50] This is the basis of traditional Japanese Reiki techniques
such as *hatsurei hô*.

These techniques were not passed on systematically to all of her
students. Some were taught them, others not.

There is no evidence that Hawayo Takata taught the chakra system and instead spoke of the 'true energy' in the body that 'lies in
the bottom of the stomach about 2 inches below the naval'.[51] This is
a reference to the *hara*.

The New Age movement became increasingly popular throughout
the world during the 1970s. Modifications made to the Indian chakra
system by many New Age practitioners during this time made it an
easily accessible system. Modern teachers perhaps found comfort in
using a 2000-year-old established tradition rather than following
Hawayo Takata's words, 'Reiki will guide you. Let the Reiki hands
find it. They will know what to do.'[52]

John Harvey Gray did teach the chakra system and admitted that
Hawayo Takata did not. Fran Brown agrees that Hawayo Takata did
not teach the chakra system.[53] Other students of Hawayo Takata's
began to use the chakra system in their teachings. It was said that
Phyllis Lei Furumoto, Hawayo Takata's granddaughter who became
a teacher in 1979, introduced the chakra system into the attunement
process – but she denies this.[54] Chakras have been grafted onto the
system of Reiki in many creative ways: One modern branch professes

[48] *The Gray Book–Reiki*, Hawayo Takata's Diary Notes, Alice Takata Furumoto, 1982.
[49] *The Gray Book–Reiki*, Hawayo Takata's Diary Notes, Alice Takata Furumoto, 1982.
[50] *The Gray Book–Reiki*, Hawayo Takata's Diary Notes, Alice Takata Furumoto, 1982.
[51] *The Gray Book–Reiki*, Hawayo Takata's Diary Notes, Alice Takata Furumoto, 1982.
Spelling is unchanged.
[52] *Hawayo Takata's Story* by Helen Haberly, Archedigm Publications, 1990.
[53] Information supplied to the authors by Robert Fueston.
[54] Information supplied to the authors by Robert Fueston.

that with each attunement a separate chakra is focused on. Another branch has broken the system of Reiki into seven levels focusing on a different chakra for each level.

Hawayo Takata Tells the History of Mikao Usui

Since the mid-1990s, more knowledge and insight into the life of Mikao Usui has been gained by Reiki practitioners worldwide. This has occurred largely through the discovery of the Mikao Usui Memorial Stone in *Tôkyô* and through research completed by various practitioners. Up until her late 70s Hawayo Takata popularized a history of Mikao Usui and his teachings. Her manner was entertaining and her stories seemed aimed more at getting a point across rather than having a strong base in reality. One of her students wrote, 'Her retelling of his story was a long, involved, dramatically highlighted, and somewhat speculative third- or fourth-hand account.'[55] Hawayo Takata taught that Mikao Usui, or Dr. Usui as she called him, was the principal of the Doshisha University in *Kyôto*. On Sundays he also became the university's minister. She called him a 'full-fledged Christian minister'. She also credited him with having traveled to the USA to study at the University of Chicago. Chûjirô Hayashi, Hawayo Takata claimed, told her this particular history of Mikao Usui. Her story went on to recount that Mikao Usui studied many religions.

The focus on Mikao Usui as a Christian may well have been a clever way for Hawayo Takata to introduce a Japanese system, initially created by a Buddhist, to the USA during World War II. To create a credible story she included in it convincing names such as the Doshisha University in *Kyôto* and the University of Chicago. It is now known that neither of these universities knew Mikao Usui as lecturer, principal, minister or student.[56] She called Mikao Usui a 'Doctor', which has often been misinterpreted as a physician. 'Doctor' may simply have been her translation for the respectful Japanese term *sensei* used for one's teacher. However, it may also have been an excellent backup to Hawayo Takata's story that Mikao Usui had received a Doctorate in Theology at the University of Chicago.

[55] *The Reiki Factor*, Barbara Weber Ray, Exposition Press, 1983.
[56] *The Spirit of Reiki*, Walter Lubeck, Frank Arjava Petter, William Lee Rand, Lotus Press, 2001.

A certain freedom of interpretation was natural for Hawayo Takata and it was not unusual for her to use the words 'church' and 'temple' when talking about identical subjects. In this same way Mikao Usui no longer solely filled the 'Christian Minister' role but is actually described as a Zen monk in some of her advertising in the 1970s. In contrast to the system of Reiki's first introduction to the USA in the 1940s and 1950s, Zen Buddhism had become a popular trend. It may even have added an attractive element to her advertisements.

Yes, Hawayo Takata told stories that changed with each telling but her nature may simply not have found these details important. Her words appeared randomly chosen depending on the moment itself. This eccentricity was accepted by most who knew her perhaps because of her dedication to her topic and the strict manner in which she taught.

It does not seem that all of Hawayo Takata's students could grasp her ease of changing the facts. After her death most clung tightly to the 'full-fledged Christian Minister' belief – this was probably what she had spoken of most convincingly. Even Helen Haberly's biography neatly sidelines this. Although she uses the words 'monk', 'Zen' and 'Buddhism' they are not written in direct combination with the name of Mikao Usui – though she was certain to have read during her research the transcripts where Hawayo Takata talks about Mikao Usui the 'Buddhist monk'. [57]

End of an Era

There have been dogmatic claims from Reiki practitioners the world over that they are the only teachers of the system of Reiki that was taught by Hawayo Takata. Interestingly they all teach something different. There is no consistency between those asserting to be the 'original' or 'traditional' method. The subjects of the contentions all differ and are as small as how to spell the word 'Reiki'[58] or as integral as how to perform an attunement. Due to the multitude of unreliable reports it is almost impossible to evaluate exactly what

[57] Transcript of a tape of Hawayo Takata talking about Mikao Usui, 1979.
[58] Posters advertising her teachings in the 1970s are written as Reiki – one word.

Hawayo Takata did teach.

Hawayo Takata invented tenets that may also have created dogma. Rules such as 'if you teach this method to anyone you will lose your healing power' are recorded as having been taught in a Level 1 course. There is nothing to substantiate this claim but it does leave the door open for further unsupported statements to be made on behalf of other Reiki teachers who believe that they, too, have the 'power'.

Additions to her teachings can be seen in the wide variety of branches of Reiki that exist today.

A certain idolization of Hawayo Takata began to occur during her lifetime and this certainly developed thereafter. Some of the statements made today about what she said or did cannot be verified and her status is fast becoming mythic. An example of this is where a student of Hawayo Takata wrote in 2006 that Hawayo Takata had claimed to be able to alchemically change silver to gold and that the student had, in fact, seen an example of this occurring.[59] [60]

The love and admiration that many felt for this small Japanese-American woman who spoke little, yet expressed herself clearly through her actions, is evident in the many tales that have entranced the global Reiki community during and after her lifetime.

Hawayo Takata died of a heart attack on 11 December 1980. Her remains were placed at a Buddhist temple on the island of Hawaii.[61]

---

[59] *Reiki Magazine International* February/March 2006, 'Spiritual Lineage' by Paul Mitchell.

[60] The authors can only guess that Hawayo Takata would have been a very wealthy woman if this were the case.

[61] *Hand to Hand*, John Harvey Gray, Xlibris Corporation, 2002.

Part III
Reiki Present

Just over 25 years on from the death of Hawayo Takata and the system called Reiki has become a globally popular complementary therapy with many individual faces.

Reiki Present looks at what occurred within the system of Reiki from 1980 until the present day. This includes the spread of the system, its dispersion and the struggle within its teaching ranks.

There is a brief analysis of what requirements (if any) are necessary to become a branch of Reiki and details of their commonalities and irregularities.

The details of some of the major branches and directions that the system of Reiki has taken are introduced by the individuals, organizations and cultures that have influenced them.

The world is fascinated with any scientific evidence that proves the existence of Reiki. Though its effects can be readily experienced by all, it is often the scientific data that truly amazes us. A summary is provided of a number of experiments that have taken place in modern times to, amongst other things, measure Reiki's effectiveness.

9 The Evolution of Reiki

Hawayo Takata's Successors

Directionless. This appeared to be the emotion that most of Hawayo Takata's 22 teacher students felt after she died. Their teacher was gone and most were not sure what was to happen next. Hawayo Takata had talked for years of naming a successor or successors who would continue in her steps but no one had officially been recognized. There were contradictory statements at that time about who she had desired as her successor. Claims were also being made for the leadership role.

Even without the naming of an official successor, the 1980s saw the attempted creation of a standardized system. One and a half years after Hawayo Takata's death, her granddaughter, Phyllis Lei Furumoto, hosted a meeting of Hawayo Takata's Reiki teachers in Hawaii.[1]

Not one of them knew that there were still traditional practitioners living and practicing Mikao Usui's teachings in Japan. They therefore assumed that their decisions would ultimately regulate the way the modern teachings would be practiced throughout the world for all time. This great responsibility was in their hands. What a great shock it was for them when they decided to compare their symbols to find that they were, to some extent, different. Regulation of the system first began when the teachers present decided upon

[1] Reiki Magazine International, February/March 2006 'The Power of Recognition' by Barbara McDaniel.

which symbols were to become the standard symbols.[2] The initial meeting may also have been held as a reaction to a stand taken by one of Hawayo Takata's teacher students, Barbara Weber. In 1979 she had become a teacher and was now claiming to be Hawayo Takata's successor. Barbara Weber did not attend this meeting.

Most of the teachers who came together apparently felt that Phyllis Lei Furumoto, Hawayo Takata's granddaughter, was the natural successor. Phyllis Lei Furumoto had already trained teachers prior to the meeting in 1982 and appeared confident in the role. Although the other teachers taught Levels 1 and 2, they had previously passed their teacher students onto Hawayo Takata, and now Phyllis Lei Furumoto would take over that role. She was said to be open to becoming Hawayo Takata's successor and the others at the meeting were happy for her to take the lead.[3]

This group eventually became known as The Reiki Alliance (teaching *Usui Shiki Ryôhô*) with the first of its inaugural meetings held in Canada in 1983. Phyllis Lei Furumoto also became known as The Reiki Alliance 'lineage bearer of the system of Reiki' and gained their official 'title of holder' of the 'Office of the Grandmaster'. This was the first time that either term had been used in the system of Reiki. Paul Mitchell wrote that, 'In those early days many of us had a simple idea of what Grandmaster meant: it was the person who was responsible for initiating others to be masters to carry on this work.'[4] Many of the teachers, therefore, sent their students who wanted to become Reiki teachers to Phyllis Lei Furumoto. Eventually, this changed with all teachers being able to train teachers.

Today there are a great many Reiki teachers in the world, of varying Reiki branches and understandings with only a very small percentage of them coming from The Reiki Alliance. The non-Reiki Alliance members do not generally consider Phyllis Lei Furumoto to be their lineage bearer or grandmaster as these terms apply only to members of The Reiki Alliance, which was formed in 1983.

---

[2] Letter written by Carrel Ann Farmer on 31 December 1997 (she was the fourth Master taught by Phyllis Lei Furumoto and was present at the first Reiki Teachers meeting in 1982).

[3] Letter written by Carrel Ann Farmer on 31 December 1997 (she was the fourth Master initiated by Phyllis Lei Furumoto and was present at the first Reiki Master Teachers meeting in 1982).

[4] *Reiki Magazine International* February/March 2006.

Meanwhile, Barbara Weber was publishing what she called the first ever Reiki book. Little did she know that there had already been a number of books published in Japan from as early as 1930 by students of Mikao Usui.[5] The first edition of her book however connects the system of Reiki with ancient Tibet and the Aquarian New Age rather than with its Japanese roots. It is true that Hawayo Takata once mentioned that Reiki is spoken of in the ancient history of Japan and the Buddhist *sutra*.[6] She was never known to have elucidated on this nor taught any information about Tibet etc. This may very well have been her manner of restating that Reiki 'can stem from the sun, or moon or stars' and that it 'is nature, it is God'.[7] Barbara Weber asserts that she had been carefully instructed in the advanced levels of the system of Reiki by Hawayo Takata and yet only goes on to explain the same three levels that *Usui Shiki Ryôhô* teaches.[8] In later editions these three levels are extended to the seven levels that are taught in her system today. The Radiance Technique® official website actually denies there was a split after Hawayo Takata died. That, their website states, is impossible as there is only one true authentic system of Reiki. Anything else is 'an imitation, a copy, a part and a fabrication'. Their website also shows copies of the original certificates Barbara Weber received from Hawayo Takata – only three are provided.

One of the 22 Reiki teachers, Virginia Samdahl, is known to have followed Barbara Weber, while many initially joined The Reiki Alliance. Virginia Samdahl actually joined both The Radiance Technique® and The Reiki Alliance. She may have been hoping to be a sensible go-between, though eventually she left The Radiance Technique®. One of the reasons given was that Barbara Weber had told her she would have to re-train with her as a Reiki teacher.[9]

[5] *Te No Hira Ryôji Nyûmon* (*Introduction to Healing with the Palms*), Toshihiro Eguchi and Kohsi Mitsui, 1930; *Te No Hira Ryôji Wo Kataru* (*A Story of Healing with the Palms*), Toshihiro Eguchi, 1954; *Reiki To Jinjutsu – Tomita Ryû Teate Ryôhô* (*Reiki and Humanitarian Work – Tomita Ryû Hands Healing*), Kaiji Tomita, 1933.

[6] 'Mrs. Takata Opens Minds to Reiki', interview with Hawayo Takata, Vera Graham, *The Times*, San Mateo, California, 17 May 1975.

[7] 'Mrs. Takata Opens Minds to Reiki', interview with Hawayo Takata, Vera Graham, *The Times*, San Mateo, California, 17 May 1975.

[8] *The Reiki Factor*, Barbara Weber Ray, Ph.D., Exposition Press, 1983.

[9] Information supplied to the authors by Robert Fueston.

Another student teacher of Hawayo Takata was Beth Gray. She went in her own direction, unaffiliated with either The Reiki Alliance or Barbara Weber and is said to have taught *Usui Shiki Ryôhô* to over 20,000 Level 1 and 2 students in the USA and Australia between 1973 and 1990[10].

Standardization

The Reiki Alliance quickly created an elite, standardized system. Elite, as it was affordable (especially in its early days) to only a small section of society: one that could afford the prices.

Course costs became identical across the board without room for individual assessment. It is believed that the amounts of US$150 for Level 1, US$500 for Level 2, and US$10,000 for the Level 3 are still being charged by them today. Teacher students are required to complete an apprenticeship (not full time) with their teacher for a period of at least one year. Once the new teacher begins to teach, it is under their teacher's supervision, and this teacher receives all course fees.

Once Phyllis Lei Furumoto gave Reiki teachers the green light to teach new teachers, many new teachers emerged with their own ideas. To counteract this development, 'guidance' provided by Phyllis Lei Furumoto stated that a teacher should teach Levels 1 and 2 for a minimum of three years before teaching new teachers.[11] In the 2005 *Reiki Magazine International* December/January edition, Paul Mitchell (whose title within The Reiki Alliance is Head of the Discipline of the Usui System) went on to say that it is recommended that teachers should teach Levels 1 and 2 for ten years before being able to teach new teachers. These changes came too late with the teachers rapidly teaching new teachers and so on, outside of any new recommendations developed by The Reiki Alliance or Phyllis Lei Furumoto.

Hawayo Takata said that the fees she charged were the same as when she trained in 1936–1938. She apparently asked her student teachers not to increase the fees even though the value of the dollar would naturally change.[12] According to a poster advertising her

---

[10] Information supplied by Barbara McGregor, teacher student of Beth Gray.
[11] *Reiki Magazine International* 2005 December/January, Paul Mitchell.
[12] Information supplied to the authors by Robert Fueston.

courses in 1975, she charged $100 for her Level 1, which went up to $125 ($25 less than The Reiki Alliance claimed) in 1976. Her Level 2 course cost $400[13] in comparison to The Reiki Alliance's $500. [14]

Money and the System

There is a major problem with charging $10,000 for Level 3. The Reiki Alliance practitioners have been known to claim that high fees differentiate between those who are genuinely interested in the teachings and those who are not. Consequently, what has happened is that instead of teaching those who sincerely wish to learn, only those with the financial wherewithal end up as Reiki teachers. Of course, there will always be exceptions to this rule, but an average person in India or Africa (even after selling their house!) could not raise such a large sum. On the other hand a well-to-do person in the USA would not think twice about paying it if he or she so wanted. The dogma may have been well intentioned as a means to protect the system of Reiki but that is not what has occurred.

The attitude that this has engendered within a minority of the system is a reflection of modern society's view toward wealth; that the 'worth' of an individual is assessed upon one's ability to pay. Not a healthy attitude for a spiritual practice.

As the system of Reiki is an energetic practice it would, perhaps, have been wiser to develop levels in line with a student's energetic development rather than financial status. In this way levels would be reached depending upon energetic expertise rather than merely upon monetary accountability. In Japan, a set monetary fee was attached to the teachings beginning with the *Usui Reiki Ryôhô Gakkai*, yet this was coupled to the teacher following a student's energetic progression at regular sessions.

Reiki branches today have found it difficult to break away from this financial structure, yet many have removed the guidance aspect provided by the teacher. This modern structure has created a system

[13] Information supplied by a student of Hawayo Takata.
[14] Unfortunately, The Reiki Alliance board have chosen not to provide basic information regarding their infrastructure for inclusion in *The Reiki Sourcebook*. Information in this chapter, apart from the quotes, has therefore been provided by students of The Reiki Alliance.

that is easily corrupted and has led to misuse by various individuals over time. It is certainly a major factor behind any 'downfall' or lack of credibility attributed to the system of Reiki in its modern form.

Conflict in the New Age

Throughout the 1980s there were struggles within the Reiki community. The Reiki Alliance may have felt undermined by a number of Hawayo Takata's teacher students who did not wish to conform to their, or The Radiance Technique's®, rulings.

Something was missing from the system of Reiki after Hawayo Takata died. Her personality, strength of character and depth of healing knowledge were sorely missed. There seemed to be a void that needed to be filled. And people began filling it!

The variety of techniques and concepts that have been introduced into the system over the last 25 years is quite astounding. In some cases new branches have been developed, in others the name of the branch has remained the same and yet its contents may be quite unrecognizable.

The 1980s was full of upheaval for the system of Reiki. In 1988, a book that listed some of Hawayo Takata's teachers was recalled due to objections. The relevant pages were cut out and the book was reissued. From those closed-door attitudes the system of Reiki then entered the rebellious 1990s. With it followed many new lineages and globalization, primarily due to the success of the Internet. Today almost every English-language Reiki website has a list of Hawayo Takata's 22 teacher students. How quickly things change. Yet, this closed-door attitude still exists in some arenas as some Reiki organizations struggle to retain or gain control of their teachings and dogma.

The problem with the creation of new branches is that, often, it is no longer understood what is 'original' anymore and no clear boundaries remain intact. One answer to this has been trademarking. Barbara Weber had already complained that the system of Reiki could be used 'by anyone for anything' and has trademarked numerous titles related to her teachings. Other branches soon followed in this trend. The next great trademarking escapade was in the mid-90s when Phyllis Lei Furumoto (The Reiki Alliance's grandmaster) attempted to trademark Reiki itself. This was a worldwide effort. In Germany the words 'Reiki', 'Usui' and *'Usui Shiki Ryôhô'* were attempted. In the USA it was 'Usui System' and *'Usui Shiki Ryôhô'* and in Canada, 'Usui System of Reiki Healing', *'Usui Shiki Ryôhô'* and 'Usui System of Natural Healing'. Other countries followed. It was stated in the USA that 'she could not identify or distinguish her goods from those of others nor do they indicate their source'.[15] As Frank Arjava Petter pointed out, it would be impossible to trademark the word Reiki in Japan. That would be like taking a shot at trademarking the word 'milk' in the USA.

Modern Japan

Since Hawayo Takata's death in 1980, many foreigners have attempted to contact traditional Japanese practitioners. The *Usui Reiki Ryôhô Gakkai* would happily have continued its peaceful existence, but this was not likely to be the case. This curiosity has changed the face of the modern system of Reiki in both Japan and elsewhere due to the exchange of information that has finally begun to occur.

Mieko Mitsui, a Japanese Reiki practitioner living in New York, visited her native country in 1985. She instigated a revival of the system of Reiki in Japan and taught the first two levels of The Radiance Technique® to many Japanese. During one stay she met a member of the *Usui Reiki Ryôhô Gakkai*, most probably Fumio Ogawa. Mieko Mitsui's interest was sparked and she began researching the roots of the system in Japan. There was an article in a Japanese magazine called *Twilight Zone* that had a photo of Fumio Ogawa reading from a book about the system of Reiki.[16] In the same article there was a photo of Mieko Mitsui demonstrating hands-on healing.

In 1991, Frank Arjava Petter moved to Japan with his then-wife, Chetna Kobayashi, to live. Briefly returning to Germany, his homeland, he studied all three levels of the system of Reiki. He claims that before long he became the first teacher to teach all three levels openly in Japan.

From 1993, Frank Arjava Petter and Chetna began researching the

---

[15] The International Center for Reiki Training's website: www.reiki.org.
[16] Fumio Ogawa was reading a book by Barbara Weber, founder of The Radiance Technique®.

system of Reiki's traditional roots. A female member of Mikao Usui's family had left a clause in a will saying that Mikao Usui's name must never be mentioned in her house. Her relative informed Frank Arjava Petter that a number of people had been in contact to find out about Mikao Usui but she preferred to be left alone because of family reasons.[17] One of these people was undoubtedly Mieko Mitsui, who had received a similar reception a number of years earlier.[18] Their research also brought them to an undisclosed current member of the *Usui Reiki Ryôhô Gakkai* in Japan. She declared that she didn't want anything to do with a system of Reiki that came from outside of Japan. However, she did offer a small amount of information that led them to Mikao Usui's memorial stone in *Tôkyô*.

The discovery of Mikao Usui's memorial stone has been a milestone in the history of modern Reiki for hundreds of thousands of practitioners around the world. It is now possible to connect to a tangible history. Funnily enough it appears that Hawayo Takata had told some of her students about the memorial stone but there had never been great interest in it. Fran Brown's book, *Living Reiki – Takata's Teachings*, writes briefly about the existence of such a memorial stone and her book was published in 1992 – a number of years before Frank Arjava Petter heard of it and consequently published his first book.

Frank Arjava Petter also gradually made contact with other Japanese people associated with Mikao Usui's traditional teachings in Japan. Among these was Fumio Ogawa who is given a special mention of thanks in Frank Arjava Petter's third book for openheartedly sharing information with him. His stepfather, Kôzô Ogawa, ran a center in *Shizuoka* for Mikao Usui during his lifetime. Kôzô Ogawa had trained the mother of another contact called Tsutomu Oishi. In 1997, Tsutomu Oishi provided Frank Arjava Petter with a photo of Mikao Usui with the five precepts in the left-hand corner. He also gave him a copy of the *Reiki Ryôhô Hikkei* (Frank Arjava Petter included a translation of the *Reiki Ryôhô Hikkei* in two of his first three books).[19]

[17] *Reiki Fire*, Frank Arjava Petter, Lotus Press, Twin Lakes, Wisconsin, 1998.
[18] 1986 article 'Mysterious Report 28' from *The Twilight Zone* by Shiomi Takai, translated by Shiya Fleming from the website: www.threshold.ca/reiki.
[19] Information supplied by Frank Arjava Petter.

Tatsumi, a teacher student of Chûjirô Hayashi, was met by two non-Japanese Reiki teachers in an out-of-the-way Japanese village. Tatsumi told them he had become a student of Chûjirô Hayashi's in 1927. Due to the changes in the system that were taking place, Tatsumi left Chûjirô Hayashi's clinic in 1931. Though Tatsumi had never taught these teachings he still had the paperwork. These included handwritten notes from Chûjirô Hayashi's teachings and copies of the four traditional symbols. His attunement has become popular amongst practitioners wishing to practice in a more traditional Japanese manner.

Some people outside Japan also claim to have met other students of Mikao Usui in Japan who have lived to a great age. These include a number of *Tendai* Buddhist nuns.

The modern system of Reiki has become increasingly popular in Japan. It has been influenced largely by the New Age movement, which spread throughout the world.

Global Movements

The 21st century continues to introduce the concept of spiritual energy to more people than ever. It is, on the other hand, debatable as to whether society itself has become more spiritual – there are no guarantees as to what people will do with the information they receive. Yet, the interest is there.

The Internet has successfully allowed people from every culture to access teachings. Reiki practitioners are communicating with ease across continents via email, forums, social networking sites and chat programs.

Fads have come and gone. Distant attunements via Internet courses, for example, became briefly popular until practitioners realized that the possible lack of integrity on the Internet meant that the risk was too great. Who could say for sure that one has actually 'received' anything? In fact, the only action taking place may have only been the buyer giving – from the hip pocket! Another aspect of the distant attunement that was not working was that people were not receiving training; they were not learning the basic tenets of the system of Reiki such as the five elements. Instead they were merely being told that they were receiving an energetic attunement of some kind. That on its own does not constitute the system of Reiki.

Initiatives such as free Reiki courses are another Internet specialty. Free courses are offered (with distant attunements of course) along with the availability of chat programs where members can come together and discuss free Reiki.

The anonymity that the Internet provides can also lead to a misuse of its astonishing powers. People gossip or create smear campaigns, all the while operating under a pseudonym and signing off with the modern Reiki signature of 'Love and Light'.

The system of Reiki is also reaching people through the greater infrastructure that is evolving from within its ranks. Initiatives such as the Council of Australian Reiki Organisations (CARO) – where Australian Reiki organizations have joined together in an attempt to support unity and dialogue within the Australian Reiki comamunity – is an excellent example of the global change that is to come.

10   Reiki Branches

Defining a Branch

> The river flows on, but something remains from the past,
> leading us through the present, and into the future, if we but
> step into the clear waters for a drink.
>
> (Excerpt from 'What is a Ryû?' Wayne Murumoto.
> Issue 8, *Furyo* —*The Budo Journal*)

How can one tell if a branch of healing or energetic work has its
foundations in Mikao Usui's teachings?

A new branch is generally created in the system of Reiki today
when teachers change the contents of what they have been taught.
They may call themselves Independent Reiki Master/Teachers or
create a new, more apt name to work under, appending the word
'Reiki' at the end. Once this new system is created it is passed on to a
student, written on certificates, advertised, etc., and the birth of yet
another new branch of the system of Reiki is complete.

The unsettling speed with which new branches arise within the
system of Reiki may be due to it being unclear to teachers whether
they are teaching Reiki as in 'the system of Mikao Usui' or Reiki as in
'spiritual energy'. If it was clearly understood that the system of Reiki
comprised a set of five elements with certain guidelines to adhere
to, then there would be relatively few new branches developed. Yet,
if one felt that Reiki represented solely 'energy' then any 'system' or
'teachings' could be applied to it. This lack of clarity is extremely
confusing for the general public and Reiki practitioners alike.

Original Methods

It is therefore to the original methods that modern practitioners look today in order to define what Mikao Usui taught. The little that is known of Mikao Usui includes that he was born into a *samurai* family with the influences on his life ranging from Japanese martial arts to Buddhism. There has always been a link in Japan between spirituality and martial arts. Lao tzu is quoted as saying, 'He who excels in combat is one who does not let himself be roused.' That is why Japanese warriors trained in peaceful hermitages – to practice their fighting *and* meditative skills. *Shûgyô*, the training that Mikao Usui is said to have completed on *kurama yama*,[1] is both a martial art and an esoteric Buddhist term.

In traditional Japanese martial arts, to be considered a founder of a style one must first have received a divine understanding through a spiritual experience – not unlike Mikao Usui's experience. It is from this seed of divine understanding that a founder then goes on to create a system or method. If this method is to remain divinely inspired then the teachings must always flow back to the founder. This is a traditional belief in Japan.

Unless it can be claimed that one has the pure source and the direct teachings from the founder (who initially received the divine guidance), then what is practiced is considered a degeneration.

This does not mean that the true method should remain stagnant. Teachers are expected to be able to teach using their own personal methods to support the original teachings. Often these teachings are called 'outside' teachings. This creates clarity as to what the original teachings are and what has been added. Remember that the method flows from the source. Innovative attempts to make a method 'better' cut its links from its divine origins. In order to maintain the method's integrity, the proximity to its origins must be close. Otherwise the teachings need to be given a new name unrelated to the original method.[2]

In this context, all branches of Mikao Usui's teachings would need to retain the original methods, which are the traditional aspects

---

[1] Mikao Usui's experience on *kurama yama* is described on the memorial stone.
[2] 'What is a Ryû?' Wayne Murumoto, Issue 8 of *Furyu – The Budo Journal*.

of the five elements of the system of Reiki, while teaching their personal add-ons openly. Apart from the continuity of teaching, a shared lineage is the other major requirement for all Reiki branches.

Lineage

Traditionally in Japan a lineage is 'passed on' when the student's mind becomes One with the teacher's. It is not to do with one's role or place within a family structure. This sense of lineage is rarely experienced within the Reiki community.

In the system of Reiki today, a lineage is merely a written lineage that traces the teacher and the teacher's teachers back to the founder of the system, Mikao Usui. Many organizations, such as associations, use this concept of lineage to ensure that what is being taught as the system of Reiki by members relates back to the teachings of Mikao Usui. Unfortunately the concept of lineage is not strong enough to guarantee that a teacher actually teaches in line with the teachings of Mikao Usui and other safeguards must be met to ensure a quality of standards. This includes that the five elements of the system of Reiki are taught and practiced.

Some new branches claim that Mikao Usui created his teachings from a far older and, often, 'more powerful' system. Egyptian, Tibetan and inter-galactic origins are often suggested. Many of these new branches are offshoots from one another, simply carrying the story along and occasionally adding to it.

From Part II, Reiki Past, it can clearly be seen that Reiki grew out of a Japanese culture. The mantras and symbols have Japanese origins (some are Japanese *kanji*) and therefore do not link in to any of these so-called histories. The traditional techniques are also specifically Japanese, originating from Shintôism, *Tendai* Buddhism and Japanese martial art practices.

It is curious that this interest in alternative histories occurred only a few short years after Hawayo Takata's death in 1980. Perhaps the trend of 'all things Tibetan' or 'mystical Egypt' at the time influenced the sale-ability of the system of Reiki to the general public? The New Age movement also introduced channeling as an acceptable form (in some circles) of acquiring information.

Verification is an issue. To seriously search for verification can mean turning up many questions and receiving few answers. Even some of the historical information that is accepted as 'true teachings' today has not been fully verified – simply accepted. Since the 1980s there have been many beliefs as to what the correct teachings are, or are not. The Radiance Technique® asserts it teaches Hawayo Takata's original system (though Barbara Weber's book *The Reiki Factor* appears to be largely influenced by the New Age movement). In a similar fashion, The Reiki Alliance (which teaches *Usui Shiki Ryôhô*) is said to have quietly standardized Hawayo Takata's teachings to create a system that was acceptable to many of her teacher students after her death.[3]

Levels

Many different names exist for the levels that one will go through to receive the highest teachings available in that branch. There are generally three levels. They might be called facets or degrees or carry Japanese names such as *shoden, okuden* or *shinpiden.*

All three levels have had information, mantras and symbols added to and taken away from them at some time. They have been broken up to create more levels (the more levels generated, the more financially lucrative teaching can become) or condensed to help impatient students cram their experiences into a briefer timeslot.

Precepts, Hand Positions and Techniques

Three of the five elements of the system of Reiki – precepts, hand positions and techniques – can be found in the majority of Reiki branches.

The precepts are often taught in a simplified version, and depending upon the version they may or may not relate to the original Japanese Reiki precepts.

Specific hand positions may be taught strictly in some branches, while others teach intuitive methods only.

Techniques, as can be seen in Part V, are enormously varied and

[3] Letter written by Carrel Ann Farmer on 31 December 1997 (She was the fourth Master initiated by Phyllis Lei Furumoto and was present at the first Reiki Masters meeting in 1982).

completely depend upon first the branch and then the individual teachers as to what is taught and how.

Mantras and Symbols

Mantras and symbols are one of the five elements of the system of Reiki. The terms 'traditional' and 'non-traditional' mantras and symbols are used in *The Reiki Sourcebook*. These terms are simply a yardstick as traditionally four mantras and symbols were taught.

As the system of Reiki is passed from one teacher to another there have naturally been alterations made in the drawing of the symbols (especially as Hawayo Takata taught without drawn copies). Many modern teachers have little understanding of the mantras and symbols and their Japanese origins and it is has, therefore, been easy for them to be drawn incorrectly. Once incorrect symbols are taught and passed on to others the flawed cycle continues.

As modern teachings have veered further away from Mikao Usui's teachings, more and more symbols are appearing. A modern view is that the symbols are seen as the 'energy'; therefore if more symbols are used it is believed that the 'energy' will become stronger. In traditional Japanese teachings it is not believed that the symbols are the power – they simply invoke certain energy.

These new symbols might be 'channeled' or taken from existing religions and cultures. As long as there are attempts to make the system of Reiki unnecessarily 'bigger and better' more symbols will continue to be added.

Attunements and Reiju

Attunements or *reiju* are also one of the five main elements of the system of Reiki. Closely linked to the different levels is the number of attunements or *reiju* that are performed. Those branches that have extended their number of levels often base each level around the receiving of the attunement.

Different branches perform an assortment of attunements and these are generally influenced by the origins of the branch. If the system is a 'channeled' form, then the founder may claim to have received, through guides, new information about the attunement process. 'Tibetan' attunements may include 'Tibetan' sounds, 'Tibetan' symbols/mantras, Tibetan deity connections, etc. An Egyptian system of Reiki may include attunements based around an Egyptian god or entity.

A teacher's lack of faith in his or her own ability may mean that parts of the attunement are repeated endlessly in the hope that it will prove more 'powerful'. The length of time that an attunement takes can be from a couple of minutes up to 45 minutes.

Major Influences on Reiki Branches

Through tracing individual influences on the system of Reiki it is possible to gain an idea of what is taught within the wide variety of teachings that exist under the banner of the system of Reiki today.

This section includes some of the major influences on the system of Reiki to date, plus a sprinkling of the branches that have evolved from that.

There are so many branches that it has been impossible to include each of them. New branches of the system of Reiki are also continually being developed.

There are some teachings that, although they may influence the system as it is known today, may not wish to be related to the system of Reiki; this includes the unverified teachings of Chris Marsh. He states that they have nothing to do with the system of Reiki and yet these teachings are claimed to be taught by a student of Mikao Usui known as Suzuki san. Chris Marsh's teachings have been called various names in the past – none named by him personally. The teachings are quite different as they are taught one-on-one only and in an ongoing manner where the student receives gradual teachings.

There are many varied 'original' histories and lots of individual creativity as far as branches of Mikao Usui's teachings are concerned. Inclusion in this section in no way indicates that a branch is legitimate. When reading through the branch information it is likely that the reader will feel confused. Don't lose sight of the fact that Mikao Usui's teachings are Japanese in origin. If the reader becomes overwhelmed by all the intergalactic activity, take a deep breath and head back to Part II: Reiki Past.

It is good to remember that nothing can (as of yet) be proven to be of a 'higher vibration', 'stronger than' or be 'more penetrating' as far as energy is concerned. This is truly subjective, and these statements will only color one's personal experience of the energy.

In spite of extensive checking it is impossible to be 100 percent correct about some of the information contained in the following pages. This is, of course, because of the changeable nature of life, Reiki practices and histories told (and not told). The authors are more than happy to update any information and offer their apologies here for any mistakes that may have slipped through.

Mikao Usui

The founder of the system of Reiki. Reiki teachings include the five basic elements of Mikao Usui's teachings. These elements are

- the five precepts
- hands-on healing for the self and others
- techniques
- four mantras and symbols
- reiju

These five elements are not, however, always taught within Reiki branches and it is then debatable whether a practice that calls itself Reiki but has limited connection with Mikao Usui's teachings should actually utilize this name at all. Since its popularity, the word Reiki has often been used as a draw card to gain attention to a practice, whether it stems from the system of Reiki or not.

Usui Reiki Ryôhô Gakkai

An organization that was developed during the last years of Mikao Usui's life, or after his death, and focused on the hands-on healing element of the system. The original members of the *Usui Reiki Ryôhô Gakkai* were officers in the Japanese Navy and the system of Reiki was utilized to support them and their naval personnel with healing. Their lists of presidents have been Jûzaburô Ushida, Kanichi Taketomi, Yoshiharu Watanabe, Hôichi Wanami, and Kimiko Koyama, with the current president being Masaki Kondô. If there was such a thing as a successor to Mikao Usui within this organization. then this would naturally have beeen the president Jûzaburô Ushida. They teach three major levels with sub-levels of proficiency with *reiju* being performed at each meeting by the *shihan* (teachers). The *Usui Reiki Ryôhô Gakkai* only accepts members by invitation and has no foreigners as members. The focus is very much on self-development through the healing techniques. Meetings are held three times a month in *Tôkyô*. It sees itself as a society rather than a branch of the system of Reiki. The *Usui Reiki Ryôhô Gakkai* teaches *hatsurei hô*, *byôsen reikan hô* and *reiji hô*.

Their teachings have changed over the years as each *shihan* introduces or takes away material, yet they do try to preserve the essence of their teachings. Mikao Usui either started the *Usui Reiki Ryôhô Gakkai* in 1922 or his students created it shortly after his death.

Chûjirô Hayashi

A retired surgeon from the Japanese Navy who was originally a student of Mikao Usui and then a member of the *Usui Reiki Ryôhô Gakkai*. He broke away to begin his own branch of the system of Reiki in 1931. He is known to have focused largely on hands-on healing and, with his staff and students, performed treatments professionally. He is considered to be the 'father' of the modern system of Reiki as it was his student, Hawayo Takata who took his teachings outside of Japan to Hawaii. This modern system is essentially an external practice which should more discernibly be known as 'Hayashi Reiki' rather than 'Usui Reiki'. Another of his students was Chiyoko Yamaguchi, who in the last years of her life at the turn of the 21st century began to teach what she had learnt as a teenager. Many of the Yamaguchi family members were practitioners trained by Chûjirô Hayashi. One of them taught her the attunement so that she could help out at a course that the relative was hosting for Chûjirô Hayashi. She was not taught *shinpiden* fully or formally. Chiyoko Yamaguchi began teaching at the turn of the 21st century when the system of Reiki became globally popular. Chiyoko Yamaguchi taught her son Tadao and Hyakuten Inamoto.

Jikiden Reiki

As taught by Tadao Yamaguchi.

Levels: Four levels. *Shoden* and *okuden* are taught over five days with five attunements in total. Level 3 is the assistant teacher level and lasts from six to 12 months. Level 4 is the teacher level.

Mantras/Symbols: Three slightly different mantras and symbols only. Comments: The lineage initially used for these teachings listed Hayashi as Mrs. Yamaguchi's teacher, but this has changed in recent years to name her uncle as her teacher instead. Chiyoko Yamaguchi passed away in August, 2003. Techniques taught are *distant reiki with one hand on the thighs, *nentatsu hô* and *ketsueki kôkan hô*.

Komyo Reiki Kai

As taught by Hyakuten Inamoto.

Levels: Four levels of *shoden, chuden, okuden* and *shinpiden*.

Mantras/Symbols: Slightly different to traditional mantras and symbols.

Comments: Komyo Reiki was developed by Hyakuten Inamoto and is based upon Chûjirô Hayashi's teachings as taught by Chiyoko Yamaguchi. Komyo Reiki claims to put an emphasis on spiritual personal transformation or *satori* (enlightenment) through Reiki practice.

Hyakuten Inamoto is a Pure Land Buddhist monk. Hyakuten Inamoto translated Mikao Usui's Memorial Stone and the Meiji Emperor's *waka* used in this book.

Hawayo Takata

Taught by Chûjirô Hayashi, Hawayo Takata brought the system of Reiki to Hawaii in the late 1930s. She controlled what was taught in the system until she died in 1980. She said that she simplified the system for the non-Japanese mind yet she appears to have been true to the basic practices of 'Hayashi's Reiki'. She set her own style by introducing a $10,000 US price tag on the Level 3 course and by removing Japanese elements of philosophy and culture. She taught 22 teacher students and called the teachings *Usui Shiki Ryôhô*. A number of branch directions stemmed from these teachings through her students, including Beth Gray, Iris Ishikuro, Phyllis Lei Furumoto, Ethel Lombardi, and Barbara Weber.

Beth Gray

A teacher student of Hawayo Takata who, without joining with any other students of Hawayo Takata, went on to teach the system throughout the USA and Australia.

Usui Shiki Ryôhô
As taught by Beth Gray.
Levels: Three levels where the first two levels are taught in large
  groups. To become a teacher (Level 3) in this lineage one must be
  chosen and study directly with the teacher for a number of years.

Iris Ishikuro

Iris Ishikuro was a student and friend of Hawayo Takata who asked her to train only three teacher students (she trained just two in total). Her student, Arthur Robertson, made many changes to the system of Reiki. These teachings influenced many of the New Age systems of Reiki that came out of the 1980s. By teaching the chakra system and bringing in techniques that are unrelated to Japanese culture and philosophy, the system of Reiki morphed into a New Age practice itself. Iris Ishikuro is thought to have taught Levels 1 and 2 together and reduced the cost of the teachings.[4]

Raku Kei Reiki
As taught by Arthur Robertson.
Levels: Four levels with Level 1 and 2 taught in one class.
Attunements: Three non-traditional attunements plus an 'initia-
  tion'.
Mantras/Symbols: Johrei Symbol.
Comments: This was one of the first branches to break away from
  Usui Shiki Ryôhô teachings and to introduce the myth of a 'Tibetan'

---

[4] Information supplied by Robert Fueston.

history to the system of Reiki. Arthur Robertson first studied with Hawayo Takata's student Virginia Samdahl in 1975. He then went on to study and work with another of Hawayo Takata's students, Iris Ishikuro, in the early 1980s. Iris Ishikuro was a member of the Johrei Fellowship and this would account for the introduction of the Johrei symbol or 'white light symbol' in these teachings. In 1983 a Raku Kei Reiki manual included non-traditional techniques such as the *breath of the fire dragon, the *hui yin* breath and the kanji hand mudras. The *water ceremony and the chakra system were also practiced in Raku Kei Reiki. Master Frequency Plates with an *antakharana inside were used by students of Raku Kei Reiki. [5]

Phyllis Lei Furumoto

In 1983 a number of Reiki teachers taught by Hawayo Takata created an organization called The Reiki Alliance. Phyllis Lei Furumoto, Hawayo Takata's granddaughter, was dubbed by them to be the grandmaster and lineage bearer of *Usui Shiki Ryôhô*.

Usui Shiki Ryôhô
As taught by The Reiki Alliance.
Levels: Three levels or degrees. The first has four attunements, the second has one or two attunements and the third level has one attunement.
Mantras/Symbols: Four traditional mantras and symbols. Three are taught in the second level and one is taught in the third level.
Comments: Some of the techniques taught are *distant Reiki, *de-programming techniques and the *finishing treatment or *nerve stroke.

Ethel Lombardi

This was the first breakaway from what people thought of as the traditional system of Reiki after Hawayo Takata's death (apart from

[5] Information regarding Iris Ishikuro and the teachings of Arthur Robertson supplied by Robert Fueston.

The Radiance Technique®). Ethel Lombardi, a student of Hawayo Takata, created it in 1983 at a time when students of Hawayo Takata were deciding how they would organize the future of the system of Reiki. Ethel Lombardi taught one teacher only.

Mari-EL
As taught by Ethel Lombardi
Levels: One level
Attunements: One attunement
Mantras/Symbols: Three non-traditional symbols were taught in the first level.

Barbara Weber

A student of Hawayo Takata who developed her own system with extra levels and symbols and energetic understandings, integrating the popularity of the New Age movement in the early 1980s. One of her students, Mieko Mitsui, was the first Japanese teacher of the Barbara Weber lineage to teach in Japan. Many of the modern Japanese Reiki teachers, including Hiroshi Doi, have studied the teachings of Barbara Weber.

The Radiance Technique®[6] (or Authentic Reiki®[7])
As taught by Barbara Weber.
Levels: Initially three levels were described in her book, *The Reiki Factor* (1983), but this changed in later editions to seven levels.
Attunements: Level 1 has four non-traditional attunements and level 2 has one non-traditional attunement. The system works like this: From Level 3 a student can teach the levels beneath them. This same system continues through to Level 7 from where the student can teach all levels.
Mantras/Symbols: The traditional symbols are taught plus non-traditional symbols. The names for the traditional symbols are different: they are Cosmic Pattern 1 (Symbol 1), Cosmic Pattern 4

[6] The Radiance Technique® is the registered trademark of The Radiance Technique International Association, Inc. (TRTIA).

[7] Authentic Reiki® is the registered trademark of The Radiance Technique International Association, Inc. (TRTIA).

(Symbol 2), and Cosmic Pattern 22 (Symbol 3). After Level 2, these are replaced with the traditional mantras.

Comments: Hawayo Takata taught Barbara Weber in 1979 as a Reiki teacher. After Hawayo Takata's death in 1980 she claimed to have been the only teacher student to have received the true teachings. The nature of these teachings appears to have changed or developed over a period of time and includes a 'Tibetan' history with New Age leanings. The Radiance Technique® uses the *deprogramming technique.

Japanese Influences

After leaving Japan, the system of Reiki gradually became influenced by popular New Age practices even within modern Japanese Reiki teachings. As a reaction to this development there has been renewed interest in the traditional Japanese aspects of the system of Reiki. Some researchers today have gone back to look at what would have been taught in Japan from the early 1900s.

Usui Reiki Ryôhô
As taught by Frans and Bronwen Stiene.
Levels: Three levels.
Mantras/Symbols: Four traditional symbols/mantras and teaches Reiki *jumon*.
Comments: Frans and Bronwen Stiene, Reiki authors and researchers, teach a simple form of the system of Reiki that focuses on its Japanese elements plus their research into the practices as taught by Mikao Usui. This includes teaching the Japanese energetic method they call The Three Diamonds which works with the *hara*, plus the five foundation elements of the system of Reiki.

Fusion Influences

A number of modern Reiki teachers from Japan have been influenced by the New Age movement and their own cultural background. They have then fused these two elements together to create their own unique systems. These are not traditional Japanese Reiki branches.

Gendai Reiki Hô

As taught by Hiroshi Doi.

Levels: Four levels being *shoden, okuden, shinpiden* and *gokui kaiden*.

Attunements: *Gokui kaiden* has one integrated attunement developed by Hiroshi Doi. *Reiju* is also performed at each level.

Mantras/Symbols: Four traditional Japanese mantras/symbols are taught.

Comments: *Gendai Reiki Hô* blends Japanese and non-Japanese practices. The techniques are claimed to be 'simplified and standardized'. Over two thirds of the techniques are influenced by the New Age movement and include: *chakra kassei kokyû hô, *communicating with your higher self, *deprogramming technique, *reiki box, *making contact with higher beings, *reiki meditation, *reiki shower and *solar image training.

Hiroshi Doi is a member of the *Usui Reiki Ryôhô Gakkai*. He has also trained in a variety of Reiki branches with teachers Mieko Mitsui, Hiroshi Ohta, Manaso and Chiyoko Yamaguchi. He claims that his lineage is an energetic lineage as he received permission from Kimiko Koyama (previous president of the *Usui Reiki Ryôhô Gakkai*) to utilize this lineage for his *Gendai Reiki Hô* teachings although he is not a *shihan* (teacher) of the *Usui Reiki Ryôhô Gakkai*.

Reido Reiki

As taught by Fuminori Aoki.

Levels: Seven levels.

Mantras/Symbols: The four traditional mantras and symbols are taught with one extra symbol called 'Koriki', which is claimed to be the Force of Happiness that brings inner peace.

Comments: *Reido Reiki* means 'to start again or be reborn'. It stresses the importance of both spiritual and emotional aspects of one's being. *Reido Reiki* claims to teach how to clear oneself and discover what is preventing one from happiness and how to attain it. The focus is on self-growth.

Satya Reiki

As taught by Shingo Sakuma.

Levels: Three levels called degrees.

Attunements: Three or four attunements in the first level, three attunements in the second level and one attunement in the third level.

Mantras/Symbols: Three traditional symbols for the second level and one for the third level.

Comments: This lineage comes through Toshiro Eguchi's student Gorô Miyazaki, student of Toshihiro Eguchi. Shingo Sakuma has been teaching in India, where it has been popular, since 1996. Satya Reiki teaches the chakra system from an Indian viewpoint, set hand positions and these non-traditional techniques: *anticlockwise energy spirals, *the morning prayer, *chakra balancing and the *symbol meditations.

Independent Reiki Master/Teachers

This is a generic term used by Reiki teachers who do not belong to a specific branch. The term Reiki Master/Teacher is also a recent term that has been developed as a response to the inappropriateness of the term Reiki Master.

Independent Reiki Master/Teachers are unaligned with a definitive branch and may teach from a number of different lineages. These teachers may or may not show clearly which branches they practice or where their styles of teachings come from.

Usui Reiki or *Usui System of Natural Healing*
As taught by an Independent Reiki teacher.
Comments: The system of Reiki has as its founder Mikao Usui. Therefore the term Usui Reiki is generic. This name does not indicate what the teacher teaches. It may include any of these non-traditional techniques such as: *antakharana, *breath of the fire dragon, *chakra balancing, *crystal healing (crystal grid), *group distant healing, *healing the past and the future, *hui yin breath, *manifesting grid, *open heart exercise, *power sandwich, *reiki aura cleansing, *reiki boost, *reiki box, *reiki guide meditation, *scanning, *symbol meditation, *smudging and *talismans.

'Tibetan' Influences

The Tibetan culture and religion, in contrast to Japan, has been forced to spread itself throughout the world due to its political situation since the Chinese occupation of Tibet in 1959. Tibetan teachings have been warmly embraced and integrated into the modern world. The New Age movement has readily adapted many of its teachings and these 'Tibetan' style teachings have then influenced New Age forms of Reiki including unverified claims that the lineage of the system of Reiki can be traced back to Buddha. There is absolutely no proven historical connection between the two eastern practices. Some of these 'Tibetan' branches include other influences such as Seichim and may also be partially 'channeled'.

Dorje Reiki
As taught by Lawton R. Smith.
Levels: Two levels.
Pre-requisites: Reiki teacher.
Mantras/Symbols: Non-traditional symbols are added as needed.
Attunements: Non-traditional attunements are performed focusing on all chakras.
Comments: Created from a combination of Reiki branches, it also has elements of 'Tibetan' tantric Buddhism and shamanism.

Jinlap Maitri Reiki
As taught by Gary Jirauch.
Levels: Five levels.
Pre-requisite: Karuna® Reiki Master.
Attunements: Non-traditional attunements based on Medicine Buddha initiations.
Mantras/Symbols: 25 non-traditional symbols.

Men Chhos Reiki (or Medicine Dharma Reiki or Universal Healing Reiki)
The claims to authenticity by the founder of this lineage, Richard Blackwell aka Lama Yeshe, are controversial.

Reiki previously called Usui/Tibetan Reiki
As taught by William Lee Rand.
Levels: Four levels. Levels 1 and 2 are taught in one class. ART or (Advanced Reiki Training) is the third level and the Usui/Tibetan Master/Teacher Level is the fourth.

Attunements: Four attunements in total with a non-traditional Usui/Tibetan Reiki Master attunement.

Mantras/Symbols: Four traditional symbols and two non-traditional 'Tibetan' initiatory symbols. One of these is a non-traditional symbol called Dumo.

Comments: Non-traditional techniques are *Reiki meditation; psychic surgery; healing attunement; distance and self-attunement; *violet breath; *manifesting; four variations of the *antakharana symbol with description and usage plus some traditional techniques. Usui/Tibetan Reiki is a mix of Raku Kei Reiki, *Usui Shiki Ryôhô* and traditional techniques. These specific courses are no longer called Usui/Tibetan, they are now called Reiki I, II, ART and IIIM/T. Offshoots can be found under branches entitled Tibetan Reiki, Tibetan/Usui Reiki and Usui/Tibetan Reiki.

Reiki Jin Kei Do

As taught by Ranga Premaratna.

Levels: Three levels followed up by four levels of a practice called Buddho-EnerSense.

Mantras/Symbols: Traditional Reiki symbols are used except that Symbol 2 is altered.

Comments: Reiki Jin Kei Do claims an alternate unverified history to the system of Reiki through an Indian and Tibetan Buddhist background.

Reiki Tummo

As taught by Irmansyah Effendi.

Levels: Three levels.

Comments: Reiki Tummo makes many claims including having been taught by Buddha himself as the way to achieve enlightenment within one lifetime.

Sacred Path Reiki

As taught by John and Paula Steele.

Comments: According to Sacred Path Reiki it is a mixture of Raku Kei Reiki, 'Tibetan' Reiki and more.

Saku Reiki
As taught by Eric Bott.
Levels: Six levels in total.
Mantras/Symbols: Traditional and non-traditional symbols are
    taught. The non-traditional 'Tibetan' Saku master symbols are
    taught in Level 6.

Other International Cultural Influences

The system of Reiki has also been integrated into teachings from
specific cultures and religions (apart from the major 'Tibetan' influence). Some of these branches may have other influences such as
Seichim and 'Tibetan' teachings or are partially 'channeled'.

Alef Reiki
As taught by Eli Machani.
Mantras/Symbols: No symbols.
Comments: This appears to be a mixture of Hebrew and Reiki teach-
    ings.

Celtic Reiki
As taught by Martyn Pentecost.
Levels: One.
Mantras/Symbols: Includes 38 Celtic essences and symbols.
Attunements: Four attunements.

Johrei Reiki or Jo Reiki
Levels: One level that covers Level 1 to 3 in two days.
Mantras/Symbols: Four non-traditional symbols.
Comments: Johrei Reiki is a combination of Raku Kei Reiki and the
    religion of Johrei. The Johrei Fellowship does not recognize it
    as part of their teachings and have since trademarked the name
    Johrei so that any unauthorized usage is forbidden. Johrei Reiki is
    no longer practiced under this name. Vajra Reiki is an adaptation
    of Johrei Reiki.

Vajra Reiki
As taught by Wade Ryan.

Levels: Three levels.

Mantras/Symbols: Four symbols and one Om-Ah-Hum Mantra all influenced by Raku Kei Reiki and Johrei.

Seichim Influences

According to its founder, Patrick Zeigler, Seichim is one of the earlier systems adopted into the Reiki community. In 1980 he travelled to Egypt and claims he spent the night in the Great Pyramid and received a powerful initiation. In New Mexico he took his first Reiki class. He asserts that from that experience, with the help of a 'channeled' Master named Marat, the first Seichim attunement was created. Since that introduction in 1984, many New Age-styled Reiki teachers have developed teachings that include both elements of Seichim and the system of Reiki. Seichim had no set price and also no set standards. This meant that it flourished easily but in many different directions. Phoenix Summerfield was the primary teacher who promoted Seichim worldwide and it was through her that many of the structures were added as well. Seichim has had many different spellings including Seichem, Sekhem and Sachem. Patrick Zeigler went on to introduce SKHM and that has since evolved into All-Love.

Some of the branches which link to Seichim are included in this section but may also be found under the Virtual Branches and the 'Channeled' and 'Tibetan' Influences sections.

Newlife Reiki Seichim
As taught by Margot Deepa Slater.
Levels: Seven levels.
Attunements: Non-traditional attunements.
Mantras/Symbols: 36 non-traditional symbols drawn from Tibetan, Chinese, Japanese and Egyptian origins. Approximately 12 non-traditional mantras are also taught.

Seichim
As taught by students of Patrick Zeigler.
Levels: Five levels called facets.
Attunements: Level 1; two attunements in Level 2; one attunement

in Level 3; one attunement in Level 4 plus separate attunements for animals and inanimate objects; one attunement in Level 5 and a personal empowerment attunement.

Mantras/Symbols: Three traditional symbols and several variations on Symbol 4. Additional symbols are added in the fourth and fifth level. Some of the symbols used under variations of Seichim are: Chokuret; Blue DKM; Pink DKM; Mai Yur Ma/Shining Everlasting Flower of Enlightenment (three versions); Tan Ku Rei; Ta Ku Rei; Shining Everlasting Living Waters of Ra; Shining Everlasting Living Facets of Eternal Compassionate Wisdom; Divine Balance; Eternal Pearl of Wisdom and Love/Blue Pearl of Wisdom; Healing Triangle; Symbol of Divinity; Heart of the Christos; Heart of Gaia; Align with God; Eeftchay; Angel Wings; Merge Consciousness; as well as the Infinity symbol.

Comments: Some of the techniques which have been taught under this name are the *power sandwich, *de-programming technique and *breath of the fire dragon or *violet breath, *distant healing and mental/emotional balancing.

As there were no manuals and no standards set for Seichim, the levels, mantras and symbols, attunements and techniques will not be consistent under this heading.

Helen Belot Sekhem®[8]
As taught by Helen Belot.
Comments: Helen Belot claims to be the re-introducer and custodian of this ancient Egyptian Energy System of Sekhem.

All-Love (evolved from SKHM)
As taught by Patrick Zeigler.

'Channeled' Influences

Within the New Age movement there has been a steadily growing popularity of the practice of 'channeling'. 'Channeling' is where one connects with a being or spirit that is not in a physical form.

This practice is unrelated to the traditional practice of the system

---

[8] Helen Belot Sekhem® is the registered trademark of Helen Belot.

of Reiki. Some modern practitioners allege to have received 'new' information such as different mantras and symbols from 'channeled' spirits (including that of Mikao Usui himself). Unfortunately this information cannot be verified as 'channeling' is a subjective practice.

'Channeled' information generally does not utilize a lineage dating back to Mikao Usui. This is due to Reiki teachers preferring to use their guides as the higher authority, dismissing their lineage as unimportant. In most cases though, the teacher was a Reiki teacher before the 'channeling' took place and it is the system of Reiki that forms the foundation for the branch's existence.

The question that many have asked is: Should systems that have altered the teachings in such a personal way still be acknowledged as the system of Reiki? The word Reiki is often tagged on to the end of a new practice, providing it with more marketing possibilities (this comment does not apply to 'channeled' material only).

The following are some of the wide variety of new-styled branches that include 'channeled' material. Their influences may also come from other aspects of the New Age movement.

Angelic RayKey
As taught by Sananda.
Levels: Three levels with approximately three days teaching for each level.
Mantras/Symbols: Traditional symbols/mantras plus non-traditional symbols as needed.
Comments: Angelic RayKey claims to be 'channeled' from the Archangel St. Michael.

Blue Star Reiki
As taught by Gary Jirauch.
Pre-requisite: Reiki teacher and Karuna® Reiki Master.
Comments: Originated from a 'channeled' system by John Williams called Blue Star Celestial Energy.

Brahma Satya Reiki
As taught by Deepak Hardikar.
Levels: Three levels plus extra levels.

Mantras/Symbols: Non-traditional symbols are 'channeled' as needed.

Karuna Reiki®[9]
As taught by William Lee Rand.
Attunements: Two attunements.
Pre-requisite: Reiki teacher.
Mantras/Symbols: 12 non-traditional symbols. Various Reiki practitioners, not including William Lee Rand, 'channeled' the symbols.
Comments: The *violet breath, *chanting and *toning, *scanning and *Reiki meditation are all taught in Karuna Reiki®. In the early 1990s William Lee Rand developed Sai Baba Reiki, which was influenced by *Usui Shiki Ryôhô* and Tera Mai™ Reiki.

Karuna Ki
As taught by Vincent P. Amador.
Levels: Three levels or just one teacher level (with one non-traditional attunement).
Pre-requisite: Reiki teacher.
Mantras/Symbols: Non-traditional symbols are used. These are the same as those used in Karuna Reiki® but with different purposes.
The development of Karuna Ki is said to initially have been a reaction to the trademarking of Karuna Reiki®. Techniques used are *violet breath, *chanting and *toning, *scanning and special *karuna ki do meditations.

Rainbow Reiki
As taught by Walter Lubeck.
Levels: Three levels.
Attunements: Level 1 has four attunements and one Rainbow Reiki initiation. Level 2 has three attunements. Level 3 has one attunement.
Mantras/Symbols: One symbol is used in Level 1 plus three Rainbow

---

[9] Karuna Reiki® is a registered trademark of the International Center for Reiki Training.

Reiki mantras. Three traditional symbols are used in Level 2 and one traditional symbol in Level 3.

Comments: Rainbow Reiki appears to be a mixture of New Age practices including *Reiki guide meditations, shamanism, feng shui, meditation, spiritual psychology/ psychotherapy, karma clearing, astral traveling, *crystal healing, inner child techniques, NLP, aura/chakra reading and channeling. Some traditional Reiki techniques are also included.

Reiki Plus

As taught by David Jarrell.

Levels: Four practitioner levels plus teacher level.

Comments: The founder claimed that his true initiation was through the spirit of a Tibetan Master.

Shamballa Multi-Dimensional Healing/Reiki

As taught by John Armitage.

Levels: Three levels.

Mantras/Symbol: 352 symbols one for each level between here and the Source.

Comments: 'Channeled' teachings relating to St. Germain. The techniques taught include *crystals; the *antakharana; *how to connect people to their higher selves; meet one's *Reiki guides, and the Ascended and Galactic Masters.

Tera Mai™¹⁰ Reiki and Tera Mai™ Seichem

As taught by Kathleen Ann Milner.

Levels: Tera Mai™ Reiki I, II and Mastership and Tera Mai™ Seichem I, II and Mastership.

Attunements: Non-traditional Egyptian attunements. The YOD initiation performed is said to connect the student with the energies of the Ark of the Covenant. Tera Mai™ Seichem has two more symbols than Tera Mai™ Reiki.

Mantras/Symbols: Some of the 'channeled' symbols are Harth, Zonar, two Double CKRs, Halu, Iava, Shanti, Sati.

Comments: The Tera Mai™ Reiki system is followed up by the

[10] Tera Mai® is the registered trademark of Kathleen Ann Milner.

Tera Mai™ Seichem system. It teaches *breath of the fire dragon technique, *deprogramming techniques, the *Reiki boost and the *water ceremony amongst other techniques.

Wei Chi Tibetan Reiki
As taught by Thomas A. Hensel and Kevin Rodd Emery.
Levels: Three practitioner levels and three teacher levels.
Branch claims: 'Channeled' teachings of Wei Chi from Tibet 5000 years ago. Wei Chi has said, via 'channeling', that he and his brothers had created the original system that is the basis of the system of Reiki today. He claims that when the system was 'rediscovered' in the 19th century, only a small portion of the original was actually found as much had been lost through the centuries.

Virtual Influences

With the increased reliance on the Internet as a teaching tool, it seems only natural that Reiki courses have become available through this avenue. Unfortunately, as the system of Reiki is an energetic practice, studying via online courses is not a viable option if one wishes to learn the system of Reiki in its entirety. Some distant learning 'opportunities' that are offered include courses that start at US$1.99 and include names like: Archangelic Reiki, Attraction Reiki, Celestial Reiki, Crystal Reiki, Dolphin Reiki, Dragon Reiki, Fairy Realms Reiki, Feiki Reiki, Gold Reiki, Money Reiki and much, much more.

Not only is the Internet an inappropriate place to study an energetic system such as Reiki, there is also a quality issue in much of the currently available material. The US$1.99 online course, for example, includes this comment from the seller 'I will be very limited as to how much I can answer your questions' – well, what would one expect at that price?

11   Scientific Studies on Reiki

Mikao Usui is quoted saying in the *Reiki Ryôhô Hikkei* that the mind and body are one. Recent studies in the world of science are beginning to finally comprehend that statement. Brainwaves and body pulses and their roles in stimulating healing are all being researched today, allowing the concept of Reiki, as spiritual energy, to be more widely understood by the medical community.

> The energy fields projected from the hands of bodyworkers are in the range of intensity and frequency that can influence regulatory processes within the body of another person.
>
> (Excerpt from *Energy Medicine-The Scientific Basis* by James L. Oschman)

The challenge, however, has been to find technology that can measure accurately what this energy is. An answer to this is not to measure the Reiki itself but its resulting benefits.

> The National Center for CAM in the USA believe a new direction for research into biofield therapies is by measuring the wellbeing of the client. 'The advantage of focusing our research on positive psychological states, such as positive meaning, is that people can be trained to increase these states, and the subsequent effects on wellbeing and health can be directly measured.'
>
> (Excerpt from *Your Reiki Treatment* by Bronwen and Frans Stiene)

An example of this type of research has been undertaken by the Brownes Cancer Support Centre in Western Australia. Their 2004 Patient Care Report concluded that there was an overall improvement in both quality of life and symptom distress scores for patients who received Reiki. There was also an improvement in these areas over the course of the Reiki sessions from treatment 1 to 6.

A report[11] in 2003 of a randomized trial using healing touch with cancer patients showed that a relaxed state was induced, with lowered respiratory and heart rates and lower blood pressure. The therapies also reduced short-term pain, mood disturbances and fatigue.

Historically, the introduction of 'Therapeutic Touch' by Dolores Krieger into nursing in the 1970s increased interest in other energetic systems such as Reiki. This in turn has boosted the amount of research that has recently been undertaken using Reiki and other forms of energetic work.

The system of Reiki is also being accepted into hospitals and hospices across the world. Patients can often bring their Reiki practitioner with them, or Reiki is made available to them.

The article 'The first Reiki Practitioner in our O.R.' by Jeanette Sawyer in 1988 in the *AORN Journal* describes the steps that were taken to allow a Reiki practitioner into the theatre at the request of a patient during a laparoscopy.

Also in 1988, patients were given the opportunity to experience a 15-minute pre-and post-surgery Reiki treatment. More than 870 patients took part and as a result there was less use of pain medication, shorter stays in hospital and increased patient satisfaction. This was discussed in the article, 'Using Reiki to Support Surgical patients' by Patricia and Kristin Aladydy in the Journal of Nursing Care Quality.

Heart surgeon Dr. Mehmet Oz, whose wife, Lisa, is a pro-active Reiki practitioner, has worked with Julie Motz, who used Reiki on his patients. These patients had received heart transplants and had experienced open-heart surgery. Motz treated 11 patients in total and none of them had the usual post-operative depression. The bypass patients had no post-operative pain or leg weakness and the trans-

[11] 'Diagnosis Cancer: The Science & Controversy Behind Touch Therapies Patients claim benefit, but some doctors question evidence.' by Jennifer M. Gangloff. *Cure.* Spring Issue 2005.

plant patients experienced no organ rejection. Motz has written about this experience in her book, *Hands of Life*.

Listed below are a number of Reiki clinical trials. For more research details, there are some Reiki books with relevant research material, or personal observations, written by both doctors and nurses. *Spiritual Healing,* by Daniel J. Benor, has listed a number of Reiki trials as well as some very interesting trials on distant healing and healing through touch in general.

There are many aspects of Reiki being researched today, some to see if Reiki speeds up healing; others to see if, how and whom it relaxes, some to measure biomagnetic fields, and others to verify the concept of distant healing.

Unfortunately, in the race to prove the efficacy of bioenergetics some recent researchers have disconnected themselves from their Reiki roots and its precepts. Using animals for research in the medical world is common, but it is unacceptable that research be undertaken on animals to 'prove' if Reiki works or not. The foundation of the system of Reiki focuses on compassion and Oneness and hurting anyone or anything goes against these basic principles. It is better to not have these scientific facts if the only way that humanity can measure energy's effectiveness is through animal research.

Here is a well-known trial completed using Reiki to examine its effect on human blood levels:

Human Hemoglobin Levels and Reiki Healing: a Physiologic Perspective

Wendy Wetzel.
Published in *Journal of Holistic Nursing,* 7 (1), pp. 47–54 (1989).
Purpose: The purpose of this study is to examine the effects of Reiki on human hemoglobin and hematocrit levels.
Procedure: The hemoglobin and hematocrit levels of 48 adults participating in a Level 1 course were measured. Demographics and motivation were also examined. An untreated control group was used to document the changes in hemoglobin and hematocrit under normal circumstances.
Findings: Using a t-test there was a statistically significant change

between the pre-and post-course hemoglobin and hematocrit levels of the participants at the p > 0.01 level. 28 per cent experiencing an increase and the remainder experiencing a decrease. There was no change for the untreated control group within an identical time frame.

Conclusions: That Reiki has a measurable physiologic effect. The data supports the premise that energy can be transferred between individuals for the purposes of healing, balancing, and increasing wellness. Some individuals found that their blood levels went up while others went down which is consistent with the concept that Reiki is balancing for each individual.

This trial tests Reiki on patients with chronic illnesses using electro-dermal screening:

The Efficacy of Reiki Hands on Healing: Improvements in Adrenal, Spleen and Nervous Function as Quantified by Electro-Dermal Screening

Betty Hartwell and Barbara Brewitt.
Published in *Alternative Therapies Magazine*, 3 (4), p. 89 (July 1997)

Purpose: The purpose of this study is to evaluate the therapeutic effects of Reiki treatments on chronic illnesses using electrodermal screening.

Procedure: This study was carried out on five patients with life-threatening and chronic illnesses: lupus, fibromyalgia, thyroid goiter, and multiple sclerosis. Eleven one-hour Reiki treatments using 4 different Level 2 practitioners and one Reiki Master were performed over a ten-week period. These Reiki practitioners systematically placed their hands over the same body positions including the neurovascular regions on the cranium, neurolymphatic points on the trunk and minor chakra points on the limbs. No new conventional or alternative medical treatments were given during this period. Initially, three consecutive treatments were given and then one treatment per week for eight weeks.

Findings: The patients were tested three times during the study.
1. Before the study commenced. 2. After their third treatment.
3. After their tenth treatment. Each individual was measured

for skin electrical resistance at three acupuncture points on hands and feet. At the cervical/thoracic point the measurements went from 25 per cent below normal to the normal range. The adrenal measurements went from 8.3 per cent below normal to normal – some time between the middle and last measurements. The spleen measurements went from 7.8 per cent below normal to normal after only three sessions. All the patients reported increased relaxation after Reiki treatments, a reduction in pain and an increase in mobility.

These trials are concerned with the effect of Reiki on pain relief and other symptoms:

Pain, Anxiety and Depression in Chronically Ill Patients with Reiki Healing

Linda J. Dressen and Sangeeta Singg.
Published in *Subtle Energies and Energy Medicine Journal*, 9 (1) (1998).
Purpose: To measure the results of Reiki and its effect on pain, anxiety, and depression in chronically ill patients.
Procedure: 120 Patients who had been in pain for at least 1 year were trialed. Their complaints included: headaches, heart disease, cancer, arthritis, peptic ulcer, asthma, hypertension and HIV. Four different styles of treatment were performed on 3 groups of 20 people. The four styles of treatment were: Reiki, Progressive Muscle Relaxation, no treatment and false-Reiki. Each of the groups received ten 30-minute treatments, twice a week over five weeks. Patients were examined before and after the series of treatments. Reiki patients were examined three months after completion.
Findings: Reiki proved significantly superior ($p<.0001$–$.04$) to other treatments on ten out of 12 variables. At the three-month check-up these changes were consistent and there were highly significant reductions in Total Pain Rating Index ($p<.0006$) and in sensory ($p<.0003$) and Affective ($p<.02$) Qualities of Pain.
Conclusion: Significant effects of Reiki on anxiety, pain and depression are shown here. Some possible variables were not controlled.

Using Reiki to Manage Pain: a Preliminary Report

alta.karino@cancerboard.ab.ca Cross Cancer Institute, Edmonton, USA.

Published in *Cancer Prev. Control,* 1 (2) pp. 108–13 (1997).

Purpose: To explore the usefulness of Reiki as an alternative to opioid therapy in the management of pain. This was a pilot study.

Procedure: 20 volunteers experienced pain at 55 sites for a variety of reasons, including cancer. A Level 2 practitioner provided all Reiki treatments. Pain was measured using both a visual analogue scale (VAS) and a Likert scale immediately before and after each Reiki treatment.

Findings: Both the instruments showed a highly significant ($p < 0.0001$) reduction in pain following the Reiki treatments.

This trial was to determine if it is possible to gauge the experience of a Reiki treatment using normal trialing procedures:

Experience of a Reiki Session

J. Engebretson and D. W. Wardell. University of Texas Health Science Center in Houston, USA Published in *Alternative Therapies in Health and Medicine,* 8 pp. 48–53 (2002).

Purpose: To explore the experiences of Reiki recipients so as to contribute to understanding the popularity of touch therapies and possibly clarify variables for future studies.

Procedure: All Reiki treatments were 30 minutes long and performed in a sound proof windowless room by one Reiki Master. There were audio taped interviews immediately after the treatment in a quiet room adjoining the treatment room. The recipients were generally healthy volunteers who had not experienced Reiki previously.

Findings: The recipients described a conscious state of awareness during the treatment. At the same time, paradoxically, they experienced sensate and symbolic phenomena.

Conclusions: Conscious awareness and paradoxical experiences that occur in ritual healing vary according to the holistic nature and individual variation of the healing experience. These findings suggest that many linear models used in researching touch therapies are not complex enough to capture the experience of the recipients.

This particular trial is not specifically about Reiki but deals with the effectiveness of *distant healing which is relevant to Reiki practitioners:

A Randomized Double-Blind Study of the Effect of Distant Healing in a Population with Advanced AIDS

Fred Sicher, Elizabeth Targ, Dan Moore II and Helene S. Smith.
Published in the *Western Journal of Medicine*, 169, pp. 356–363 (December 1998).
Purpose: To find the effect of distance healing (DH) on AIDS patients during a six-month double-blind study.
Procedure: Forty patients with advanced AIDS were randomly divided into two groups. Half the patients received DH in addition to their usual medical care. They were not told they were being given DH. Forty healers from various locations throughout the US with an average of 17 years of experience were used. The healers practiced a variety of healing methods including Christian, Jewish, Buddhist, Native American, shamanism, meditative, and bioenergetics. Each of the treated subjects received DH for one hour a day for six days from each of a total of ten different healers, and this was performed over a period of ten weeks.
Findings: After six months, treated patients had significantly fewer outpatient visits and hospitalizations, less severe illnesses, fewer new illnesses, and improved mood.

Other research and articles relating to Reiki research include:

Alternative Medicines Gain in Popularity, Merit Closer Scrutiny.
Journal of the National Cancer Institute
1999, July. Vol. 91, No. 13. pp. 1104–1105.
Katherine Arnold

Autonomic nervous system changes during Reiki treatment: a preliminary study.
Journal of Alternative and Complementary Medicine
2004, December. Vol. 10. No. 6: 1077–1081.
N. Mackay, S. Hansen, O. McFarlane

Diagnosis Cancer: The Science & Controversy Behind Touch Therapies Patients claim benefit, but some doctors question evidence.
Cure
Spring Issue 2005.
Jennifer M. Gangloff

Effect of Reiki Treatments on Functional Recovery in Patients in Poststroke Rehabilitation: a Pilot Study.
Journal of Alternative and Complementary Medicine
2002 December
S.C. Shiflett, S. Nayak, C. Bid, P. Miles, S. Agostinelli

Evaluation of Healing by Gentle Touch in 35 Patients with Cancer.
European Journal of Oncology Nursing
2004, 8, 40-49.
C. Weze, H.L. Leathard, J. Grange, P. Tiplady, & G. Stevens

In Vitro Effect of Reiki Treatment on Bacterial Cultures: Role of Experimental Context and Practitioner WellBeing.
Journal of Alternative and Complementary Medicine
2006, January. Vol. 12. No. 1: 7–13.
Beverly Rubik, Ph.D., Audrey J. Brooks, Ph.D., Gary E. Schwartz, Ph.D.

Long-term Effects of Energetic Healing on Symptoms of Psychological Depression and Self-perceived Stress.
Alternative Therapies Health and Medicine
2004, Vol. 10. Issue 3, Pages 42–48.
A. G. Shore

The Use of Reiki in Psychotherapy.
Perspectives in Psychiatric Care
2005, October. 41 (4). 184–187.
Mary Ann LaTorre

Part IV

Reiki Future

Looking to the future, there is more knowledge and education in the Reiki community than ever before. This allows for Reiki practitioners to be informed about what they choose to align themselves with, within the diversity that is the system of Reiki in the 21st century.

New questions arise with each new generation of Reiki practitioners. In the last decade the questions were largely of an historical nature as practitioners attempted to find their feet and piece together more precise information about their practice. Due to the greater amount of educative material available it has been possible to move through to a new phase in the system of Reiki.

Within this phase new questions abound. They have a change of focus and come from a more centered, educated and aware background. Relevant issues for practitioners today relate to professionalism, representation, community, and standards. How practitoners view themselves as Reiki practitioners and world citizens with a voice and a choice is upmost in many minds. At the same time the age old questions, which sit uncomfortably at the base of every individual on the planet, continue to prod for an answer to the meaning of it all. This search for a meaningful and ongoing spiritual practice awaits the exploration of every modern Reiki practitioner.

What, for example, will happen to The Reiki Alliance and its lineage bearer, Phyllis Lei Furumoto? With fewer and fewer people willing to pay $10,000 to become Reiki teachers (there are many other options today), will it continue to exist? In 2006 Phyllis Lei Furumoto, in an article entitled 'What Does a Grandmaster Do?'[12], wrote that it was time to put attention to the development of a 'common form for the preparation and initiation of masters' and that a protocol 'for the recognition and support of the next Grandmaster' needed to be created. At this time the largest Reiki associations around the world are not affiliated with The Reiki Alliance or their grandmaster. The Reiki Alliance is a small minority within a very large and diverse global community. *The Reiki Sourcebook* asks: Is the Reiki community interested in actually having a grandmaster? There is little more that can be said on

---

[12] *Reiki Magazine International* February/March 2006. In 2007 the *Reiki Magazine International*, a publication focusing mainly on interviews with The Reiki Alliance members, was unable to continue publication due to 'Mainly the decreasing numbers of subscriptions'.

this matter: the Reiki community must find its own way and its own truth.

Looking at the bigger picture, what can Reiki practitioners do to support the planet in its hour of need?

Humans are fouling their own nests, tramping blindly forward to the beat of a globalizing world. Humanity has forgotten what it means to come from a space of balance, a connected place that moves forward from the Heart. *The Reiki Sourcebook* asks: What can Reiki practitioners do to support the planet?

What will happen to the myriad of New Age Reiki practices (such as 'Tibetan' and 'channeled' Reiki teachings) that have sprung up in the last 25 years?

When the recent New Age movement was at its height, many healing and meditation techniques developed. The majority of the techniques have fallen by the wayside as they lacked a solid foundation and path for the practitioners to follow. That is why traditional practices such as *Tai Chi, Qi Gong,* yoga and other traditional practices still exist thousands of years later; their foundation grew from a solid and well-tested base.

The Reiki Sourcebook asks: Will the system of Reiki fall down the same hole of no return that many flakey practices have disappeared into? Or will it stand the test of time and practice to be a support to humanity and a path for its practitioners to follow and grow with?

12   Reiki and Global Warming

The Intergovernmental Panel on Climate Change (IPCC) has projected that within the next 100 years there will be a global warming of 11.5 °F (6.4 °C) due largely to greenhouse gas emissions. Meaning that the glaciers will melt, the sea levels rise and that there will be an increase in extreme weather events. Change in the climate will affect not only quality of human life, but also that of the flora and fauna with species' extinctions and a change in agricultural yield.

Governments worldwide are discussing how to reduce and counteract this effect. Global warming is a hot political issue. People talk of reducing carbon emissions and how, as individuals, people need to be more conscious of the cars they buy, the light bulbs they use, the fuel they burn, the appliances they buy and so on.

Finally, it seems humanity is catching on that this lifestyle of have and have more is creating an unbalanced world where one may no longer be able to exist (let alone co-exist) with the environment. What a pity that such drastic changes, on such a massive scale, must first occur before humanity opens its ears, minds and selves to nature's voice.

Where does the Reiki practitioner fit into this picture of a greedy world, ravaging its natural resources and fouling its bed? Is there a Reiki solution?

The first thing many Reiki practitioners might think of as a solution is to 'send' distance healing to the planet using the techniques they studied in Level 2. Certainly a concerted energetic effort at supporting the natural flow of the Earth's energy can be beneficial.

There are a number of Reiki groups actively working with dedication at such projects. But what more can be done? Is there another Reiki solution?

Practitioners find that by delving deeper into their own existence, using the five elements of the system of Reiki, new understandings occur. These include a full-bodied sense of connection with the natural elements. As this develops, the science classes from one's youth take on a more meaningful and experiential turn; one that is actually lived rather than read of.

By working on oneself then, could it be possible that one can positively affect global warming?

There grows from inner work a natural sense that, yes, without trees humanity is bereft of oxygen. There is a sense that when one walks in the forest, trees are one's natural companions. Without rain, one can also sense that the world is thirsty and that the opportunity for growth becomes stunted. The links within the cycle of existence are as intuitively apparent as the links that one follows through a daily routine.

Such daily cycles also take on a more complete picture when the inner work strengthens.

One begins to understand reciprocity. Everything that is created comes from somewhere else. Nothing is created out of nothing. Life is a constant flux of influences and it is from them that one draws to create. A flower grows through tender loving care. And then beauty, knowledge and wisdom are given back. The joy felt is shared.

With inner growth, there comes an awareness of an innate responsibility toward that which is created. Where was it created and from what? What was taken from the Earth to make this product? And when it is finished with – what will be returned to the Earth and in what form? A plastic container, a wrapper, foam, a used diaper?

In this current state of greed there is the constant attitude of buy and throw away. In taking, the Earth is stressed. In returning damaged products to the Earth, the environment is not nourished – instead a knife is stuck into its core.

A person who is in touch with the natural elements begins to realize that there is no need to take, take, take. Materialism does not create happiness. The more a practitioner works on him or herself, the stronger the realization that life is in how one lives it, rather than what one can take from it. Living in sync with nature, one no longer stresses the Earth; one learns and listens from its wisdom.

Tales are told of yogis living deep in the wilderness, in damp caves, or on top of mountains surviving extreme climates. And they do survive. Is this accomplished by destroying the environment? No, the yogis look within and develop an ability to co-exist with their natural surroundings. In the depths of winter an inner heat is created that gives them strength and warmth and impacts the outside world imperceptibly.

Such effective techniques are common in spiritual practices from Japan, China, Tibet and other countries. In Japan, for example, a monk or nun practices *misogi* (purification) by standing under ice-cold waterfalls, preferably in winter. Being able to withstand such extreme temperatures toughens the mind and body, supporting the development of a flexible form.

These stories are not just tales, but true practices and can be performed by any individual – with practice. In fact, Genshin Fujinami Ajari, the current head Tendai Buddhist 'marathon monk', states 'Human beings are not special, there are no special things.' That statement is made from a place of Oneness and expresses the understanding that anyone who works on him or her self can achieve anything. Reiki practitioners are given these very tools of self-practice.

In Levels 2 and 3 Reiki practitioners work strongly with this concept of Oneness. Becoming One with the environment, after much practice, means the possibility of regulating one's body temperature – perhaps not something that many practitioners think about. It is not impossible; it is merely the result of submersion in a practice. If, for example, Reiki practitioners could evolve their personal practice to the point that their bodies could deal with more extreme temperatures, that might mean less need for wood for a fireplace, or less electricity for a heater. The domino effect from this would be less stress on the forests and the Earth. Perhaps that would reflect on materials required to be manufactured for clothing, less strain on fields and consequently less spraying of poisonous chemicals to create bumper crops.

It is a thought.

And when one knows deep within one's being that everything is interlinked, one's consequent actions may begin to make a dent in this cycle of greed.

With the clarity of mind that comes with self-practice, a world of friendship between all natural forces opens to be explored and lived in.

All that is required to achieve this comes first from within.

Is it a pipe dream – or is it the practice of a serious-minded practitioner who rejects the lifestyle of a world that refuses to sustain itself viably? Can Reiki practitioners work through their practice to help positively affect global warming?

13 Reiki Dô

In Japanese the word for 'path' is *dô*.

Dô, itself, has many meanings that are similar to path; like 'way' and 'passage'. In Japanese Buddhist terms, *dô* is the path leading toward enlightenment, the absolute or unhindered path.

Many Japanese arts and ways use the word *dô* to indicate a specific path or way. These include *jûdô, chadô, shodô, budô* and *aikidô*. In relation to these practices the translation of *dô* is said to mean 'the way of harmony with your spirit' or 'the way of unifying life energy'.

A common thread between these *dô* or paths is that they all utilize The Three Diamonds: the energetic understanding of Heaven (*ten*), Earth (*chi*) and humanity (*jin*).

The origins of the word *dô* can be traced back to the Chinese word *Dao*. In Chinese *kanji* this character is depicted as a sage with unbound hair walking the path. Its literal translation is 'the way that one comes to see and understand oneself in relationship with the universe'. Could this be the meaning behind the mystery teachings, *shinpiden*, that Mikao Usui taught – the practitioner unlocking the mysteries of the universe?

The old Daoist masters believed that it is through the mind that the *Dao* manifests itself. The path to realizing this manifestation is the integration of Heaven and Earth so that the Daoist practitioners (humankind) can become One with the divine or *Dao*.

In English the word 'path' may relate to a method, plan, or means for attaining a goal. This is similar to the way of *aikidô* or the old teachings of the Daoist masters and for that matter the system of Reiki as Mikao Usui taught it.

Lose your way
And you will
Enter a bad path;
Do not give rein to the
Wild stallion of your heart.

From ancient times,
Deep learning and martial valor
Have been the two wheels of the Path;
Through the virtue of practice
Enlighten both body and soul.

(Excerpt from *The Philosophy of Aikidô* by John Stevens)

Before a student takes the first step on the path, the student needs to have a clear understanding as to where this path is heading. Is its aim to enjoy a short course, or is it an actual path to walk?

In Mikao Usui's time, it was of great import that the teacher was available to guide the student on the right path. Naturally the teacher was required to know this path him or herself prior to sending a student off along it. Without clear guidance the student might become lost or stray from the correct path. It is not unlike the student requiring an experienced mountaineering guide for the trek up a treacherous mountainside. The responsibility for any mishap will lay not only with the student's inability to follow direction, but also the lack of guidance provided by the teacher. Not only is the guide required to support the student on the path, but also to find the top of the mountain.

To walk the path in Mikao Usui's time it was important to follow an entire process. Within this process there is a foundation structure, such as the five elements of the system of Reiki. This structure can be seen as one entire entity; a complete practice where each element requires dedication and perseverance. In modern forms of the system of Reiki, some of these elements receive focus while others are often ignored. When these elements are taught as separate entities, the whole path falls away. The result is no path to walk on. This in turn creates a space of stuck energy where a practitioner is aimless and disconnected, unable to flow with the natural movements of the universe.

In many Japanese *dô* there is a special relationship between the teacher and the student. The teacher provides the student with a practice to work on, to perfect. The student takes this away and practices, returning to report progress and experiences. This information guides the teacher in supporting the student on his or her path and when the student is ready, the teacher provides another practice to be worked with. Thus, slowly, the student walks the path.

The path is not only meant to be understood intellectually but most of all through the student's direct experience; only through direct experience can it become a true path. This practice of walking and climbing and experience are all a part of being the practice and making it a lifelong commitment.

> A man has been practicing a particular *kata* [formal exercise] for a couple of months and then he says with a weary sigh, "No matter how hard I train, I can not master this *kata*. What shall I do?" A couple of months! How could he master a *kata* in a couple of months?
>
> (Excerpt from *Karate-Dô – My Way of Life* by Gichin Funakoshi)

Seeing one's Reiki practice as life itself is the Reiki movement of the moment. If one's spiritual practice is considered a separate action in one's life, it will remain an unintegrated practice that cannot lead to spiritual fulfillment. The direction that the evolution of the practice of Reiki will take may well be shaped by this change.

14 Positive Outcomes

These latest questions accompanied by their answers are forcing many new directions upon practitioners, their associations and the Reiki community in general. If the system does not flounder because of its previous lack of commonality of practice, then there is certain to be growth in many areas that have already begun to blossom.

A more comprehensive level of understanding of what it means to practice the system both professionally, personally and as a responsible citizen is leading to:

- Practitioners not merely accepting what they are being told but using their intellect and experience to guide them
- Practitioners working toward developing their credibility professionally through greater education and experience
- A greater availability of experienced teachers providing ongoing support
- Stronger Reiki community support for credible practitioners
- This credibility being a promotion for the system of Reiki in the broader community, resulting in a wider respect and understanding
- Acknowledgement that the Reiki community needs to remember the simplicity and profundity of the system and not create further confusion with 'new' unrelated concepts and branches
- Support being provided through further factual Japanese research
- Reiki practitioners living their experience and this being reflected in their actions

- Professional practitioners confidently approaching organizations to offer their services as paid professionals
- Reiki treatments and courses being accepted as integrative healthcare by insurance companies and healthcare organizations
- Associations tightening their entry requirements to support professional practitioners and the credible Reiki community in general
- The further creation of Reiki organizations with Member Organizations that span a multitude of diverse Reiki branches

There is a greater openness within the Reiki community and this can only grow as any left-over superstitions and narrow-minded attitudes are removed. The fundamental requirement in moving forward is that it must be remembered that this is a system, a practice – not just a name. And within this system, the well-being of the world can be supported.

Although there may not be consensus as to what the system of Reiki is at this moment in time, the discussion is there. Through discussion the system can evolve into a stronger, more grounded practice that will eventually fulfill its potential.

The call for the move to a stronger, more grounded practice is getting louder.

Part V

Reiki Techniques

A student is poorly trained if he learns many [techniques] but only possesses a shallow understanding of performing them.

(Excerpt from Funakoshi Gichin's 'Tanpenshu' by
Patrick and Yuriko McCarthy)

Techniques are one of the five integral elements in the system of Reiki. The term 'technique' can be qualified here to include exercises that aid the development of the individual's personal practice along with methods of using Reiki to achieve certain ends for the self and others.

There are a wide variety of techniques taught within the system of Reiki around the world. The descriptive terms 'Western' and 'Japanese' were utilized in the first edition of *The Reiki Sourcebook* to define the origins of Reiki techniques. This line is often blurred as a number of techniques taught in modern Japanese branches actually originated in the West and were later introduced to Japan from the mid-1980s onward. The Japanese then integrated these New Age techniques into their own teachings. For this reason the terminology of 'traditional' and 'non-traditional' has been adopted instead.

Traditional techniques were introduced to the system of Reiki in Japan and evolved from the Japanese culture and philosophy. Many of these work at aiding the practitioner's own self-development by building energy in the *hara*, clearing one's energy and teaching sensitivity to it. A number of these techniques have their roots in traditional Eastern energy work such as *ki ko* (Japanese *Qi Gong*), *Tendai* Buddhism, *Mikkyô*, martial arts and *Shintô*.

Of the few Reiki techniques taught by Hawayo Takata, who brought the system of Reiki to Hawaii, there remained in each a kernel of these traditional techniques. After Hawayo Takata's death, however, an influx of non-traditional add-ons from individuals and the New Age movement were grafted onto the system of Reiki. Many of these additions claim to have their foundation in Tibetan, Indian or Egyptian origins and do not relate to the Japanese origins of the system. The Indian chakra system was grafted onto the system of Reiki by some of Hawayo Takata's students and has become almost inseparable from a modern Reiki course even in Japan. Some non-traditional techniques center on various ways of using Reiki to achieve an end result with the use of *talismans or *manifesting grids for example. A concern here is that the more complex and dramatic additions to the system may lessen the connection with Reiki itself though provide a connection to other forms of esoteric arts.

Overlapping techniques between traditional and non-traditional include *enkaku chiryô hô* and *distant Reiki; *shûchû reiki* and group Reiki; *ketsueki kôkan hô* and the *nerve stroke; *byôsen reikan hô* and *scanning and *gedoku hô* and the x-ray technique.

The system of Reiki is taught in steps, with a practitioner's knowledge gradually growing and expanding through theoretical and practical experience. As practitioners progress through the various levels of the teachings, new techniques are studied. Techniques from each of the three levels are included in this sourcebook.

Today the system of Reiki is so diverse that it would be almost impossible to list all the variations on each technique. Therefore the included techniques are merely representative of what is taught in a branch or branches. They are also written in a summarized form as succinctly and accurately as possible. To achieve optimal results from any technique, it is best to practice with the assistance of a teacher. The authors do not accept any liability for the use or misuse of any techniques in this book.

15 Traditional Reiki Techniques

Mikao Usui's teachings were initially created as a form of self-development for his students. Many of the traditional techniques are based on building the energy flow through the meridians and strengthening the *hara*. This, in turn, clears the body emotionally, physically, mentally and spiritually, thus raising one's vibration level until one becomes lighter and lighter; shedding one's human ties and bonds to become One with the natural energetic flow of life. Many of the traditional techniques train the mind that energy or *ki* is entering the body through the breath. By breathing in this manner access to *ki* becomes unlimited.

But where exactly did these techniques come from?

Mikao Usui's teachings appear to have been developed rather than 'rediscovered' as has been stated. This indicates that it was an evolving process and leaves open the possibility that his 21 teacher students may have been taught slightly different techniques to work with depending upon when they were taught.

The teachings were broken up into three major divisions.[1] This ensured that those with different capabilities worked with the appropriate energetic techniques. Each division was created to achieve the same outcome. The three approaches are listed below:

1. Experienced practitioners such as advanced meditators were taught meditation techniques.
2. Experienced practitioners who were martial arts practitioners and *Shintô* followers were taught 4 mantras without any symbols. The mantras are chanted in a different manner to that in the third division.

[1] Information supplied to the authors by Chris Marsh.

247

3. Lay people like farmers or naval personnel (this would have included Chûjirô Hayashi and possibly *Usui Reiki Ryôhô Gakkai* members) were taught 4 mantras and 4 symbols. The focus of these teachings was to aid those who were unfamiliar with energy work.

Techniques listed in this section were either taught by Mikao Usui or are practiced in Japanese branches of Reiki that claim to teach in a traditional manner. The modernized system of Reiki is relatively popular in Japan and therefore some Japanese Reiki branches actually practice non-traditional techniques alongside more traditional ones[2].

Since Mikao Usui's death in 1926, his teachings were not always practiced in an overt manner. Once these teachings made their way to the USA in the late 1930s, the system of Reiki gradually became popular. By the 1980s the teachings swept their way around the world, finally finding themselves back in the land of their origin. Mieko Mitsui is credited with introducing a branch of the system of Reiki, The Radiance Technique®, to Japan in 1986, where she began teaching Levels 1 and 2[3]. These modern styles of Reiki quickly gained in popularity in Japan due to their ease of availability; they were short courses that were quick to complete.

It is noted beside each traditional technique whether it is still practiced today and what its origins are where known. The techniques, or their variations, are taught in branches such as *Gendai Reiki Hô, Jikiden Reiki, Komyo Reiki Kai, Usui Reiki Ryôhô* and the *Usui Reiki Ryôhô Gakkai*.

The Japanese Energetic Method

For an understanding of how the Japanese consider energy and the body to work together, information has been included on the Japanese energetic method. There are three major symbolic energy centers in the body according to Japanese philosophy. In one of our

---

[2] An example is *Gendai Reiki Hô* as it practices a mixture of both traditional and non-traditional techniques.

[3] 1986 article 'Mysterious Report #28' from the *Twilight Zone* by Shiomi Takai – translated by Shiya Fleming:www.threshold.ca/reiki.

other books, *The Japanese Art of Reiki*, they are described as The Three Diamonds of Earth *Ki*, Heart *Ki*, and Heaven *Ki*. For simplicity's sake they are listed here using their physical position in the body as their reference name. Each of these centers has its own function and when developed through the Reiki techniques they combine to create a powerful healing system.

1. Earth *Ki*. Found in the belly or hara (approximately 3 inches (8cms) below the naval).

   In this center one's original energy is stored. This is the energy one is born with, the energy that is the essence of your life and supports your life's purpose. Original energy is not only the energy one receives from one's parents when one is conceived but most importantly it is the energetic connection between the practitioner and the universal life force. It is through this center that one connects with the strength of the Earth.

2. Heart *Ki*. Found in the middle of the chest.
   The energy in this center is connected with emotions. This 'human' energy connects one fully with the human experience. Through this center one learns life's process; from childhood through to adulthood and back to being a child. When one is a child, one is without experience, yet as one grows older one becomes a child with experience.

3. Heaven *Ki*. Found in the head.
   Here exists energy connected with one's spirit: Heavenly energy. When connected with this center, one may see colors or develop psychic ability. It is important to remain balanced and centered when working with this energy. Working in combination with the other energy centers supports one in this.

Practicing the Techniques

Techniques described in this chapter include their Japanese *kanji* and literal translation for a deeper understanding of their purpose.

The levels in which the techniques may be taught, and the specific branches that practice them, are listed here. This is just a guideline and may alter depending upon the branch that teaches them.

Some historical information relating to the techniques is included plus any relevant points of interest relating to their practice.

The particular technique is then explained in detail. Within one branch a technique may be approached from different viewpoints and therefore the details may not be matching.

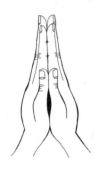

The techniques, as described, generally all use the *gasshô* position. This is where the palms of both hands are placed against one another, with thumbs closest to the body and fingertips pointing upward. It is often called the 'prayer position' or 'namaste position' in English as it is commonly used in many cultures. When practiced in conjunction with Mikao Usui's teachings it represents the balance of the body, harmony, respect for the energy, practitioner and client, and humility. It is also an aid in setting intent clearly. *Gasshô* is used before and after all Japanese techniques and before and after treating clients.

When practitioners are asked to sit while practicing a technique they can either sit in *seiza* or on a chair with feet flat on the ground.

The techniques may also ask that practitioners close their eyes. The eyes may be fully closed or partially. Partially closed eyes means that the practitioner is in fact gazing in an unfocused manner at the ground about 3 feet (1 meter) from the body. The advantage of partially closed eyes is that the practitioner is more likely to retain awareness of the practice.

Byôsen Reikan Hô 病前霊感法

Sensing imbalances

byôsen 病前 – before illness
reikan 霊感 – inspiration, sacred
intuition
hô 法 – method

- *Shoden* or *okuden* technique

- Taught in *Gendai Reiki Hô, Usui
  Reiki Ryôhô, Usui Reiki Ryôhô
  Gakkai* and once practiced by
  Chûjirô Hayashi and Hawayo
  Takata

Byôsen reikan hô is where hands glide over the body to sense
imbalances. Reiki is then offered to the area to restore balance.
Imbalances can be sensed on physical, mental, emotional or spiritual
levels.

1. *Gasshô* – to center the mind and set intent.
2. Move the hands approximately 2 to 6 inches (5–15 cm) over the
   sitting, standing or lying body. Wait, without expectation,
   for a sensation known as *hibiki* to occur in your hands. *Hibiki*
   might include sensations of heat/cold/tingling/pain/itchiness/
   pulsating, etc.
3. When you sense *hibiki,* place your hands on that part of the body.
4. Remain in that position until the *hibiki* has passed before
   moving on.
5. *Gasshô* – to give thanks.

Enkaku Chiryô Hô 遠隔治療法

Remote healing

enkaku 遠隔 – distant, remote
chiryô 治療 – treatment, cure, remedy
hô 法 – method

- *Okuden* technique

- Taught originally by Mikao Usui in a
  different format and practiced today in all
  Japanese branches of Reiki

This technique can be practiced in a number of different ways.

According to traditional Japanese teachings, practitioners do not *send* Reiki or even need to connect to another person – instead the practitioner becomes One with that person. The concept is that one is already One with everything and does not need to make this connection happen.

Some say Mikao Usui used a photograph to practice *enkaku chiryô hô*. In the early 1900s photography was not as common as it is today, making it likely that he and his students also focused on their intent alone. With the development of one's energetic skill, the use of a tool such as a photograph would also be unnecessary. The system using a photograph is commonly practiced today.

1. Obtain a photo of the person and write their name, age, location and condition on the back. If you cannot get a photo write the name, age, location and condition of the person on a piece of paper. This is to help you focus on the person. If it is someone you know you can simply visualize the person between your hands. Naturally the more specific details you can access to help connect to the individual, the easier it is. However, if detailed specifics are unavailable it does not mean that the technique will be unsuccessful.
2. *Gasshô* – to center the mind and set intent.
3. Hold the photograph in your hands and feel the connection to Reiki.
4. Focus on the person you are going to connect with.
5. Visualize or draw the symbols 3, then 2, then 1 while repeating their accompanying mantras onto the photo.
6. Continue focusing on the person for as long as you feel the energy moving.
7. *Gasshô* – to give thanks.

Gasshô Kokyû Hô 合掌呼吸法

(see **seishin toitsu*)

Gasshô Meditation 合掌

A meditation method concentrating on the hands

gasshô 合掌 – to place the two palms together

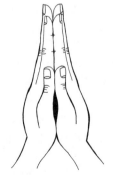

- *Shoden* technique
- This technique is taught by Frank Arjava Petter and is claimed to be a traditional Japanese Reiki technique

This is a meditation technique that aims to calm and focus the mind.

1. Sit and *gasshô* to center the mind and set intent. Close your eyes.
2. Breathe in naturally, focusing on the point where your two middle fingers come together. When your mind wanders, use this physical point as your focus to bring yourself back to this single-pointed meditation.
3. Continue the meditation for up to 30 minutes.
4. *Gasshô* – to give thanks.

Gyôshi Hô 凝視法

A method of healing by staring

gyôshi 凝視 – stare, eye-focus
hô 法 – method

- *Shoden* or *okuden* technique
- Taught in *Gendai Reiki Hô*, *Reido Reiki*, *Usui Reiki Ryôhô* and once practiced by the *Usui Reiki Ryôhô Gakkai*

In the *Reiki Ryôhô Hikkei* it states that Reiki emanates from all parts of the body and is strongest in the hands, eyes and the breath. *Gyôshi hô* is a technique for directing Reiki with the eyes. This is a useful technique when working with people you may not be able to touch. It may be used during a treatment in conjunction with hands-on practice or simply on its own.

1. Gaze with soft, unfocused eyes at the chosen part of the body.
2. Intend that the Reiki flows and visualize it moving from your eyes to the body.
3. Continue until you sense that the body has drawn the energy that it needs for now and finish the technique or move on to the next position.

Hanshin Kôketsu Hô 半身交血法 (see *ketsueki kôkan hô* and *zenshin kôketsu hô*)

Half body blood exchange or cleansing

hanshin 半身 – half-body
kôketsu 交血 – blood exchange
hô 法 – method

- *Okuden* or *shinpiden* technique

- Taught in *Gendai Reiki Hô, Jikiden Reiki, Reido Reiki, Usui Reiki Ryôhô* and once practiced by the *Usui Reiki Ryôhô Gakkai,* Chûjirô Hayashi and Hawayo Takata

If the client has diabetes, reverse the direction of the sweeps, beginning at the base of the spine and working up toward the neck.

1. *Gasshô* – to center the mind and set intent.
2. Begin at the top of the spine and sweep (with one hand on either side of the spine) out to the side of the body. Work down the back, one hand width at a time, until you reach the coccyx. Repeat 10 to 15 times.
3. Place index and middle fingers at the base of the neck on either side of the spine. Hold the breath and press down sweeping to the base of the spine. Press fingers into the bottom of the spine and breathe out. Repeat 10 to 15 times.
4. Place the hands about 1 to 2 inches (3 to 5 cm) above the neck. Hold the breath and sweep down the back to the coccyx. At the coccyx, separate the hands and move them toward the feet.
5. *Gasshô* – to give thanks.

Hatsurei hô 発霊法

A method for generating greater amounts of spiritual energy

hatsu 発 – to generate
rei 霊 – spirit
hô 法 – method

- *Shoden* or *okuden* technique
- Practiced by the *Usui Reiki Ryôhô Gakkai* and versions of it are taught in *Gendai Reiki Hô, Reido Reiki* and *Usui Reiki Ryôhô*

Method 1

This method cleanses the body using energy, in turn allowing for a greater flow of energy through the body. In some branches *hatsurei hô* is initially broken into different techniques and taught separately. These are *kenyoku hô, jôshin kokyû hô* and *seishin toitsu*. This particular version is based on one taught by Hiroshi Doi. He also states that *reiju* is performed during *jôshin kokyû hô*. When practiced today the 5 precepts and the *waka* are generally not included.

1. Sit in *seiza* with hands in *gasshô* – to center the mind and set intent. Close your eyes.
2. Recite *waka* written by the Meiji Emperor.

   Kenyoku Hô
3. a) Place your right hand on the left shoulder (where collarbone and shoulder meet). Breathe in, and on the out breath, sweep diagonally down from the left shoulder to right hip.
   b) On the in breath place your left hand on the right shoulder, and on the out breath, sweep down diagonally from right shoulder to left hip.
   c) Breathe in, returning your right hand to the left shoulder. On the out breath, sweep diagonally down from left shoulder to right hip.
4. a) With the left elbow against your side and with your left arm horizontal to the ground, place your right hand on the left forearm. Breathe in, and on the out breath, sweep downward along the arm to the fingertips.
   b) With the right elbow against your side and with your right arm horizontal to the ground, place your left hand on the right forearm. Breathe in, and on the out breath, sweep down along the arm to the fingertips.
   c) Breathe in, and with the left elbow against your side and with your left arm horizontal to the ground, place your right hand on the left forearm. On the out breath, sweep down along the arm to the fingertips.

   Jôshin Kokyû Hô
5. Place your hands in your lap, palms facing upward.
6. With each in breath, feel the energy coming in through the nose, moving down to the *hara* and filling the body with energy.
7. On the out breath, expand the energy out of the body, through your skin and continue to expand the energy out into your surroundings.
8. Repeat steps 6 and 7 until finished. The exercise may take anywhere from 5 minutes to half an hour. If you begin to feel dizzy, finish the exercise and slowly build on the amount of practice time.

   Seishin Toitsu
9. Place your hands in the *gasshô* position. Focus on your *hara*. On

the in breath begin to bring the energy into your hands. Feel the energy move along your arms, down though your body and into the *hara*.

10. On the out breath visualize energy moving from the *hara* back up through the body and then to the arms and out through the hands.

11. Repeat steps 9 and 10 until finished. The exercise may take anywhere from 5 minutes to half an hour. If you begin to feel dizzy then finish the exercise and slowly build on the amount of practice time.

12. Recite the 5 precepts.[4]

13. *Gasshô* – to give thanks.

Method 2

This method is a translation of *hatsurei hô* from a 1933 book by a student of Mikao Usui. The author was Kaiji Tomita, a well-known healer in his own right. The book is called *Reiki To Jinjutsu – Tomita Ryû Teate Ryôhô (Reiki and Humanitarian Work – Tomita Ryû Hands Healing)*. Kaiji Tomita considered this technique to be the fundamental technique for working with spiritual energy.

To begin, sit down and concentrate on unifying the mind and body. Choose a quiet place or somewhere comfortable where you can relax. Included in the text are two different readings of the word *seiza*. One means to sit still and is the first part of the technique the other relates to the physical action of sitting in *seiza*.

Seiza (lit. Japanese – to sit still)

1. Sit in the *seiza* position and perform *gasshô* with the objective to gather/concentrate the energy from the heart into the palms of the hands. Hold the hands together without using force from the arms or the shoulders. Drop the shoulders and clasp the hands, joining the fingers lightly and feel the alignment of the posture. Close your eyes.

Jôshin Hô (Mind purification method)

2. The aim of *jôshin-hô* is to unify and purify the mind. Once the sitting upright is achieved, recite (silently) some *waka* poetry and feel at One with its meaning.

Following is an example of *waka* that can be used for *jôshin hô:*

---

[4] This is understood to be included when the *Usui Reiki Ryôhô Gakkai* practice **hatsurei hô*.

あさみどりすみわたりたるおほそらの
広きををのがこころともがな

asami dori sumi watari taru o hosora no
    hiroki wo wo no ga kokoro tomo gana (ten)

As a great sky in clear light green
    I wish my heart could be as vast (sky)

Hatsurei hô

3. If you have followed the previous steps and stayed focused on the palms of your hands, they start to become warm. This is what Kaiji Tomita calls *reiha* 霊波 (wave of *rei*). It describes the tingling sensation that is comparable to an electrical current. The heat created and the wave of *rei* are what constitute spiritual energy. Even if the sensations are weak at first, they should become stronger as you keep concentrating.

5. Day plan

4. Repeat the above steps for 5 consecutive days, and concentrate for at least 30 minutes, progressively increasing the allotted time until you reach an hour.

Heso Chiryô Hô 臍治療法

A method of healing at the navel

heso 臍— navel

chiryô 治療 – treatment, cure, remedy

hô 法 – method

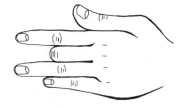

- *Okuden* technique
- Taught in *Gendai Reiki Hô, Komyo Reiki Kai, Reido Reiki, Usui Reiki Ryôhô,* and once practiced by the *Usui Reiki Ryôhô Gakkai*

This method works on the umbilical connection at the navel and is associated with your mother connection (either real or symbolic). Your kidneys are also strengthened by connecting with an important kidney acupuncture point. This technique can be practiced on yourself or others.

1. Sit or stand and *gasshô* – to center the mind and set intent.
2. Place one hand flat over the navel area or place the middle finger gently in the navel, feeling the pulse. Place the other hand flat on the body's back over the corresponding area.
3. Hold until you feel that the body is balanced.
4. *Gasshô* – to give thanks

Hikari No Kokyû Hô 光の呼吸法 (see *jôshin kokyû hô*)

Jakikiri Jôka Hô 邪気きり浄化法

A method for energetically cleansing and enhancing inanimate objects

jaki 邪気 – bad, negative
kiri きり – cut
jôka 浄化 – purification, cleansing
hô 法 – method

- *Shoden* technique
- Taught in *Gendai Reiki Hô, Reido Reiki, Usui Reiki Ryôhô* and once practiced by the *Usui Reiki Ryôhô Gakkai*

This technique is only to be used on inanimate objects such as crystals, stones, jewellery, furniture, houses, etc. Not to be practiced on humans, plants or animals. While 'chopping' with the hand, focus on your *hara* and hold the breath.

1. Sit or stand and *gasshô* – to center the mind and set intent.
2. Hold the object in your non-dominant hand.
3. Place your dominant hand over the object approximately 2 inches (or 5 cm) away, with your palm facing the object. Chop three times in the air above the object. Hold the object and perform Reiki.
4. Chop three times above the object to seal the energy in.
5. *Gasshô* – to give thanks.

Jôshin Kokyû Hô 定心呼吸法 (also called *hikari no kokyû hô*)

Focusing the mind on one thing with breath

jôshin 定心 – focusing the mind
kokyû 呼吸 – breath, respiration
hô 法 – method

- *Shoden* technique
- Practiced by the *Usui Reiki Ryôhô Gakkai* as a part of *hatsurei hô* and taught as a separate exercise in *Gendai Reiki Hô, Komyo Reiki Kai, Reido Reiki* and *Usui Reiki Ryôhô*

It is used to focus the mind, clear the meridians and to build energy in the *hara*.

1. Sit and *gasshô* – to center the mind and set intent. Close your eyes.
2. Place your hands in your lap, palms facing upward.
3. With each in breath, feel the energy coming in through the nose, moving down to the *hara* and filling the body with energy.
4. On the out breath, expand the energy out of the body, through your skin and continue to expand the energy out into your surroundings.
5. Repeat steps 3 and 4 until finished. The exercise may take anywhere from 5 minutes to half an hour. If you begin to feel dizzy, finish the exercise and slowly build on the amount of practice time.
6. *Gasshô* – to give thanks.

Kenyoku hô 乾浴法

A method of dry bathing or brushing off

kenyoku 乾浴 – dry bath
hô 法 – method

- *Shoden* technique
- Practiced by the *Usui Reiki Ryôhô Gakkai* as a part of *hatsurei hô and taught as a separate exercise in *Gendai Reiki Hô, Komyo Reiki Kai, Reido Reiki* and *Usui Reiki Ryôhô*

This is a practice to purify the body, heart and spirit. This technique is generally used before and after the practice of any energy work. It is based on a *Shintô misogi* technique.[5]

    You clear the tension of the shoulders, the heart, the stomach and liver with stroke 1. Stroke 2 clears the tension of the shoulder, heart,

---

[5] *Misogi* is a purification rite and these are a vital part of Shintôism. *Shintô* priests practice *kenyoku hô* or the dry bath method. One *Shintô* practitioner said that he performed a similar ritual with a group of men from his village where they wore only a red loincloth at the *hekogaki* festival (putting on the loincloth festival).

stomach and spleen. Strokes along the arms specifically clear the arm and hand meridians.

1. *Gasshô* – to center the mind and set intent while standing or sitting.

2. a) Place your right hand on the left shoulder (where collarbone and shoulder meet). Breathe in, and on the out breath, sweep diagonally down from the left shoulder to right hip.
   b) On the in breath place your left hand on the right shoulder, and on the out breath, sweep down diagonally from right shoulder to left hip.
   c) Breathe in, returning your right hand to the left shoulder. On the out breath, sweep diagonally down from left shoulder to right hip.

3. a) With the left elbow against your side and with your arm horizontal to the ground, place your right hand on the left forearm. Breathe in, and on the out breath, sweep downward along the left arm to the fingertips.
   b) With the right elbow against your side and with your right arm horizontal to the ground, place your left hand on the right forearm. Breathe in, and on the out breath, sweep down along the arm to the fingertips.
   c) Breathe in, and with the left elbow against your side and with your arm horizontal to the ground, place your right hand on the left forearm. On the out breath, sweep down along the left arm to the fingertips.

4. *Gasshô* – to give thanks

Ketsueki Kôkan Hô 血液交換法

(also called *kôketsu hô **see variations ****hanshin kôketsu hô* **and *** *zenshin kôketsu hô***)**

Blood exchange method
ketsueki 血液— blood
kôkan 交換 – exchange
hô 法 – method

This technique is described in detail under its different variations. It is to be practiced by the practitioner on the client's bare back,

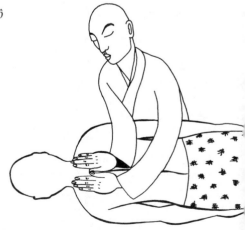

and massage oil may be used. If the client has diabetes, reverse the direction of the sweeps, beginning at the base of the spine and working up toward the neck. This technique is mentioned in the *Ryôhô Shishin*, or Healing Guide, in the *Reiki Ryôhô Hikkei*, as well as in Chûjirô Hayashi's *Ryôhô Shishin*. Modern variations are the *finishing treatment or *nerve stroke.

Kôketsu Hô 交血法 (also called *ketsueki kôkan hô*)

Koki Hô 呼気法

A method of sending *ki* with the breath

koki 呼気 – breathing *ki*
hô 法 – method

- *Okuden* technique
- Taught in *Gendai Reiki Hô, Komyo Reiki Kai, Reido Reiki* and *Usui Reiki Ryôhô* and once practiced by the *Usui Reiki Ryôhô Gakkai*

You can incorporate this technique into a regular treatment or use it on its own. It is useful in situations where you cannot touch.

1. *Gasshô* – to center the mind and set intent.
2. Breathe in through your nose, focus on your *hara*, and feel your lungs filling with this energy.
3. Blow the energy out through your 'O' shaped mouth at the intended area.
4. *Gasshô* – to give thanks.

Nadete Chiryô Hô 撫手治療法

A method of stroking with the hands

nadete 撫手 – stroking with the hands
chiryô 治療 – treatment, cure, remedy
hô 法 – method

- *Okuden* technique
- Taught in *Gendai Reiki Hô, Usui Reiki Ryôhô* and once practiced by the *Usui Reiki Ryôhô Gakkai*

You can incorporate this technique into a regular treatment or use it on its own.

This technique stems from Traditional Chinese Medicine and has its roots in *Qi Gong* and Chinese Massage (*tui-na*). Important in this technique is that you hold the intent to clear the energy of meridians and organs when stroking. To perform the stroke, work with the palm of your hand using either one hand or one hand on top of the other.

Emotional links of the organs: Heart: hurt, pain, joy, excitement, shock

Stomach: sadness, worry
Liver: anger
Spleen: depression, frustration, resentment, pensiveness
Kidneys: fear

Front of the body:
1. Start at the heart (middle of chest) then move to the stomach, down to the liver and all the way down the outside of the leg, flicking off the energy at the toes. Complete with one long stroke.
2. Start at the heart (middle of chest) then move to the stomach, down to the spleen and all the way down the outside of the leg; flicking off the energy at the toes. Complete with one long stroke.
3. Begin at the heart, move up to the shoulders and down the arm; flicking off energy at the fingers.
4. Place the index and middle fingers of both hands between the eyebrows with finger tips touching and hold for about 20 seconds. Then stroke slowly toward the temples along the eyebrows and hold the fingers at both temples for another 20 seconds. Continue the stroke to the ears and flick off energy.
5. Place the index and middle finger of both hands on either side of the nose just below the eyes and hold for about 20 seconds. Follow the cheekbones till you reach the ears and flick off the energy.

The areas to stroke on the back of the body:
1. Start at the base of the neck and stroke down along the spine all the way to the tailbone. This will clear the heart, kidneys and spinal meridians.

Nentatsu Hô 念達法 (also called *seiheki chiryô hô*)

A method of sending thoughts

nen 念 – thought

tatsu 達 – reach, attain, notify

hô 法 – method

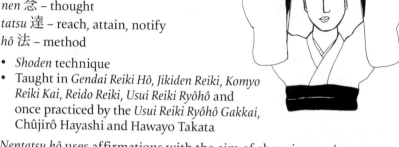

- *Shoden* technique
- Taught in *Gendai Reiki Hô, Jikiden Reiki, Komyo Reiki Kai, Reido Reiki, Usui Reiki Ryôhô* and once practiced by the *Usui Reiki Ryôhô Gakkai*, Chûjirô Hayashi and Hawayo Takata

Nentatsu hô uses affirmations with the aim of changing one's set behavioural beliefs. It is valuable for achieving goals, overcoming set beliefs, and ridding oneself of bad habits. In *seiheki chiryô hô* the symbols and mantras are added to this practice.

1. Create the affirmation you wish to use. To make an affirmation always set your sentence in the present. Keep the sentence positive by focusing on what you want in life rather than what you don't want.
2. Sit or lie down and close your eyes and breathe regularly.
3. *Gasshô* – to center the mind and set intent.
4. Place one hand on your forehead and the other hand at the base of the neck.
5. Repeat your affirmation for as long as 5 minutes – saying it out loud or to yourself.
6. Remove your hand from your forehead while keeping the other hand in place and relax for up to 5 minutes. You may wish to place the hand that was on your forehead next to, or on to, your body as you relax.
7. *Gasshô* – to give thanks.

Oshite Chiryô Hô 押手治療法

A method of using pressure with the hands

oshite 押手 – hand pressure

chiryô 治療 – treatment, cure, remedy

hô 法 – method

- *Okuden* technique

Taught in *Gendai Reiki Hô, Usui Reiki Ryôhô* and once practiced by the *Usui Reiki Ryôhô Gakkai*

This technique is useful for areas of the body that are experiencing pain or stiffness. You can incorporate this technique into a regular treatment or use it on its own. Practice it regularly for as long as the pain persists.

1. *Gasshô* – to center the mind and set intent.
2. Push the area of pain or problem with your fingertips. This sends Reiki through to the section you are focusing on.
3. *Gasshô* – to give thanks.

Reiji Hô 霊冶法

A method of being guided by spirit

rei 霊 – spirit
ji 冶 – show
hô 法 – method

- *Okuden* technique
- Taught in *Gendai Reiki Hô, Usui Reiki Ryôhô, Usui Reiki Ryôhô Gakkai* and once practiced by Chûjirô Hayashi and Hawayo Takata[6]

Once a student is confident working with *byôsen reikan hô*, then *reiji hô* is taught. This technique guides your hands like magnets to places on the body in need of treatment. Practicing *reiji hô* will heighten your sensitivity to energy work. It can be practiced on yourself or others. The hands are placed in *gasshô* in front of the forehead, thus stimulating the intuitive center, which helps to sense the body's imbalances.

1. Sit or stand and *gasshô* to center the mind and set intent.
2. From this position, move your hands, maintaining them in the *gasshô* position, to the center of your forehead.
3. Now allow your hands to be drawn to the areas of the body that require Reiki.
4. Once in a position, hold it until you feel that the section has extracted all the Reiki it currently needs.
5. Move on to the next position that lures your hands.

---

[6] Hawayo Takata wrote in her diary in May 1936 that Chûjirô Hayashi had granted and bestowed on her *Leiji hô* (this is a spelling mistake and was probably meant to read *reiji hô*).

6. Continue to allow your hands to be drawn to the different parts of the body until the process is finished.
7. *Gasshô* – to give thanks.

Reiki Mawashi 霊気回し[7]

A current of spiritual energy

rei 霊 – spiritual
ki 気 – energy
mawasu 回す – pass on

- *Shoden* technique
- Practiced in *Gendai Reiki Hô, Komyo Reiki Kai, Reido Reiki* and *Usui Reiki Ryôhô*

This technique helps to sensitize practitioners to feel energy flow. A group of practitioners make a circle, hold hands and allow Reiki to flow first to the right and then to the left.

1. Practitioners sit in a circle and *gasshô* – to center the mind and set intent. Close the eyes.
2. Each practitioner's left palm faces up and right palm faces down with hands out to the side of the body. In this way your right hand is on top of your neighbour's left and so on around the circle. Although the palms are facing each other, they do not touch.
3. The teacher begins sending Reiki to the right. This increases in strength as it passes from one student to another. Practice this for a couple of minutes.
4. Now swap your hands and place the right palm facing upward. Once again the teacher sends Reiki through the circle, this time through the left hand.
5. *Gasshô* – to give thanks.

Reiki Undô 霊気運動

Movement of Spiritual Energy

rei 霊 — spiritual
ki 気 — energy
undô 運動 – movement

---

[7] Hiroshi Doi listed this technique as non-traditional in 2000 and as traditional in his 2005 *Gendai Reiki Hô* manual.

- *Shoden* technique
- Practiced in *Gendai Reiki Hô* and *Usui Reiki Ryôhô* and was introduced by previous *Usui Reiki Ryôhô Gakkai* president Kimiko Kôyama

This technique uses physical movement to cleanse and release the body's energy. Energy guides the physical body once you totally let go. For each person the movement is completely unique. Release may also be expressed through movement, sound, breath work, or silence. This is originally a *Qi Gong* practice.

1. Stand with your feet shoulder-width apart. Knees slightly bent.
2. *Gasshô* – to center the mind and set intent. Close your eyes.
3. Reach your hands up to the sky with both hands facing each other, forming a funnel shape. Feel the connection to Reiki.
4. Once you sense the energy moving down through your hands, in between your hands, and onto your head, let your arms flop relaxed to the side.
5. With each in breath, feel the energy coming into your body, filling the *hara*.
6. As you breathe out, expand the energy through your body and surroundings.
7. Repeat steps 5 and 6 until there is a strong flow of energy.
8. Now let your body totally relax and breathe normally. You will want to spontaneously move with the energy that is pulsing through the body. Let go but don't force yourself to move either.
9. Take as long as you feel you need. At each practice session you will find yourself giving over to the energy more and allowing it to move the body as it feels the need.
10. *Gasshô* – to give thanks.

Seiheki Chiryô Hô 性癖治療法 (see **nentatsu hô*)

Seishin Toitsu 精神統 (also known as **gasshô kokyû hô*)

Creating a unified mind

seishin 精神 – spirit, mind, soul, intention
toitsu 統 – to unite, unify (to make one)

- *Shoden* technique

- Practiced by the *Usui Reiki Ryôhô Gakkai* as a part of *hatsurei hô* and taught as a separate exercise in *Gendai Reiki Hô, Reido Reiki* and *Usui Reiki Ryôhô*

This technique clears your mind, develops sensitivity in your hands, and strengthens the *hara*. In Japanese branches slightly different versions of this technique are practiced.

1. Sit and *gasshô* – to center the mind and set intent. Close your eyes.
2. Focus on your *hara*.
3. On the in breath, begin to bring the energy into your hands. Feel the energy move along your arms, down though your torso, and into the *hara*.
4. On the out breath, visualize energy moving from the *hara* back up through the body and then to the arms and out through the hands.
5. Repeat for as long as you wish.

Shûchû Reiki 集中霊気 (also called *shûdan reiki)

Concentrated spiritual energy

shûchû 集中 – concentrated
rei 霊 – spiritual
ki 気 – energy

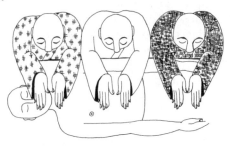

- *Shoden* technique
- Practiced in most Japanese branches especially those that are influenced by Chûjirô Hayashi and taught by Hawayo Takata

This is a technique where several practitioners work on one person. Often practiced during a *shoden* class, practice groups, meetings and/or share evenings. *Shûchû reiki* is generally performed over a shorter timeframe than a regular treatment due to the intensity of working together with other practitioners.

1. *Gasshô* – to center the mind.
2. Each practitioner places hands on the body of the person lying down.
3. The practitioners cover the main parts of the body and any known imbalances.
4. *Gasshô* – to give thanks.

Shûdan Reiki (see **shûchû reiki*)

Tanden Chiryô Hô 丹田治療法 (also called **gedoku hô*)

A detoxifying and purifying method

tanden 丹田 – the point below the navel where all the body's energy concentrates
chiryô 治療 – treatment, cure, remedy
hô 法 – method

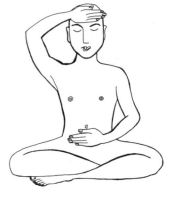

- *Okuden* technique
- Taught in *Gendai Reiki Hô, Komyo Reiki Kai, Reido Reiki, Usui Reiki Ryôhô* and once practiced by the *Usui Reiki Ryôhô Gakkai*

This technique is used to purify and clear the body. The hand on the *hara* connects to your original nature and Earth energy. Meanwhile the hand on the forehead makes the connection with the mind and Heavenly energy. When you bring the hand from the forehead down to join the hand at the *hara* you are reminding your consciousness about your original nature, bringing the dualities of Heaven and Earth into one. There is a similar detoxifying technique called *gedoku hô* where one hand is placed on the front and the other on the back of the *hara*.

1. Sit and *gasshô* to center the mind and set intent. Close your eyes.
2. Place one hand on the *tanden* or *hara* and the other hand on the forehead.
3. Connect with the Heavenly energy at the forehead. Hold this position for approximately 5 minutes.
4. Remove your hand from the forehead and now place it on top of the hand at the *hara*. Hold for approximately 20 minutes.
5. *Gasshô* – to give thanks.

Uchite Chiryô Hô 打手治療法

A method of patting with the hands

uchite 打手 – patting with the hand
chiryô 治療 – treatment, cure, remedy
hô 法 – method

- *Okuden* technique
- Taught in *Gendai Reiki Hô, Usui Reiki Ryôhô* and once practiced by the *Usui Reiki Ryôhô Gakkai*

You can incorporate this technique into a regular treatment or use it on its own. It is used to encourage the flow of energy. This technique stems from Traditional Chinese Medicine and has its roots in *Qi Gong* and Chinese Massage (*tui-na*).

When patting it is important that you hold the intent to clear the energy of either the organs or the meridians. There are 4 different ways to pat with the hand. You can work with the:

- palm of the hand
- back of the hand
- side of the hand
- fingers

Work from the wrist and not with the force of the whole arm.

1. Start at the heart (middle of chest), patting with the back of the hand and moving down in a straight line to the hara. Be careful not to pat too hard on the abdomen and be careful not to cross personal physical boundaries.
2. Begin just below the collarbone, moving up to the shoulder and down along the inside of the arm. Again, pat with the back of the hand.
3. Start to pat just above the hip bone and follow the outside of the leg to the knee, then move to the inside of the leg, finishing at the feet. Flick off the energy at the toes.
4. Or start to pat just above the hip bone and follow the outside of the leg to the knee, then move to the front of the leg to the feet. Flick off the energy at the toes.

On the back you can pat either with your palm, the side of your hand or the back of your hand as the back is not as sensitive as the front of the body.

1. Begin at the base of the neck and pat all the way down to the tailbone along the spine. This helps to clear the meridians that travel alongside the spine.

Zenshin Kôketsu Hô 全身交血法 (see*ketsueki kôkan hô and * hanshin kôketsu hô)

Whole-body blood exchange or cleansing

zenshin 全身 – whole body

*kôketsu*交血 – blood exchange

hô 法 – method

- *Okuden* or *shinpiden* technique
- Taught in *Gendai Reiki Hô, Jikiden Reiki, Komyo Reiki Kai, Reido Reiki, Usui Reiki Ryôhô* and once practiced by the *Usui Reiki Ryôhô Gakkai,* Chûjirô Hayashi and Hawayo Takata

If the client has diabetes, reverse the direction of the sweeps, beginning at the base of the spine and working up toward the neck.

1. *Gasshô* – to center the mind and set intent.
2. Complete a full treatment covering head, lungs, heart, stomach and intestines.
3. Begin at the top of the spine and sweep (with one hand on either side of the spine) out to the side of the body. Work down the back, one hand width at a time, until you reach the coccyx. Repeat 10 to 15 times.
4. Place index and middle fingers at the base of the neck on either side of the spine. Hold the breath and press down sweeping to the base of the spine. Press fingers into the bottom of the spine and breathe out. Repeat 10 to 15 times.
5. Place the hands about 1 to 2 inches (3 to 5 cm) above the neck. Hold the breath and sweep down the back to the coccyx. At the coccyx, separate the hands and move them toward the feet.
6. Rub and sweep both arms from the shoulder to the tips of the fingers several times.
7. Sweep down from the thighs to the toes.
8. *Gasshô* – to give thanks.

16 Non-Traditional Reiki Techniques

Non-traditional Reiki techniques have been sourced from many fields. Naturally, some are variations on traditional Reiki techniques while others are obvious imports. As seen in the previous section there are numerous traditional techniques so it is a wonder that it has been necessary to include new techniques at all.

In tracing the evolution of techniques, it appears that the student of Mikao Usui, Chûjirô Hayashi, taught only 4 or 5 of the Japanese techniques to his students Hawayo Takata and Chiyoko Yamaguchi. This may mean that Chûjirô Hayashi did not know them to pass on, did not place an emphasis on them or the other techniques were not introduced till a later date. Hawayo Takata was not known to add any new techniques to the teachings during her lifetime.

The aims of the techniques practiced outside of Japan are varied. These include methods to clear the meridians and chakras allowing the body to heal and become One with the universal energy – not unlike the traditional techniques. Enhancing existing energetic modalities is also a common method as in the examples of *crystal grid work or *talismans. Other techniques are said to, themselves, enhance Reiki such as the *hui yin breath and *antakharana meditation. Modern techniques can also focus on the achieving of a specific result which may sometimes have a materialistic aim; for example using Reiki as a tool for manifestation.

Not only have techniques been added to the system of Reiki but so have mantras, symbols, hand positions, beliefs and attunement methods. Why have there been so many add-ons? What is the motivation for changing the system of Reiki?

Humans continually attempt to improve and do their best.

Though what one thinks is the best could be quite different as to what another's view is of the best – it's relative to one's own experiences in life and knowledge gained from within that. One practitioner may believe that the system works best when it includes a favourite breathing technique or physical movement. That practitioner tells their student that this is in fact the best way to do it and then that student tells their student and … this pattern repeats itself over and over again and is in fact the game commonly known as Chinese Whispers. It can make humans feel powerful to have changed an existing system 'for the better'. It can also reflect an attitude of knowing better than any existing system.

Reiki techniques are technically valuable in helping the individual continue to develop a stronger energetic understanding. They sensitize practitioners, offering them deeper insights into their true nature. The techniques are also valuable as a means to stimulate intent. When a technique is practiced with dedication a very clear intent is set. This intent affects the practitioner's ability to perform the exercise and that strength of character thus dominoes into every aspect of life. When these techniques from Mikao Usui's teachings were omitted, it is no wonder that new techniques replaced them.

New Age Additions

A most beautiful facet of energy work is its ability to adapt to any situation.

The New Age movement has been active rediscovering ancient ways. Egyptian, Tibetan, South American, Indian, Celtic and Chinese cultures have had many of their mysteries extracted for use by New Age believers.

Mikao Usui's teachings were not New Age based although mystical and energetic elements of the New Age have been included into what is now known as the system of Reiki today. This has naturally weakened the connection to the original teachings while redirecting practitioners into New Age practices. Some of these are:

- Talismans – originating from the Western magical tradition.
- Energy bodies and auras – adapted from either Victorian spiritualism, Theosophy, eastern yogic practices or all of these.
- Spirit guides – definitely shamanistic, yet witches have also been

said to have familiars. Mystics, too, have been guided throughout the centuries by what they believed were angelic beings, so the concept of spiritual guidance is quite broad based.

- Chakra system – is yogic in nature and the New Age movement has adapted it from the energetic method written about in the Indian Vedas. Traditionally the chakras or energy centers are pictured as multi-petalled lotus flowers, each associated with different deities, symbols, colors, syllables and animals. Today it is generally taught that there are 7 major chakras and that they begin at the base of the spine with the root chakra and work their way up to the crown chakra at the top of the head.

Listed below are some of the basic qualities of chakras as written about by medical intuitive Caroline Myss:

Root Chakra – groundedness, family identity, bonding
Sacral Chakra – creativity, survival instincts, sexuality
Solar Plexus Chakra – self respect, self esteem, ethics
Heart Chakra – love and compassion
Throat Chakra – choice, faith, personal authority
Third-eye Chakra – wisdom, intellectual skills, inspiration
Crown Chakra – inner divinity, inner guidance

Mikao Usui did not teach the chakra system, instead using the Japanese energetic system. Hawayo Takata noted her awareness of the *hara* (the foundation of the Japanese energetic method) in her practice in her diary and is not known to have taught the chakra system in the USA. A number of her students added the chakra system to the modern teachings of Reiki, and it can be found in the techniques, mantra and symbol descriptions, and the attunement process.

> It [Reiki] is nature's greatest cure, which requires no drugs. It helps in all respects, human and animal life. In order to concentrate, one must purify one's thoughts in words and to meditate to let true 'energy' come out from within. It lies in the bottom of the stomach about 2 inches below the naval.
>
> (Excerpt from Hawayo Takata's diary writing about the *hara*, 10 December 1935)

Practicing the Techniques

Each technique description consists of the levels that the technique may be taught, and the specific branches that practice them. There are so many split-offs from branches, as well as vague groupings, such as the generic term Usui Reiki, that it is often impossible to know what one school teaches in comparison with others, even if they do belong to the same branch.

Historical information relating to where a technique originates is included where possible. Many New-Age additions unfortunately do not have a clear background. Any important points relating to the practice of the technique are also cited.

The particular technique is then described in detail. Mantras and symbols are linked as one in modern teachings (unlike Mikao Usui's traditional teachings) therefore, unless noted, the word 'symbol' will stand for both. Symbol 1, Symbol 2, Symbol 3 and Symbol 4 have been used to represent both the mantra and the symbol.

Antakharana

A non-traditional Reiki healing symbol

- Level 3a (or Advanced Reiki Training) technique
- Introduced to the system of Reiki in Raku Kei Reiki and practiced in Usui/Tibetan Reiki and by various Independent Reiki Master/Teachers

In Sanskrit, this non-traditional Reiki technique is said to mean 'internal instrument such as mind, intellect, ego and the subconscious mind'. The antakharana is a two dimensional cube with three sevens on its faces. Myth has it that this symbol originated from Tibet and China. Apart from it being called a cure-all, it is said if you meditate on the antakharana you will connect the conscious with the unconscious.

Meditation 1

1. Simply gaze at the antakharana symbol drawn on a piece of paper or make a 3 dimensional cube and draw sevens on it.
2. Meditate on the image and experience the energy.

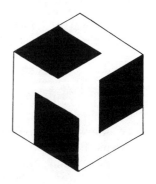

Anti-Clockwise Energy Spirals

To ease the client into a change that is about to happen

- Level 1 technique
- Introduced to the system of Reiki in the West and practiced in Satya Reiki

It is easy to become very relaxed during a Reiki treatment. This method is used to bring someone's awareness back to the treatment room gently.

1. Draw anti-clockwise spirals with the tip of the index finger, just touching the client's skin, from the shoulder down to the feet and from the shoulders to the fingers.

Blue Kidney Breath (see *breath of the fire dragon)

Breath of the Fire Dragon (also known as blue kidney breath, Reiki breathing)

Non-traditional breath technique used with non-traditional attunement process

- Level 3 technique
- Introduced to the system of Reiki in the West. Different variations are practiced in Johrei Reiki, Karuna Ki, Karuna Reiki®, Reiki Jin Kei Do, Seichim and Tera Mai™

A variation of this technique is the *violet breath.

1. Begin the **hui yin* breath
2. While you hold the contractions, begin by breathing blue into your kidneys and white out. Repeat 3 times.
3. Visualize a white mist cloud above your head. Breathe the white light in all the way down to your root chakra.
4. Hold your breath.
5. Allow the energy to rise up the center of your spine. Once it reaches your brain it then turns white, sapphire blue, royal purple and gold.
6. Draw each symbol once and repeat their mantras, breathing the symbols out.

Chakra Balancing

Balancing the chakras with each other

- Level 1 technique
- Introduced to the system of Reiki in the West and practiced in Satya Reiki and by various Independent Reiki Master/Teachers

This chakra-balancing technique may be used on yourself or on

another person. Remember never touch a person's private parts. If necessary, place your hands a couple of inches/centimeters above the body – this is just as effective as hands-on. This technique takes up to 15 minutes to execute and the crown chakra is not used. The crown chakra will naturally fall into line if the other chakras are balanced. Do feel free to use different combinations with all 7 chakras if you intuitively feel this is appropriate.

The chakra system was grafted onto the system of Reiki by a number of Hawayo Takata's students, but was not taught by her.

1. Lie on your back and place one hand on your third eye and one on your root chakra.
2. Leave your hands there until you feel that the energy has been absorbed into the body or for up to 5 minutes.
3. Place one hand on your throat chakra and one on your sacral, your lower abdomen. Leave your hands there until you fell that the energy has been absorbed into the body or for up to 5 minutes.
4. Place one hand on your heart chakra and one on your solar plexus. Once again, leave your hands there until you feel that the energy has been absorbed into the body or for up to 5 minutes.

Chakra Kassei Kokyû Hô

Breathing method to activate the chakras

- Level 1 technique
- Introduced to the system of Reiki by Hiroshi Doi and practiced in *Gendai Reiki Hô*

kassei 活性 – active or activate
kokyû 呼吸 – breath, respiration
hô 法 – technique, method or way

Set up

1. Sit and *gasshô* to center the mind and set intent. Close your eyes.
2. Reach your hands up to the sky with both hands facing each other (forming a funnel shape). Feel the connection to Reiki. Once you feel the energy moving down through your arms and onto your head,

place your hands on your knees, facing upward.

3. With each in breath, feel the energy coming in through the crown chakra (top of the head), moving down through the body and filling the body with energy. On the out breath the body relaxes.

Basic Exercise Pattern: Root – Heart – Crown

4. a) Breathe in through the root chakra (base of spine), bring the energy to the heart, pause, and breathe out through the heart chakra (center of the chest).

b. Breathe in through the heart chakra, take the energy to the crown, pause, and breathe out through the crown chakra.

c. Breathe in through the crown, take the energy back to the heart, pause, and breathe out through the heart chakra.

d. Breathe in through the heart chakra, take the energy to the root chakra, pause, and breathe out through the root chakra.

e. Repeat this exercise a number of times.

f. *Gasshô* – to give thanks.

It is possible to work with each of the chakras individually using this technique.

Chanting

Enhancing the qualities of symbols with the sound of mantras

- Level 2 technique
- Introduced to the system of Reiki in the West, and different variations are practiced in Karuna Ki and Karuna Reiki®

Chanting mantras is a technique used throughout the world in many cultures. This specific technique uses non-traditional symbols and non-traditional mantras. Chanting is used at any time during a treatment or during meditation and is preferably practiced out loud. It is said to intensify the flow of energy in the top chakras while protecting the body, allowing it the space to heal.

1. Start the treatment with your hands on the temples of the client's head.

2. Chant 'Om' seven times, then wait for the energy to move.

3. Continue with the rest of the treatment.

Communicating With Your Higher Self

Re-connecting with the Higher Self

- Level 3 technique
- Introduced to the system of Reiki by Hiroshi Doi and practiced in *Gendai Reiki Hô*

1. Sit and *gasshô* to center the mind and set intent. Close your eyes.
2. Draw Symbol 4 in the air and say the mantra 3 times.
3. Reach your hands up to the sky with both hands facing each other (forming a funnel shape). Feel the connection to Reiki.
4. Place your dominant hand on the center of your chest. Repeat 'My higher self, my soul' to yourself 3 times. Note any sensation.
5. Repeat step 4 with the non-dominant hand.
6. Communicate with the higher self through the hand on the chest.
7. *Gasshô* – to give thanks.

Crystal Healing With Reiki

Crystals are renowned as excellent healers. There are so many versions of crystal healing being used in the Western system of Reiki that it is hard to decide which one to print. It is generally advised to clear and charge crystals before using them in any of the following techniques.

Method 1

Crystal Chakra Healing

Helps people who have very low energy
- Level 1, 2 or 3 technique
- Introduced to the system of Reiki in the West and practiced by various Independent Reiki Master/Teachers

For this technique you will need 10 crystal quartz stones, preferably Rose quartz.

1. Place one on each of the seven chakras (be aware of people's boundaries), in the palms (minor chakras) of the hands, and one on the ground in between the feet.
2. Perform a complete one-hour Reiki treatment, starting with the head, working your way down the body. Also treat the hands and the feet.

Method 2

Crystal Grid

Sending continual energy to a person, place or event

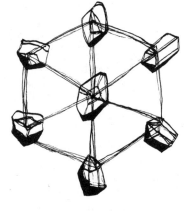

- Level 3a (or Advanced Reiki Training)
- Introduced to the system of Reiki in the West and practiced in Usui/ Tibetan Reiki and by various Independent Reiki Master/Teachers

1. Choose eight similarly sized quartz crystals. From these, have one as a center quartz crystal (sphere, cluster, or multi-terminated).
2. Cleanse all the crystals.
3. Pick up each crystal, empowering them with all three of the symbols. Set the intention that the crystal's abilities are enhanced with Reiki.
4. Find a special place for the grid.
5. Place the center crystal in the middle.
6. From the rest of the crystals, intuitively choose one that feels like it has strong energy as the 'charging crystal'.
7. Place the six remaining crystals, points facing inward toward the center crystal, in a circle, evenly distributed like the numbers on a clock.
8. Pick up the charging crystal and place it in your dominant hand, point downward over the grid of crystals. Place the point of the charging crystal over the center crystal and draw pie-shaped triangles over each of the crystals in a anti-clockwise direction. Draw a line from the center crystal out to one of the crystals, then move anti-clockwise to the next crystal, then back to the center, then back out to the crystal you just left, and move anti-clockwise to the next crystal, moving around the circle several times, until you feel that the grid is strongly empowered.
9. The intent is to charge this grid with Reiki. Every couple of days

you can recharge the grid by repeating step 8.

10. Now place your list of persons, places, or things to be healed into the center of the grid with the intent to send energy to every individual on the list.

De-Programming Techniques

There are two traditional Japanese techniques that work on releasing set mental patterns. One is *nentatsu hô* and the other is *sei heki chiryô hô*. They are the same technique except that the latter is practiced in *okuden* (or Level 2) and uses mantras and symbols. In the West a number of variations of these techniques are practiced. Chûjirô Hayashi and Hawayo Takata taught these traditional techniques, as do some other traditional Japanese branches.

To make affirmations, always set your sentence in the present. Keep the sentence positive by focusing on what you want in your life instead of what you don't want.

Method 1

Works on the removal of bad habits
- Level 2 technique
- Variations are practiced in *Gendai Reiki Hô*, Tera Mai™ Reiki, The Radiance Technique®, *Usui Shiki Ryôhô* and by various Independent Reiki Master/Teachers

Create an affirmation for the habit you wish to work with.

1. Place one hand on the back of the head.
2. Draw Symbol 4, Symbol 3, and Symbol 2 on the head with the other hand and chant the mantra.
3. Now place one hand on the forehead and one on the back of the head with the intent that light is filling up the head.
4. Repeat the affirmation for the bad habit three times in your mind.
5. Repeat this exercise every day for 6 days.

Method 2

A method for changing mental patterns
- Level 2 technique
- Practiced in Seichim by Diane Shewmaker

Create the affirmation you wish to use together with your client.

1. The client sits with eyes closed, breathing regularly.
2. Draw Symbol 1 over the client's head and repeat the mantra 3 times.
3. Place your left hand on the back of the head just above the neck.
4. With your right hand, draw Symbol 2 over the crown or third eye and repeat its mantra 3 times.
5. Place your right hand across the crown or forehead of the client.
6. Call the client's name in your mind three times, then repeat the affirmations silently or aloud. The client may also repeat the affirmations at the same time. Stay with your hands in that position for as long as you feel that it is necessary.
7. Give a written copy of the affirmations to the client and ask them to repeat them several times a day.

Distant Healing (also known as Distant Reiki)

Send Reiki to a person, place or thing in the past, present or future

- Level 2 technique
- Originally taught by Chûjirô Hayashi and Hawayo Takata (based on the traditional Japanese Reiki technique *enkaku chiryô hô*)

There are many, many versions of this technique. Some people hold a teddy bear and pretend that the bear is the client to whom the Reiki is being sent. Some pretend that their thigh is the body of the client. Others have the intent that their own bodies are representative of the person they are sending Reiki to and simply perform Reiki on themselves.

Below is a simple version of distant healing:

1. Hold a photo of the person, place or event you wish to send Reiki to in between your hands.
2. Focus on the photo.
3. Visualize or draw the Symbols 3, 2, and 1, with their accompanying mantras, onto the photo with your finger.
4. Allow the energy to move through the body until you feel that it is finished.

Finishing Treatment (also called the Nerve Stroke)

Blood-cleansing method

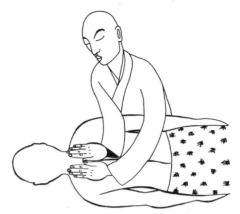

- Level 2 technique
- Originally taught by Chûjirô Hayashi and Hawayo Takata (based on the traditional Japanese Reiki technique *ketsueki kôkan hô*)

Hawayo Takata used the finishing treatment at the end of a treatment. Chûjirô Hayashi often recommended the blood-exchange technique, as he called it, for various diseases.[1]

1. Place the fingers of both hands on either side of the spine. In one fluent stroke, move your hands from the neck to the coccyx. For diabetes, always move from the coccyx upward.
2. Place hands flat on shoulder blades, palms facing down, and perform anti-clockwise circular movements. Move hands down a hand width and repeat until the coccyx is reached.
3. Place one hand on the tailbone and one on the back of the neck.
4. Using one fluid stroke from the shoulder to the hand on both arms, stroke down from the hip to the feet. For diabetics, stroke toward the heart.

Grounding

A method of connecting to the center of the Earth energetically

- Level 1, 2 or 3 technique
- Practiced throughout the world in many cultures

Grounding techniques energetically center a person by connecting to the Earth's energy. Most of these techniques can easily be practiced within the system of Reiki. Below is just one of the many grounding techniques used within this system. Level 1 practitioners can practice it without using the

[1] From Chûjirô Hayashi's *Ryôhô Shishin*.

symbols.
1. Sit calmly with your hands relaxed in your lap and your eyes closed.
2. Visualize Symbol 3, Symbol 2, and Symbol 1, and repeat each appropriate mantra 3 times.
3. Place your hands on the forehead and the back of your head and intend to send Reiki.
4. Place your hands on your sacrum and send Reiki.
5. Place your hands over your knees and send Reiki.
6. Place your hands over your feet and send Reiki.

Group Distant Healing

A method where a group of Reiki practitioners send Reiki to a person, place or event

- Level 2 technique
- Introduced to the system of Reiki in the West and practiced by various Independent Reiki Master/Teachers

This is one variation of *distant healing in a group:
1. Practitioners sit in a circle facing the each other.
2. Visualize Symbol 3, Symbol 2, and Symbol 1, and repeat each appropriate mantra 3 times.
3. The name, age, and any other information about the person to be treated are read out.
4. The practitioners send Reiki to the person, who is then visualized in the center of the circle.

Group Reiki

Healing with Reiki in a group
- Level 1 technique
- Practiced in the West stemming from Chûjirô Hayashi and Hawayo Takata (based on traditional Japanese technique *shûchû reiki)

This is a technique where several practitioners practice on one person. Often practiced during a Level 1 course or at practice groups, meetings, and/or share evenings. Group Reiki is generally performed over a shorter timeframe than a regular Reiki treatment due to the intensity of working together with

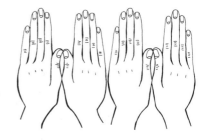

other practitioners. Chûjirô Hayashi had two people working on one client at the same time in his clinic.

1. Each practitioner places hands on the body of the person lying down.
2. The practitioners cover the main parts of the body and any imbalances.

Guide Meditation

Meet your Reiki Guide

- Level 3a or Advanced Reiki Training technique
- Concept introduced to the system of Reiki in the West and popularized by teachers such as Diane Stein, William Lee Rand and Walter Lubeck; now practiced by various Independent Reiki Master/Teachers

Guide work is used in shamanic traditions throughout the world. Here it has been adapted to create a non-traditional Reiki meditation. Unlike Reiki, with guide work it is traditional to use protection before undertaking such methods. Protection can be as simple as visualizing yourself surrounded by protective white light.

1. Sit and close your eyes.
2. Imagine yourself engulfed by Reiki and divine light.
3. See a figure coming toward you through this light.
4. As the figure comes closer you gain a clearer image of what the figure looks like.
5. To begin to connect ask some simple questions and listen to the answers. Know that you will remember these answers. What is the name, gender, appearance or even smell of your Reiki guide?

6. Take the hand of the figure and see if you recognize it. Feel the energy of the Reiki guide.
7. Now ask why this guide has come to you and what its message is for you.
8. Ask the Reiki guide how you will recognize it in the future and if you may call on it at any time you need assistance.
9. Know that the guide will always be there for you.
10. Come back to the room and open your eyes.

Hadô Kokyû Hô 波動呼吸法

A method of vibrational breathing

hadô 波動— wave, vibration

kokyû 呼吸 – breathing

hô 法 – method

- Level 3 technique
- Taught in *Gendai Reiki Hô* and used in some traditional Japanese Reiki branches

The 'Haa' sound brings us to a different vibration level. The breathing improves the functioning of the immune system and detoxifies the blood and body tissues. It raises your level of energy and brings about relaxation and calm. Various Japanese branches use different versions of this technique. Depending upon the branch it is not always taught in Level 3. This technique is practiced in traditional Japanese *ki* traditions[2] and in some Buddhist traditions[3] as well.

1. Sit and *gasshô* – to center the mind.
2. Place your hands on your knees, facing upward with eyes closed.
3. Breathe in and then breathe out from mouth with a 'haa' sound and hold it as long as you can. The out breath will gradually lengthen as you become more practiced. The final aim is to hold the 'haa' sound for approximately 40 seconds. Focus solely on the 'haa' sound as you breathe out until you reach your limit.
4. When you finish the sound you release the tension in your abdomen. This creates a natural inhalation.
5. Repeat steps 3 and 4 with the aim of creating a free flowing breath without tension.
6. *Gasshô* – to give thanks.

[2] *Ki-A Practical Guide for Westerners*, William Reed, Japan Publications Inc. 1986.
[3] Information supplied by Hiroshi Doi.

Hadô Meisô Hô 波動瞑想法

A method of vibrational meditation

hadô 波動 – wave, vibration

meisô 瞑想 – meditation, contemplation

hô 法 – method

- Level 3 technique
- Introduced by Hiroshi Doi and taught in *Gendai Reiki Hô*

This technique can bring you into a deep state of meditation.

1. Sit and *gasshô* to center the mind and set intent. Close your eyes.
2. Reach your hands up to the sky with both hands facing each other (forming a funnel shape). Feel the connection to Reiki. Once you feel the energy moving down through your hands and into the body bring your arms out to the side until they are parallel to the ground, palms facing the ground.
3. Bend your elbows and move the hands in front of the chest, fingertips touching, palms still facing the ground.
4. Breathe out, doing the hadô breath of 'haa' with the hands pushing down to the ground.
5. Move your hands up to the forehead as you breathe in. Move the hands slowly down while breathing out with the hadô breath with palms facing the body.
6. Complete step 5 three times. Now feel the energy move throughout the body. You can repeat step 5 as often as you want.
7. *Gasshô* – to give thanks.

Healing the Past and the Future

Send Reiki to yourself to heal your past, present and future

- Level 2 technique
- Introduced to the system of Reiki in the West as an extension to *distant Reiki and practiced by various Independent Reiki Master/Teachers
1. Begin on Day 1 (after completing your regular treatment on yourself) by visualizing yourself in your mother's womb. Were you feeling happy, fearful, relaxed? Try to imagine exactly how you felt. Hold that image.

2. Now, imagine yourself in the future. Choose a date 10, 20, 30 years from now and visualize how you would like to be. Are you a fit and healthy 80-year-old with a passion for life? Choose an image that will be the ideal you.
3. Now, attempt to visualize the older you making contact with the past you. It is a beautiful meeting and now you are going to send Reiki to the image.
4. Use Symbol 3 and its mantra repeated three times.
5. Then Symbol 2 with its mantra also repeated three times.
6. Mentally draw Symbol 4 repeating its mantra three times.
7. Wait peacefully as the energy is sent.
8. On Day 2 visualize yourself as 1-year-old and see if you can remember back to events happening within that year. Perhaps someone has told you about yourself at this age, use this information as well. Then visualize that the 1 year old you, will meet the future you.
9. On Day 3 visualize yourself as a 2-year-old, etc. etc.
10. Continue until you reach your present age.
11. Repeat this technique as often as you wish beginning from in the womb.
12. Try to remember both good and bad experiences from your life and Reiki will heal all that you wish.

Hui Yin Breath

Non-traditional breath technique used with attunement process

- Level 3 technique
- Introduced to the system of Reiki in Raku Kei Reiki and practiced in Karuna Ki, Karuna Reiki®, Usui/ Tibetan Reiki as well as by many Independent Reiki Master/Teachers

This breath technique originates from Chinese *Qi Gong* practices. The *hui yin* technique is sometimes used in conjunction with the *breath of the fire dragon or *violet breath.

1. Contract your perineum (between your anus and genitals).
2. Place the tip of the tongue against the top soft palate (behind the upper teeth).
3. Hold the breath.

Jiko Jôka Hô 自己浄化法

A method of self-purification

jiko 自己 – self

jôka 浄化 – purification

hô 法 – method

- Level 2 technique
- Introduced by Hiroshi Doi
  and taught in *Gendai Reiki Hô*

1. Stand relaxed with your feet hip width apart. Knees slightly bent.
2. *Gasshô* – to center the mind and set intent. Close your eyes.
3. Reach your hands up to the sky with both hands facing each other (forming a funnel shape). Feel the connection to Reiki. Once you feel the energy moving down through your hands and into the body, bring your arms out to the side until they are parallel to the ground. Palms facing the ground.
4. Bend your elbows to bring the hands in front of the chest, palms still facing the ground with fingertips touching.
5. On the out breath release a 'haa' sound, pushing your hands down to the ground. Feel imbalances leaving the body as you do this.
6. On the in breath fan arms out to the side of the body and up in a circular movement until your hands are above your head in a funnel shape.
7. Bring your hands down (palms facing the ground and fingertips touching) past the forehead to the chest.
8. Continue pushing down repeating steps 5, 6 and 7 until you feel clear and fresh.
9. *Gasshô* – to give thanks.

Making Contact with Higher Beings

Connecting and asking for guidance from higher beings

- Level 3 technique
- Introduced to the system of Reiki by Hiroshi Doi and practiced in *Gendai Reiki Hô*

1. Close your eyes. Draw Symbol 4 in the air and say the mantra 3 times.
2. Reach your hands up to the sky with both hands facing each

other (forming a funnel shape).
3. Feel the connection to Reiki.
4. Focus your intent on the higher being and sense its vibration.
5. *Gasshô* and melt into that vibration level. Your consciousness becomes One with it.
6. Now send your question to this higher being.
7. You will receive your answer in your everyday life or dreams.

Manifesting

Manifest what you need or want

- Level 2 technique
- Introduced to the system of Reiki in the West and practiced in Usui/ Tibetan Reiki and by various Independent Reiki Master/Teachers

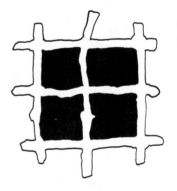

The ethics of manifesting with Reiki are simple and clear. If you must ask for something in such a way that it will deprive someone else, it is unethical. In asking for a job, for example, it is wrong to ask for someone else's job simply ask for the BEST POSSIBLE employment of your own. If you want someone else's love but they are in a relationship with someone else, it is unethical to ask for this relationship to end. Ask instead for the BEST POSSIBLE relationship for you, without designating who the person is. To manifest a relationship, make a list of all the qualities you wish for in the BEST POSSIBLE mate and use this list as a focal point.

1. Visualize your wish with you in it.
2. Place the Earth behind you and your wish.
3. Bring a golden grid over the picture, spiraling from Heaven to Earth.
4. Draw the Symbol 1 over the whole picture.
5. Hold the image for as long as you can, then let go.

Metta Meditation

Meditation focusing on goodwill and sending love and compassion to all beings

- Level 2 technique
- Introduced to the system of Reiki in the West and practiced in Reiki Jin Kei do

Metta – loving kindness (lit. Pali)

This technique is a well-known Mahayana Buddhist practice. There are many Metta meditations depending on what your particular intention is. This Reiki Jin Kei do technique is an adaptation of the Metta Golden Light meditation. You may wish to send Metta to your family, your fellow travellers, to world leaders, etc.

1. Sit in a chair with palms in the lap, right over left.
2. Focus on your heart chakra.
3. Focus on goodwill and loving kindness toward yourself and as you inhale visualize the heart area as a lotus flower opening on the in breath. Feel compassion for yourself and gently feel the energy blooming in the heart chakra.
4. As you exhale visualize compassion expanding from the heart as a beam of light. Send goodwill and loving kindness to all beings. This light expands in every direction throughout the whole universe benefiting all beings.
5. After a few minutes visualize the energy coming from the flower in the heart chakra as a silver mist. It spreads from the heart to every single cell in your body filling you with compassion and love.
6. Visualize this compassion expanding from your physical body outwards in all directions filling the whole universe benefiting all beings.

Morning Prayer

Prayer to be practiced each morning

- Level 1 technique
- Introduced to the system of Reiki by Shingo Sakuma and practiced in Satya Reiki

1. Make a bow to the Sun two times, thanking God and existence.
2. Clap your hands two times, purifying the space around you.
3. Repeat three times:
   HARAE – TAMAE, cleanse all
   KIYOME – TAMAE, purify all
   MAMORI – TAMAE, protect all
   SAKIHAE – TAMAE, may all beings be happy.
4. Say the Sun's Mantra:
   A-MA-TE-RA-SU OO MI-KAMI.
5. Make a personal wish.
6. Repeat three times:
   KAMNAGARA – TAMACHI – HAEMASE, as the God wishes
7. Make a bow to the Sun one time and thank God.

Nerve Stroke (see *finishing treatment)

Open Heart Exercise

Creates a trusting and open relationship with others

- Level 1, 2 and 3 technique
- Introduced to the system of Reiki in the West and practiced by various Independent Reiki Master/Teachers

Reiki is about opening up your heart and living life in a compassionate, loving way. Here is a technique to open students up to each other before experiencing the first Level 1 attunement.

1. Stand opposite your partner.
2. Place your palms flat against theirs (right against left).

3. Your right hand gently clasps their left wrist.
4. Make and maintain eye contact throughout the whole exercise.
5. When you feel the link is made at eye-to-eye level and you begin to feel your partner's energy, place their left hand on your heart chakra.
6. Now move your hands so that you and your partner are palm to palm again.
7. Slowly bring all four hands together to form a diamond shape.
8. Bring this up to eye level and maintain your eye-to-eye contact through the diamond's center.
9. Raise your arms up as far as you can reach above, still maintaining eye-to-eye and palm-to-palm contact.
10. Fan your arms slowly out horizontally and then embrace each other.

Power Sandwich

Increases effectiveness of hands-on or distant treatments

- Level 2 technique
- Introduced to the system of Reiki in the West and practiced in Seichim and by various Independent Reiki Master/Teachers

This technique is practiced with the belief that Symbol 1 activates the other symbols.

1. Repeat the symbols in this sequence as an alternative to using just one symbol.
2. Symbol 1, 3, 1, 2, 1

Preparative Mini Reiki Session (see *Reiki boost)

Quick Treatment (see *Reiki boost)

Reiki Aura Cleansing

Clearing the aura of heavy energy
- Level 3 technique

- Introduced to the system of Reiki in the West and practiced by various Independent Reiki Master/Teachers

This clearing technique can be used for both the client or on the self. There are many versions of this in use and below is just one example.

1. Stand and close your eyes.
2. Reach your hands up to the sky with both hands facing each other (forming a funnel shape). Feel the connection to Reiki.
3. Visualize Symbol 4, then visualize energy coming down into your body through the crown chakra, filling the whole body and hands, inside and out, with a white light.
4. Now visualize Symbol 1 in three dimensions. The top of the symbol is just above the head. Let the energy spiral around you in a clockwise direction moving downward. As it spins around see Reiki removing blockages and strengthening the aura as it goes. Repeat the mantra 3 times.
5. Repeat step 4 nine times.
6. Visualize Symbol 4 starting above the head and going down to below the feet. Repeat the mantra 3 times. See Reiki as a white mist and breathe it in. Expand your energy out to the rest of the universe as you breathe out.
7. Open your eyes when you feel ready.

Reiki Boost (also called the *quick treatment, *preparative mini Reiki session)

Balances and harmonizes the chakras allowing a greater flow of Reiki in the body

- Level 1, 2, or 3 technique
- Introduced to the system of Reiki in the West and variations are practiced in Tera Mai™ Reiki, The Radiance Technique®, and other various Independent Reiki Master/Teachers (see *seated chakra treatment for Reiki Jin Kei do version)

The chakra system was incorporated into the system by a number of

Hawayo Takata's students but was never taught by her.

This technique can be used before a student receives an attunement. The intent is that it harmonizes the energy of the body so that the student can then receive full benefit from the attunement.

1. Stand the client sideways in front of you.
2. Place your hands on his or her shoulders to develop an energetic connection.
3. Begin by placing your hands above the crown chakra, palms facing down and hold for 2–5 minutes.
4. Third-eye chakra – palms facing each other on the front and back of the head and hold for 2–5 minutes.
5. Throat chakra – palms facing each other front and back and hold for 2–5 minutes.
6. Heart chakra – palms facing each other front and back and hold for 2–5 minutes.
7. Solar plexus chakra – palms facing each other front and back and hold for 2–5 minutes.
8. Sacral chakra – palms facing each other front and back and hold for 2–5 minutes.
9. Root chakra – palms facing each other front and back and hold for 2–5 minutes.
10. Knees – palms facing each other front and back and hold for 2–5 minutes.
11. Turn palms upward and slowly lift the energy up to the crown chakra.
12. Sweep down the aura to the knees.
13. Snap your fingers to break the energy connection.

Reiki Box

Send Reiki to a person, place or event in the past, present or future

- Level 1 or 2 technique
- Introduced to the system of Reiki in the West and practiced in *Gendai Reiki Hô* and by various Independent Reiki Master/Teachers

This is a technique for sending Reiki

without having to use symbols or mantras. You will need a non-metallic box and paper and pen.

1. Write or draw any intentions you wish to send Reiki to on a piece of paper.
2. Put the papers in the box and keep it in a special place.
3. Send Reiki to the box every day by placing your hands on it with the correct intention.
4. Remove the paper once the intentions have been realized or you feel that it is no longer relevant.

Reiki Breathing (see *breath of the fire dragon)

Reiki Meditation

Meditation using Reiki to increase sensitivity and connection to the source

- Level 3 technique
- Introduced to the system of Reiki by Hiroshi Doi and practiced in *Gendai Reiki Hô*

1. Close your eyes. Reach your hands up to the sky with both hands facing each other (forming a funnel shape). Feel the connection to Reiki and feel the energy moving down through your hands, in between your hands and onto your head.
2. Bring your hands down in front of your face in the *gasshô* position. Feel the energy moving through the whole body. Breathe in and out through your fingertips.
3. Raise the non-dominant hand a little higher and place your dominant hand, facing up, on your lap. Once again sense the energy running through the body. Place your dominant hand on any body areas that feel unbalanced.
4. Bring your non-dominant hand down onto the dominant hand in the lap. Relax into the energy.
5. Bring one hand to the heart and send Reiki to your higher self and say an affirmation.
6. Then bring one hand to the forehead and one to the back of the head and say an affirmation.

Reiki Shower

A cleansing technique that also increases energy flow in the body

- Level 1 technique
- Introduced to the system of Reiki in the West and variations are taught in *Gendai Reiki Hô* and Reiki Jin Kei do

This technique has been adapted from *Qi Gong*. In another version of this you can keep your hands in the area where you feel any imbalances to rebalance the energy.

1. Close your eyes. Reach your hands up to the sky with both hands facing each other (forming a funnel shape). Feel the connection to Reiki and feel the energy moving down through your hands, in between your hands and onto your head.

2. Once you can sense the energy coming over and into the body like a shower, bring the hands slowly down over and just off the body. Your palms are facing you with the visual idea that you are washing and cleaning yourself with energy. Move the hands over and across the body and finally down to the ground, sending the 'dirty' energy down to the Earth.

3. Repeat this as often as you wish reconnecting to the energy each time.

Saibo Kassei Kokyû Hô 細胞活性呼吸法

A method of vitalizing the cells through breath

saibo 細胞 – cell

kassei 活性 – activate, vitalize

kokyû 呼吸 – breathing

hô 法 – method

- Level 2 technique
- Introduced by Hiroshi Doi and taught in *Gendai Reiki Hô*

1. Sit or stand and *gasshô* – to center the mind. Close the eyes.

2. Reach your hands up to the sky with both hands facing each other (forming a funnel shape). Feel the connection to Reiki by sensing the vibrations of light. Once you feel this move your hands down and onto your head then place your hands on your knees, facing upward.
3. Slowly scan down the body with your mind's eye.
4. Where you sense an imbalance, breathe in, and on the out breath send Reiki to that area. Talk to the area, showing your gratefulness for the insight that you receive and for the balance that is currently taking place in your life. After a while you can just say 'thank you' and then eventually there will be a natural gratefulness attached to this technique and it will not be necessary to voice these words at all.
5. *Gasshô* – to give thanks.

Scanning

Sensing imbalances in the energy field

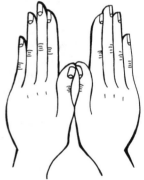

- Level 1, 2 or 3
- Practiced in the West and taught by Karuna Ki, Usui/Tibetan Reiki and various Independent Reiki Master/ Teachers. A different version was originally taught by Chûjirô Hayashi and Hawayo Takata and is called *byôsen reikan hô*

Scanning is placing your hands into a person's energy field and trying to sense energetic differences. This may be practiced on yourself or on a client before or during a treatment. In *byôsen reikan hô,* as you scan you place your hands immediately on any imbalances, but in scanning, you first scan the whole body before placing your hands anywhere.

1. The client lies or sits and closes the eyes.
2. Stand at the crown with hands about 2 to 6 inches (5–15cm) above the body. Move your hands from the crown to the feet and back up again. This may take a few passes.
3. See if you can feel heat/cold/tingling/pain/itchiness/pulsating, etc., in your hands.
4. This is useful in finding places that may need extra attention before or during a healing session.

Seated Chakra Treatment

Stimulating the chakras

- Level 1 technique
- Introduced to the system of Reiki in the West and taught in Reiki Jin Kei Do (variation of *Reiki boost)

The chakra method was grafted onto the system by a number of Hawayo Takata's students but was never taught by her.

1. Seat the client and ask them to close their eyes.
2. Place your hands above the crown sensing the energy.
3. Begin to move both hands in a circular motion. After a while, begin to move your hands in an upward expanding motion. Then return to the circular movements contracting the energy.
4. Place the palms of both hands at the back of the head and bring the fingertips around to rest on the temples covering the ears to seal the energy.
5. Stand to the side of the client and move your right hand in front of the forehead and your left hand to the back of the head and repeat the motions of step 3. Seal the energy in by holding the back of the head and moving the right hand in small circular movements in front of third eye.
6. At the throat chakra, repeat the motions of step 3. Then place your left hand on the back of the throat while the right hand is off the body at the front of the neck, sealing the energy in in small circular movements.
7. At the heart chakra, repeat the motions of step 3. Then place your left hand on the back of the heart while the right hand is off the body at the front of the heart chakra, sealing the energy in in small circular movements.
8. At the solar plexus, repeat the motions of step 3. Then place your left hand on the back of the solar plexus while the right hand is off the body at the front of the solar plexus, sealing the energy in in small circular movements.
9. At the sacral chakra, repeat the motions of step 3. Then place your left hand on the back of the sacral chakra while the right hand is off the body at the front of the sacral chakra, sealing the energy in in small circular movements.

10. At the root chakra, repeat the motions of step 3. Then place your left hand off the back of the root chakra, while the right hand is off the body at the front of the root chakra, sealing the energy in in small circular movements.
11. Stand behind the client and at the shoulders. Repeat the motions of step 3. Then place your hands on both shoulders to seal the energy in.
12. Stand at the side of the client again, hold the left hand above the crown, and the right hand between the legs, balancing the energy.
13. Stand at the front of the client, and from the root chakra sweep upward with both hands. Repeat three times.

Sekizui Jôka Ibuki Hô 脊髄浄化息吹法

A method of cleansing the spinal cord with breath

sekizui 脊髄 – spinal cord

jôka 浄化 – purification, cleansing

ibuki 息吹 – breath

hô 法 – method

- Level 3 technique
- Introduced by Hiroshi Doi and taught in *Gendai Reiki Hô*

In Japan it is said that the spinal cord records our karma.[4] This technique works solely on the spinal cord, rebalancing it and consequently balancing the rest of the body.

1. Sit and *gasshô* – to center the mind and set intent. Close your eyes.
2. Reach your hands up to the sky with both hands facing each other (forming a funnel shape). Feel the connection to Reiki. Once you feel the energy moving down through your hands, in between your hands and onto your head, then place your hands on your knees, facing upward.
3. Imagine that your spine is a pipe from the crown of your head down to the coccyx. As you breathe you practice the *hadô* breathing cleaning the dirt out of the body from the crown to the coccyx.

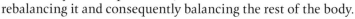

[4] *Modern Reiki Method for Healing*, Hirosho Doi, Fraser Journal Publishing, 2000.

4. Breathe in through your nose and at the same time imagine pure water entering your coccyx and going up the pipe to the area in between the eyes on the forehead.
5. On the out breath, feel the water leaving the coccyx.
6. Repeat steps 4 and 5 seven times and counting 5 breaths in one cycle.
7. *Gasshô* – to give thanks

Seventh Level Technique

Activating the gateway chakra

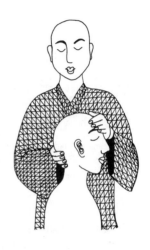

- Level 7 technique
- Introduced to the system of Reiki in the West and practiced in the Seven Level system (based on The Radiance Technique® where extra levels were added)

The chakra method was grafted onto the system of Reiki by a number of Hawayo Takata's students but was never taught by her.

This technique uses the gateway chakra that is situated where the neck meets the base of the skull.

1. Hold one hand over the gateway chakra and the other on the crown for 5 minutes.
2. Move the hand from the crown and place it over the third-eye chakra for 5 minutes.
3. Now place one hand on the crown chakra and one on the third-eye chakra for 5 minutes.

Six Point Meditation for Energy Awareness

Creating an even flow of energy in the body

- Level 2 technique
- Introduced to the system of Reiki in the West and practiced in Reiki Jin Kei Do
1. Center yourself by taking 3 breaths.
2. Bring your awareness to your crown chakra. Sense the energetic changes

that may be taking place.

3. Bring your awareness to your third-eye chakra. Sense any changes that may be taking place.
4. Bring your awareness to your throat chakra. Sense any changes that may be taking place.
5. Bring your awareness to your heart chakra. Sense any changes that may be taking place.
6. Bring your awareness to your palms chakras. Sense any changes that may be taking place.
7. Repeat as often as you feel necessary to create an even sense of energy flow.

Smudging

Using the vibration of smell to affect energy

- Level 1, 2 or 3 technique
- Introduced to the system of Reiki in the West and practiced by various Independent Reiki Master/Teachers

Sense of smell is far more important than one imagines. Smudging is used for clearing the energetic space in a room or around a person. Level 2 or 3 practitioners can draw the symbols with the incense sticks while clearing.

1. Client stands with their feet and arms spread out while the practitioner wafts an incense stick around the front and back of the body and under their feet, encasing them in the energetic vibration.

Solar Image Training

Method to lose dependency on symbols

- Level 3
- Introduced to the West by Hiroshi Doi and practiced in *Gendai Reiki Hô*

This technique uses images instead of symbols to help the student lose their dependency on the symbols. Symbol 1 uses the Earth or red color, Symbol 2 uses the sun or gold color, Symbol 3 uses the moon or blue color and Symbol 4 uses white light. Below is the technique using Symbol 2.

1. Close your eyes.
2. Reach your hands up to the sky with both hands facing each other (forming a funnel shape). Feel the connection to Reiki and its light.
3. Face your palms toward each other and visualize a golden sun in between them. Count to 10. Use a blue, cool sun if you have high blood pressure.
4. Place your hands on either side of your head at the level of the third-eye chakra and visualize the sun in and around it. Count to 10.
5. Place your hands on the sides of your neck at the throat chakra. Visualize the sun having grown larger and encompassing it, too. Count to 10.
6. Place your hands on the heart chakra. Visualize the sun having grown larger and encompassing it, too. Count to 10.
7. Place your hands on the solar plexus chakra. Visualize the sun having grown larger and encompassing it, too. Count to 10.
8. Place your hands on the sacral chakra. Visualize the sun having grown larger and encompassing it, too. Count to 10.
9. Place your hands on the root, chakra. Visualize the sun having grown larger and encompassing it, too. Count to 10.
10. Relax and sense the sun's energy, expanding from your body.

Symbol Exercises

Increase your connection to Reiki by meditating on the symbols

When students learn Level 2, they are traditionally taught 3 mantras and 3 symbols. In Level 3 they are traditionally taught 1 mantra and 1 symbol. Depending upon the branch of Reiki you practice, this may vary as non-traditional branches will often teach more mantras and symbols. Below are a number of methods shown to aid the student with their mantra and symbol practice.

Method 1

Sense the energy of the symbols and mantras
- Level 2 technique
- Introduced to Reiki in the West and practiced in
  Satya Reiki
  1. With the palm flat and facing away from you, draw the symbol.
     Repeat the mantra out loud. Breathe in and sense the energy.
  2. Look at the symbol and whisper the mantra. Breathe in and
     sense the energy.
  3. Now visualize the symbol in your mind and repeat the mantra to
     yourself while holding the breath.

Method 2

Gain a deeper understanding of the energy of the symbols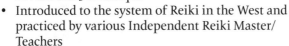
- Level 2 and 3 technique
- Introduced to the system of Reiki in the West and
  practiced by various Independent Reiki Master/
  Teachers
  1. With the palm flat and facing away from you, draw Symbol 1.
     Repeat the mantra 3 times and step into the space where the
     symbol was drawn. Feel the energy of the space.
  2. Repeat step 1 for each of the symbols.

Method 3

Connect with the symbols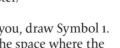
- Level 2 or 3 technique
- Introduced to the system of Reiki in the West and
  practiced by various Independent Reiki Master/Teachers

If you have not yet studied Level 3 then practice this technique using
Level 2 symbols only.
  1. Seat yourself and place your hands on your knees, or if you wish,
     in your lap with the right hand over the left, palms up.
  2. Close your eyes and breathe into your sacral chakra. Do not
     force the breath. Remember that while meditating your mind
     will start to wander. Do not chastise yourself or continue to
     put energy into these thoughts. Let them float away – you can
     imagine a fluffy white cloud coming along and taking them
     gently away. Let them go and concentrate on this specific
     meditation.
  3. To begin the meditation, intend that Reiki enters through your
     crown chakra and fills your body in a golden glow. Continue

to breathe into your sacral chakra, filling your organs, arteries, bones, and skin with Reiki. The in breath brings the energy into you and the out breath expands it through the body. Now begin the visualization.

4. The first symbol to visualize is Symbol 4. You can draw it in front of you or visualize it in your mind. Allow the energy to flow into you and then ask the energy for any message that this symbol might have for you. Remain focused on the symbol and allow the Reiki to flow through you showing you its meaning. Continue for at least 15 minutes. You can now finish the meditation or continue with the three other symbols finding your personal connection with each symbol.

5. Visualize Symbol 1 in a yellow color, Symbol 2 as a blue color and Symbol 3 as a red color. You may change these colors if you wish – just follow your intuition.

6. To finish the meditation, draw your symbols while saying their mantras, and thank the energy.

7. It might be necessary to ground yourself after this meditation. You can do whatever it is that is appropriate for you. You can place your hands on your sacral chakra and send energy there, drink a glass of water, stand solidly on the ground with your feet slightly apart, and wring your hands or lie down and imagine the root of a tree growing downward from your root chakra into the Earth.

Talismans

A method of manifesting using an image as the focus

- Level 2 technique
- Introduced to the system of Reiki in the West and practiced by various Independent Reiki Master/Teachers

You can use a talisman to manifest and to send distance healing. The time and energy spent on making a talisman may strengthen your intent. Once the talisman is finished hang it, or place it (in an envelope so that it is private) somewhere where you see it often, e.g., in the kitchen or next to your bed. Every time you look at the talisman, you are sending energy to that person, place, or wish. Replace it with a new talisman

when you feel the need. Some people burn the old talismans after seven days and make new ones.

1. On a sheet of paper write down the person, place, or wish in detail in violet.
2. In the corners, draw Symbol 1s in yellow.
3. Top and bottom, either side of the page, draw Symbol 2s in blue.
4. Over your wish, draw one large red Symbol 3.
5. These are just suggested colors; you may also make a talisman completely in gold or black if you wish.

Toning

A method of using the voice as a healing tool

- Level 3 technique
- Introduced to Reiki in the West and variations are practiced in Karuna Ki and Karuna Reiki®

This technique is used to amplify the Karuna energies and can bring you to higher levels of energy. Toning is not like singing and may even be off key. The purpose is not to be pitch perfect but to trust that the perfect healing will take place. Always inform your client of the actions you will undertake in a technique so that the client is comfortable with touch, sound etc.

1. Place your hands approximately 3 inches (6cm) to 2 feet (50cm) from the body of the client with your palms facing them.
2. First mentally begin toning the names of the symbols. You can create patterns by mixing the symbols together using your intuition.
3. Take a deep breath and begin the toning out loud. Allow the vowels to resonate.
4. Focus on the part of the body where you wish to direct the energy.
5. Continue for as long as you feel necessary.

Violet Breath

Non-traditional breath technique used with attunement process

- Level 3 technique
- Introduced to the system of Reiki in Raku Kei Reiki. Different variations are practiced in Johrei Reiki, Karuna Ki, Karuna Reiki®, Reiki Jin Kei Do, Seichim, Tera Mai™, and Usui/Tibetan and practiced by various Independent Reiki Master/Teachers

A variation of this technique is *breath of the fire dragon.

1. Visualize a white mist around you.
2. Contract the *hui yin* point and place your tongue behind the upper teeth.
3. Visualize a white light coming down through the crown chakra, through the tongue, and out and down the front of the body. It then moves through the *hui yin* point and up the spine to the center of the head.
4. Visualize white mist filling the head.
5. Visualize the white mist turning blue, then indigo blue, and then to begin rotating clockwise. Now it begins to turn violet.
6. In the violet mist, visualize a golden Dumo symbol.
7. In an attunement, blow this breath out onto the student's crown chakra, visualizing the symbol going into the head as you say the mantra 3 times.

Water Ritual

Changing water into energized healing water

- Level 3 technique
- Introduced to the system of Reiki in the West and taught in Tera Mai™ Reiki

This is often used as a preparation for an attunement.

1. Students sit in chairs back to back with about 4 feet (1¼ meters) between them or in a circle.

2. The teacher uses Symbol 3 over cups of water.
3. Each student holds a cup of water at the solar plexus.
4. Students take a deep breath, hold it and close their eyes, exhaling forcibly a blue mist into the water.
5. After each breath, the students pass the cup to the person on their right.
6. Throughout the technique, the teacher will place the left hand on the crown, saying Symbol 2 while using the *hui yin* breath.
7. Students hold the cup in their left hand and then with their right hand and draw Symbol 1 over the cup (horizontally), saying: 'I exorcise thee O SUI CHING (spirit of the water) to receive the Divine Benediction of Fire. That as I partake of this water, so shall I receive the Divine Benediction of Fire. I declare this to be True, and so in the name of the Holy of Holies – So Be It.'
8. Students draw Symbol 1 over the top of the cup again (vertically) and drink the water.
9. Students are now ready for the attunement.

Part VI

Directory

Those interested in the system of Reiki appreciate finding places where they can meet like-minded people, receive treatments, continue their training, and find research facilities. It can be lovely as a Reiki practitioner if you move to a new area or your teacher no longer teaches to be able to connect with others. A variety of resources have been collated and included here as a support system.

17 Reiki Centers

This directory lists Reiki centers throughout the world. They are from an array of branches with some centers teaching more than one branch of Reiki. These centers are not personal recommendations, simply a list compiled for the reader's interest and convenience. It is also obviously not a complete list of teachers worldwide, but is aimed at being a starting point for those who are searching out some one in their area.

Argentina:

Sólo Reiki
Claudio Márquez
Buenos Aires
Phone: 4787 6414
Email: reiki@reikihoy.com.ar

Australia:

International House of Reiki
Frans and Bronwen Stiene
Sydney, NSW
Toll Free: 1800 000 992 within Australia
Website: www.reiki.net.au & www.thereikishow.com
Email: info@reiki.net.au

Belgium:

Anne Fredholm
Website: http://users.telenet.be/annreiki
Email: usui-doka@telenet.be

Ute Wehrend-Segers and Harry Segers
Mol
Phone: 0032 14 706554 – 0476 942195
Email: Ute-harry@telenet.be

Canada:

Brentwood Integrative Health Clinic
Catherine Harvey
Victoria, BC
Phone: 250 665 7685
Website: www.ReikiShamanicJourneys.com
Email: reikivictoria@gmail.com

Centre de Référence Reiki du Québec
Jean Cornudet
Repentigny, Québec
Phone: 450 657 1126
Website: www.centrereikiquebec.com
Email: info@centrereikiquebec.com

Komyo Reiki Kai – Toronto Centre
James Wells
Toronto, ON
Phone: 416 966 2685
Email: jwells_reiki@yahoo.ca

Queenswood Centre
Sister Eileen Curteis
Victoria, BC
Phone: 477 382 2230 or 250 665 7685
Website: www.queenswoodcentre.com

Reiki Therapy Centre
Maria Fatima Barros
Toronto, Ontario
Phone: 416 588 5686
Website: www.alderlygroup.com/reikitherapy
Email: falcon01@Sympatico.ca

Chile:

Escuela de Reiki Gendai Hikari
Claudio Robe Oyaneder
Santiago
Phone: 56 02 2749111
Website: www.reikigendai.cl
Email: escuelahikari@gmail.com

Finland:

Matti Täppinen
Vantaa
Phone: 358 40 7590579
Email: reikiborealis@gmail.com

France:

Cabinet Emergence
Anne-Aurelie Demory
Roquebrune-sur-Argens
Phone: 33 6 13 82 26 04
Website: http://www.cabinet-emergence.fr
Email: cabinet.emergence@wanadoo.fr

Mahayana Reiki
Pascale Lemaire
Bullion
Phone: 01 30 41 38 63
Email: chamanastral@aol.com

Germany:

Hiroko Kasahara
Brühl
Phone: 49 2232 941872
Website: www.reikischulekoeln.de
Email: hiroko.kasahara@t-online.de

Shizuoka Reiki
Stefanie Krupp
Hamburg Lokstedt/Eppendorf
Phone: 0 176 48 61 07 60
Website: www.shizuokareiki.com
Email: reiki@shizuokareiki.com

Ute Wehrend-Segers and Harry Segers
Brekendorf
Phone: 0032 14 706554 – 0476 942195
Email: Ute-harry@telenet.be

Greece:

Center of Light
Lumi Vasile – Dimitris Katsiavalos
Rhodes
Phone: 0030 6976 604623 – 6974 456017
Website: www.reiki-centeroflight.gr
Email: luminaria333@yahoo.com

Hong Kong:

Crystal Age
Angeline Pui Yee Yeung
Kowloon
Phone: 852 23997390
Website: www.crystalage.com.hk
Email: angeline@crystalage.com.hk

Italy:

Associazione Culturale 'Reiki On'
Firenze
Website: www.usuireiki.it
E-mail: cristian@harno.it

Animazen
Matteo Cervi
Legano (Mi)
Phone: 39 328 9712895
Website: www.animazen.it
Email: reiju@email.it

Japan:

Komyo Reiki Kai
Hyakuten Inamoto
Kyoto, 612-0019
Phone: 81-75-645-3263, 81-90-1910-5015
Website: www.komyo-reiki.jp
Email: komyo100@yahoo.co.jp or hyakuten@komyo-reiki.jp

Reiki Retreat 'Refrepia'
Mr. Yasuhide Tanaka
Chiba prefecture
Phone: 81 475 80 1313
Website: www.reikijapan.com
Email: healing@reikijapan.com

The Netherlands:

De Kern Boz
Bergen op Zoom
Phone: 0164-210700
Website: www.dekernboz.nl
Email info@dekernboz.nl

Sunspirit Reikicentrum
Els van Dusseldorp
Renkum
Phone: 0317 310899
Website: www.sunspiritreikicentrum.nl
Email: info@sunspirit.nl

Praktijk De Adelaar
Edwin Heus
Almere
Phone: 036 537 28 78
Website: www.adelaarnet.nl
Email: Edwin@adelaarnet.nl

Praktijk Parcival
Monique Hendriks
Kloosterzande
Phone: 0114 681898
Website: www.praktijkparcival.nl
Email: info@praktijkparcival.nl

New Zealand:

Southern School of Reiki
Julie Anderson
Invercargill
Phone: 03 2130776
Email: jewles@es.co.nz

Wonderful Works
Rachel Watson
Auckland
Phone: 64 21576869
Email: rwatson@nz1.ibm.com

South Africa:

Beverley Marsden
Sandton, Gauteng
Phone: 011 656 5401
Website: www.reikihealing.co.za
Email: maniacs@iafrica.com

Switzerland:

Reiki Therapie – Raum Frangipani
Maria Karrer
Basel
Phone: 41 079 758 48 18
Website: www.reiki-karrer.ch
Email: info@reiki-karrer.ch

Urs Wernli
Ormalingen
Phone: 41 61 983 10 80
Website: www.gesund.ch/verz/plz4200.htm
Email: urs.wernli@magnet.ch

UK:

Angel Inspirations
Nina Fotara
Essex, CM3 5ZB
Phone: 01245425715
Websites: www.angelinspirations.co.uk & www.usuireikiryoho.biz
Email: mail@angelinspirations.co.uk

Complete Therapy
Vivienne Whitehead
Peterborough, Cambridgeshire
Phone: 01733 235254
Website: www.complete-therapy.com
Email: info@complete-therapy.com

Doreen Sawyer, Business & Training
Doreen Sawyer
Andover, Hampshire
Phone: 01264 792779 or 07990 620660
Website: www.manteia.co.uk
Email: training@manteia.co.uk

Highest Touch Reiki
Andrea K. Bradley
Greenwich, London
Phone: 07979960378
Email: andreakbradley@hotmail.com

Manor Reiki Centre
Angela Robertshaw
Albrighton, Wolverhampton
Phone: 0190 237 4697
Website: www.reiki-train.co.uk
Email: angela@reiki-train.co.uk

Namkha Reiki Training
Rebecca Holton
Brighouse, West Yorkshire
Phone: 01484 721534
Website: www.namkha.co.uk
Email: MoonSongstress@aol.com

Reiki Inspirations
Helen Galpin
Winchcombe, Gloucestershire
Website: www.reikiinspirations.co.uk
Email: reikiinspirations@hotmail.co.uk

Reiki: Pure & Simple
Colin Powell
Eccles, Manchester
Phone: 0161 288 0593
Website: http://homepage.ntlworld.com/reiki.colin/reiki.htm
Email: reiki.pureandsimple@ntlworld.com

Rita Bishop
Little Plumstead, Norwich
Phone: 01603 720737
Website: www.RitaBishop.co.uk
Email: ritabish@aol.com

The Beacon of Healing Light
Graham King & Angie Buxton-King
Hemel Hempstead, Hertfordshire
Phone: 01923 267552
Website: www.angiebuxton-king.com
Email: angel.beacon@virgin.net

The Kelso Reiki Room
Cathleen Hepburn-Klemm
Kelso
Telephone: 07738 638486
Website: www.nutritionally-u.com
Email: cat@nutritionally-u.com

USA:

Animal Paradise Communication & Healing
Janet Dobbs
Oak Hill, VA
Phone: 703 648 1866
Website: www.animalparadisecommunication.com
Email: janet@animalparadisecommunication.com

Animal Reiki Source
Kathleen Prasad
San Rafael, California
Phone: 415 420 9783
Website: www.animalreikisource.com
Email: info@animalreikisource.com

International Association of Reiki
Mari Hall
Houston, Texas
Phone: 832 282 4454
Website: www.wisechoices.com
Email: mari@wisechoices.com

Intensegrity
Joseph W. Moon
Downingtown, PA
Phone: (610) 873-4514
Website: www.reikihealingcenter.org/reikiteachers.htm
Email: jwmoon@verizon.net

Midwest Institute of Usui Reiki Ryôhô
Timothous L. Seaton
Kansas City, KS
Phone: 9135792952
Website: www.miurr.org
Email: admin@miurr.org

New York Reiki Dojo
Janet Dagley Dagley
New York, New York
Phone: 917 512 1330
Website: www.reikidojo.net
Email: janet@healingmovement.com

Reiki and Storyweaving
Carol Burbank
Accokeek, MD
Phone: 301 891 7450
Website: www.storyweaving.com
Email: cburbank@storyweaving.com

Robert N. Fueston
Lexington, KY
Phone: 859 273 1011
Website: www.robertfueston.com
Email: info@acupunctureky.com

Sundar Kadayam
Cincinnati, Ohio
Phone: 513 708 1910
Website: http://kadayam.com
Email: skadayam@gmail.com

The Ark Reiki
Carrie Ann Calay
Rancho Cordova, San Francisco Bay Area, California
Phone: 510 652 4770
Website: www.thearkreiki.com
Email: carrieanncalay@juno.com

The Center for Japanese Reiki
James Johnson
Washington UT
Email: fireheart@q.com
Website: www.japanesereiki.org

18 Reiki Associations

Associations have been set up throughout the world to provide a place of community for Reiki practitioners. They are also there to set and keep standards. Each association has its own views as to what these standards are and how they should be implemented.

Some associations are created for specific branches of Reiki while others have an open membership for all Reiki practitioners. There is even an association for registered nurses.

It is important that an association is there for its members rather than for those who direct it. For associations to be successful they must meet the needs of their members and, at the same time, the needs of the general public.

This is not a complete list of all Reiki associations but a guide to some of the associations available.

Argentina:

> Asociación Argentina de Reiki
> Av. Los Incas
> Phone: 4787 6414
> Website: www.reikihoy.com.ar
> Email: info@reikihoy.com.ar

Australia:

> Australian Reiki Connection (ARC)
> Toll free: 1300 130 975
> Website: www.australianreikiconnection.com.au
> Email: arcpres@australianreikiconnection.com.au

> Council of Australian Reiki Organisations (CARO)
> Website: www.caro.org.au
> Email: chair@caro.org.au

Canada:

Atlantic Usui Reiki Association
Nova Scotia
Email: jsettle@atcon.com

Canadian Reiki Association
Vancouver, BC
Phone: 1800 835 7525
Website: www.reiki.ca
Email: reiki@reiki.ca

Croatia:

Croatian Reiki Society
Zagreb, Croatia
Phone: (385) 1619 00 99 or 619 22 99
Email: verica.aleksander@zg.tel.hr

France:

Maison Internationale des Arts Energétiques
Paris
Website: www.minaren.blogspirit.com
Email: minaren@wanadoo.fr

Ireland:

Celtic Reiki Federation
Website: http://celticreikifederation.org
Email: info@celticreikifederation.org

Reiki Federation of Ireland
Website: www.reikifederationireland.com
Email: info@reikifederationireland.com

Italy:

European Reiki Association
Varese VA, Italy
Phone: (0332) 966064
Email: caocis@tin.it

The Netherlands:

Nederlandse Vereniging van Reiki Masters
Phone: 073-5220501
Website: www.nvrm.nl

New Zealand:

Reiki New Zealand Inc.
Auckland, NZ
Website: www.reiki.org.nz
Email: reiki@ihug.co.nz

South Africa:

The Reiki Association of Southern Africa
Phone: (2782) 857 5999
Website: www.reikiassociation.co.za
Email: karen@reikiassociation.co.za

UK:

National Federation of Spiritual Healers
Website: www.nfsh.org.uk

The Guild of Professional Healers
Website: www.cancertherapies.org.uk   Email: info@cancertherapies.
   org.uk

UK Reiki Federation
Website: www.reikifed.co.uk
Email: enquiries@reikifed.co.uk

USA:

International Association of Reiki Professionals
Nashua, NH
Phone: 603 881 8838
Website: www.iarp.org
Email: info@iarp.org

19 Reiki Newsletters

Resonance

UK Reiki Federation Magazine
Phone: 01264 791 441
Website: www.reikifed.co.uk
Email: resonance@reikifed.co.uk
Members' magazine

The Reiki Digest

Editor: Janet Dagley Dagley
New Jersey
Phone: 917 512 1330
Website: www.thereikidigest.com
Email: editor@thereikidigest.com
Free weekly online newsletter

The Reiki Newsletter

International House of Reiki
Editors: Bronwen and Frans Stiene
Toll free: 1800 000 992 within Australia
Website: www.reiki.net.au
Email: info@reiki.net.au
Free e-mail newsletter from the authors of *The Reiki Sourcebook*

20 Reiki Internet Resources

One of the greatest inventions of the last century must be the Internet. The World Wide Web has laid the globe at our feet. Billions of pages of information are accessible with just a tap of the fingers and a click of a mouse.

The Internet is a weird and wonderful place. Listed below are sites for chatting, joining forums, registering for free distant Reiki and sites to help practitioners become pro-active and heal the earth. Hopefully none of these sites will have been hacked into and turned into sex sites by the time they are logged onto.

An added element of caution has also entered our lives with the advent of the Internet. In the writing of this book many wonderful sites have been accessed and some strange ones too. It is true that you can't believe everything you read. Keep that in mind as you ride the Reiki roller web. Reiki pages have taken to the Internet like a duck to water and there is no shortage of viewpoints out there. Their validity is another point entirely. Once again the chats, forums and distant healing groups are not here through special recommendation – their existence is simply noted.

Life on the Internet can be short-lived for many sites, so if any changes are found, please contact the authors so that we can update our information.

Reiki Chat/Forum

Practitioners from all levels can come together and chat over the Internet to ask questions, provide information and make friends.

Australian Reiki Connection

> Website: www.australianreikiconnection.com.au
> Australian forum

Healthy Pages

> Website: www.healthypages.net/forum
> UK forum

Reiki-4 all

> Website: www.reiki-4-all.com
> Worldwide forum

Reiki Centrum Belgie

> Website: www.reikicentrum.be
> Belgian forum

Reiki Centrum Nederland

> Website: www.reikicentrum.nl
> Dutch forum
> Reiki Forum
> Website: www.reikiforum.de
> German forum

Reiki Forums

> Website: www.reikiforums.nl
> Dutch forum

Reiki Meetup

> Website: www.reiki.meetup.com
> Worldwide forum

Reiki Stromingen

> Website: www.reikistromingen.nl/forum/
> Dutch forum

Reiki Suche Forum

> Website: www.reiki-suche.de/forum
> German forum

The Reiki Café

> Website: www.nexuscafe.com/bin/bbs.cgi/ShowBoardList/reiki
> Worldwide forum

Reiki Projects

Healing Hands Network
Contact person: Sandra Griffiths
Tenbury Wells, Worcestershire
Phone: 44 0 1885 410620
Website: www.healinghandsnetwork.org.uk
Email: hhnadmin@btconnect.com

Healing Hands Network sends professionally trained complementary therapists to treat people suffering from physical and emotional trauma following war or disaster. They have been working in Sarajevo, Bosnia & Herzegovina since 1996, treating over 20,000 people who have lost limbs, homes and loved ones, or who have been raped or tortured. The therapies used include Reiki, massage, reflexology, aromatherapy and acupuncture and they treat anyone, regardless of race, gender or creed. They have also begun a project in Nairobi, Kenya, where local therapists treat the victims of gender violence.

S.P.A.R.K.
Spirited Action, Release and Kindness, Inc. (SPARK)
Contact person: Dave Gorczynski
New York, NY
Phone: 212 737 7391
Website: www.sparkenergy.org
Email: info@sparkenergy.org

S.P.A.R.K. is a New York-based nonprofit offering free and accessible energy work services and workshops to the general public, nonprofit organizations and other institutions.

Reiki Articles

www.reikiarticles.com

Reiki Podcasts

www.thereikishow.com

Reiki Wiki

www.reiki-wiki.com

Reiki Videos

www.youtube.com/user/IntHouseReiki

Distant Healing

These sites provide distant healing for the general public and the environment and are open for practitioners to join as members.

> Innate Foundation
> Website: www.innatefoundation.com

> The Circle of Light
> Website: www.yourangels.com

> The Distant Healing Network
> Website: www.the-dhn.com

Reiki Research

The site below is dedicated to collecting data from Reiki practitioners about their treatments. Interesting to either take part in or, at least, to read the results.

> Reiki and Meridian Therapy Centre (formerly Rose Carr Reiki Centre)
> Contact person: Joe Potter
> Lancashire, UK
> Website: www.reiki-research.co.uk
> Email: joe_potter@lineone.net

Appendices

A. Glossary

 A

Advanced Reiki Training – Sometimes called ART, 3a, or Reiki Master/Practitioner. It originates from Usui/Tibetan Reiki but has also been adopted by many Independent Reiki teachers. Some techniques taught at this level are *crystal grid work, a healing attunement, *Reiki guide meditation, psychic surgery, *Reiki symbol meditation and the *antakharana symbol. Students are taught what is called the Master Symbol (Symbol 4 and/or Dumo) but not how to perform the attunement.

Aikidô – A form of self-defence martial arts founded by Morihei Ueshiba, who is said to have been an acquaintance of Mikao Usui. Morihei Ueshiba stated that *aikidô* is a, 'study of the spirit'. It is often called 'The Way of Harmony'.

Amida Nyorai – This deity is taught as the connection to SHK and Symbol 2. Amida Nyorai is the main deity of Pure Land Buddhism. Amida is the Japanese transliteration for the Sanskrit for Amitabha which means Infinite Light. Amida's compassion is therefore also infinite. The main practice of the Pure Land sect is to recite *Namu-Amida-Butsu*, which is an expression of Oneness. *Namu-Amida-Butsu* translates to, 'I take refuge in Amida Nyorai Buddha'.

Animals – Reiki treatments can be performed on animals. Hand positions are applied on or near the animal. Often Reiki first aid procedures are used where hands are not placed in any specific sequence. In this situation hands are placed directly on the animal's area of complaint. Animals will clearly indicate to the Reiki practitioner if they are accepting of the treatment or not. Animals may show the practitioner that the treatment is finished by moving away.

Anshin Ritsumei – Hiroshi Doi, founder of *Gendai Reiki Hô*, states that Mikao Usui 'came to recognize that the purpose of life is to attain a state of *anshin ritsumei*. It means *to learn a fact *that man given a role to play is being sustained by the universe,* and *to fulfill one's role with a calm mind by trusting the universe and leaving all to the universe no matter what happens in the course of life.'* Hyakuten Inamoto, founder of *Komyo Reiki Kai,* states that *anshin ritsumei* means, 'to stay clam and peaceful without any attachment or expectation after having surrendered to the divine will' or simply put, 'absolute inner peace'.

*Antakharana Symbol – Non-traditional Reiki symbol. This symbol has been added to the system of Reiki by some Reiki teachers, including Arthur Robertson, and is used in Usui/Tibetan Reiki as a meditation technique. The antakharana is a two dimensional cube with three sevens on its face. Myth has it that this symbol comes from Tibet and China. It is claimed that if you meditate on the antakharana you will connect the physical brain with the Higher Self.

*Anti-Clockwise Energy Spirals – Non-traditional technique that claims to ease the client into a change that is about to happen.

Araki, George – One of Hawayo Takata's 22 teacher students. According to Robert Fueston, George Araki initially became a Reiki teacher when he was head of the Department of Natural Healing at San Francisco State University and was interested in completing a study about it. He did not teach many people, preferring to refer them to either Fran Brown or Shinobu Saito.

Attunement – Attunements are one of the five elements of the system of Reiki. There are many different attunement methods as teachers have added to, or taken away from, traditional processes. The origin of the attunement is the Japanese *reiju* which does not include mantras and/or symbols. There are no limits to the number of *reiju* one can receive. It is believed that Chûjirô Hayashi may have created the basic attunement process that is taught today by adding symbols and mantras to the *reiju*. The attunement is sometimes known as an initiation, empowerment, or transformation.

Aura – A supernatural energy field around all objects that some claim to be able to see. The aura is said to be linked with the function of the chakras. These concepts have been adopted into New Age movement beliefs and consequently some recent branches of the system of Reiki.

 B

Baba, Dorothy – One of Hawayo Takata's 22 Reiki teacher students. According to Robert Fueston, she was a social worker.

Baylow, Ursula (1911–1996) – One of Hawayo Takata's 22 Reiki teacher students.

Beaming – Non-traditional technique in which Reiki is said to be directed to a person/place or thing by turning the palms toward them/it. This technique does not include touch. It is taught in Usui/Tibetan Reiki and is practiced by some Independent Reiki Master/Teachers.

Beggar Story – Most modern Reiki practitioners know the 'beggar story' as a parable told by Hawayo Takata. Usuing Mikao Usui and his experience trying to help a beggar as an example she taught practitioners that Reiki must be paid for or it will not be respected.

Many teachers dispute this concept today and there exist groups of teachers and practitioners who offer Reiki treatments and Reiki courses for free.

There is an account of the 'beggar story' in *Living Reiki – Takata's Teachings* by Fran Brown.

Benefits – The bodymind knows how to heal itself – the system of Reiki supports that innate healing process.

One of the most fundamental concepts of Reiki is that the body draws on more energy to clear its stagnant energy. This is a non-diagnostic system that accepts that the body draws the energy to where it is most needed.

This system began as a spiritual development practice at the beginning of the 1900s. Once a practitioner feels spiritually whole, the physical body follows.

Blockage – Sometimes the word blockage is used to express the lack of movement of energy in a specific area of the body. A more positive view of this experience is that stagnant energy is stimulated by working with Reiki, resulting in change for the client.

Blue Book, The – Paul Mitchell and Phyllis Lei Furumoto wrote *The Blue Book – Reiki* in 1985. It includes historical information as taught by Hawayo Takata, some information about The Reiki Alliance plus photos of Mikao Usui, Chûjirô Hayashi, Hawayo Takata and Phyllis Lei Furumoto.

Bockner, Rick – One of Hawayo Takata's 22 Reiki teacher students.

Bowling, Patricia – One of Hawayo Takata's 22 Reiki teacher students.

Branch of Reiki – The system of Reiki began in the early 1900s. Since the death of its founder Mikao Usui, a number of different branches of the system have developed in Japan.

Since 1980, a great variety of Reiki branches and teachings inspired by the system of Reiki have also been created outside of Japan. This has led to many individual teachings which may or may not relate to what was once taught by Mikao Usui.

Over the last 30 years the system of Reiki has become one of the most popular forms of energy healing. Its structure of three levels with its interesting mix of self-help and mysticism has been replicated many times over with slight variations. This has meant the word 'Reiki' has been adopted for use in systems and practices unrelated to the system of Reiki.

*Breath of the Fire Dragon – Non-traditional breath technique used with a non-traditional attunement process. Variations of this are the blue kidney breath, Reiki breathing and *violet breath. It was originally taught in Raku Kei Reiki.

Brown, Barbara (1915?–2001) – One of Hawayo Takata's 22 Reiki teacher students. The inaugural Reiki Alliance meeting was held at Barbara Brown's house in British Columbia in 1983.

Brown, Fran – One of Hawayo Takata's 22 Reiki teacher students. She published a book entitled *Living Reiki – Takata's Teachings*.

Buddhism – Chinese Buddhism travelled across to Japan from the 7th century, and over the last 1,400 years has developed its own unique Japanese form. A Japanese form of Buddhism called *Tendai* is said to have been a large influence on the teachings of Mikao Usui. Suzuki san, a Tendai nun and student of Mikao Usui, claims that he was a *Tendai* lay priest.

In the 1980s and 1990s, other forms of Buddhism such as Tibetan Buddhism were claimed to lie at the foundation of the system of Reiki. That is unlikely, however, as Buddhism originated in India and moved to China and Tibet independently of each other. Japanese esoteric Buddhism is a term that includes *Mikkyô* and *Shugendô* practices. Within these forms esoteric rituals involving mantras, *mudras*, and mandalas are used.

Budô – Refers to the traditional art of self-defence in Japan. Some different kinds of budo are *jûdô, karate, aikidô,* kendô, and iaidô. It is claimed that Mikao Usui studied martial arts and gained *menkyo kaiden*, the highest license of proficiency.

*Byôsen Reikan Hô 病腺霊感法 – Sense imbalances in the body. Traditional technique similar to the modern technique of scanning.

C

Certificate – Certification is often given to students at the end of a Reiki course. There is no one true form of Reiki certification. A certificate today signifies that a student has simply completed whatever it is that the Reiki teacher teaches. There are no across-the-board standards. It is possible to finish Levels 1, 2, or even 3 in a weekend. This leaves the student feeling temporarily powerful without actually becoming empowered. When an individual receives attunements over a couple of days, the body's energy cannot differentiate between having received a Level 1, 2, or 3 certificate.

The system of Reiki is not about certification – it is about personal practice. In traditional Japanese teachings a certificate is given to indicate that certain levels of proficiency have been reached and that the student is just beginning that actual level.

Chakra – Chakra is a Sanskrit word often translated as 'wheel of energy'. There are a minimum of seven major chakras in the body. The chakra system, though Indian in origin, is popular in many New Age forms of energetic work. Chakras have also recently been included in some modern forms of the system of Reiki.

There is no record of Mikao Usui, or his students Toshihiro Eguchi, Kaiji Tomita, or Chûjirô Hayashi working with chakras.

Hawayo Takata wrote of the 'true energy' in the body that 'lies in the bottom of the stomach about 2 inches below the navel' in *The Gray Book,* compiled by her daughter, Alice Takata Furumoto, from her diary notes. Here Hawayo Takata is referring to the *hara* energetic method that is used in Japan.

Chakras have been taught in the system of Reiki by a number of Hawayo Takata's students, including John Harvey Gray and Iris Ishikuro. Barbara Weber also bases The Radiance Technique® on the chakra system. In some modern branches of Reiki, it is claimed that an attunement clears or opens a particular chakra. This is, however, a recent interpretation of the system.

*Chakra Balancing – Non-traditional technique to balance the chakras with one another. Taught in Satya Reiki.

*Chakra Kassei Kokyû Hô – Non-traditional breathing technique to activate the chakras.

Channel (1) – When a Reiki practitioner stimulates Reiki to move through the body this is often called channeling (different to Channel (2)).

A practitioner does this by practicing techniques to strengthen his/her energy, by receiving *reiju* or attunements, and by focusing with a clear intent.

Channel (2) – Another meaning of channel has to do with mediumship and communicating with those who have passed away or exist in another dimension. Some recent branches of the system of Reiki aligned with New Age movement beliefs claim to 'channel' information from sources that are not physically alive.

Chiba – The name of Mikao Usui's ancestors. The *Chiba* clan was one of the most famous and influential *samurai* families in all of Japan according to the *Chiba* family records. The Usui memorial stone states that the famous *samurai* Chiba Tsunetane (1118–1201) was Mikao Usui's ancestor. This may be incorrect as Hiroshi Doi states it was the *samurai* Chiba Toshitane instead. The Usui family crest, otherwise known as the *Chiba mon*, is a design comprising the moon and a star. These were also the symbols of Myoken Bodhisattva. Myoken was once an icon for the *samurai*.

Chiba Toshitane – A famous *samurai* warlord from the 1500s. In 1551 he conquered the city Usui and thereafter all family members acquired that name. The memorial stones states that the famous *samurai* Chiba Tsunetane (1118–1201) was Mikao Usui's ancestor. Hiroshi Doi notes that this was incorrect and that it was in fact Chiba Toshitane.

Chiba Tsunetane (1118–1201) – The memorial stone states that the famous *samurai* Chiba Tsunetane was Mikao Usui's ancestor.

Chiryô Hô 治療法 – Treatment. This term is used in the description of a number of Japanese Reiki techniques.

Christianity – The system of Reiki is not a religion and is used by people of all religions around the world. Many Christians, including some Catholic nuns and priests, practice the system of Reiki on themselves and others.

CKR – As the traditional mantras of the system of Reiki are considered as sacred by many, pseudonyms are used in *The Reiki Sourcebook* rather than the true mantras. The pseudonym for the first traditional mantra is the initials CKR.
The main modern characteristic of CKR is Power and it is spoken three times in conjunction with Symbol 1.
The main traditional characteristic is Focus. In Japan, the mantra is not necessarily used in conjunction with the symbol. The early teachings of Mikao Usui claim that CKR develops a Reiki practitioner's link to the energy of Earth.

Cleansing – With any form of natural healing, there is a cleansing. This may happen during or immediately after a Reiki treatment, or within a few days.
During a treatment the client's body draws in energy, which washes through, clearing the body out on a physical, mental, emotional, and/or spiritual level. This cleansing may be obvious or very subtle and is sometimes called a clearing or a healing crisis. See also Three-Week Cleansing Process.

Clearing – See Cleansing.

Client – A person who receives a Reiki treatment from a Reiki practitioner. A Reiki client is not referred to as a patient as that would indicate that the client was sick, which is not necessarily the case. Using the word 'patient' is also suggestive of a quasi-medical environment that may inappropriately represent the treatment as diagnostic.

*Communicating with Your Higher Self – Non-traditional technique where one re-connects with the Higher Self.

Connection – In some Japanese teachings this word is used to describe the characteristic of HSZSN and Symbol 3. This mantra and symbol help one remember that a connection between everything already exists, stimulating Oneness between the Reiki practitioner and client. If a practitioner becomes One with everything, it becomes unnecessary to 'send' Reiki to someone or something. The symbol itself is Japanese *kanji* meaning, 'My original nature is a correct thought'.

*Crystal Healing – Crystals are renowned as excellent healers. There are now many versions of crystal healing being used in modern branches of the system of Reiki.

D

Dainichi Nyorai – Symbol 4 helps practitioners connect to this deity. Dainichi Nyorai is the Great Shining Buddha because this Buddha is the 'Life force of the Buddhas that Illuminate Everything'. Dainichi dispels the darkness of the world by casting light everywhere, giving life to and nurturing all living things. The wrathful face of Dainichi Nyorai is Fudô Myôô.

Daiseishi Bosatsu – Symbol 1 helps practitioners connect to this Buddhist deity. The name means 'He who Proceeds with Great Vigour'.

Degree – Another name for the word 'level' used within the system of Reiki.

Deity – God or Goddess.

Den 伝 – Legend, tradition and teachings.
In some Japanese branches of Reiki the name of the levels ends with -den, for example *shoden* (first teachings). This system originates from Japanese martial arts.

Denju – Handing down of the teachings.
This Japanese Buddhist term has recently been adopted by some Reiki practitioners to replace the word *reiju*. Denju could be interpreted to mean *reiju* but may more accurately indicate the entire teachings.

*De-programming Techniques – There are two traditional Japanese techniques that work on releasing set mental patterns. One is **nentatsu hô* and the other is **seiheki chiryô hô*. In modern teachings, a number of variations of these techniques are practiced.

Dharani – A spell.
From the 13th century in Japan, it was thought that *waka* achieved supernatural effects because they were *dharani* or spells. Mikao Usui included in his teachings 125 *waka* penned by the Meiji Emperor.

Distance Symbol – The name is sometimes applied to HSZSN and Symbol 3 in modern forms of the system of Reiki. The mantra and symbol are commonly used for distant healing. According to the modern system of Reiki they create a bridge between the sender and receiver.
In traditional teachings the characteristic of the mantra and symbol is considered to be Connection.

Distant Attunement – Attunements and *reiju* are initially performed in person but with globalization, attunements are now being sent by distance. This method is an extension of the concept of distant healing, which has been used in the system of Reiki. If a practitioner wishes to learn the system of Reiki then solely receiving an attunement is not enough – one must study the five elements of the system of Reiki.

*Distant Healing – Distant healing is used to send Reiki for the purpose of healing to someone who is not physically present. Symbol 3 is said to activate this technique and is taught at Level 2. Numerous techniques are used in conjunction with distant healing, including the photo technique and healing lists. The related traditional technique is called *enkaku chiryô hô*.

*Distant Reiki – Send Reiki to a person, place or thing in the past, present or future with distant healing.

DKM – As the traditional mantras of the system of Reiki are considered as sacred by many, pseudonyms are used in *The Reiki Sourcebook* rather than the true mantras. The pseudonym for the fourth traditional mantra is the initials DKM.

The *kanji* of the true mantra of DKM is actually Symbol 4.

The main modern characteristic of DKM is as the Master Symbol and it is spoken three times in conjunction with Symbol 4.

The main traditional characteristic is Empowerment. In Japan, the mantra is not necessarily used in conjunction with the symbol. The early teachings of Mikao Usui claim that DKM develops a Reiki practitioner's true nature.

This mantra is not used only within Mikao Usui's teachings. It can be found in some Japanese martial arts as well as in *Mikkyô*, *Shugendô*, and some of the new religions like *Shunmei*.

Dô 道 – Way or method. A term commonly used in Japan to describe a teacher's method, like *aikidô* and *jûdô*.

Doctor – Mikao Usui was given the title 'Doctor' by Hawayo Takata. This led to some believing that

he was actually a physician even thought it was not the case. Using this type of terminology can be misleading for clients and students, leading them to believe that the system of Reiki's origins are allopathic. Constant repetition of this misinformation does not promote the system of Reiki as a reputable practice.

However, a student of Mikao Usui, Chûjirô Hayashi, was a doctor and his medical background is claimed to have helped Mikao Usui create the *Usui Reiki Ryôhô Gakkai's* healing guide.

Doi, Hiroshi – Teacher of *Gendai Reiki Hô*. Hiroshi Doi is also a member of the *Usui Reiki Ryôhô Gakkai*. He officially joined the society on 22 October 1993. Hiroshi Doi has studied many styles of Reiki as well as numerous energetic and spiritual techniques. He was one of the first Japanese to study Levels 1 and 2 with Mieko Mitsui who was teaching Barbara Weber's The Radiance Technique® in Japan. He also studied all three levels of a system of Reiki called Neo Reiki and trained with Chiyoko Yamaguchi.

Dôjô – A place of the path. Generally speaking, a place where something is learnt. This term is most often used in martial arts like *jûdô*, *karate*, *kendô*, etc. On Mikao Usui's memorial stone it states that he set up a *dôjô* at *Nakano* in *Tôkyô*.

E

Earth – In Japan, Earth is often described as one half of the universe with Heaven being its opposite force. An ancient Japanese cosmological theory states that through the union of these dual forces all things were born. In Mikao Usui's early teachings the CKR and Symbol 1 are said to be associated with the energy of the Earth: heavy, powerful and grounding. Hiroshi Doi has stated, 'In the Gakkai the words *harmony of ten-chi-jin* and *Oneness of Great Universe (the macrocosm) and Small Universe (humans or the microcosm)* are often used.' *Ten* is Heaven, *chi* is Earth, and *jin* is humanity.

Eguchi, Toshihiro (1873–1946) – Professor Judith Rabinovitch has been collecting research about Toshihiro Eguchi from material that includes his diaries and monographs. She states that he was both a student and longtime friend of Mikao Usui. According to a recently published Japanese book by Mihashi Kazuo on Toshihiro Eguchi's life, *Tenohira-ga Byoki-o Naosu*, he was born in *Kumamoto*, studied at *Tôkyô* University, and was principal of a junior high school. He also wrote *waka*.

As his health had never been very good, as an older man he claimed that only two good things had happened in his life: that he had started practicing hands-on healing and found a good husband for his daughter. His daughter's husband was Gorô Miyazaki, a hands-on healing student of Toshihiro Eguchi. Due to Toshihiro Eguchi's popularity as a teacher of hands-on healing, he is most likely to have influenced many hands-on healing teachings at that time.

Toshihiro Eguchi created the *Tenohira Ryôji Kenkyû kai* (Hand Healing Research Center) in 1928 and wrote a number of books: *Te No Hira Ryôji Nyûmon* (*Introduction to Healing with the Palms*) in 1930 and *Te No Hira Ryôji Wo Kataru* (*A Story of Healing with the Palms*) in 1954. Hiroshi Doi states that Toshihiro Eguchi studied Mikao Usui's teachings between 1925 and 1927.

Toshihiro Eguchi was a member of the *Usui Reiki Ryôhô Gakkai* for two years but, according to Mihashi Kazuo, he apparently found the 50 yen admission fee to be too expensive. At that time Taketomi Kanichi was teaching and as he was a financially well-off naval officer, Toshihiro Eguchi could not understand why such large sums of money were required. At every meeting members were also asked to pay 1 yen. Eventually Toshihiro Eguchi wrote a letter to the *Usui Reiki Ryôhô Gakkai* president, Jûzaburô Ushida, resigning from the society.

According to Mihashi Kazuo, he taught specific hand positions, meditations, the recitation of the Meiji Emperor's *waka* by students on a daily basis, and principles for an ascetic life.

In 1929 he taught members of the *Ittôen* community his system, with some families still practicing these hands-on healing practices today. Professor Judith Rabinovitch states that, '*Ittôen* folks have told me that there were no levels, no formal rituals or attunements in Eguchi's way of doing things.' His teachings became very popular with about 150 to 300 people in attendance at a teaching. A book by his student Kôshi Mitsui about the teachings increased this popularity. He even travelled to Pusan in Korea to teach. Toshitaka Mochizuki states in his book that Toshihiro Eguchi taught approximately 500,000 students. This large number may include all students who have studied his teachings over the years.

According to Suzuki san, it was Toshihiro Eguchi who was responsible for adding the 3 mantras or *jumon* from Shintôism into Level 2 of the system of Reiki.

Empowerment (1) – This word is often used to describe the *reiju* and/or the attunement process.

Empowerment (2) – In some Japanese teachings this word is used to describe the characteristics of DKM and Symbol 4.

Energy Exchange – This term is a modern concept that ensures students take responsibility for their own health. The client is asked to return the favour of a Reiki treatment by doing 'something' for the Reiki practitioner. In this way the client is more respectful of the treatment, leaving him/her with a sense of self-responsibility for his/her own health. Hawayo Takata taught using a parable which is commonly called the 'beggar story'.

Enjudô – A hall where one's life is lengthened.
This is a specific hall within a Japanese monastery where monks and nuns perform healing. This healing can take place on either a physical or spiritual level.

*Enkaku Chiryô Hô 遠隔治療法 – Remote healing.
This practice is related to the technique called *distant healing.

En-no-Gyoja – The ascetic En.
The legendary founder of *Shugendô*, also known as En-no-Ozunu. He is said to have been born in 634. From the age of 32 he practiced esoteric Buddhism and laid the foundations for *Shugendô* (esoteric mountain Buddhism).
Researchers today claim that Mikao Usui practised *Shugendô* and that many of the understandings of the system of Reiki grew from it.
Due to the outlawing of *Shugendô* in 1872, the author of *Shugendô*, Miyake Hitoshi, wrote that many new religions sprang up 'to take its place and respond to the human need for fulfilling worldly aspirations.' *Shugendô* thus became the central foundation for many of these new religions. Reiki is not a religion. It was created as a system that could be

openly practiced by individuals regardless of their beliefs. It does however have similar origins to many of the new religions of that particular time in Japanese history.

Enryaku ji – Main *Tendai* temple on *hiei zan*, near *Kyôto*, Japan. There are claims that Mikao Usui trained and studied here and that old *sutra* copies still bear his Buddhist name.

 F

Facet – A variation of the word 'level' used by some branches of Reiki e.g., Facet 2 instead of Level 2.

*Finishing Treatment – A blood cleansing technique that is also called the *nerve stroke. In Japan, traditional versions of this are *zenshin kôketsu hô, *hanshin kôketsu hô, and *ketsueki kôkan hô. Hawayo Takata taught this technique at Level 2.

First Aid – In the mid-1920s Mikao Usui taught hands-on healing to a group of naval officers. The intention was that while at sea they would be able to work energetically on themselves and others, especially in first aid situations. This group were the founding members of a society that still exists in Japan today called the *Usui Reiki Ryôhô Gakkai*. To use Reiki as a form of first aid immediately place the hands on or near the area of need. Myths have abounded that Reiki should not initially be

used on broken bones as it would too quickly set the bone. Overtime this myth and others have proved themselves to be merely superstitions. If Reiki could heal a bone as quickly and consistently as this myth suggests then surely Reiki would be indispensable in all hospitals.

Five Elements of the System of Reiki – No matter what the background, all Reiki courses should have a minimum of five elements in common. These elements are all rituals that are created to help Reiki practitioners develop structure and routine. The five elements that every student receives are: attunements or *reiju*, hand positions, the precepts, symbols and mantras (from Level 2 onward), and meditations and/or techniques.

Five Head Positions – A number of hand positions on the head are included in the *Reiki Ryôhô Hikkei* and Chûjirô Hayashi's *Ryôhô Shishin*.

Five similar head positions below are claimed by Suzuki san to have been taught by Mikao Usui.

They are:

zentô bu – forehead

sokutô bu – both temples

kôtô bu – back of your head and forehead

enzui bu – either side of neck

tôchô bu – crown on top of head

Toshihiro Eguchi, a well-known hands-on healer and friend of Mikao Usui, used a similar set of hand positions in his manuals and added one last position at the stomach. Following is a translation of his five head positions taken from his joint publication with Kôshi Mitsui. The positions are:

haegiwa – hairline

komekami – temples (you can do both sides with both hands at once) *kôtôbu no takai tokoro* – rear of head, high up

kubisuji – nape of neck

atama no chôjô – top of head (crown)

ichoo – stomach, intestines

Five Precepts

For today only:

Do not anger

Do not worry

Be humble

Be honest in your work

Be compassionate to yourself and others

These precepts are the cornerstone of Mikao Usui's teachings and are guidelines to aid students in their spiritual development journey. The *Usui Reiki Ryôhô Gakkai* perform *Gokai Sansho* (chanting of the five precepts three times) at the end of their regular group meetings called *kenkyû kai*.

The precepts are spiritual teachings rather than religious teachings and students are asked to consider them in their daily actions. They are also a part of the ritualism of the system of Reiki. The words are used to connect Reiki practitioners to certain thoughts in order to help move energy. Without these initial words and their intentions, practitioners would not know where to begin. After much personal work using these precepts, it is possible to tap into

their energy without the words themselves. This occurs when the practitioner is totally in the flow of his or her practice. Recently, it has been asserted that the origins of the five precepts actually date back to 9th-century Japanese Buddhist precepts. The precepts translated above originate from the *Usui Reiki Ryôhô Gakkai* and may have been developed to suit the *Usui Reiki Ryôhô Gakkai's* first members, Japanese naval officers.

Focus – In some traditional teachings this word is used to describe the characteristics of CKR and Symbol 1.

Fudô Myôô – Fudô Myôô is the wrathful face of Dainichi Nyorai. Fudô Myôô is often depicted with flames (to consume passions), a sword in his right hand (to conquer and cut through ignorance, greed, anger and injustice), and a rope in his left hand (to bind demons). In esoteric Japanese Buddhism Fudô Myôô is connected to the mantra taught at Level 3 of the system of Reiki.

Fueston, Robert – Reiki researcher who focuses mainly on Hawayo Takata, her teachings, and her students. Fueston has trained with some of Hawayo Takata's teacher students as well as Japanese teachers such as Hiroshi Doi and Hyakuten Inamoto.

Funakoshi Gichin (1868–1957) – Founder of modern *karate*. He is said to have known Mikao Usui. Shinpei Goto knew both Gichin Funakoshi (he wrote a calligraphic work for Gichin

Funakoshi's first book in 1922) and Mikao Usui. In 1922 Mikao Usui moved his seat of learning to *Tôkyô*, where Gichin Funakoshi taught and Shinpei Goto lived.

Furumoto, Alice Takata – The daughter of Hawayo Takata and the mother of Phyllis Lei Furumoto. Alice Takata Furumoto compiled *The Gray Book* (called *Leiki*), which was handed out to some of Hawayo Takata's teacher students.

Furumoto, Phyllis Lei – The granddaughter of Hawayo Takata. She is a Reiki teacher and a trained psychologist. Phyllis Lei Furumoto is said to have apprenticed with her grandmother for a year and a half. She is also a founding member of The Reiki Alliance. The Reiki Alliance state they have honoured her with their 'title of holder' of the 'Office of the Grandmaster' and also called her the 'lineage bearer' of the system of Reiki.

Futomani Divination Chart – The *Futomani* Divination Chart stems from the *Hotsuma Tsutae*. Copies of the *Hotsuma Tsutae* have been stored in *iwamuro* (cave storage) in a *Tendai* temple at *enryaku ji* (*hiei zan, Kyôto*). These copies were given to Saichô (767–822), the founding priest of *enryaku ji*. The origin of this text is controversial. *Tendai* priests were believed to give lectures on the *Hotsuma Tsutae*. The divination chart has 48 syllables attributed to deities that form the matrix of magic signs. One of the letterforms in the divination

chart, the *wa*, resembles the essence of Symbol 1.

 G

Gasshô 合掌 – To place the two palms together. This is a Japanese gesture of respect, gratitude, veneration and humility. This simple act balances both the mind and body. There are many varieties of *gasshô*.

*Gasshô Kokyû Hô 合掌呼吸法 – *Gasshô* breathing technique. Also called **seishin toitsu* and is part of the technique **hatsurei hô*.

*Gasshô Meditation – A meditation technique where one concentrates on the hands.

*Gedoku Hô – A similar technique to **tanden chiryô hô*. One hand is placed on the front of the *hara* and the other hand on the back of the *hara*. This technique is listed in the *shiori* (manual) for *Usui Reiki Ryôhô Gakkai* members.

Gokai 五戒 – Five precepts.

Gokai no sho – Book of five precepts.
This is a calligraphic scroll of the five Reiki precepts and is entitled *'Mikao Usui Sensei Ikun Gokai'* (The Five Precepts, an admonition of the late Mikao Usui).
Chiyoko Yamaguchi had such a work, brushstroked by her teacher, Chûjirô Hayashi. Although Chûjirô Hayashi created his own organization, he still showed his respect for the teachings of Mikao Usui by teaching classes in front of this scroll.

Gokai Sansho 五戒三唱 – To sing the five precepts three times. This is a Buddhist term. It is still practiced by the *Usui Reiki Ryôhô Gakkai* at the end of their meetings.

Gokui Kaiden – Ultimate stage of proficiency.
Teacher level in *Gendai Reiki Hô*, Hiroshi Doi's branch of Reiki.

Go Shimbô ご辛抱 – Patience, endurance or perseverance.
This is a *Tendai* Buddhist ritual that has similarities to the *reiju* and is known as 'Dharma for Protecting the Body'. Sometimes written as *Go Shinbô*.

Goto Shinpei (1857–1929) – After studying at medical school he worked in various important Government positions. He became well known for advocating philanthropy and the principle of a 'Large Family' when he took the position of Governor of the Standard of Railways. As a politician his nickname was 'Big Talker'.
Shinpei Goto became the Mayor of *Tôkyô* in 1920 and it has been said that Mikao Usui had worked for him.
Shinpei Goto wrote a calligraphic work in Gichin Funakoshi's first book in 1922 called *Ryukyu Kempo: Tode*. Gichin Funakoshi is also said to have been an acquaintance of Mikao Usui.
After the *Kanto* earthquake in September 1923, he played an active role in rebuilding *Tôkyô*.
In 1924, Citizen's forerunner, the Shokosha Watch Research Institute produced its first pocket watch. As a well-known Japanese personality Shinpei Goto had the honor of naming the watch CITIZEN with the hope that the watch (a luxury item) would become widely available to ordinary citizens and be sold throughout the world.

Grandmaster – The term grandmaster was never used by any Reiki teacher prior to the early 1980s. Therefore none of today's more well-known teachers such as Mikao Usui, Chûjirô Hayashi or Hawayo Takata used the term.
It was introduced in the early 1980s by The Reiki Alliance. Phyllis Lei Furumoto, Hawayo Takata's granddaughter, received the title 'Office of the Grandmaster' from this association.
Today some teachers of Reiki have self-nominated themselves as grandmasters or even great-grandmasters. It is generally accepted that this is a marketing ploy rather than having anything to do with the system of Reiki.

Gray, Reverend Beth – Beth Gray was a friend and teacher student of Hawayo Takata. In 1976, Beth Gray ordained Hawayo Takata as a minister on the basis of the spiritual nature of her teachings. Beth Gray founded a large Reiki center in the USA and Australia. A stroke in 1993 meant the end of her teaching career and she passed on on 14 May 2008.

Gray Book, The – Also called the *Leiki* booklet by some. Alice Takata Furumoto compiled this booklet in 1982. It includes notes and photographs of Hawayo Takata, a copy of Hawayo

Takata's certificate signed by Chûjirô Hayashi, a list of Hawayo Takata's teacher students and the *Ryôhô Shishin* (*Healing Guide*). Chûjirô Hayashi wrote this guide especially for American distribution. It shows hand positions for treating specific illnesses.

Gray, John Harvey – One of Hawayo Takata's 22 Reiki teacher students. He was once married to Beth Gray but has since remarried. He is the author of *Hand to Hand – The Longest-Practicing Reiki Master Tells His Story*, published in 2002.

*Grounding – A technique to reconnect to the center of the Earth energetically. An excellent practice for those who work solely with their intuitive skills and find that they are feeling regularly ungrounded.

*Group Distant Healing – A technique where a group of Reiki practitioners send Reiki to someone or something not present.

*Group Reiki – Working with Reiki in a group environment. A number of Reiki practitioners place their hands on or near the client at the same time to support the client's healing process. Based on a traditional Japanese technique called **shûchû Reiki*.

Gyoho (Gyotse) – Claimed by some to be Mikao Usui's Buddhist name. This name is written on the memorial stone in *Tôkyô*. It has been claimed that there are copies of old *sutra* with Mikao Usui's Buddhist name on it at *hiei zan*. Others claim that Gyoho

was either a pen name or extra name.

Gyosei 御製 – *Waka* written by the Emperor.

It is said that the Meiji Emperor wrote over 100,000 *waka* and his Empress Shoken over 30,000. Mikao Usui taught over 100 *gyosei*, according to the *Usui Reiki Ryôhô Gakkai*, to support spiritual development. The *Usui Reiki Ryôhô Gakkai* recite *gyosei* at the beginning of their meetings (*kenkyû kai*).

Kaiji Tomita, a student of Mikao Usui, writes in his 1933 book *Reiki To Jinjutsu – Tomita Ryû Teate Ryôhô* (*Reiki and Humanitarian Work – Tomita Ryû Hands Healing*) that **hatsurei hô* is a meditation using *gyosei*.

Toshihiro Eguchi also taught *gyosei* in his teachings according to the author Mihashi Kazuo.

*Gyôshi Hô 凝視法 – Healing by staring technique.

Gyôsho – *Kanji* drawn in a modern, semi cursive style.

A simplification of the standard style of writing *kanji*, allowing it to be written in a more flowing and faster manner.

 # H

*Hadô Kokyû Hô 波動呼吸法 – Vibrational breathing technique.

*Hadô Meiso Hô 波動瞑想法 – Vibrational meditation technique.

Hand Positions – Hand positions refer to the specific hand positions that are used when performing a Reiki treatment. Reiki practitioners place their hands on specific body regions with the intention of assisting the energy to move through the body. The purpose is to clear and strengthen the client's spiritual and energetic connection.

A one-hour Reiki treatment consists of a practitioner placing hands on or near the body of the client. Hand positions are also taught to be used by the practitioner for self-healing.

It is claimed that in Mikao Usui's early teachings, only five head positions were used. Professor Judith Rabinovitch has translated a book by Toshihiro Eguchi (a friend and student of Mikao Usui), co-written with his student Kôshi Mitsui, and it shows a similar set of five hand positions for the head.

A number of head positions are written up in related healing guides such as the *Ryôhô Shishin* by Chûjirô Hayashi and the *Usui Reiki Ryôhô Gakkai*'s manual called the *Reiki Ryôhô Hikkei*. In this latter manual, Mikao Usui is quoted as saying, 'My method is beyond modern science so you do not need knowledge of medicine. If brain disease occurs, I treat the head. If it's a stomachache, I treat the stomach. If it's an eye disease, I treat eyes.'

It is claimed that Hawayo Takata taught 12 positions (including the head, front and back of torso). Her teacher, Chûjirô Hayashi, is thought to have formalized Reiki treatments in his clinic where he had two practitioners working together on one person. His treatments are often considered to be the foundation for Reiki treatments taught in modern branches of Reiki.

The ritual of set hand placements on the body gives practitioners a structure to work from. This builds their confidence and energetic wisdom. As practitioners' inner understanding of the system of Reiki grows, it is then possible for them to leave the ritual behind and work from a solely intuitive understanding.

Hands-on Healing – When hands are placed on or near the body during a Reiki treatment this is called hands-on healing. The basic premise is that healing exists *within* each person rather than outside. The client's body draws on energy to stimulate his/her own energy via the Reiki practitioner's hands. This helps move stagnant energy and to support balance in the body. Hands-on healing was very popular in Japan at the turn of the 20th century. The generic Japanese word for hands-on healing is *teate*. When discussing a specific structure to hands-on healing, the word *tenohira* is used.

Hanko – A *hanko*, is also called an *inkan* and is a personal seal. This seal is used to sign formal and legal documents in conjunction with a signature. Without this seal, business in Japan would stagnate. The *hanko* is necessary for filling in application forms or banking slips, or for when you receive registered mail. There are different kinds of *hanko*: cheap ready made ones – *sanmon ban*; ones that are officially registered – *jitsu in*; and those that are for banking mainly – *ginkô in*. Mikao Usui would have used his *hanko* on his documents. The use of *hanko* will help modern researchers verify the authenticity of any documents that lay claim to Mikao Usui as their writer.

*Hanshin Kôketsu Hô 半身交血法 – Half-body blood exchange technique.

This is a part of the technique **ketsueki kôkan hô*.

Hara 腹 – Belly or abdomen.

The *hara* is the foundation of the Japanese energetic system. Within this system, called The Three Diamonds, are two other energetic centers; one is at the head and the other is at the heart.

The *hara* is like a battery that can be recharged through physical and spiritual techniques. Energy is stored at this point. From here it expands throughout the entire body. It is connected to Earth energy.

In Mikao Usui's and the *Usui Reiki Ryôhô Gakkai's* teachings many techniques are known to stimulate the *hara* centers. This is not unique in itself as the *hara* is an innate element of Japanese philosophy and culture. Whether practicing *go* (a Japanese game), *sadô* (flower arrangement), or *budô* (martial arts), the focus is on the *hara*.

Harajuku – *Harajuku, Aoyama, Tôkyô*. The place where Mikao Usui started his first official seat of learning in 1922.

Harmony – In some Japanese Reiki teachings this word is used to describe the characteristic of SHK and Symbol 2.

Hatamoto 旗下 – The *hatamoto* were the Shogun's personal guard. Mikao Usui's family was *hatamoto samurai* – a high level within the ranks of *samurai*.

*Hatsurei hô 発霊法 – Technique to generate greater amounts of spiritual energy.

This technique includes the techniques **kenyoku hô*, **joshin kokyû hô* and **seishin toitsu*.

Hiroshi Doi claims that the *Usui Reiki Ryôhô Gakkai* also practice a version of this technique.

Kaiji Tomita describes another version of this technique, using *waka*, in his book *Reiki To Jinjutsu – Tomita Ryû Teate Ryôhô*, published in 1933.

Hayashi, Chie – The wife of Chûjirô Hayashi. She continued on at her husband's clinic after his death, becoming the second president of the *Hayashi Reiki Kenkyû kai*.

Hayashi, Chûjirô (1880–1940) – One of the 21 teacher students of Mikao Usui. According to Hyakuten Inamoto, he was a *Sôtô Zen* practitioner who naturally included *Shintô* into his personal practices. According to his student Hawayo Takata, Chûjirô Hayashi met and became a student of Mikao Usui in 1925. He was a retired naval officer (still in the reserves) and surgeon. The length of his study with Mikao Usui was relatively short as he only studied the teachings for approximately 10 months before

Mikao Usui's death in March 1926. According to Hiroshi Doi, he was the last *shinpiden* student of Mikao Usui. It is interesting to note that Chûjirô Hayashi didn't teach the *reiju* but instead taught an attunement, which included the mantras and symbols, according to his student Chiyoko Yamaguchi.

Once he became a *shihan*, or teacher, he was expected to either 'engage in the spread of *Reiki Ryôhô* and in Reiki treatments at the Gakkai Head Office' or open up his own branch. As Chujirô Hayashi was a medical doctor, Mikao Usui felt that he should open a clinic for treatments. This, according to Hiroshi Doi, would 'promote the efficacy of *Reiki Ryôhô* from a medical doctor's point of view'. Naturally all results were to feed back to the *Usui Reiki Ryôhô Gakkai*. However, he broke away in 1931 developing his own branch called *Hayashi Reiki Kenkyû Kai*.

Chûjirô Hayashi is not known to have been recognized as the successor to Mikao Usui – if there was a successor within his known circle of fellow practitioners it would have been the president of the *Usui Reiki Ryôhô Gakkai*, Jûzaburô Ushida. Chûjirô Hayashi created a healing guide called the *Ryôhô Shishin*. It appears to be an almost exact copy of the *Ryôhô Shishin* in the *Reiki Ryôhô Hikkei*, the healing guide from the *Usui Reiki Ryôhô Gakkai* of which Chujiro Hayashi had previously been a member. It is believed

that he may have written both of these due to his medical expertise.

Chûjirô Hayashi wrote in 1938 that there were 13 fully qualified Reiki Masters but it is not known who all of these people were. From various reports it is believed that some of his teacher students were Tatsumi, Hawayo Takata, Chie Hayashi, and Chiyoko Yamaguchi plus Shûô Matsui who was not a teacher student.

Chûjirô Hayashi passed away on 10 May 1940. Hawayo Takata reported that he died ceremoniously of a self-induced stroke, Chiyoko Yamaguchi recounts that he had killed himself by 'breaking an artery', while others say that as he was a military man the honourable method of death would certainly have been *seppuku*.

Hayashi Reiki Kenkyû Kai 林霊気研究会 – Hayashi Spiritual Energy Research Society. Chûjirô Hayashi started this society in 1931, according to Hiroshi Doi. After his death, his wife, Chie Hayashi, became known as the second president. The name of his society indicates that he had adapted Mikao Usui's teachings. In Japan, it is customary to keep the teaching's name intact. The name would only be changed if the teachings were similarly altered. So it is possible to see that Chûjirô Hayashi had changed the system which Mikao Usui taught. Chûjirô Hayashi definitely displayed respect to Mikao Usui as he always taught in front of the calligraphic scroll of Mikao Usui's precepts called the *gokai no sho*.

Chûjirô Hayashi continued to use the same three level system as the *Usui Reiki Ryôhô Gakkai* which included *shoden*, *okuden* and *shinpiden*.

Head Positions – See Five Head Positions.

Healer – Many Reiki practitioners struggle with the concept of whether they are healers or not. A basic principle of the system of Reiki is that everyone and everything is a natural healer. Mikao Usui is quoted in the *Reiki Ryôhô Hikkei* as saying, 'Every existence has healing power'. The system of Reiki teaches how to bring awareness and strength to that quality.

Yet a practitioner never states that he/she heals someone as it is not the practitioner that is doing the healing. The practitioner facilitates healing but the responsibility to heal always remains in the hands of the client.

Healing – The word 'heal' has many different interpretations with the word 'whole' often being used to describe it. 'To make whole' means to balance out all aspects of being human: mind, body and heart. It embraces the connectedness of each of these aspects and does not accept that one is more important than the other. The system of Reiki works at stimulating and strengthening each of these aspects of humanity and is therefore considered to be a system that supports and promotes healing.

One of the five elements of Reiki is hands-on healing. The other four elements of the system (symbols and mantras, precepts, attunements or *reiju*, techniques) also support healing. Together these elements create an entire and effective system.

By focusing only on one's hands within the system of Reiki, the ability to heal and become whole is limited. By strengthening and balancing one's inner energy, using all elements of the system of Reiki, not only is one's life affected beneficially, but those of everyone the practitioner comes into contact with. This is healing in the microcosm (the human, the small universe) and, consequently, the macrocosm (the greater universe).

Mikao Usui is quoted as saying in the *Reiki Ryôhô Hikkei* 'Every existence has healing power. Plants, trees, animals, fish and insects but especially a human'.

Healing Attunements – This non-initiatory attunement was developed with the intent that it focus on healing the self rather than the ability to 'do' Reiki. However the perception that attunements give the student the ability to 'do' Reiki is not held by all systems of Reiki. There is within the system of Reiki a general understanding that everyone consists of universal energy. If this is so then all that is needed is intent when placing hands on the body to support healing by drawing on this innate ability.

Traditionally in Japan, the *reiju* did not 'make' one into

something, e.g., a Level 1 practitioner. The *reiju* was seen as a support for the student's personal growth.

The system of Reiki is a number of practices that when brought together teach one how to use Reiki for healing and spiritual development, this is not governed solely by an attunement or *reiju*.

Healing Crisis – See Cleansing.

Healing List – Non-traditional technique where a Reiki practitioner writes a list of people, places or things that he/she wishes to send Reiki to. The list is held in the hands and a distant healing technique is performed on it.

*Healing the Past and the Future – Non-traditional technique where you send distant healing to yourself or others to heal the past, present and future.

Heart Sutra – A *sutra* practised in *Tendai* Buddhism presenting the essence of the transcendental wisdom of the void. The Heart *Sutra* is widely practiced in Japan and aids in the understanding of Oneness. The concept of Oneness lies at the base of *distant healing.

Heaven – In Japan, Heaven is often described as one half of the universe with Earth being its opposite force. An ancient Japanese cosmological theory states that through the union of these dual forces all things were born.

In Mikao Usui's early teachings, SHK and Symbol 2 are said to be associated with the energy of Heaven: intuitive and clear.

Hiroshi Doi has stated, 'In the Gakkai the words *harmony of ten-chi-jin* and *Oneness of Great Universe (the macrocosm) and Small Universe (humans or the microcosm)* are often used.' *Ten* is Heaven, *chi* is Earth, and *jin* is humanity.

*Heso Chiryô Hô 臍治療法 – Healing at the navel technique.

Hibiki 響き – Sound, echo, vibration.

Hibiki is sensed when the body is being scanned or treated. It may feel like heat/cold/tingling/pain/ itchiness/pulsating, etc., in the palm of the hand.

Hiei Zan 比叡山 – Mt. Hiei near *Kyôto*, Japan.

There is a main *Tendai* temple complex, *enryaku ji*, on *hiei zan*. Mikao Usui is said to have studied *Tendai* Buddhism there. It has been suggested that old *sutra* copies on *hiei zan* have Mikao Usui's Buddhist name of Gyoho or Gyotse on them.

Higher Self – Terminology used in the New Age movement to refer to an eternal, conscious, and intelligent being. This terminology has been adopted into some modern branches of Reiki.

*Hikari No Kokyû Hô 光の呼吸法 – Breathing in the light technique. Also called **jôshin kokyû hô* and is a part of the technique **hatsurei hô*.

Hikkei 必携 – Companion, often translated as manual.
See *Reiki Ryôhô Hikkei*.

Hiragana – *Hiragana* is used to write the inflectional endings of the conceptual words that are written in *kanji*. It is also used for all types of native words not written in *kanji*. This was an attempt to cut down on the amount of *kanji* needed to express a multi-syllabic Japanese word.

Hô 法 – Method or technique. This word is used in the description of a number of Japanese Reiki techniques.

Hokke-Zanmai – The lotus *samadhi*.
A meditation technique based on the Lotus *Sutra*. One chants the Lotus *Sutra* while circumambulating the temple hall. This meditation is said to have been practiced by Mikao Usui. *Zazen shikan taza* is a modern simplified form of the *Hokke-Zanmai* that excludes a lot of the more difficult elements of the practice.

Hotsuma Tsutae – Its first parts, 'Book of Heaven' and 'Book of Earth', were recorded and edited around 660 B.C. (according to the *Nihonshoki* calendar) by Kushimikatama-Wanihiko. His descendant, Ootataneko, recorded the third part, 'Book of Man', which contains the stories after Emperor Jinmu (660 B.C.), and offered the complete *Hotsuma Tsutae* to Emperor Keiko (the 12th Emperor) in A.D. 126. The origin of the *Hotsuma Tsutae* is controversial. It is guessed to be very old while some researchers challenge the dates written above. Copies of *Hotsuma Tsutae* have been stored in *iwamuro* (cave storage) in a *Tendai* temple at *enryaku ji* (*hiei zan*, *Kyôto*). These copies may have been given to Saichô (767–822), the founding priest of *enryaku ji*.

Tendaï priests were also known to give lectures on the *Hotsuma Tsutae*.

Hrih – This is an ancient Sanskrit Indian seed syllable (a syllable used for meditation).
The Japanese seed syllable *kiriku* is derived from the *hrih*. Symbol 2 appears to have evolved from the *kiriku*.

HSZSN – As the mantras of the system of Reiki are commonly classified as sacred, pseudonyms are used in *The Reiki Sourcebook* rather than the true mantras.
The pseudonym for the third traditional mantra is the initials HSZSN.
The *kanji* of the true mantra of HSZSN is actually Symbol 3. The modern characteristic of HSZSN is as the Distance Symbol and it is spoken three times in conjunction with Symbol 3.
The main traditional characteristic is Connection. Traditionally the mantra is not necessarily used in conjunction with the symbol. The early teachings of Mikao Usui claim that HSZSN develops a Reiki practitioner's link to the energy of the Heart. It is within the Heart that the concept of Oneness is embraced.

*Hui Yin Breath – Non-traditional breath technique introduced via the New Age movement into the attunement process of some modern branches of Reiki including Raku Kei Reiki. This technique originally comes from China and lies at the base of practices such as Chinese *Qi Gong*. It stimulates the energy to rise up the back energy channel and harmonise with the energy descending down the front energy channel, helping to balance the body's energy.

 I

Ichinyo – Oneness.

The concept of Oneness is linked to the HSZSN and Symbol 3 in Mikao Usui's early teachings. When working with this concept one starts to realise the non-existence of 'I'. When the 'I' disappears the notion of 'others' will disappear too. Once this occurs it is no longer possible to make the separation between 'I' and 'others', and there arises the desire to protect and help others as oneself.

Imperial Rescript on Education – The Imperial Rescript was written by the Meiji Emperor in 1890 and is an edict that became a fundamental Japanese moral code until the end of World War II.

Kanô Jigorô, the founder of *jûdô*, also used this text as a moral code in his teachings. There are claims that he was an acquaintance of Mikao Usui. According to one Reiki researcher, the five precepts are based on this rescript.

In – A physical sign often using the hands.

More commonly known by its Sanskrit name of *mudra*.

Inamoto, Reverend Hyakuten – Teacher of *Komyo Reiki Kai*. He has studied the system of Reiki under Chiyoko Yamaguchi. He is also a translator for Hiroshi Doi and a Pure Land Buddhist monk. Hyakuten Inamoto's translation of the memorial stone and the Meiji Emperor's *waka* is included in *The Reiki Sourcebook*.

In and Yô 陰陽 – *Yin* and *yang*. These are the cosmic dual forces of Heaven and Earth. The *samurai* of the 17th century used these principles along with Chinese Confucianism. The first two mantras and symbols in Mikao Usui's early teachings are said to help the student become One with *in* and *yô*.

Hiroshi Doi wrote in his book *Iyashino Gendai Reiki-ho* that, 'Usui-*sensei* gave his training based on the truth that heaven and earth's nature makes humans greater.'

It is believed that Mikao Usui deliberately created a system that was unaligned to any specific religion. However, he naturally drew elements from his personal religious and energetic experiences to create the system. To develop a practice in this way was quite common in Japan. Some of his influences were Buddhism, *Shintô*, martial arts and *Shugendô*. The book *Religions of Japan in Practice* states, 'Japanese religious practice drew from many sources, accommodating both the imported religion of Buddhism and the native *Shintô* tradition, while accepting Chinese *yin-yang* beliefs and other aspects of religious Taoism.'

Independent Reiki Master – Independent Reiki Master is a term used to describe people who are Reiki teachers but are not aligned with a particular branch of Reiki. They might use an eclectic approach drawing on techniques from many branches and/or include New Age practices.

Individual Attunement – An attunement is a ritual performed on students (often on their back and front while they are seated) by Reiki teachers. This ritual is generally performed as an individual attunement meaning that the teacher completes the attunement on each student individually before moving to the next student. With the advent of large class sizes some teachers began to line students up and walk down the front of the line – performing the first part of the attunement and then walking down the back of the line – completing the back. Some teachers have expressed concern that the individual energetic link between teacher and student is broken or weakened by this 'group' method.

Initiation – This word is often used to describe the *reiju* and/ or attunement process. Its Latin origins mean 'beginning'.

Integrated Attunement – Attunement created and taught by Hiroshi Doi in the *gokui kaiden* level of *Gendai Reiki Hô*. He claims that it integrates all mantras and symbols into one attunement.

Intent – A Reiki practitioner sets intent by anticipating an outcome. This anticipation guides the practitioner in his/her planned course of action. The clearer a practitioner's energy becomes through self-practice, the more focused, and therefore more effective, the intent is.

Ishikuro, Iris (?–1984) – One of Hawayo Takata's 22 Reiki teacher students. She was told to only train three people to the teacher level and trained just two people to this level, her daughter and Arthur Robertson.
Arthur Robertson worked with Iris Ishikuro and together they had an immense impact on the future of the system of Reiki with the system Raku Kei Reiki. Arthur Robertson was responsible for a great deal of what is called 'Tibetan' information today. This included the 'Tibetan' symbols, the Johrei symbol and 'Tibetan' techniques such as breath of the fire dragon and the *hui yin* breath. This information is supplied by Robert Fueston.

Islam – The system of Reiki is not a religion and is used by people of all religions around the world.

Ittôen – Toshihiro Eguchi, a friend and student of Mikao Usui, taught a form of hands-on healing to the *Ittôen* community. Some families still practice this today although there are only about 100 residents remaining in the community. The present leader is the grandson of the founder, Nishida Tenko, and his name is Takeshi.
According to Professor Judith Rabinovitch, the *Ittôen* community is not a religion

but more of a philosophical system. At its core are popular Buddhism, Zen Buddhism, Confucianism, and even some Christian teachings.

 J

*Jakikiri Jôka Hô 邪気きり浄化法 – A technique that energetically cleanses and enhances inanimate objects.

*Jiko Joka Hô 自己浄化法 – Self-purification technique.

Jiro, Asuke – A well-known hands-on healing student of Kaiji Tomita. Kaiji Tomita was a student of Mikao Usui.

Jisshû kai 実習会 – Practice or training meetings.
The *Usui Reiki Ryôhô Gakkai* once held *jisshû kai*. These practice meetings, where techniques were taught and practiced, took place after the shûyô kai or the group meetings.

Jôdo Shû 浄土宗 – School of the Pure Land sect.

*Jôshin Kokyû Hô 浄心呼吸法 – Technique to focus the mind with the breath.
Also called **hikari no kokyû hô* and is a part of *hatsurei hô*.

Judaism – The system of Reiki is not a religion and is used by people of all religions around the world. There is even a branch of Reiki based on the Hebrew alphabet called Alef Reiki.

Jûdô – Modernized, sport-oriented form of *jujutsu*. Founded by Jigorô Kanô, who is said to have been an acquaintance of Mikao Usui.

Jumon 呪文 – Spell, incantation. *Jumon* is a sound that invokes a specific energetic vibration. In modern forms of the system of Reiki it is commonly called by the Sanskrit word mantra.
In Mikao Usui's early teachings it is said that the *jumon* made the teachings more accessible for *Shintô* followers. They can be used as a focus point for meditation.
According to Suzuki san, it was Toshihiro Eguchi who introduced the three *okuden jumon* to Mikao Usui.

 K

Kaicho – Title of the president of the *Usui Reiki Ryôhô Gakkai*.

Kaimyô 漢字 – A posthumous Buddhist name.
Also called *hômyô*. It is a posthumous Buddhist name given to the soul of the newly departed person by the priest at a funeral.
Originally it was a Buddhist name given to devout believers who took the Buddhist precepts. Each sect has its own way of giving *kaimyô*, but as a rule it is made up of several *kanji*.
Mikao Usui's kaimyo is *Reizan-in Shuyo Tenshin Koji*.

Kaisho – *Kanji* in modern, standard style.
This style is similar to the printed style of *kanji*, and is taught in schools.

Kanji 漢字 – *Kanji* are Japanese

written characters that are both pictographs (pictures that represent ideas) and ideographs (symbols that represent the sounds that form its name). In China, *kanji* originated in the Yellow River area about 2000 B.C.. During the 3rd and 4th centuries A.D. it was brought across from China and Korea to Japan. Until that time Japan had only ever used the spoken language. The Chinese characters were used phonetically to represent similar sounding Japanese syllables but the actual meaning of the characters was ignored.

Kanji Hand Mudras – *Kanji* are Japanese written characters. *Mudra* is a Sanskrit word and represents the stimulating of specific energy through body postures and hand movements. Kanji Hand Mudras were introduced to the system of Reiki in an Omega Dawn Sanctuary of Healing Arts manual in 1983 from the branch Raku Kei Reiki, according to Robert Fueston. That manual was created by Arthur Robertson.

Kannon – This deity is sometimes taught as the connection to Symbol 3. Kannon is the 'Bodhisattva who Perceives the Sounds of the World'.

Kanô, Jigorô (1860–1938) The founder of *jûdô*. There are some claims that he knew Mikao Usui. It was once thought that Jigorô Kanô was in a photo with Mikao Usui from Toshitaka Mochizuki's book *Chô Kantan Iyashi No Te*. This however could not be verified by the *Kodokan*

Jûdô Institute in Japan.

Katakana – *Katakana* became phonetic shorthand based on Chinese characters (*kanji*). It was used by students who, while listening to classic Buddhist lectures, would make notations on the pronunciations or meanings of unfamiliar characters, and sometimes wrote commentaries between the lines of certain passages.

Katsu – This is a method of infusing life into a person and is mentioned on page 35 of Chûjirô Hayashi's *Ryôhô Shishin* as a method to aid resuscitation.

Kenkyû kai 研究会 – Research or study society. This is the name that the *Usui Reiki Ryôhô Gakkai* uses today for its regular meetings. Previously these meetings were called *shuyô kai*.

*Kenyoku hô 乾浴法 – Dry bathing or brushing off technique. This is similar to purification methods practiced in *Shintô*. Purification rites are a vital part of *Shintô*. A personal purification rite might be purification by water, also known as *misogi*. This would involve standing under a waterfall.

*Ketsueki Kôkan Hô 血液交換法 – Blood exchange technique. Variations are *hanshin kôketsu hô, *zenshin kôketsu hô, *finishing treatment or *nerve stroke. Also called *kôketsu hô.

Ki 気 – Universal energy. In Japan, *ki* is considered to be an integral element in the success of daily life. Many Japanese traditions are based on a strong connection to *ki*.

Apart from martial arts and religious training, the success of the Japanese tea ceremony, the ancient game of *go* and the art of calligraphy are all based on the practitioner's ability to channel free-flowing *ki*.

Ki Ko – *Qi Gong* or energy cultivation.
These techniques have their origins in Chinese physical and meditative practices called *Qi Gong*. They help to regulate the body, mind and breath and are both Taoist and Buddhist in origin.

Kiriku – A seed syllable is a letterform used solely for meditation and is a part of esoteric Buddhism practiced in China and Japan. Its Sanskrit origins can be traced back to the seed syllable *hrih*.
The *kiriku* calls upon the energy of Amida Nyorai. Amida Nyorai is the main deity in Pure Land Buddhism.
Symbol 2 in the system of Reiki appears to be derived from the *kiriku*.

Koizumi, Tetsutarô – Toshitaka Mochizuki has listed a number of early Japanese Reiki practitioners in his book *Chô Kantan Iyashi No Te*. He relates that Tetsutarô Koizumi was a member of the *Usui Reiki Ryôhô Gakkai* and taught Reiki at their headquarters and in regional areas.

*Kôketsu Hô 交血法 – An abbreviation of **ketsueki kôkan hô*.

Kôki Hô 後期 – Second half.
The second part or grade within *okuden*.

*Koki Hô 呼気法 – Sending *ki* with the breath technique.

Kondô, Masaki – Seventh and current president of the *Usui Reiki Ryôhô Gakkai*. He is also a university professor.

Kotodama 言霊 – Words carrying spirit.
Hiroshi Doi uses the word *kotodama* rather than *jumon* to address the mantras taught in the system of Reiki. Morihei Ueshiba, the founder of *aikidô* who is said to have been an acquaintance of Mikao Usui, also used *kotodama* in his teachings. He belonged to the *Oomoto* sect who had formulated effective meditation techniques and powerful chants based on *kotodama*. *Kotodama* in *Shintô* invoke specific energies/deities.

Koyama, Kimiko (1906–99) – Sixth president of the *Usui Reiki Ryôhô Gakkai*. According to her student, Hiroshi Doi, she always said that 'Reiki is the light of love'.
In Toshitaka Mochizuki's book *Chô Kantan Iyashi No Te* he states that as president she held meetings four times a month.
For the 50th anniversary of the *Usui Reiki Ryôhô Gakkai*, Kimiko Koyama published the *Reiki Ryôhô Hikkei* for members. The *shiori* booklet, created for society members, was also written by Kimiko Koyama and Hôichi Wanami.

Kuboi, Harry M. – One of Hawayo Takata's 22 Reiki teacher students.

Kun Yomi 訓読み – Here Chinese *kanji* are used to express Japanese words that have a similar meaning to the original Chinese word. When a Japanese word's sound uses *kanji,* this is then called a *kun yomi* reading.

Kurama Yama 鞍馬山 – Mt. Kurama near *Kyôto,* Japan.

It states on the memorial stone of Mikao Usui that he became enlightened while performing a meditation on *kurama yama.* According to the Kurama Temple, Mikao Usui has no specific connection to them. Many martial arts practitioners, like Morihei Ueshiba, also practiced on *kurama yama.*

Kushu Shinren – Painful and difficult training.
A form of *shûgyô. Kushu shinren* was the word used on the memorial stone for Mikao Usui's practice on *kurama yama.*

 L

Leiki – Hawayo Takata sometimes wrote Leiki instead of Reiki. This seems to be a translation mistake. To pronounce the word Reiki in Japanese, it is necessary to forego any preconceptions about language that you may have. The first sound in 'rei' is neither an 'R' nor an 'L', as some believe. In Japanese the sound is in fact somewhere in between the two letters. The Japanese language has no correlation with English or its pronunciations. The *kanji* for 'rei' is officially spelt with an 'R' when translating into English and is therefore pronounced with an 'R' (even though the Japanese pronunciation might sound similar to what is understood as

an 'L' in English).

Level – There are three levels of training with the system of Reiki with some branches dividing these levels up.
Between each level students are required to practice the techniques and principles that they have been taught as preparation for moving forward to the next level.
In modern times the levels have varying names including degree or facet. In Japan, the three major levels are called *shoden, okuden* and *shinpiden.*
In the *Usui Reiki Ryôhô Gakkai* manual, called the *Reiki Ryôhô Hikkei,* Mikao Usui is quoted as saying about who he would accept at Level 2 as students, 'I will teach it to people who have learned *shoden* (Level 1) and who are good students, [with] good conduct and enthusiasts [enthusiasm].'

Level 1 – Called *shoden* in some Japanese branches. Students are taught how to heal themselves and friends and family. They are given a self-healing practice routine to continue and develop before moving on to Level 2.

Level 2 – Called *okuden* in some Japanese branches. Students are taught the three mantras and symbols and how to put these to practice. Once again students are asked to develop their personal practice before moving to Level 3.

Level 3 – Called *shinpiden* in some Japanese branches. Here students are taught the fourth mantra and symbol and how to perfume attunements or *reiju* and teach.

Lineage – Teachings that are handed down to a student are the student's 'lineage'. A lineage is expressed as a list of teacher's names in chronological order. The lineage should be able to be traced back to the founder of the system, in the case of the system of Reiki this is Mikao Usui. In modern times an imbalance has developed in the teachings. The importance of the attunement has grown disproportionately to the rest of the five elements of the system of Reiki. In fact many people today say 'I've had my Level 1 attunement therefore I am now a Reiki practitioner'. What has actually occurred is that they have completed a course (which included attunements) and they have now set off on the path of a Reiki practitioner. In this case some of the modern Reiki teachings believe that an attunement 'makes' you into something, e.g., a Level 1 or 2 practitioner. Here the idea of the attunement being the course itself has taken over.

In the earlier teachings of Mikao Usui, an attunement or *reiju* is performed to support a practitioner in his or her practice. For this reason the *Usui Reiki Ryôhô Gakkai* (that still exists today) offers *reiju* to members at each gathering. Therefore the lineage of a student will depend upon the teachings that the student has received. This means not just the style of attunement or *reiju*, or just the five elements of the system of Reiki or even just the energy of the teacher. It is the entire teachings that are being handed down. This is what a student has acquired by the time he or she walks out of the door.

Ling Chi – This is the pronunciation of the two *kanji* that represent the word 'Reiki' in Chinese.

The *Ancient Book of Lu* states that "even a blade of grass or clump of dirt contains *Ling Qi*." *Ling Qi* is the spiritual energy that envelops and forms all things. In order to connect with and perceive the *Ling Qi* contained within the environment, an individual must first cultivate his or her own personal *Ling Qi*. (Excerpt from *Chinese Medical Qigong Therapy Volume 1* by Professor Jerry Alan Johnson)

Lombardi, Ethel – One of Hawayo Takata's 22 Reiki teacher students. She went on to create a system called MariEL. Though this was based on the system of Reiki it was filled out with her own interpretations. She did not wish to be a member of any of the post-Hawayo Takata organizations.

Lotus Sutra – A *sutra* practiced in *Tendai* Buddhism. In Japanese it is called the *Hoke-kyo* or *Myohorenge kyo* and forms the basis on which *Tendai* Buddhism is established.

Love and Light – The salutation 'Love and Light' is used by some modern Reiki practitioners. Curiously this salutation has similarities to the characteristics of the deities who represent *kurama yama*. These three characteristics are power, light and love. *Kurama yama* is where the memorial stone states that Mikao Usui meditated.

 M

*Making Contact with Higher Beings – Non-traditional technique of connecting and asking for guidance from higher beings.

*Manifesting – Non-traditional technique to manifest what you need or want.

Mantra – A power-laden syllable or series of syllables that manifest certain cosmic forces. Traditionally, there are only four mantras in Mikao Usui's teachings. The mantras were given to students as a device for tapping into specific elements of energy.
In some Japanese branches of Reiki the mantras are practiced independently of the symbols. However in modern teachings the mantra is chanted three times as the symbol is drawn. The Japanese words to describe the word mantra are either *kotodama* or *jumon*.

Master Symbol – This name is sometimes applied to DKM and Symbol 4 in modern forms of the system of Reiki.
Its traditional characteristic is considered to be Empowerment.

Matsui, Shûô – He studied with Chûjirô Hayashi in 1928. His first level was completed in five 90-minute sessions. Shûô Matsui wrote in an article called 'Treatment to Heal Diseases,

Hand Healing' in the magazine *Sunday Mainichi*, 4 March 1928, about the levels *shoden* and *okuden* and mentioned that there were further unknown levels.

McCullough, Barbara Lincoln – One of Hawayo Takata's 22 Reiki teacher students.

McFadyen, Mary Alexandra – One of Hawayo Takata's 22 Reiki teacher students. According to Robert Fueston, Mary McFadyen has written two German Reiki books entitled *Die Heilkraft des Reiki. Lehren einer Meisterin* and *Die Heilkraft des Reiki. Mit Händen heilen. Schnellbehandlung.*

Meditation – Some practices taught in the system of Reiki are meditation practices. Depending on the branch of Reiki their origins may be Japanese or taken from other cultural and spiritual backgrounds.

Meiji 明治 – Name of an era.

Meiji Emperor (1852–1912) – The Meiji Emperor ruled Japan from 1867–1912. Mikao Usui, Toshihiro Eguchi (Mikao Usui's friend and student), Kaiji Tomita and the *Usui Reiki Ryôhô Gakkai* used *waka* written by the Meiji Emperor in their teachings. This poetry was called *gyosei*.

Memorial Stone – This is the engraved memorial stone relating elements of Mikao Usui's life at a gravesite at the Pure Land Buddhist *Saihôji* Temple in *Tôkyô*. The stone was placed there by a number of Mikao Usui's students just one year after his death in 1927. The memorial stone is one aspect of Mikao Usui's life as seen through the eyes of his students from the *Usui Reiki Ryôhô Gakkai*. Some state that the students who wrote this information did not consult with Mikao Usui's family and therefore may have left out information that was relevant in a memorial about his life.

Menkyo Kaiden – License of complete and total transmission. It is a certificate given in traditional arts to show full proficiency for a lineage or style. It normally denotes a license indicating a very high level of skill. For some lineages, it might be given to the headmaster. It is said that Mikao Usui received *menkyo kaiden* in a specific branch of martial arts.

Mental/Emotional Symbol – The name is sometimes applied to SHK and Symbol 2 in modern forms of the system of Reiki. Traditionally its characteristic is considered to be Harmony.

Meridians – These are interconnected energy lines in the body. This understanding of the body's energetic system originates from Traditional Chinese Medicine.

*Metta Meditation – Non-traditional meditation focusing on goodwill and sending love and compassion to all beings.

Mikkyô 密教 – The secret teaching, esoteric Buddhism. There are five general areas taught in *Tendai* Buddhism. They are the teachings of the Lotus *Sutra*; esoteric *Mikkyô* practices; meditation practices; precepts; and Pure Land teachings. This form of Buddhism reached Japan at the beginning of the 9th century. There is a clear connection between Mikao Usui's teachings and *Mikkyô*. For example: the physical aspects of the *reiju* called *Go Shimbô* and the origins of the fourth *jumon* DKM.

If, as is claimed, Mikao Usui was a *Tendai* lay priest, he would have studied *Mikkyô* as it is an integral part of *Tendai* Buddhism.

Mine, Imae – According to Toshitaka Mochizuki's book, *Chô Kantan Iyashi No Te*, she was a musician and the wife of fellow Reiki practitioner Umataro Mine. In 1967 specific details about Mikao Usui's students were written of in her book *Kyujyu Nen No Ayumi*. She was involved with teaching Reiki until the age of 103.

Mine Umataro (1865–1934) – According to Toshitaka Mochizuki's book, *Chô Kantan Iyashi No Te*, he was one of the teachers of the *Usui Reiki Ryôhô Gakkai*. Toshitaka Mochizuki's book also includes a full page photo of him. His wife, Imae Mine, also taught Reiki.

Misogi 禊 – Purification. Purification rites are a vital part of *Shintô*. A personal purification rite is purification by water; this may involve standing under a waterfall, which is known as *misogi*.

In Mikao Usui's teachings there is a technique called **kenyoku hô* – a method of dry bathing or brushing off, which is a form of *misogi*. *Shintô* priests practice techniques such as **kenyoku hô*. One *Shintô* practitioner said that he performed a similar ritual with a group of men from his village where they wore only a red loincloth at the *hekogaki* festival (putting on the loincloth festival).

Mitchell, Paul – One of Hawayo Takata's 22 Reiki teacher students. He is a founding member of The Reiki Alliance and works closely with Phyllis Lei Furumoto.

Mitsui, Kôshi – A student of Toshihiro Eguchi. According to a recently published Japanese book by Mihashi Kazuo on the life of Toshihiro Eguchi, Kôshi Mitsui was a village Mayor who wrote and reviewed *waka*. He introduced Toshihiro Eguchi's teachings in a book, which increased their popularity, and he also helped facilitate the actual teachings.

He was also a good friend of fellow student Gorô Miyazaki.

Mitsui, Mieko – A Japanese Reiki practitioner living in New York who visited her native country in 1985. She began a revival of the system of Reiki in Japan by teaching the first two levels of The Radiance Technique®. In Japan, she met Ogawa Fumio, a member of the *Usui Reiki Ryôhô Gakkai*. In 1986 there was an article in a Japanese magazine called *Twilight Zone* with a photo of her practicing Reiki and of Fumio Ogawa reading a book written by Barbara Weber, founder of The Radiance Technique®. Hiroshi Doi claims to have been one of the first Japanese to study Levels 1 and 2 with Mieko Mitsui.

Miyazaki, Gorô – Student of Toshihiro Eguchi. According to a recently published Japanese book by Mihashi Kazuo on the life of Toshihiro Eguchi, Gorô Miyazaki was married to the daughter of Toshihiro Eguchi. He also wrote *waka* and books, and got on very well with a fellow student called Kôshi Mitsui.

After Toshihiro Eguchi's death he focused more on writing than the actual teaching of the practices.

The popularity of Toshihiro Eguchi's teachings gradually tapered away after Gorô Miyazake's death.

Mochizuki ,Toshitaka – Author of two Japanese Reiki books and founder of the Vortex branch in Japan. In his 2001 book, *Chô Kantan Iyashi No Te*, there is a photo of Mikao Usui and 19 of his students, family and friends in 1926. In the first edition of this book, *Iyashi No Te* (*Healing Hands*), Toshitaka Mochizuki claims to have healed 3,000 people. In his 2001 condensed version with pictures he claims to have healed up to 5.200 people.

Reiki To Jinjutsu – Tomita Ryû Teate Ryôhô (*Reiki and Humanitarian Work* – *Tomita Ryû Hands Healing*), a book written by Kaiji Tomita in 1933 was re-published in 1999 with the help of Toshitaka Mochizuki. Included in this book are many anecdotes about healing, hand positions for specific diseases and an interesting version of the technique *hatsurei hô.

Mon or Kamon – Family crest. *Mon* originated in the 11th century when court nobles and warriors used emblems as symbols of their families. The designs were drawn from a variety of objects like the sun, moon, stars, animals, geometrical patterns and letters. Families marked their clothing, banners and many other things with their crest.

The most famous crest is the Imperial family's 16-petalled chrysanthemum.

Mikao Usui's *Chiba* crest is a circle with a dot at the top. The circle represents the universe, and the dot or Japanese star represents the North Star. The North Star never moves while the universe circles around it.

Money and Reiki – It is believed that Mikao Usui initially saw his teachings as spiritual practices that he himself undertook and passed onto others. There was no formalized system at first.

Once he began teaching the Japanese naval officers, this changed. At least one healing guide was written up, and a formal *dôjô* was created. There are no records available that state whether or not he charged for his teachings and healings. From a sensible perspective, money would have had to come from somewhere to maintain the *dôjô*, whether that was from patrons, students, or clients.

After Mikao Usui died the *Usui Reiki Ryôhô Gakkai* is known to have charged large sums of money for the teachings. There is an account from an article written in 1928 where a famous Japanese playwright studied with the society (with Chûjirô Hayashi in fact) and questioned why it was so expensive. Professor Judith Rabinovitch states that in Toshihiro Eguchi's diaries she learnt that he actually resigned from the society because he could not understand why a well-to-do naval officer would charge so much money. As Toshihiro Eguchi was a friend of Mikao Usui's, his resignation from the society would signify that Mikao Usui had not charged his students and clients large sums of money.

Hawayo Takata had more or less regular fees that she charged her students. She supposedly requested that her students ask the same fees as she herself had.

There has always been controversy over the pricing of Reiki courses and Reiki treatments. Today some feel that they should all be free and others believe that $10,000, Hawayo Takata's asking price, should be required for a Reiki teacher class. One cannot pay for energy – it is subjective and intangible. For this reason a sensible suggestion is that the client and student pay only for the *quality* of the treatment or course that they receive.

*Morning Prayer – Non-traditional prayer to be practiced each morning. This is a prayer that is practiced in Satya Reiki.

Mudra – A Sanskrit word which means ritualistic signs performed with the fingers and hands.

Some branches of Reiki have added *mudra*s into their practice and teachings. However in traditional eastern practices like esoteric Buddhism, martial arts or *Qi Gong*, these *mudras* are only taught to students who have a deep understanding of emptiness or void. If the student has not integrated emptiness into the mind, body, or spirit, then practising a *mudra* is useless.

Muryo-Ju – Infinite life and light. This is another name for Amida Buddha. It is also the name (not mantra) of Symbol 2 taught in *Komyo Reiki Kai*.

 N

*Nadete Chiryô Hô 撫手治療法 – Stroking with the hands technique.

Nagana, Harue – Student of Mikao Usui according to Hiroshi Doi.

Nagao, Tatseyi – He completed Levels 1 and 2 with Hawayo Takata in Hawaii and while in Japan in 1950 received *shinpiden* from Chie Hayashi (Chûjirô Hayashi's widow). He returned to Hawaii to teach the system of Reiki to students and died in 1980. This is stated by William Lee Rand.

Nakano – A suburb of *Tôkyô* where Mikao Usui moved his *dôjô* to in February 1925, according to the memorial stone.

Naval Officers – In 1922, Mikao Usui formalized his teachings and began to teach hands-on healing to a group of naval officers. These men went on to create the *Usui Reiki Ryôhô Gakkai*, claiming Mikao Usui as their first president. The society still exists in Japan today.

One member of the original society was Chûjirô Hayashi, whose teachings created the backbone for modern forms of the system of Reiki.

*Nentatsu Hô 念達法 – A technique to send thoughts. Also called **seiheki chiryô hô*.

*Nerve Stroke – Also called **finishing stroke*, **zenshin kôketsu hô* or **ketsueki kôkan hô*. Hawayo Takata taught this technique in Level 2.

New Age Movement – The search for universal truths in the late 20th century created a loose network of spiritual teachers, healers and searchers. They have become known as the New Age movement and draw on mythical and religious historical material to develop their understandings of life. From 1980 onward the New Age movement has had a great impact on the system of Reiki.

New Religions – In Japan, the term 'new religions' relates to all sects founded since the middle of the 19th century. In Japanese they are called *shinshûkyô*. That includes a great diversity of sects. Most are influenced by much older traditional religions including *Shintô*, Buddhism, and *Shugendô*. Some well known new religions are *Oomoto*, *Shunmei*, *Tenrikyo* and *Mahikari*. The system of Reiki, though not a religion, has some similarities to these new religions as it, too, has drawn on traditional Japanese religious elements. Some similar elements include the system's practice of hands-on healing, *jumon* and *kotodama* use, and even the *reiju*.

Non-traditional – This term is used to represent teachings that are not directly related to the Japanese origins of the system of Reiki. The term largely includes add-ons from the New Age movement but may relate to Reiki practices taught in Japan as well as elsewhere today.

  O

Okada, Masayuki – He was a student of Mikao Usui and composed the text of Mikao Usui's memorial stone erected at the *Saihôji* Temple in *Tôkyô* in 1927 one year after the death of Mikao Usui.

Ogawa, Fumio (1908-1998) – Member of the *Usui Reiki Ryôhô Gakkai* who by 1943 completed six grades of proficiency (two levels) in 14 months. His certificates were shown in a Japanese magazine called *Twilight Zone* in 1986. In the same magazine was a photo of him reading a book written by Barbara Weber, founder of The Radiance Technique®. Fumio Ogawa's stepfather, Kôzô Ogawa, ran a healing center in *Shizuoka* during Mikao Usui's lifetime. Fumio Ogawa's certificates read: *rokkyû, gokyû, yonkyû, sankyû, okuden zenki,* and *okuden kôki*. The first four were grades within the Level 1. The last two were grades within the Level 2. These dated from 1942 to 1943.

According to Toshitaka Mochizuki, in 1991 he self-published a book called *Reiki Wa Darenidemo Deru*.

Ogawa, Kôzô – The stepfather of Fumio Ogawa. He ran a Reiki center in *Shizuoka* during Mikao Usui's lifetime.

Okudan 奥段 – Innermost level.

Okuden 奥伝 – Inner teachings. This is the name of Level 2 taught in most Japanese branches of Reiki. Hawayo Takata was taught *okuden* (she actually wrote *okudan* in her diary but her spelling of Japanese words was inaccurate). The *Usui Reiki Ryôhô Gakkai* includes two grades within *okuden*. One is called *zenki* and the other is *kôki*. This Japanese term signifies that you have begun working at this level – it does not signify that you have completed the level.

Oneness – A concept where you become One with the universe. No separation, you are the Universe and the Universe is you. Oneness is absolute truth. To face Oneness means to face everything – yourself, the world, every being, and everything – in its absolute truth.
Oneness is considered to be a characteristic of the mantra HSZSN and Symbol 3.

On Yomi – There are two methods of pronouncing Japanese *kanji*. One is *on yomi* where the Chinese reading and meaning are attached to the *kanji*. The other is *kun yomi*.

Oomoto Religion – *Oomoto* is the name of a *Shintô* sect considered to be one of the new religions of Japan. One influential member was Morihei Ueshiba, the founder of *aikidô*. It has been suggested that he knew Mikao Usui.

The true Reiki mantra of the pseudonym CKR is also used within the *Oomoto* religion. *Oomoto* have extracted it from the *Shintô* teachings.

A spokesman for *Oomoto*, Masamichi Tanaka, states that the true mantra (not the pseudonym) of CKR literally means 'Direct Spirit' and that it is a part of the Divine Spirit which all of us are bestowed with from God, the Creator of the universe. He writes that, 'This is a word (or term) we use at *Oomoto* and *Shintô*.'

One more interesting point is that *Oomoto* appears to have no concern about writing or discussing the complete mantra with those outside the religion, unlike some within the system of Reiki. This attitude can help Reiki practitioners to understand that it is not the mantra or symbol that is 'powerful' but rather the practitioner's personal work with them.

*Oshite Chiryô Hô 押手治療法 – A hand pressure technique.

 P

Phaigh, Bethel (?–1986) – One of the 22 Reiki teacher students of Hawayo Takata. She wrote two books, one called *Gestalt and the Wisdom of the Kahunas,* and the other, *Journey into Consciousness* (unpublished). According to Robert Fueston, she studied over a short period of time with Hawayo Takata and wrote in *Journey into Consciousness,* 'The lessons (in life that I needed to learn) may have been particularly painful because my initiations had been timed so closely together. I had left Hawaii that spring not knowing of Reiki. I return this winter as a Reiki Master, a very green one.'

Photo Technique – This is a technique used to send distant healing and is based on the Japanese technique *enkaku chiryô hô. A simple version of this is where a photo is held in the hands with the intent that Reiki be sent to whom or whatever is in the photo.

Power Symbol – The name sometimes applied to CKR and Symbol 1 in moderns forms of the system of Reiki.

In Japan its characteristic is considered to be Focus.

Precepts – See Five Precepts.

Protection – Some modern branches of Reiki claim that a Reiki practitioner must protect him or herself against the energy of others with certain techniques and practices. These are often developed with practices taken from the New Age movement.

It is true that one can affect others with energy and if someone wishes to do harm energetically, then it might be possible. This is commonly called a psychic attack. Traditionally, it is taught that to protect oneself from outside influences, one must be strong within. Therefore the most effective protection that the system of Reiki could offer a practitioner would be the ongoing practice of a technique like *hatsurei hô*. With this technique the practitioner's original energy strengthens, and offers a deeper awareness of energy. In this way the practitioner can sense what is happening and yet is not necessarily affected by it.

Proxy Methods – Proxy methods are modern techniques used to send *distant healing and are based on the Japanese technique *enkaku chiryô hô*. There is the Knee method, Pillow method or Teddy Bear method. These items or parts of the body are used as a proxy for the individual that Reiki is being sent to. This concept is intended to help those who have difficulty setting clear intent when performing distant healing.

Psychic Attack – See Protection.

Pure Land – Hônen brought Pure Land Buddhism to Japan. It is also known as *Jôdo Shû*. The goal of this Buddhist school is to be reborn in the Pure Land of Amida Nyorai. The main practice of Pure Land Buddhism is to recite *Namu-Amida-Butsu*, which is an expression of Oneness. *Namu-Amida-Butsu* translates as 'I take refuge in Amida Nyorai Buddha'.

Mikao Usui is buried in a Pure Land temple in *Tôkyô* and Hyakuten Inamoto believes that Mikao Usui belonged to this sect. According to some of the early teachings of Mikao Usui, it is claimed that Symbol 2 is connected to Amida Nyorai.

 Q

Qi Gong – A Chinese word meaning energy cultivation. This term refers to exercises that improve health and longevity as well as increase the sense of harmony within oneself and in the world. Japanese *ki ko* techniques are based on *Qi Gong*.

 R

Rabinovitch, Professor Judith – Professor Judith Rabinovitch., Ph.D., Harvard University; Currently Karashima Professor of Japanese Language and Culture Department of Foreign Languages and Literatures, University of Montana, USA. She studied *Tenohira ryôji* with Miss Endo (an original student of Toshihiro Eguchi) for one week. 'Miss Endo (then aged around 97 in 1994), [was] an original *Ittôen* student of Toshihiro Eguchi ca 1929 or 1930. She initiated me without my knowing it, just by putting my hands under hers (I had no idea what for at the time) for a longish period of time and then telling me just to 'keep practicing', saying my hands were very good. This sort of informal initiation and a call for practice seems to have been the way at *Ittôen*.'

Professor Judith Rabinovitch reports feeling great energy in her body and hands thereafter, and she continued to practice for 10 years. She went on to train through to the teacher level with a Japanese priest in 2002. Professor Judith Rabinovitch has copies of Toshihiro Eguchi's diaries and monographs and is interested in continuing her research into spiritual healers from the early 1900s in Japan.

Re-Attune – Some teachers claim to be able to re-attune you. As an attunement is a clearing of the body's energy it is impossible to be able to undo this or 'wipe it out'. Each attunement received takes the student a step further to realigning oneself with the natural function of the body – either mentally, physically, emotionally or spiritually.

Reiha 霊波 – Wave of *rei*. According to the 1933 book *Reiki To Jinjutsu – Tomita Ryû Teate Ryôhô* (*Reiki and Humanitarian Work – Tomita Ryû Hands Healing*) by Kaiji Tomita, a student of Mikao Usui, it describes the tingling sensation that is comparable to an electrical current. The heat created and the wave of *rei* are what he believed constituted spiritual energy.

*Reiji Hô 霊示法 – Being guided by spirit technique.

Reiju 霊授 – Spiritual offering or blessing. This is the Japanese origin of what is known today as attunements, initiations or transformations. *Reiju* is one of the five elements of the system of Reiki. It helps to strengthen students' connection with spiritual energy and raises their personal energy levels.

This in turn gives a sense of reconnection to one's true self. It also helps to clear the meridians, allowing students to conduct more energy through the body. *Reiju* is the same for each level – there are no differences as it is the student's ability to draw on more energy that creates the differences, not the *reiju* itself. No symbols or mantras are used in the *reiju*. The *reiju* appears to have links to practices from within the more esoteric elements of *Tendai* Buddhism called *Mikkyô*. It mirrors a *Tendai* ritual called *Go Shimbô*, also known as 'Dharma for Protecting the Body'.

Reiki 霊気 – Spiritual energy. The two *kanji* for Reiki represent the name of the energy that is used within the system of Reiki. It is the energy of everything. Kimiko Koyama, former president of the *Usui Reiki Ryôhô Gakkai*, told her student Hiroshi Doi that, 'Reiki is the light of love'.

Reiki (The System of) – This system has its origins in the early 1900s. It is believed that it was heavily influenced at that time by *Tendai* Buddhism, *Mikkyô*, *Shugendô*, *Shintô* and the general popularity of spiritual and healing systems that were blossoming at that time. There are five elements within the system of Reiki. They are attunements or *reiju*, hand positions, the precepts, symbols and mantras (from Level 2 onward), and meditations and/or techniques. It is believed that Mikao Usui did not call his teachings by this name. The word 'Reiki' appeared often in conjunction with his teachings but this was merely to point out that the teachings worked with Reiki, i.e., spiritual energy.

Professor Judith Rabinovitch states that the terms 'rei' and 'reiki' in Japan at the turn of the 20th century 'were of course widely known and had many meanings in the healing world, connoting spiritual matters/ spiritual forces of various sorts.'

Reiki Alliance, The – An organization formed by some of Hawayo Takata's teacher students after her death in 1980. In 1982 they all came together, according to Carel Anne Farmer, and compared symbols and mantras (and attunements according to John Harvey Gray). They were surprised when they found that they differed. This group then standardized these elements of the system of Reiki.

Hawayo Takata's granddaughter, Phyllis Lei Furumoto, was named as their grandmaster and lineage bearer – the first time that these words had ever been used by anyone in conjunction with the system of Reiki.

*Reiki Aura Cleansing – Non-traditional technique for clearing the aura of 'heavy' energy.

*Reiki Boost – Non-traditional technique that balances and harmonizes the chakras allowing a greater flow of Reiki in the body. Also called the quick treatment, harmonizing Reiki prior to a session, and the preparative mini Reiki session.

*Reiki Box – Non-traditional technique to send Reiki to a person, place or event in the past, present or future. A list is written up, placed in a box, and Reiki is offered to it.

Reiki Circle – A coming together of Reiki practitioners where *group Reiki is practiced.

Reiki Course – Traditionally there are three levels in the system of Reiki. By studying a Reiki course the student begins to work at that level. The five elements of the system of Reiki will be experienced at each of the levels, with the student gradually discovering them in greater depth as he or she progresses.

*Reiki Guide Meditation – Non-traditional technique to meet your Reiki guide.

Reiki Guides – The concept of guides is an add-on to the system of Reiki. It might stem from shamanism, yet witches were also believed to have familiars. Mystics, too, have been guided throughout the centuries by what they believed to be angelic beings – so the concept of spiritual guidance is quite broad based. It has been popularized in the modern system of Reiki.

Reiki Master – Someone who has completed Level 3 or *shinpiden* and is allowed to teach other people the system of Reiki. The title might not necessarily mean that this individual can guide you on your spiritual path or even understands the concept of Reiki. Some branches may only teach the attunement to their teacher students while others may offer an extensive training. The term Reiki Master is becoming less popular today as practitioners realize that it is not likely that one can master spiritual energy. One can teach about how to work with spiritual energy, however, and therefore the terms of either Reiki Master/Teacher or simply Reiki Teacher are gaining in popularity and use.

Reiki Master/Practitioner – A modern title developed for someone who has completed only half of the third level of the system of Reiki. This is a new innovation. It means that the student has not learnt the attunement, only the fourth mantra and symbol. Commonly used in 'Tibetan'-influenced branches of Reiki.

Reiki Master/Teacher – A relatively new title that is utilized for two different purposes. One is to signify that the student has completed both levels of a form of Reiki where the third Level is split in two. See Reiki Master/Practitioner.

The second purpose is that many Reiki teachers today do not believe that the term 'Master' is relevant as a description of what they do. There is the suggestion that it is arrogant to call one's self a 'Master' after what is generally a brief course and if one has not mastered spiritual energy. The title Master/Teacher is meant to suggest that the person is in fact a teacher rather than a guru of some sort. Although the title Reiki Master is still an accepted term for a Reiki

teacher perhaps it is good to keep this quote from Yukiyoshi Takamura (1928–2000) in mind: 'Anyone who refers to himself as a master, isn't.'

*Reiki Mawashi 霊気回し – A current of spiritual energy.

*Reiki Meditation – Non-traditional meditation using Reiki to increase sensitivity and connection to the source.

Reiki Practitioner – Anyone who has completed a minimum of Level 1 in the system of Reiki. If one wishes to practice professionally then it is suggested that at least Level 2 be first completed. Mikao Usui is quoted in the *Reiki Ryôhô Hikkei* as saying, 'If you can't heal yourself, you can't heal others'. Today the name also indicates someone who provides Reiki treatments for others.

Reiki Ryôhô Hikkei 霊気療法必携 – Spiritual Energy Method Manual.

The *Reiki Ryôhô Hikkei* is a 68-page document divided up into four sections. There is the introduction or explanation by Mikao Usui; a question and answer section with Mikao Usui; the *Ryôhô Shishin* or healing guide with specific hand positions and 125 *gyosei* (poetry of the Meiji Emperor).

It was given to *shoden* (Level 1) students of the *Usui Reiki Ryôhô Gakkai*.

It is believed that Chûjirô Hayashi created the healing guide for the *Usui Reiki Ryôhô Gakkai* as it is similar to his own healing guide which was developed after 1931 when he left the society. The creation of this first healing guide may have been prior to, or after, Mikao Usui's death.

Kimiko Koyama, former president of the *Usui Reiki Ryôhô Gakkai*, compiled the *Reiki Ryôhô Hikkei* for the society's 50th anniversary from past *Usui Reiki Ryôhô* material. Therefore, although the *Reiki Ryôhô Hikkei* has been promoted as Mikao Usui's manual, it is unclear how original to Mikao Usui the material is.

Reiki Salad – Hawayo Takata was renowned for her 'Reiki Salad' as she called it. Some of her recommended recipes for better health included sunflower seeds, red beet, grape juice and almonds. Two students of Virginia Samdahl's wrote a book in 1984 called *The Reiki Handbook*, which included Reiki recipes.

Reiki Shares – See Reiki Circle.

*Reiki Shower – Non-traditional cleansing technique that also increases energy flow in the body.

Reiki Stacks – Non-traditional technique used for sending distant Reiki. This is similar to the technique Reiki box and the healing lists where lists are written up and Reiki is offered to them.

Reiki Teacher – A Reiki Master that does not wish to use the word 'Master' due to its implications of having perfected working with spiritual energy. See also Reiki Master/Teacher.

Reiki Treatment – Also known as Reiki Session. Reiki treatments come in all shapes and sizes. A treatment can be performed on the self or on others.

If working on others, the client lies or sits and the Reiki practitioner's hands are placed on or just above the body. It is unnecessary for the client to remove one's clothes and no private parts of the body should be touched. There is no place for sexual contact or inference within the system of Reiki. The practitioner channels energy through his/her body and the client draws what he or she requires at that point in time. The treatment may take from about five minutes to an hour. Reiki treatments may also be used as a form of first aid.

*Reiki Undô 霊気運動 – Movement of spiritual energy technique.

Reizan-in Shuyo Tenshin Koji – Mikao Usui's posthumous Buddhist name (called *kaimyô* in Japanese).

Hyakuten Inamoto states that this is a typical Pure Land Buddhist name.

Ritual – Within the system of Reiki a number of rituals are practiced. Ritual is in place to teach practitioners the ground rules and give guidance. Once one knows and understands these rituals, it is time to free oneself of them and move to integration or Oneness with the true meaning of the practice. This may take many years or even a whole lifetime. In fact, a Reiki practitioner may never reach the stage where he/she can fully detach from the need for ritual.

All five elements of the system of

Reiki can be seen as rituals. They are: the practicing of attunement or *reiju*, symbols and mantras, precepts, hand positions, and techniques and meditations.

Robertson, Arthur (?–2001) – He first studied with Hawayo Takata's student, Virginia Samdahl in 1975, and then went on to study and work with another of Hawayo Takata's students, Iris Ishikuro, in the early 1980s. He created Raku Kei Reiki. According to Robert Fueston, in a 1983 Raku Kei Reiki manual the non-traditional techniques taught included the breath of the fire dragon, the *hui yin* breath and the kanji hand mudras. This appears to be the first time that they had been used in connection with the system of Reiki. Arthur Robertson also worked with Master Frequency Plates with an *antakharana inside. These additions to the system of Reiki have made a profound impact on how it is taught today. Many of the 'Tibetan'-influenced branches have stemmed from Arthur Robertson's teachings.

Ryôhô – Healing method.

Ryôhô Shishin 療法指針 – Healing guide.

There are two Japanese healing guides that are known of. The first belongs within the *Usui Reiki Ryôhô Gakkai*'s larger manual called the *Reiki Ryôhô Hikkei*. The other is from a later date and was written by Chûjirô Hayashi for his students. They contain almost identical hand positions for treating specific illnesses. Due to their similarities it is

believed that both were created by the doctor, Chûjirô Hayashi. He was originally a member of the *Usui Reiki Ryôhô Gakkai* who then went on to start his own organization in 1931.

The front cover of the second healing guide reads *Ryôhô Shishin* and explains that it had been set up for American distribution. The branch name on the cover is the *Hayashi Reiki Kenkyû Kai* (Hayashi Spiritual Energy Research Society). It also states that it is not for sale and is a copy of the original. The actual manual is written in Japanese. Hawayo Takata is known to have handed it to a number of her students including Harue Kanemitsu. John Harvey Gray also received a copy from Alice Takata Furumoto, Hawayo Takata's daughter.

 S

Sacred – The word sacred is often used to explain why some Reiki practitioners do not show their symbols and mantras to those who have not studied the appropriate levels of the system of Reiki. Some Reiki practitioners even believe that the symbols and mantras are secret.

For these reasons, *The Reiki Sourcebook* uses pseudonyms for the mantras instead. They are CKR, SHK, HSZSN, and DKM.

The symbols are listed by their numbers from 1 to 4 as is taught in traditional branches.

In Japan some of the symbols and mantras are of use in the public arena and can be found today in martial arts, *Shintô*, and some new religions.

*Saibo Kassei Kokyû Hô 細胞活性呼吸法 – Vitalizing the cells through the breath technique.

Saihôji Temple – Pure Land Buddhist Temple in *Tôkyô*. The exact address is *Toyotama* district, 1-4-56 *Umesato, Suginami Ku, Tôkyô*. Here you can visit the memorial stone that was engraved by Mikao Usui's students in 1927, one year after his death. Masayuki Okada composed it with brush strokes written by the president of the *Usui Reiki Ryôhô Gakkai*, Jûzaburô Ushida, in 1927. The memorial stone is one aspect of Mikao Usui's life as seen through the eyes of his students from the *Usui Reiki Ryôhô Gakkai*.

Sakoku 鎖国 – National isolation. From 1639 to 1854, Japan was shut under a policy called *sakoku,* which had left it culturally prosperous though far behind many other countries technologically and militarily. Foreigners were forbidden to enter Japan and trade. Only the Dutch were permitted. Through the small port of *Dejima* in *Nagasaki*, the Dutch traders became Japan's single link to the outside world for more than two centuries. This privilege was only extended to contact with Japanese merchants and prostitutes.

Any Japanese who dared to venture abroad during this period were executed on their return to prevent any form of 'contamination'.

The Meiji Emperor (1852–1912) introduced Japan to modernization and industrialization. Christianity was legalized in 1877.

Samdahl, Virginia (? -1994) – One of Hawayo Takata's 22 Reiki teacher students. Robert Fueston states that he was told that Virginia Samdahl introduced Barbara Weber to Hawayo Takata. This may account for the fact that after Hawayo Takata's death, Virginia Samdahl was a member of two of the groups that claimed to carry on Hawayo Takata's teachings. One was The Reiki Alliance, and the other was Barbara Weber's The Radiance Technique®.

Samurai 侍 – Warrior. Mikao Usui's family was *hatamoto samurai* – a high level within the ranks of *samurai*.

San – This is a neutral title, and can be used in most situations when addressing people. In formal situations it may not be polite enough.

Sanskrit – An ancient Indian language created over 2000 years ago. It is the language of Hinduism, the Vedas and classical Indian literature but it is only used for religious purposes today. Some elements of Buddhism can be traced back to their Sanskrit origins.

The origin of the Japanese symbol called *kiriku* can be traced back to the Sanskrit meditation symbol called *hrih*. Symbol 2 in the system of Reiki appears to be derived from the *kiriku*.

Satori – Spiritual enlightenment or awakening.

The method of attaining spiritual enlightenment would differ depending on which Buddhist sect you belonged to. Zen emphasized meditation as a means of experiencing awakening while the Pure Land sect uses the chanting of *Namu-Amida-Butsu* (I take refuge in Amida Nyorai Buddha).

*Scanning – Non-traditional technique sensing imbalances in the energy field.

*Seated Chakra Treatment – Non-traditional technique stimulating the chakras.

Sect – A small religious group that has branched off from a larger established group.

*Seiheki Chiryô Hô 性癖治療法 – Treatment of mental patterns technique.

This is the same treatment as nentatsu hô but with the inclusion of mantras and symbols.

*Seishin Toitsu 精神統一 – Mental concentration.

This technique is also called **gasshô kokyû hô* and is a part of the technique **hatsurei hô*.

Seiza (1) 正座 – Correct sitting.

Seiza is a traditional Japanese style of sitting on top of the ankles, with the legs folded underneath and the back erect. It is a formal way of sitting on a tatami.

Sitting cross-legged is called *agura* which is more informal or casual. *Seiza* is used when you attend a formal occasion while *agura* would be used for informal occasions.

Seiza (2) 静座 – Sit still.

This is a different reading of the word *seiza*. It relates to a part of the technique **hatsurei hô* that can be found in the 1933 book, *Reiki To Jinjutsu – Tomita Ryû Teate Ryôhô (Reiki and Humanitarian Work – Tomita Ryû Hands Healing)* written by a student of Mikao Usui called Kaiji Tomita.

*Sekizui Jôka Ibuki Hô 脊髄浄化息吹法 – Cleansing the spinal cord with breath technique.

Self-healing – In the *Reiki Ryôhô Hikkei* Mikao Usui is asked the question, 'If I can heal others, can I heal myself?' His answer is, 'If you can't heal yourself, how can you heal others?'

Self-healing is integral to all Reiki practices.

Self-Treatment – Reiki practitioners place their hands on or just off their own bodies, often in a structured form, to support self-healing.

Sensei 先生 – Teacher, master.

This is an honorific title, which people call their teachers, doctors or any professional who offers a service or instructions. In Japan the founder of the system of Reiki is often referred to as Usui *sensei*.

As it is an honorific title, it is inappropriate to call oneself *sensei*.

Seppuku – Suicide by disembowelment. Chûjirô Hayashi may have committed *seppuku*.

Shakyo – *Sutra* copying.

Sutra are copied by hand as a meditative practice within *Tendai* Buddhism. It is said that Mikao Usui's hand-copied *sutra* still exist on *hiei zan,* signed with the name Gyoho.

Shihan 師範 – Instructor or teacher. This term is used in some Japanese lineages such as the *Usui Reiki Ryôhô Gakkai* and *Gendai Reiki Hô.*

Shiki – Way. This word is used within the name of the branch of Reiki called *Usui Shiki Ryôhô* (Usui Way Healing Method).

Shinobu, Saito – One of Hawayo Takata's 22 Reiki teacher students. Robert Fueston states that Hawayo Takata hoped she would help take the system of Reiki back to Japan.

Shinpiden 神秘伝 – Mystery teachings. Japanese name for Level 3 or Reiki Master or Reiki Master/Teacher. Hawayo Takata was taught *shinpiden* (she actually wrote 'Shinpeten' in her diary in 1936 but her spelling of Japanese words was inaccurate) and the *Usui Reiki Ryôhô Gakkai* use the term too. This Japanese term signifies that you have begun working at this level – it does not signify that you have completed the level.

Shintô 神道 – The way of the *kami* (gods). *Shintô* is the indigenous faith of the Japanese people, and it is as old as the culture itself. The *kami,* or gods, are the objects of worship in *Shintô.* It has no founder and no sacred scriptures like the *sutra* or the Bible. Initially, it was so unselfconscious that it also had no name. The term *Shintô* came into use after the 6th century, when it was necessary to distinguish it from the recently imported Buddhism. It is not unusual for Japanese people to be followers of both Buddhism and *Shintô.* Today many people visit *Shintô* shrines for self-purification services. Purification rites are a vital part of *Shintô.* A personal purification rite is the purification by water; this may involve standing under a waterfall, which is known as *misogi.* In Mikao Usui's traditional teachings there is a technique called **kenyoku hô,* which is a kind of *misogi.* The use of *jumon* or *kotodama* is an aspect of *Shintô* that is also reflected in Mikao Usui's teachings.

Shiori 栞 – Guide, usually for beginners. It is also known as the *Reiki Ryôhô No Shiori.* This is a booklet exclusively for members of the *Usui Reiki Ryôhô Gakkai* and was written by Hôichi Wanami and Kimiko Koyama, both presidents of the *Usui Reiki Ryôhô Gakkai.* It consists of: the purpose, history and administrative system of the *Usui Reiki Ryôhô Gakkai* and includes the names of 11 of the 21 *shinpiden* students taught by Mikao Usui; how to strengthen Reiki and includes techniques such as **byôsen reikan hô, *gedoku hô, *kôketsu hô* and **nentatsu hô*; a teaching from Mikao Usui; a guide to treatment; characteristics of the

Reiki healing method; remarks by medical doctors and an explanation of the *Ryôhô Shishin* (*Healing Guide*).

Shirushi 印 – Symbol.

SHK – As the traditional mantras of the system of Reiki are considered as sacred by many, pseudonyms are used in *The Reiki Sourcebook* rather than the true mantras. The pseudonym for the second traditional mantra is the initials SHK.

The main modern characteristic of SHK is mental/emotional and it is spoken three times in conjunction with Symbol 2. The main traditional characteristic is Harmony and the mantra is not necessarily used in conjunction with the symbol. The early teachings of Mikao Usui claim that SHK develops a Reiki practitioner's link to the energy of Heaven.

Shodan 初段 – Beginner's level.

Shoden 初伝 – First teachings. This is the Japanese name for Level 1. Hawayo Takata was taught *shoden* (she actually wrote *shodan* in her diary but her spelling of Japanese words was inaccurate). The *Usui Reiki Ryôhô Gakkai* use the term, too.

This Japanese term signifies that you have begun working at this level – it does not signify that you have completed the level.

Shogun 将軍 – A General.

***Shûchû Reiki** 集中霊気 – Concentrated spiritual energy. Also called *shûdan Reiki. This is what is called *group Reiki today.

***Shûdan Reiki** 集団霊気 – Group spiritual energy. Also called *shûchû Reiki.

Shugendô – The path of training and testing.
En-no-Gyoja is the legendary founder of this esoteric form of Buddhism. For 30 years from the year 666, En-no-Gyoja practiced in the mountains, gaining miraculous powers. *Shugendô* practitioners were called *shugenja*.

Shugendô is a mix of shamanism, Taoism, Buddhism and *Shintô*. In fact *Shugendô* was outlawed around 1870 by the Meiji Emperor's regime because of this typical scenario of the combination of specifically Buddhist and *Shintô* elements. The government wanted a separation between *Shintô* and Buddhism, which had become interwoven. The distinction between religions supported the Meiji regime in establishing *Shintô* as the state religion. This unifying action promoted patriotism in Japan. *Shugenja* were, therefore, made to choose which sect to belong to: Buddhist (either *Tendai* or *Shingon*) or *Shintô*.

Shugenja – Someone who practises *Shugendô*.
Also known as *yamabushi*. These were the 'mountain men' who were able to draw on the power of the *kami* (gods) through their magical powers acquired by esoteric practices. *Shugenja* would often heal disease, offer religious services, perform divination, exorcism and obtain oracles.
It is claimed that Mikao Usui was a *shugenja*.

Shûgyô 修行 – Deep mind/body

training.

Shûgyô is a training performed in pursuit of deeper levels of consciousness. It is usually quite demanding, requiring unlimited amounts of effort, mindfulness and refinement.

Mikao Usui performed a form of *shûgyô* on *kurama yama* called *kushu shinren*.

Shûyô Kai 修養会 – Group meetings.

Shûyô means to cultivate one's mind or improve oneself. *Shûyô kai* was the name the *Usui Reiki Ryôhô Gakkai* once gave to their group meetings. After the shûyô kai there was the *jisshû kai*, the practical gathering, where some techniques were performed.

Today the *Usui Reiki Ryôhô Gakkai* group meeting is called the *kenkyû kai*.

*Smudging – Non-traditional technique using the vibration of smell to affect energy.

*Solar Image Training – Non-traditional technique to aid in letting go of dependency on symbols.

Sôsho – *Kanji* in modern, cursive style.

This is a kind of simplified shorthand that is drawn according to aesthetic standards.

Sôtô Zen – One of the two most important schools of Zen Buddhism in Japan. The *zazen shikan taza* meditation which Hiroshi Doi states may have been practised by Mikao Usui is heavily stressed in this school.

Stagnant energy – Universal energy flows through each and everything in life.

The human body has the ability to create obstacles to this natural flow. When the energy is not flowing in accordance with the natural flow, this is called stagnant energy.

The system of Reiki stimulates and strengthens energy flow in the body.

Sugano, Wasaburo – Uncle of Chiyoko Yamaguchi. He lived in the North of Japan and studied Reiki with Chûjirô Hayashi in 1928 in *Sakai, Osaka*. His motivation to learn Reiki came about due to the sense of helplessness he felt at the loss of his two childrens' lives.

It was Sugano Wasaburo who taught Chiyoko Yamaguchi how to perform an attunement.

Sutra – A Sanskrit word meaning rope or thread.

They are the records of religious texts.

Suzuki, Bizan – Author of a book called *Kenzen No Genri* (*The Principles of Health*) written in 1914. It includes precepts similar to those taught by Mikao Usui. A translation of this similar section in Bizan Suzuki's book is: 'Today do not be angry, do not worry and be honest, work hard and be kind to people'.

Another interesting fact is that the *kanji* for Bizan can be read as Miyama. *Miyama cho* is the modern name of Mikao Usui's town of origin.

Suzuki, Sadako (?–1946) – Mikao Usui's wife. She died on 17 October 1946.

Her posthumous name on the gravestone is *Te shin ing on ho jo ning dai shi*.

Suzuki san (1895–) – It is said that

Suzuki san is a *Tendai* nun who studied with Mikao Usui and is still alive as of 2008. She is the cousin of Mikao Usui's wife. Her formal training with him began in 1915 when she was 20 years old and her relationship with him continued on a less formal basis until his death in 1926. The teachings which Suzuki san passes down have no correlation to the system of Reiki other than that they originated with Mikao Usui. There are no symbols and mantras, no physical attunements, a different set of precepts and no hand positions.

Symbol – Traditionally, there are four symbols in the system of Reiki. Symbols 1 and 2 are clearly 'real' symbols while 3 and 4 are actual Japanese *kanji*. However anything can be used as a symbol and in this case the four symbols are extra tools whose purpose is to make it easier for students to practice the teachings.

The names of the traditional Reiki symbols are Symbol 1, 2, 3 and 4. In modern branches the symbols are called by their accompanying mantras rather than by numbers.

The symbols and mantras are considered sacred but in some modern teachings there is also a sense of forced secrecy around them. It is interesting to note that most of these mantras and symbols are openly discussed in Japan when they are used in martial arts, *Shintô*, and new religions, unlike the system of Reiki.

Reiki practitioners can learn from this traditional attitude to mantras and symbols to overcome what may be exaggerated modern mysticism. This traditional perspective also supports the understanding that it is not the mantra or symbol that is 'powerful' but rather the strength of the practitioner's commitment to practice.

Symbol 1 – This is the first symbol of Reiki taught in *okuden* or Level 2. It is known as the Power Symbol in modern teachings.

Symbol 2 – This is the second symbol of Reiki taught in *okuden* or Level 2. It is known as the Mental/Emotional Symbol in modern teachings.

Symbol 3 – This is the third symbol of Reiki taught in *okuden* or Level 2. This symbol is not really a symbol but *kanji*. Its meaning is 'my original nature is a correct thought'. This is known as the Distance Symbol in modern teachings.

Symbol 4 – This is the fourth symbol of Reiki taught in *shinpiden* or Level 3. This symbol is not really a symbol but *kanji*. It means 'Great Bright Light'. This *kanji* is not used solely within Mikao Usui's teachings. It can be found in some Japanese martial arts as well as in *Mikkyô*, *Shugendô*, and some of the new religions like *Shunmei*.

*Symbol Exercises – Non-traditional techniques to increase your connection to Reiki by meditating on the symbols.

T

Takata, Hawayo (1900–1980) – One of 13 Reiki teacher students of Chûjirô Hayashi according to her certificate from Chûjirô Hayashi. Hawayo Takata was born in Hawaii and studied with Chûjirô Hayashi in Japan from 1936 to 1938. She brought Chûjirô Hayashi's teachings to Hawaii. For 40 years she offered treatments and taught people about the system she called Reiki. Before she died in 1980 she had taught 22 Reiki teachers to carry on her teachings.

Taketomi, Kanichi (1878–1960) – Third president of the *Usui Reiki Ryôhô Gakkai* and a Rear Admiral in the Japanese Navy. He became a member of the society in 1925 and was taught by Mikao Usui.

*Talismans – Non-traditional technique of manifesting using an image as the focus.

Tanden – The abdomen below the navel.
Also called *hara*.

*Tanden Chiryo Hô 丹田治療 法 – Detoxifying and purifying technique.

Taniai – Birthplace of Mikao Usui. He was born on 15 August 1865 in this village in the *Yamagata* county of the *Gifu* Prefecture, Japan. This village is now called *Miyama cho*.

Tatsumi (?–1996) – According to a modern Reiki practitioner he was a teacher student of Chûjirô Hayashi.

Teate 手当 – Hands-on healing.

This is the generic term used for the many forms of hands-on healing that took place during the 20th century in Japan. A variety of groups were practicing *teate*, with some of the teachings spreading worldwide. *Tenrikyo, Johrei,* and *Mahikari* were just some of these.

Technique – Techniques are one of the five elements of the system of Reiki.
Some of them originate in Japan and others have been introduced over the last 25 years from influences such as the New Age movement.

Tendai – Buddhist sect in Japan. Mikao Usui is said to have been a *Tendai* lay priest and to have studied on *hiei zan*, the main *Tendai* temple complex in Japan. *Tendai* was brought to Japan by Saichô in the early 9th century and names Nagarjuna as its patriarch. *Tendai* practitioners believe that the Lotus *Sutra* is Buddha's complete and perfect teachings.
There are five general areas taught in *Tendai*. They are the teachings of the Lotus *Sutra*; esoteric *Mikkyô* practices; meditation practices; precepts; and Pure Land teachings.

Tenohira – Hands-on healing. This is a term for a structured form of hands-on healing.

Tenohira Ryôji Kenkyû Kai 手の ひら療治研究会 – Hand Healing Research Center. Toshihiro Eguchi, a student and friend of Mikao Usui, created this hands-on healing society.

Tenon in – The Buddhist name for Mariko Obaasan, who it is claimed was a student of Mikao Usui from 1920–1926.

Three-Week Cleansing Process – The cleansing process is also known as a healing crisis. It is a response to an attunement, *reiju* or Reiki treatment.

The body is attempting to remove toxins and re-balance and this can often be felt physically, emotionally, mentally or spiritually.

After an attunement it is often said that the student will undergo a 21-day cleansing process in which the student must practice Reiki to aid the process. Though this is likely to be a recent addition to the system of Reiki it certainly has had its share of esoteric interpretations.

21-Day practices can also be found in Japanese forms such as *Shugendô* and *Tendai*. For example; traditional meditations, like the Buddhist *hokkesen*, are practiced for the duration of 21 days, but these are quite different to the three-week cleansing process.

Basically, the popularity of the three-week cleansing process concept can be put down to the fact that it is successful – it achieves its aim. That aim as far as the system of Reiki is concerned is to get people practicing. After practicing Reiki for three weeks students don't want to stop practicing – it feels too good!

Tomita, Kaiji – A student of Mikao Usui. He wrote a book called *Reiki To Jinjutsu – Tomita Ryû Teate Ryôhô (Reiki and Humanitarian Work – Tomita Ryû Hands Healing)* in 1933. The book was re-published in 1999 with the help of Toshitaka Mochizuki. Included in Kaiji Tomita's book are case studies, the technique **hatsurei hô* (which includes the use of *waka*), and hand positions for specific illnesses. The name of his organization was *Tomita Teate Ryôhô Kai* and it taught four levels *shoden, chuden, okuden* and *kaiden*.

Tomita Teate Ryôhô Kai – Name of the organization created by Kaiji Tomita, a student of Mikao Usui. In his organization he used four levels called *shoden, chuden, okuden* and *kaiden*.

*Toning – Non-traditional technique of using the voice as a healing tool.

Traditional – This term is used in *The Reiki Sourcebook* to represent teachings that are directly related to the traditional Japanese origins of the system of Reiki rather than modern Japanese teachings or other recent additions from outside of Japan.

Transformation – This word is often used to describe the *reiju* and/or the attunement process.

Tsuboi, Sonoo – Student of Mikao Usui according to Hiroshi Doi.

Twan, Wanja – One of Hawayo Takata's 22 Reiki teacher students. She wrote *In the Light of a Distant Star: A Spiritual Journey Bringing the Unseen into the Seen*, and her daughter Annelli has compiled a book called *Early Days of Reiki: Memories of Hawayo Takata*.

U

*Uchite Chiryô Hô 打手治療
法 – Patting with the hands
technique.

Ueshiba, Morihei (1883–1969)
– Founder of *aikidô*. Morihei
Ueshiba is claimed to have
been an acquaintance of Mikao
Usui. Morihei Ueshiba taught
kotodama in his method, not
unlike Mikao Usui.

Ushida, Jûzaburô (1865–1935) –
Second president of the *Usui Reiki
Ryôhô Gakkai*. He was also a rear
admiral in the Japanese navy.
Jûzaburô Ushida was taught
by Mikao Usui and became a
member of the society in 1925.
Ushida Jûzaburû drew the
brush strokes on Mikao Usui's
memorial stone in 1927.
If there had been a successor to
Mikao Usui within *Usui Reiki
Ryôhô Gakkai* practitioners, it
would most likely have been
Jûzaburô Ushida.

Usui, Fuji (1908–1946) – Mikao
Usui's son. He was a teacher at
Tôkyô University.

Usui, Mikao (1865–1926) – Mikao
Usui is the founder of the
system of Reiki. He was born
on 15 August 1865, in the village
of *Taniai mura* in the *Yamagata*
district of the *Gifu* Prefecture,
in Japan. His father's name was
Uzaemon and they were from
the *Chiba* clan.
Mikao Usui married Suzuki
Sadako and they had two
children, a boy, Fuji, and a girl,
Toshiko. He is thought to have
studied on *hiei zan* and practiced
certain meditations on *kurama
yama*. It is said that Mikao Usui
practiced *Shugendô* and that his
teachings are founded in this
practice of mountain Buddhism.
His teachings included using
waka, the five precepts,
meditations and techniques,
mantras and/or symbols, and
reiju.
Professor Judith Rabinovitch
writes that, 'Japan was in a great
popular health movement from
the teens onward and continuing
well up through the 30s, only
hampered by Japan's entry into
WWII. Hand healers, psychics,
intuitives, and every imaginable
kind of psychic healer plied their
trades all around the country.
However deeply respected and
influential he was among his
immediate healer-peers and
disciples, Usui was but one island
of healing activity.'
The names of 11 of the 21 Master
students of Mikao Usui have
been recorded in a booklet used
by the *Usui Reiki Ryôhô Gakkai*.
Mikao Usui's posthumous
Buddhist name noted at the
memorial stone site is *Reizan-in
Shuyo Tenshin Koji*.

Usui Reiki Ryôhô – Usui Spiritual
Energy Healing Method.
Hawayo Takata referred to the
system of Reiki she learned from
Chûjirô Hayashi as *Usui Reiki
Ryôhô* in a recording of 1979.
Her certificates call it *Usui Shiki
Ryôhô*.
The memorial stone, erected
by early members of the *Usui
Reiki Ryôhô Gakkai*, called the
teachings *Reiki Ryôhô*.

There is also a branch of Reiki called *Usui Reiki Ryôhô*. It attempts to trace the history of the system of Reiki basing its principles on what Mikao Usui taught.

Usui Reiki Ryôhô Gakkai 臼井霊気療法学会 – Society of the Usui Spiritual Energy Healing Method.

The *Usui Reiki Ryôhô Gakkai* claims to have been created by Mikao Usui in 1922. The society still exists today, and has its seventh president.

It includes no foreigners in its ranks and members are asked not to discuss the details of the society with non-members. When this society was first started, members of the Japanese navy largely attended it. There were once 80 divisions of the *Usui Reiki Ryôhô Gakkai* throughout Japan but today there are, at the most, five, with the teachings taking place in *Tôkyô*. The society does not advertise and has not actively made contact with Westerners apart from one member, Hiroshi Doi.

Hiroshi Doi has told about his experience of the meetings, *kenkyû kai*, held by former president Kimiko Koyama in the 1990s when she visited *Kyôto* once a month. The members would sit in a circle (on chairs rather than in *seiza*). Kimiko Koyama would talk about various topics based on her life experiences. The *gyosei* were recited followed by **kenyoku hô*, **jôshin kokyû hô* and **gasshô*. This was followed by **seishin toitsu* as all members received *reiju*. Kimiko Koyama and one of the *shihan*s performed *reiju*. There was then a three time recitation of the five precepts, answers to questions, **Reiki mawashi* and **shûchû Reiki*.

There are three major levels in the *Usui Reiki Ryôhô Gakkai*. These are *shoden, okuden* and *shinpiden* (the teacher level). Within these levels there are six grades of proficiency. Each member is supplied with the *Reiki Ryôhô Hikkei* and *shiori*.

Here is a list of presidents from Mikao Usui to modern day:
- Mikao Usui (1865–1926)
- Jûzaburô Ushida (Rear Admiral, 1865–1935)
- Kanichi Taketomi (Rear Admiral, 1878–1960)
- Yoshiharu Watanabe (Schoolteacher, ? ? –1960)
- Hôichi Wanami (Vice Admiral, 1883–1975)
- Kimiko Koyama (1906–1999)
- Kondô Masaki (University Professor)

Usui Shiki Ryôhô 臼井式療法 – Usui Way Healing Method. Hawayo Takata used this name on the certificates she issued. There are a number of branches of Reiki that use the title *Usui Shiki Ryôho* and yet there are variations in the teachings. Phyllis Lei Furumoto, Beth Gray and other teachers have used this name to represent their teachings. Today the majority of Reiki practitioners state that they teach Usui Reiki or the Usui Natural System of Healing. By these terms they are referring to aspects of *Usui Shiki Ryôhô* in one of its many forms.

Usui, Toshiko (1913–1935) – Mikao Usui's daughter.

 W

Waka 和歌 – Japanese verse.
The word *waka* is made up of two parts: *wa* meaning 'Japanese' and *ka* meaning 'poem' or 'song'. *Waka* is a short form of poetry that contains 31 syllables. In English it is typically divided into five lines of 5,7,5,7 and 7 syllables. – In the 13th century in Japan, people began to believe that *waka* were *dharani* or spells that could achieve supernatural effects.. – *Waka*, as written by the Meiji Emperor, is one of the components of Mikao Usui's teachings.
The *waka* Mikao Usui used in his teachings are written down in the *Reiki Ryôhô Hikkei*, a manual used by the *Usui Reiki Ryôhô Gakkai*.
Kaiji Tomita, a student of Mikao Usui, wrote in his 1933 book that the technique *hatsurei hô* included the student becoming One with the essence of the *waka*.
Toshihiro Eguchi, a friend and student of Mikao Usui, also used the Meiji Emperor's *waka* in his teachings according to the author Mihashi Kazuo.
It was a popular cultural social interaction at the turn of the 20th century and was very common among well-educated sections of the population.

Wanami, Hôichi (1883–1975) – Fifth president of the *Usui Reiki Ryôhô Gakkai* who was taught by Jûzaburô Ushida. He was also a vice admiral in the Japanese navy.

Watanabe, Yoshiharu (?–1960) – Fourth president of the *Usui Reiki Ryôhô Gakkai* who was taught by Mikao Usui. He was a professor at the Takaoka Commercial High School.

*Water Ritual – Non-traditional technique of changing water into energized healing water.

Weber, Barbara – One of Hawayo Takata's 22 Reiki teacher students. She founded the American Reiki Association in 1980 (now called the American-International Reiki Association) and The Radiance Technique®. She wrote a book in 1983 called *The Reiki Factor* that later changed its name to *The Reiki Factor in The Radiance Technique*. In later editions of this book she states that there are seven levels in the system of Reiki. The first edition notes that there are just three levels (the same as Hawayo Takata's other Reiki teacher students).

 Y

Yamabushi – Those who sleep in the mountain.
These are practitioners of

Shugendô, also called *shugenja*. They live in the mountains and engage in ascetic practices.

Yamaguchi, Chiyoko (1920/21–2003) – Chiyoko Yamaguchi was taught Levels 1 and 2 by Chûjirô Hayashi in 1938. She said that she learnt both *shoden* and *okuden* together over five consecutive days.

Many of her family members were Reiki practitioners and it was her uncle Sugano Wasaburo that taught her how to perform the attunement.

Yamaguchi, Tadao – Son of Chiyoko Yamaguchi, and the founder of *Jikiden Reiki*. He has also been the Secretary General of a new religious group named *Sekai Kyusei-kyo*, founded by Okada Mokichi (1882–1955). *Sekai Kyusei-kyo* performs Johrei healing.

Yamashita, Kay – One of Hawayo Takata's sisters and trained by Hawayo Takata as a Reiki Master.

Yuri in (1897–1997) – It is claimed that this Buddhist nun studied Mikao Usui's teachings alongside Tenon in from 1920–1926.

 Z

Zaike 在家 – Lay priest.
A lay priest resides in his own home, not in a monastery. Mikao Usui is said to have been a *Tendai zaike*.

Zazen Shikan Taza – A *Tendai* meditation practice that was supposedly practiced by Mikao Usui on *kurama yama*.

Zenki 前期 – First stage.
The first part or grade within *okuden*.

*Zenshin Kôketsu hô 全身交血法 – Whole body blood exchange. Also called **ketsueki kôkan hô*. Hawayo Takata taught this as the **finishing treatment or *nerve stroke in her Level 2 classes. By this inclusion it is apparent that she knew some of the more traditional techniques.

B. Mikao Usui's Memorial Stone

Reiho Choso Usui Sensei Kudoku No Hi

(Memorial of the merits of Usui *Sensei*, the founder of *Reiho* (*Reiki Ryôhô*))

That which is attained within oneself after having accumulated the fruits of disciplined study and training is called '*Toku*' and that which can be offered to others after having spread a path of teaching and salvation is called '*Koh*'. Only with high merits and great virtues can one be a great founding teacher. Sagacious and brilliant men of the olden time or the founders of new teachings and religious sects were all like that. Someone like Usui *Sensei* can be counted among them. *Sensei* newly founded the method based on Reiki of the universe to improve the mind and body. Having heard of his reputation all over, people crowded around to seek his teachings and treatments. Ah, how popular it is!

Sensei, commonly known by the name 'Mikao', with an extra name 'Gyohan' is from *Taniai-mura* (village), *Yamagata-gun* (county), *Gifu-ken* (prefecture). He is descended from Chiba Tsunetane. His father's name was Taneuji, and was commonly called Uzaemon. His mother was from the Kawai family.

Sensei was born on 15 August of the first year of Keio (1865 A.D.). From his youth he surpassed his fellows in hard work and endeavour. When he grew up he visited Europe and America, and studied in China. Despite his will to succeed in life, he was stalemated and fell into great difficulties. However, in the face of adversity he strove to train himself even more with the courage never to yield.

One day, he climbed *kurama yama* and after 21 days of a severe discipline without eating, he suddenly felt One Great Reiki over his head and attained enlightenment and he obtained *Reiki Ryôhô*. Then, he tried it on himself and experimented on his family members. The efficacy was immediate. *Sensei* thought that it would be far better to offer it widely to the general public and share its benefits than just to improve the well-being of his own family members. In April of the eleventh year of Taisho (1922 A.D.) he settled in *Harajuku, Aoyama, Tôkyô* and set up the Gakkai to teach *Reiki Ryôhô* and give treatments. Even outside of the building it was full of pairs of shoes of the visitors who had come from far and near.

In September of the 12th year (1923 A.D.) there was a great earthquake and a conflagration broke out. Everywhere there were groans of pain from the wounded. *Sensei*, feeling pity for them, went out every morning to go around the town, and he cured and saved an innumerable number of people. This is just a broad outline of his relief activities during such an emergency.

Later on, as the *dôjô* became too small, in February of the fourteenth year (1925 A.D.) the new suburban house was built at *Nakano* according to divination. Due to his respected and far-reaching reputation many people from local districts wished to invite him. *Sensei*, accepting the invitations, went to *Kure* and then to *Hiroshima* and *Saga*, and reached *Fukuyama*. Unexpectedly he became ill and passed away there. It was 9 March of the 15th year of Taisho (1926 A.D.), aged 62.

His spouse was Suzuki, and was called Sadako. One boy and one girl were born. The boy was named Fuji and he succeeded to the family. *Sensei*'s personality was gentle and modest and he never behaved ostentatiously. His physique was large and sturdy. He always wore a contented smile. He was stout-hearted, tolerant and very prudent upon undertaking a task. He was by nature versatile and loved to read books. He engaged himself in history books, medical books, Buddhist scriptures, Christian scriptures and was well versed in psychology, Taoism, even in the art of divination, incantation, and physiognomy. Presumably *Sensei*'s background in the arts and sciences afforded him nourishment for his cultivation and discipline, and it was very obvious that it was this cultivation and discipline that became the key to the creation of *Reiho* (*Reiki Ryôhô*).

On reflection, *Reiho* puts special emphasis not just on curing diseases but also on enjoying well-being in life with correcting the mind and making the body healthy with the use of an innate healing ability. Thus, before teaching, the Ikun (admonition) of the Meiji Emperor should reverently be read and Five Precepts be chanted and kept in mind mornings and evenings.

First it reads, 'Today do not anger', second it reads, 'Do not worry', third it reads 'Be thankful', fourth it reads, 'Work with diligence', fifth it reads, 'be kind to others'.

These are truly great teachings for cultivation and discipline that agree with those great teachings of the ancient sages and the wise. *Sensei* named these teachings 'Secret Method to Invite Happiness' and 'Miraculous Medicine to Cure All Diseases'; notice the outstanding features of the teachings. Furthermore, when it comes to teaching, it should be as easy and common as possible, nothing lofty. Another noted feature is that during sitting in silent meditation with *gasshô* and reciting the Five Precepts mornings and evenings, the pure and healthy minds can be cultivated and put into practice in one's daily routine. This is the reason why *Reiho* is easily obtained by anyone.

Recently the course of the world has shifted and a great change in thought has taken place. Fortunately with the spread of this *Reiho*, there will be many that supplement the way of the world and the minds of people. How can it be for just the benefit of curing chronic diseases and longstanding complaints?

A little more than 2000 people became students of *Sensei*. Those senior disciples living in *Tokyo* gathered at the *dôjô* and carried on the work (of the late *Sensei*) and those who lived in local districts also spread the teachings. Although *Sensei* is gone, *Reiho* should still be widely propagated in the world for a long time. Ah, how prominent and great *Sensei* is that he offers the teachings to people out there after having been enlightened within!

Of late the fellow disciples consulted with each other about building the stone memorial in a graveyard at *Saihôji* Temple in *Toyo-tamagun* so as to honour his merits and to make them immortalized and I was asked to write it. As I deeply submit to *Sensei's* greatness and am happy for the very friendly teacher/disciple relationships among fellow students, I could not decline the request, and I wrote a summary in the hope that people in the future shall be reminded to look up at him in reverence.

> February, the second year of *Showa* (1927 A.D.)
> Composed by: *Ju-sanmi* (subordinate third rank),
> *Kun-santo* (the Third Order of Merit)
> Doctor of Literature Okada Masayuki
>
> Calligraphy by: Navy Rear Admiral,
> *Ju-yonmi* (subordinate fourth rank)
> *Kun-santo* (the Third Order of Merit)
> *Ko-yonkyu* (the distinguished service fourth class)
> Ushida Juzaburo

C. Zazen Shikan Taza

Tendai Ceasing and Contemplation Meditation
Mikao Usui is said to have studied this particular *Tendai* meditation when meditating on *kurama yama* for 21 days. The following meditative practice is offered as a means of providing aspirants with a concrete, usable component of authentic *Tendai* Ceasing and Contemplation Meditation.

A. OUTSIDE THE MEDITATION HALL OR SPIRITUAL PRACTICE AREA

1. *Shikan Zen Yo No Ichi Ge* (The Verse Displaying the Main Point of Samatha-Vipasyana Meditation)

Recite once:

In the genuine practice of entering Nirvana, apparently there are a multitude of roads. But if one thinks about only the most vital necessities, two methods stand out. The first, Samatha, quiets one's evil passions, and the second, Vipasyana, further leads one to deny unwholesome desires. When Samatha (stopping) results in one's winning entry into Dhyana-Samadhi (meditation trance), then Vipasyana (insight) becomes the foundation of Prajna (wisdom). When both Samatha and Vipasyana are successfully practiced, the meditator enters Samadhi and receives Prajna. In that state, the Dharma's altruistic goal of helping both self and others is fully completed.

2. *Kokoro No Ryo* (Verse on Food for the Heart/Mind)

Recite once each:
Practicing the Dharma includes food and clothes, but in food and clothes the practice of Dharma is not found. Monetary wealth is not a national treasure; a person who brightens a single corner is a national treasure. The height of compassion is to welcome evil onto myself while giving good deeds to other people, and to forget myself while doing good for others. By holding grudges and repaying with hatred, hatred never ends; but by repaying with virtue, hatred is completely exhausted. Rather than bearing grudges about the things happening in this long night's dream called the world, cross the boundary into the Dharma realm of the true Buddha.

3. Method of Entering the Hall

Line up outside the Hall. Recite the Sange Mon (Repentance Verse) once:
Ga Shaku Sho Zo Sho Aku Go, Kai Yu Mu Shi Ton Jin Chi, Ju Shin Go I Shi Sho Sho, Issai Ga Kon Kai Sange
From beginningless time I have generated negative karma through my misdirected thoughts, words and deeds. I wish to acknowledge and atone for all.
Enter the hall.

B. WITHIN THE MEDITATION HALL OR SPIRITUAL PRACTICE AREA

4. *San Rai* (Three Prostrations)

Recite three times, each time performing a Grand Prostration:
Isshin Chorai Jippo Hokai Joju Sanbo

5. Ten Non-Virtuous States of Mind (The Recitation on Self Discipline)

This is done individually. Contemplate:

Reflecting on my own life, I should abandon those heart states in which bad actions accumulate, namely the realms of shells, animals, hungry ghosts, fighting entities, mundane life, heavens, evil spirits, Hinayana followers, professional priests and conflicting emotions.

6. *Godai Gan* (Five Great Vows)

Shujo Muhen Segan Do Fukuchi Muhen Segan Shu Homon Muhen Segan Gaku Nyorai Muhen Segan Ji Mujo Bodai Segan Jo Goji Busshi Jodaigan

Sentient Beings are limitless; I vow to save them all.
Knowledge and wisdom are limitless; I vow to accumulate them all.
The Dharmas are infinite; I vow to study them all.
The Tathagatas are endless; I vow to serve them all.
Supreme Enlightenment is unsurpassed; I vow to attain it.
May this seeker of enlightenment fulfill these vows.
Take your seat for meditation.

7. Entering *Samadhi*

First, check one's posture. If sitting in the half-lotus position, place the left leg over the right leg. Pull it close to the body, with the left toes and the right heel equally spaced. Loosen the belt and arrange the clothes neatly so as to cover the legs. Form the meditation *Mudra* with the hands in the lap, right palm on top of the left palm, with the tips of the thumbs lightly touching, pulled close under the stomach. Twist the body left and right a number of times, coming to rest in a correct, straight posture. The backbone should not be curved, and the shoulders are thrown back. If the posture should relax, without hurrying, quickly correct it. Clear the air passages, expelling muddy spirits. Exhale with the mouth open, releasing the stagnant air slowly while leaning slightly forward. Don't exhale quickly or slowly, but continue until you are satisfied. Breathe all defects out during exhalation, completely exhausting them. Then straighten up again, and through the nose breathe in endless, pure spirit. Imagine it entering through the top of the head, in and out three times. Then with the torso straight and relaxed, allow the diaphragm to move in tandem with the movement of air through the nose. Close the mouth, teeth lightly together, tongue against the upper palate. With the eyes half-closed to reduce the brightness of the outside light, let the line of sight fall about six feet in front. Second, check the breathing. Listening to the sound of the in and out breaths, it should not be loud, not gasping or sucking in air, not jerky, puckering or sliding. Allow the breathing to remain in a natural state, as if in a closed system. Third, check the activity of the thoughts. Separate the attention from the breathing and concentrate it at the red field. Abandon those thoughts outside the practice, such as gross thoughts, random thoughts, daydreaming, thoughts about emotional ups and downs, or relaxed and uptight states.

8. Dwelling in *Samadhi*

Observe the harmony of the Three Mysteries of the body, the breath and the thoughts. Note when the three are not in harmony, and continually apply mindfulness and recollection to again produce unity and harmony of the body, breath and thoughts. Rely on this practice to cross over. One sits single-pointedly, not being shaken by thoughts or activities of daily life, not even if enveloped in raging flames.

9. Exiting *Samadhi*

First, release the mind from Samadhi, and establish connections and relations. Next, open the mouth and breathe deeply so as to release the spirit. Next, move the body very slightly. Then move the hands, arms, elbows, shoulders, neck and head. Next, rub the pores of the whole body, then rub the palms together, using the warmth to cover the eyes. Next, open the eyes behind the palms. Finally, light incense or recite *sutra* depending on the time.

10. Method for Leaving the Hall

If there is time, recite *sutra*. This can be the Heart *Sutra*, the Ten-Verse Kannon *Sutra*, portions of the Lotus *Sutra*, the *Sutra* of Saintly Fudo or any other *sutra* you choose. You may also chant the *Nembutsu* and dedicate merit.

Finally, recite the *San Rai* (Three Prostrations) again, three times, each time performing a Grand Prostration.

Isshin Chorai Jippo Hokai Joju Sanbo

Depart the hall.

From the Mount Hiei Summer Ango Translated by Keisho, compiled by Jiho Edited from the original by Jion © *Tendai* Lotus Teachings

D. Imperial Rescript on Education

It has been suggested that Mikao Usui taught the Imperial Rescript on Education to his students. Some suggestions have also been that the five precepts are based on the rescript.

Copies of this rescript were distributed to every school in Japan and hung alongside the Emperor's portrait, where all made obeisance to them. In such awe were they held that on occasion teachers and principals risked their lives to rescue them from burning buildings. All moral and civic instruction after 1890 was based on the principles – largely Confucian – set forth here. Issuance of the rescript at that time reflected a powerful reaction to the modernizing tendencies of the early Meiji Period, yet there can be no doubt that this type of thinking was already strongly prevalent and only reinforced by the indoctrination of the new public schools. This rescript was the work of many hands, as were most of Emperor Meiji's pronouncements, but principally those of Inoue Kowashi, a Kumamoto *Samurai* known for his Chinese learning and later minister of education.

(This commentary is from a book entitled *Japanese Education*, by a scholar named Kikuchi. It is found in *Tsunoda and Debary, Sources of Japanese Tradition*, p. 139.)

Included are two versions of the Rescript: one, in ornate vocabulary, capturing the difficult style of the original. The second is in more standard modern English and both are printed with permission from Andrew Gordon's book, *A Modern History of Japan*.

1. Imperial Rescript on Education

October 30, 1890 (23rd year of the Meiji Era)

Know ye, Our subjects: Our Imperial Ancestors have founded Our Empire on a basis broad and everlasting, and have deeply and firmly implanted virtue; Our subjects ever united in loyalty and filial piety have from generation to generation illustrated the beauty thereof.

This is the glory of the fundamental character of Our Empire, and herein also lies the source of Our education. Ye, Our subjects, be filial to your parents, affectionate to your brothers and sisters; as husbands and wives be harmonious, as friends true; bear yourselves in modesty and moderation; extend your benevolence to all; pursue learning and cultivate arts, and thereby develop intellectual faculties and perfect moral powers; furthermore, advance public good and promote common interests; always respect the Constitution and observe the law; should emergency arise, offer yourselves courageously to the State; and thus guard and maintain the prosperity of Our Imperial Throne coeval with heaven and earth.

So shall ye not only be Our good and faithful subjects, but render illustrious the best traditions of your forefathers.

The way set forth here is indeed the teaching bequeathed by Our Imperial Ancestors, to be observed alike by Their Descendants and the subjects, infallible for all ages and true in all places. It is our wish to lay it to heart in all reverence, in common with you, Our subjects, that we may all attain to the same virtue.

2. Imperial Rescript on Education

October 30, 1890 (23rd year of the Meiji Era)

I, the Emperor, think that my ancestors and their religion founded my nation a very long time ago. With its development a profound and steady morality was established. The fact that my subjects show their loyalty to me and show filial love to their parents in their millions of hearts all in unison, thus accumulating virtue generation after generation is indeed the pride of my nation, and is a profound idea and the basis of our education.

You, my subjects, form full personalities by showing filial love to your parents, by making good terms with your brothers and sisters, by being intimate with your friends, by making couples who love each other, by trusting your friends, by reflecting upon yourselves, by conveying a spirit of philanthropy to other people and by studying to acquire knowledge and wisdom.

Thus, please obey always the constitution and other laws of my nation in your profession in order to spread the common good in my nation. If an emergency may happen, please do your best for Our nation in order to support the eternal fate and future of my nation. In this way, you are my good and faithful subjects, and you come to appreciate good social customs inherited from your ancestors. The way of doing this is a good lesson inherited from my ancestors and religion which you subjects should observe well together with your offspring.

These ideas hold true for both the present and the past, and may be propagated in this nation as well as in the other countries. I would like to understand all of this with, Our subjects, and hope sincerely that all the mentioned virtues will be carried out in harmony by all of you subjects.

E. The Heart *Sutra*

When Bodhisattva Avalokiteshvara was practicing the profound Prajna Paramita, he illuminated the Five Skandhas and saw that they are all empty, and he crossed beyond all suffering and difficulty.

Shariputra, form does not differ from emptiness; emptiness does not differ from form. Form itself is emptiness; emptiness itself is form. So too are feeling, cognition, formation, and consciousness.

Shariputra, all Dharmas are empty of characteristics. They are not produced, not destroyed, not defiled, not pure; and they neither increase nor diminish. Therefore, in emptiness there is no form, feeling, cognition, formation, or consciousness; no eyes, ears, nose, tongue, body, or mind; no sights, sounds, smells, tastes, objects of touch, or Dharmas; no field of the eyes up to and including no field of mind consciousness; and no ignorance or ending of ignorance, up to and including no old age and death or ending of old age and death. There is no suffering, no accumulating, no extinction, and no Way, and no understanding and no attaining.

Because nothing is attained, the Bodhisattva through reliance on Prajna Paramita is unimpeded in his mind. Because there is no impediment, he is not afraid, and he leaves distorted dream-thinking far behind. Ultimately Nirvana! All Buddhas of the three periods of time attain Anuttara-samyak-sambodhi through reliance on Prajna Paramita. Therefore know that Prajna Paramita is a Great Spiritual Mantra, a Great Bright Mantra, a Supreme Mantra, an Unequalled Mantra. It can remove all suffering; it is genuine and not false. That is why the Mantra of Prajna Paramita was spoken. Recite it like this:

Gaté Gaté Paragaté Parasamgaté
Bodhi Svaha!
Copyright © Buddhist Text Translation Society.

Bibliography

Abé, Ryûichi. *The Weaving of Mantra*, Columbia University Press, New York, 1999.

Arnold, Larry and Nevius, Sandra. *The Reiki Handbook*, PSI, 1992.

Ashton, W.G. (translated by) *The Nihongi*, 1896.

Bary De, WM Theodore. *Sources of Japanese Tradition*, Columbian University Press, New York, 2001.

Barnett, Libby. *Reiki Energy Medicine*, Healing Arts Press, Vermont, 1996.

Benor, Daniel, J. MD. *Spiritual Healing*, Vision Publications, Michigan, 2001.

Blacker, Carmen. *The Catalpa Bow – A Study of Shamanic Practices in Japan*, Japan Library, Richmond, 1999.

Bohm, David. *Wholeness and the Implicate Order*, Routledge & Kegan Paul, London, Boston, 1980.

Breen, John and Mark Teeuwen. *Shintô in History – Ways of the Kami*, Curzon Press, Surrey, 2000.

Brennan, Barbara Ann. *Light Emerging*, Bantam Books, New York, 1993.

Brown, Fran. *Living Reiki – Takata's Teachings*, Life Rhythms, California, 1992.

Chadwick, David. *Thank You and Ok! An American Zen Failure in Japan*, Penguin Books, London, 1994.

Chadwick, David. *The Life and Zen Teachings of Shunryu Suzuki*, Thorsons, London, 1999.

Cleary, Thomas. *The Japanese Art of War – Understanding the Culture of Strategy*, Shambala Publications, Boston, 1991.

Cleary, Thomas. *The Book of Five Rings*, Shambala Publications, Boston , 1994.

Cleary, Thomas. *The Code of the Samurai – A Contemporary Translation of the Bushido Shoshinshu of Taira Shigesuke*, Tuttle Publishing, Boston, 2000.

Cleary, Thomas. *The Inner Teachings of Taoism*, Shambhala Publications, Boston, 1986.

Dalai Lama. *The Power of Compassion*, HarperCollins, 1995.

Davey, H.E. *Living the Japanese Arts & Ways*, Stone Bridge Press, Berkeley, 2003.

Davey, H.E. *Japanese Yoga – The Way of Dynamic Meditation*, Stone Bridge Press, Berkeley, 2001.

David-Neel, Alexandra. *Initiations and Initiates in Tibet*, Rider and Company, London, 1970.

Doi, Hiroshi. *Modern Reiki Method for Healing*, Fraser Journal Publishing, British Columbia, 2000.

Eguchi, Toshihiro. *Te No Hira Ryôji Nyûmon*, Arusu Publishing, Japan, 1930.

Eguchi, Toshihiro. *Te No Hira Ryôji Dokuhon*, Kaikosha Publishing, Japan 1936.

Eguchi, Toshihiro. *Te No Hira Ryôji Wo Kataru*, Japan, 1954.

Floyd, H. Ross. *Shintô: The Way of Japan*, Greenwood Publishing Group, Westport, 1965.

Funakoshi, Gichin. *Karate-dô – My Way of Life*, Kodansha America Inc., New York, 1975.

Furumoto, Alice Takata. *The Gray Book – Reiki*, 1982.

Gordon, Andrew. *A Modern History of Japan: From Tokugawa Times to the Present*, Oxford University Press, Oxford, 2002.

Gray, John Harvey and Lourdes. *Hand to Hand*, Xlibris Corporation, 2002.

Groner, Paul. *Saicho – The Establishment of the Japanese Tendai School*, University of Hawaii Press, Honolulu, 2000.

Haberly, Helen J. *Reiki – Hawayo Takata's Story*, Archedigm Publications, Maryland, 2000.

Hadamitzky, Wolfgang and Spahn, Mark. *Kanji & Kana – A Handbook and Dictionary of the Japanese Writing System*, Tuttle Publishing, Boston, 1981.

Hanh, Thich Nhat. *Opening the Heart of the Cosmos – Insights on the Lotus Sutra*, Paralax Press, Berkeley, 2003.

Hanh, Thich Nhat. *The Diamond that Cuts Through Illusion – Commentaries on the Prajnaparamita Diamond Sutra*, SCB Distributors, Gardena, 1992.

Hayashi Chûjirô. *Ryôhô Shishin*, Japan.

Hensel, Thomas A. and Emery, Kevin Ross. *The Lost Steps of Reiki*, Lightlines Publishing, Portsmouth, 1997.

Herrigel, Eugen. *Zen in the Art of Archery*, Vintage, London, 1999.

Hitoshi, Miyake. *Shugendô – Essays on the structure of Japanese Folk Religion*, The University of Michigan, Michigan, 2001.

Hitoshi, Miyake. *The Mandala of The Mountain: Shugendô and Folk Religion*, Keio University Press Inc., Tokyo, 2005.

Honna, Nobuyuki and Hoffer, Bates. *An English Dictionary of Japanese*

Culture, Yuhikaku Publishing Co. Ltd., *Tôkyô*, 1986.

Ikeda, Mitsuru (translated by Andrew Driver). *The World of the Hotsuma Legends*, Japan Translation Center, *Tôkyô*, 1996.

Ikegami, Eiko. *The Taming of the Samurai: Honorific Individualism and the Making of Modern Japan*, Harvard University Press, Cambridge, 1995.

Irie, Taikichi and Aoyama, Shigery (translated by Thomas I. Elliott). *Buddhist Images*, Hoikusha Publishing Co Ltd. Osaka, 1999.

Inagaki, Hisao. *A Dictionary of Japanese Buddhist Terms*, Nagata Bunshodo, *Kyôto*, 2003.

Japanese Journals of Religious Studies, Nanzan Institute for Religion and Culture, Japan.

Johnson, Jerry Alan. *Chinese Medical Qigong Therapy – Volume 1*, The International Institute of Medical *Qi Gong*, Pacific Grove, 2002.

Johnson, Jerry Alan. *Chinese Medical Qigong Therapy – Volume 2*, The International Institute of Medical *Qi Gong*, Pacific Grove, 2002.

Jarell, David G. *Reiki Plus Natural Healing*, Reiki Plus, Key Largo, 1997.

Jung, C.G. (edited by Jolande Jacobi). *C.G. Jung – Psychological Reflections*, ARK Paperbacks, London, 1989.

Kaiguo, Chen and Shunchao, Zhen. Translated by Thomas Cleary. *Opening the Dragon Gate*. Tuttle Publishing, Boston, 1998.

Kamalashila. *Meditation – The Buddhist Way of Tranquility and Insight*, Windhorse Publications, Glasgow, 1992.

Keegan, John. *A History of Warfare*, Vintage, 1994.

Keene, Donald. *Emperor of Japan – Meiji and His World*, 1852-1912, Columbia University Press, New York, 2002.

Kelly, Maureen J. *Reiki and the Healing Buddha*, Lotus Press, Twin Lakes, Wisconsin,, 2000.

Koans – The Lessons of Zen, Hyperion, New York, 1997.

Kohno, Jiko. *Right View, Right Life*, Kosei Publishing Co., *Tôkyô*, 1998.

Kushi, Michio. *The Dô-In Way*, Square One Publishers, New York, 2007.

LaFleur, William R. *The Karma of Words – Buddhism and the Literary Arts in Medieval Japan*, University of California Press, Los Angeles, 1986.

Leyi, Li. *Evolutionary Illustration of Chinese Characters*, Beijing Language and Culture University Press, 2000.

Leyi, Li. *Tracing the Roots of Chinese Characters*, Beijing Language and Culture University Press, 1997.

Lubeck, Walter, Petter, Frank Arjava, and Rand, William Lee. *The Spirit of Reiki*, Lotus Press, Twin Lakes, Wisconsin, 2001.

Maruyana, Koretsohi. *Aikidô with Ki*, Ki-no-Kenkyûkai, *Tôkyô*, 1984.

Matsumoto, Yoshinosuke (translated by Andrew Driver). *An Unknown History of Ancient Japan, The Hotsuma Legends – Paths of the Ancestors*, Japan Translation Center, *Tôkyô*, 1999.

McCarthy, Patrick and Yukio. *Funakoshi Gichin's Tanpenshu*, International Ryukyu Karate Research Society, Brisbane, 2002.

Mihashi Kazuo. *Tenohira-ga Byoki-o Naosu*, Chuo Art Publishing Co, Ltd. Japan, 2001.

Milner, Kathleen. *Reiki & Other Rays of Touch Healing*, 1994.
Mitchell, Paul David. *Reiki – The Usui System of Natural Healing (The Blue Book)*, Idaho, 1985.
Mizutani, Osamu and Nobuku. *An Introduction to Modern Japanese*, Japan Times Ltd., *Tôkyô*, 1977.
Mochizuki, Toshitaka. *Iyashi No Te*, Tama Shuppan, *Tôkyô*, 1995.
Mochizuki, Toshitaka. *Chô Kantan Iyashi No Te*, Tama Shuppan, *Tôkyô*, 2001.
Murumoto, Wayne. '*What is a Ryu?*' Issue 8, Furyu – The Budo Journal, Tengu Press, Hawaii.
Myss, Caroline. *Anatomy of the Spirit*, Random House, New York, 1997.
Nelson, Andrew N. *The Modern Reader's Japanese-English Character Dictionary*, Tuttle Publishing, Boston, 1972.
Nishida, Tenko. *A New Road To Ancient Truth*, Horizon Press, New York, 1972.
Oda, Ryuko. *Kaji-Empowerment and Healing in Esoteric Buddhism*, Kineizan Shinjao-in Mitsumonkai, Japan, 1992.
Oki, Masahiro. *Meditation Yoga—The Meiso Yoga of Okidô*, Oki Yoga Publications, Shizuoka-Ken, 1978.
Oschman, James L. *Energy Medicine – The Scientific Basis*, Churchill Livingstone, London, 2000.
Papinot, Edmond. *Historical and Geographical Dictionary of Japan*, Tuttle Publishing, Boston, 1972.
Pert, B. Candace. *Molecules of Emotion: The Science Behind Mind-Body Medicine*, Simon and Schuster, 1999.
Petter, Frank Arjava. *Reiki Fire*, Lotus Press, Twin Lakes, Wisconsin,, 1998.
Prosser, Jion. *Trekking through Hell to find Heaven*, USA, 2007.
Ray, Barbara Weber. *The Reiki Factor*, First Edition, Exposition Press, New York, 1983.
Reed, William. *Ki – A Practical Guide for Westerners*, Japan Publications Inc., *Tôkyô*, 1986.
Reiki Ryôhô Hikkei, Usui Reiki Ryôhô Gakkai, Japan.
Sargent, Jiho. *Asking About Zen – 108 Answers*, Weatherhill, Inc., New York, 2001.
Saso, Michael. *Tantric Art and Meditation*, Tendai Education Foundation, Honolulu, 1990.
Saunders, E. Dale. *Mudra – A study of Symbolic Gestures in Japanese Buddhist Sculpture*, Princeton University Press, Princeton, 1985.
Shewmaker, Diane Ruth. *All Love – A Guidebook to Healing with Sekhem – Seichim Reiki and SKHM*, Celestial Wellspring, Olympia, 1999.
Shizuka, Shiragawa. *Kanji Ruihen (Japanese Etymological Dictionary)*.
Stevens, John. *Sacred Calligraphy of the East*, Shambala Publications, Boston, 1996.
Stevens, John. *The Essence of Aikido*, Kodansha International, New York, 1999.
Stevens, John. *The Philosophy of Aikido*, Kodansha, 2001.
Stevens, John. *The Marathon Monks of Mount Hiei*, Shambhala Publications, Boston 1988.

Stevens, John. *Three Budo Masters*, Kodansha International Ltd, New York, 1995.

Stiene, Bronwen and Frans. *A-Z of Reiki Pocketbook*, O Books, Winchester 2006.

Stiene, Bronwen and Frans. *Reiki Techniques Card Deck – Heal Yourself Intuitively*, O Books, Winchester, 2006.

Stiene, Bronwen and Frans. *The Japanese Art of Reiki*, O Books, Winchester, 2005.

Stiene, Bronwen and Frans. *Your Reiki Treatment*, O Books, Winchester, 2007.

Suzuki, D.T. *Buddha of Infinite Light – The Teachings of Shin Buddhism, The Japanese Way of Wisdom and Compassion*, Shambala Publications, Boston, 1998.

Suzuki, Shunryu. *Zen Mind, Beginners Mind*, Weatherhill, New York, 1970.

Suzuki, Shunryu. *Branching Streams Flow in the Darkness: Lectures on the Sandokai*, University of California Press, Berkeley, 1999.

Suzuki, Shunryu. *Not Always So – Practicing the True Spirit of Zen*, HarperCollins, New York, 2002.

Tanabe, George J. Jr. *Religions of Japan in Practice*, Princeton University Press, Princeton, 1999.

The Encyclopedia of Eastern Philosophy and Religion, Shambhala Publications, Boston, 1994.

Thondup, Tulku. *The Healing Power of Mind*, Penguin Books, Victoria, 1997.

Tohei, Koichi. *Ki in Daily Life, Ki-no-Kenkyûkai*, Tôkyô, 1980.

Tohei, Koichi. *Book of Ki – Coordinating Mind and Body in Daily Life*, Japan Publications Inc., Tôkyô, 1976.

Tolle, Eckhart. *The Power of NOW*, Hodder Headline Australia, Sydney 2000.

Tomita, Kaiji. *Reiki To Jinjutsu – Tomita Ryû Teate Ryôhô*, BAB Japan, Tôkyô, 1999.

Trungpa, Chogyam. *Cutting Through Spiritual Materialism*, Shambala Publications, Boston, 1999.

Turnbull, Stephen. *Ninja – The True Story of Japan's Secret Warrior Cult*, Firebird, 1992.

Twan, Annelli. *Early Days of Reiki, Memories of Hawayo Takata*, B.C. 2001.

Twan, Wanja. *In the Light of a Distant Star*, B.C.

Unno, Taitetsu. *River of Fire – River of Water – An Introduction to the Pure Land Tradition of Shin Buddhism*, Doubleday, New York, 1998.

Varley, Paul. *Japanese Culture* (Fourth Edition), University of Hawai'i Press, Honolulu, 2000.

Watson, Brian N. *The Father of Judo – A Biography of Jigoro Kano*, Kodansha America Inc., New York, 2000.

Watson, Burton. *The Lotus Sutra*, Columbia University Press, New York, 1993.

Winfield, Pamela D. *Curing with Kaji Healing and Esoteric Empowerment in Japan*, Japanese Journal of Religious Studies, Nanzan Publications, 2005.

Wilson, William Scott. *The Demon's Sermon on the Martial Arts*, Kodansha

International, Tokyo, 2006.

Wilson, William Scott. *The Unfettered Mind*, Kodansha International, Tokyo, 1986.

Yamahata, Hôgen Daido. *On The Open Way – Zen Teachings for Today by Living Zen Master Hôgen Daido Yamahata*, The Open Way Australia and Buddhist Practitioners Network, Inc., Byron Bay, 1995.

Yamaguchi, Tadao, and Petter, Frank Arjava. *Hayashi Reiki Manual*. Lotus Press, 2003.

Yamaguchi, Tadao. *Light on the Origins of Reiki*, Lotus Press, 2008.

Yamakage, Motohisa. *The Essence of Shintô – Japan's Spiritual Heart*, Kodansha International, Tokyo, 2007.

Yuho, Tseng. *A History of Chinese Calligraphy*, The Chinese University Press, 1993.

Yun, Hsing. *Lotus in a Stream*, Weatherhill, Inc., Trumbull, 2000.

Index

B O O K S

O books
O is a symbol of the world, of oneness and unity. In
different cultures it also means the "eye", symbolizing
knowledge and insight, and in Old English it means "place
of love or home". O books explores the many paths of
understanding which different traditions have developed
down the ages, particularly those today that express
respect for the planet and all of life.

For more information on the full list of over 300 titles
please visit our website
www.O-books.net

A-Z Reiki Pocketbook
Everything you need to know about Reiki
Bronwen & Frans Stiene

The pick of the crop for our Reiki harvest. My copy of this little pocketbook is already looking a bit dog-eared because I've been flipping through it a lot. Fortunately, it seems to be of very sturdy construction, so it can probably stand to be thumbed through frequently for years to come. Most any Reiki term you might think of can be found in this book, along with some you've never even heard of or imagined. People, techniques, Reiki terminology in both Japanese and English, Reiki styles and organizations, as the cover states: "Everything About Reiki" has been crammed into this tiny 254-page portable reference book. **Janet Dagley**, *The Reiki Digest*
1905047894 272pp **£7.99 $16.95**

Japanese Art of Reiki
Bronwen & Frans Stiene

This is a sequel to the aclaimed "Reiki Sourcebook." For those of us in the West who see adverts for weekend Reiki Master courses and wonder about the authenticity of the tradition, this book is an eye-opener. It takes the reader back to the Japanese roots of the tradition in a way that conveys its inspirational power and cultural flavour. The book is illustrated and is full of practical guidance for both practitioners and general readers. **Scientific and Medical Network Review**
1905047029 208pp **£12.99 $19.95**

Your Reiki Treatment
How to get the most out of it
Bronwen & Frans Stiene

Especially helpful and insightful. A down-to-earth book which can be recommended to Reaiki practitioners and clients alike. If you are new to reiki, then this is definitely THE book for you. **Mercury**
1846940133 196pp **£9.99 $19.95**

Reiki Meditations for Beginners
with free CD
Lawrence Ellyard

One of the few Reiki books which really covers something new and valuable. Reiki and Meditation is a core topic for everyone who likes to use Usui-Reiki as a spiritual path. This is why Mikao Usui emphasized so much to meditate every morning and every evening. A must read for every serious Reiki-Practitioner! **Walter Lübeck**, co-author of *The Spirit of Reiki*
9781846940989 176pp **£12.99 $24.95**

Ultimate Reiki Guide for Beginners
Lawrence Ellyard

Everything you will ever need to know about setting up a professional, successful and rewarding Reiki practice, from working with clients to teaching Reiki yourself. Lawrence's clear love of his subject and his years of experience in working with Reiki combine to make this a book that every serious Reiki professional should have. A well researched and utterly indispensable resource for anyone involved with this healing system. Highly recommended. **Steve Gooch,** author of *Reiki Jin-Kei Do*
1905047487 208pp **£12.99 $24.95**

Shamanic Reiki
Expanded Ways of Working with Universal Life Force Energy
Llyn Roberts and Robert Levy

The alchemy of shamanism and Reiki is nothing less than pure gold in the hands of Llyn Roberts and Robert Levy. Shamanic Reiki brings the concept of energy healing to a whole new level. More than a how-to-book, it speaks to the health of the human spirit, a journey we must all complete. **Brian Luke Seaward, Ph.D.,** author of *Stand Like Mountain, Flow Like Water, Quiet Mind, Fearless Heart*
9781846940378 208pp **£9.99 $19.95**

What a Body Knows
Finding Wisdom in Desire
Kimerer L. LaMothe PhD

I simply cannot praise the book enough! The prose is positively brilliant. It is full of sparkling gems of insight and astonishing, concise yet profound formulations. The nature passages remind me of Annie Dillard. It is truly a remarkable achievement! **Miranda Shaw, Ph.D.,** Professor of Religion, University of Richmond, Author of *Passionate Enlightenment: Women in Tantric Buddhism* and *Buddhist Goddesses of India*
978-1-84694-188-7 340pp **£11.99 $24.95**

An Exchange of Love
Madeleine Walker

A lovely book with a gentle and profound message about how closely our animal companions are linked to our triumphs and traumas, and an astonishing insight into how willing they are to be a surrogate for our stress symptoms and how instrumental they can be in our healing. Madeleine Walker is one of the best animal intuitives in the world. **Kindred Spirit**
978-1-84694-139-9 240pp **£9.99 $19.95**

Reiki Jin Kei Do
The Way of Compassion and Wisdom
Steve Gooch

This book is the first of its kind in Reiki in that it explores and challenges the origins and history of this therapy, and it would be a good read for both the beginner and the more accomplished Reiki Master. This was a book I couldn't put down, and I think even those that don't feel a strong interest in Reiki itself would find this an interesting and informative read.
Choice Magazine
1905047851 240pp **£12.99 $21.95**

In the Light of Meditation
Mike George

A classy book. A gentle yet satisfying pace and is beautifully illustrated. Complete with a CD of guided meditation commentaries, this is a true gem among meditation guides. **Brainwave**
1903816610 224pp **£11.99 $19.95**

Crystal Prescriptions
Judy Hall

Another potential best-seller from Judy Hall. This handy little book is packed as tight as a pill-bottle with crystal remedies for ailments. It is written in an easy-to-understand style, so if you are not a virtuoso with your Vanadinite, it will guide you. If you love crystals and want to make the best use of them, it is worth investing in this book as a complete reference to their healing qualities. **Vision**
1905047401 172pp **£7.99 $15.95**

Colours of the Soul
June Mcleod

An excellent book! June Mcleod knows her subject extremely well. Comprehensive, it is jam-packed with excellent exercises. Definitely worth purchasing, there is something in this book for everyone. Pure magic! **Vision**
1905047258 176pp **£11.99 $21.95**

Passage to Freedom
A Path to Enlightenment
Dawn Mellowship

*"Passage to Freedom" is an inspiring title that combines a spiritual treasure trove of wisdom with practical exercises accessible to all of us for use in our daily lives. Illustrated throughout with clear instructions, the information and inspiration emanating from Dawn Mellowship is a major achievement and will certainly help all readers gain insight into the way through and around life's problems, worries, and our own emotional, spiritual and physical difficulties.***Sandra Goodman PhD,** Editor and Director, Positive Health
9781846940781 272pp **£9.99 $22.95**

The Good Remembering
A Message for our Times
Llyn Roberts

Llyn's work changed my life. "The Good Remembering" is the most important book I've ever read. **John Perkins**, *NY Times* best selling author of *Confessions of an Economic Hit Man*
1846940389 96pp **£7.99 $16.95**